Arithmetic for Teachers

Arithmetic for Teachers

2nd Edition

Wilbur H. Dutton
PROFESSOR OF EDUCATION
VICE CHAIRMAN, DEPARTMENT OF EDUCATION
UNIVERSITY OF CALIFORNIA, LOS ANGELES

Colin C. Petrie
PROFESSOR OF MATHEMATICS
SANTA MONICA CITY COLLEGE

L. J. Adams

Prentice-Hall, Inc., Englewood Cliffs, N. J.

PRENTICE-HALL INTERNATIONAL, INC., *London*
PRENTICE-HALL OF AUSTRALIA PTY. LTD., *Sydney*
PRENTICE-HALL OF CANADA LTD., *Toronto*
PRENTICE-HALL OF INDIA PRIVATE LTD., *New Delhi*
PRENTICE-HALL OF JAPAN, INC., *Tokyo*

Printed in the United States of America

Preface

Arithmetic for Teachers was first published in 1961, co-authored by Wilbur H. Dutton and L. J. Adams, Chairman of the Mathematics Department of Santa Monica City College, now deceased. The 2nd Edition provides a systematic coverage of the basic mathematics topics emphasized by leaders of the mathematics revolution that is now under way. We have stressed the kind of mathematics needed for social competence as well as that needed for individual efficiency. Each topic is developed from simple introductory concepts to complex and abstract concepts. Basic mathematical principles and mathematical models are used both in the presentation of each topic to aid the reader in understanding concepts and to show the relationships between operations.

The basic method for stimulating children to learn new mathematics concepts is presenting *meaningful learning through guided discovery*. Suggestions are given in each chapter for introducing mathematics concepts so that the new concepts are meaningful to the pupil. The learning experiences recommended are based upon the structure of our number system and the maturity of the learner. Careful attention is given to the necessity for pupils to learn the language of mathematics as well as the English language needed for accurate communication of mathematical ideas.

Appropriate research studies have been consulted and cited to support the use of basic teaching procedures and for the introduction of mathematics topics to children. Particular importance has been attached to the use of behavioral objectives to guide instructional practices and to provide a sound foundation for evaluating pupil achievement and teacher efficiency. Problem solving work has been redefined and guidelines have been given for creative instruction in this important aspect of the mathematics program.

We sincerely hope that the reader will acquire a new appreciation of the meaningful approach to mathematics instruction. We hope that through increased understanding of basic mathematical concepts the teacher will become an enthusiastic supporter of *meaningful learning through guided discovery.*

WILBUR H. DUTTON
COLIN C. PETRIE

Westwood, California

Contents

3   LANGUAGE AND OPERATIONS USED IN SUBTRACTION

4   MULTIPLICATION

5 DIVISION   98

6 MEASUREMENT   116

7 PROBLEM SOLVING   140

10 PER CENT AND MAKING RELATIVE COMPARISONS 216

11 AN INTRODUCTION TO ALGEBRA 235

12 AN INTRODUCTION TO PLANE GEOMETRY 253

13 LOGIC, PROBABILITY, ODDS, AND PERMUTATIONS   276

14 EVALUATION IN ELEMENTARY SCHOOL MATHEMATICS   287

Arithmetic
for
Teachers

1

Fundamental Principles

1.1 The Need for Mathematics in an Age of Science

We are living in a new culture. This is the culture of science. Man's triumphant walk on the moon is only one dramatic example of the scientific age. Every aspect of modern living is influenced by scientific discoveries and applications. One has only to reflect upon the basic needs for living in our culture to grasp some measure of the impact of modern science. The clothing we wear contains synthetic materials enhancing beauty as well as durability. Homes are constructed to facilitate the use of machines for lightening the work load of the housewife, conditioning the temperature, and pleasing the aesthetic aspects of modern living. One twists a button to secure beautiful color television or throttles an engine to roar across water or space for recreational purposes. Mechanical devices and miracle drugs are renovating and rejuvenating the human body. Complex and expensive systems protect us and promise a chance for survival in an era of push-button warfare. To become educated one is increasingly aware of retrival systems, data processing, and computer operations. Mathematics and numerical operations are also an indispensable part of this scientific age. To keep pace with the astounding accumulation of knowledge, the research and discovery processes have become increasingly more complex and this in turn has necessitated the need for new mathematics and arithmetic.

1

The modern elementary school is responsible for basic education for all of America's children. This education would fail in its aims if careful attention were not given to one of the dominating forces of our culture. In our scientific culture the specialists as well as the nontechnically oriented citizens need to understand numerical operations and to be familiar with the applications of mathematical principles. Mathematics is the language of science, and arithmetic is the cornerstone of mathematics. Thus today's elementary schools must provide instruction in arithmetic and mathematics.

The kind of arithmetic program needed for social competence and maximum individual growth in an age of science should be based upon the following principles.

1. Provision must be made for the use of arithmetic and other mathematics in the total school program.

Arithmetic (the art of computing with figures) is needed in each elementary school subject to enable children to solve problems involving the use of numbers. Arithmetic also provides a language for communicating scientific facts and discoveries which are so important in an industrial nation. Mathematics (the science dealing with measurement, properties, and relationships among quantities) is needed to enrich and extend the elementary school arithmetic program. Problems pertaining to size, shape, form, structure, location, or numerical controls are best answered by using mathematical concepts and formulas.

Neglecting the use of arithmetic and other mathematics in functional classroom or school situations cheats the child out of vital learning experiences and makes the teaching of elementary school subjects dull and meaningless.

2. Individual differences must be provided for so that the gifted will not be suppressed and the slow or average will not be penalized.

Practically all elementary-age children are in school. They come to school younger than ever before in the history of American education and they stay in school longer. Children within any one classroom, however, differ widely in general and special abilities, and these differences increase with age. Many research studies have been made on individual differences, and many new plans for classroom organization have been developed, but the individual teacher still has the responsibility for adapting instruction to the differences found among his pupils. The improvements in instructional materials to use with various ability groups, the flexibility of school policies enabling grouping within each class, and the general concern of professional and lay groups are indications of the progress made in this important aspect of the school program.

3. A practical balance must be achieved between the teaching of basic number facts and processes and the use of social applications of arithmetic.

These two aspects of the arithmetic program are frequently referred to as the *mathematical phase* and the *social phase*. Achieving a balance between the social and the mathematical phases of arithmetic has been stressed in recent years, because of research findings and increased knowledge about content, learning theory, and children.

The *social* aspect of arithmetic has to do with the importance of arithmetic while the *mathematical* aspect has to do with meaning. These two phases are approached differently. Social situations involving the use of arithmetic do not insure meaning, so that these must be supplemented by meaningful arithmetic work. At times the mathematical aspects need to be divorced from the social so that specific study may be provided. Good teaching, then, involves achieving a proper balance between the social and mathematical aspects of arithmetic: first developing concepts, and second assisting pupils in understanding how quantitative ideas are needed and used in school and in society.

4. The search for a desirable organization of learning experiences in arithmetic, based upon social and individual needs, should be intensified and extended.

As the needs of children and the society in which they live change, the elementary school has the responsibility for providing a program which will keep pace with these changes. Considerable attention is being given to enrichment programs, mathematics laboratories, and the setting up of special classes for children who learn at a relatively slow rate.[1]

The search for better ways to organize, extend, and enrich the arithmetic experiences for children should be intensified. Research efforts should be concentrated on securing evidence useful in directing meaningful curriculum improvement.

5. The important contributions of arithmetic and mathematics to the solution of everyday problems and to effective communication should be stressed.

The main purpose of arithmetic instruction is to assist the learner in developing abilities necessary to solve problems of daily living, now and in the future. Mathematics provides skills, processes, and *a special kind of language* which enables pupils to sharpen their thinking, to perfect communication, and to find precise formulation for new concepts. One writer has taken this

---

[1]See National Council of Teachers of Mathematics, *Enrichment in Mathematics, Twenty-seventh Yearbook* (Washington, D.C.: The Council, 1963), pp. 41–63.

important view on this topic: "If mathematics is the language of precise communication, arithmetic may be considered its alphabet."[2]

Arithmetic, as a branch of mathematics, has a function to perform in assisting individuals to solve everyday problems and to understand the discoveries of our rich and stimulating technological society.

These five principles provide the framework for a *desirable arithmetic program*. Our next concern shall be with theories of teaching.

1.2   Evolving Theories of Teaching

Traditionally, arithmetic has for many centuries been an important part of the elementary school curriculum. While a study of the history of teaching arithmetic in America can be rewarding and helpful to most teachers, we shall consider here only those theories of teaching developed during the twentieth century. The beginnings of a revolution in the psychology of teaching, however, date back to the writings of Warren Colburn. He wrote *First Lessons in Intellectual Arithmetic* in 1821. According to Vincent J. Glennon, Colburn made one of the most important research efforts of the past 300 years in his logical analysis of the interaction of the teaching act and the organization of the child's textbook page.[3] Colburn's textbook was revised several times and brought about a revolution in the psychology of teaching, learning, and curriculum organization of his day.

In the evolution of teaching arithmetic, four theories can be identified and possibly a fifth theory anticipated.

1. Drill theory, 1920–1935
2. Incidental and social theories, 1935–1945
3. Meaning theory, 1945–1957
4. Discovery theory (modern math), since 1957

The "drill theory," according to Brownell, consisted of four main points: (1) arithmetic, for the purpose of learning and teaching, may be analyzed into a great many units of knowledge and skill which are comparatively separate and unconnected; (2) the pupil must master these elements whether he understands them or not; (3) the pupil is to learn these elements in the form in which he will subsequently use them; and (4) the pupil will attain these ends most economically and most completely through formal repetition.[4]

[2]Everet T. Welmers, "Arithmetic In Today's Culture," *Instruction in Arithmetic, Twenty-fifth Yearbook* (Washington, D.C.: The National Council of Teachers of Mathematics, 1960), p. 30.
[3]Vincent J. Glennon, "Research Needs in Elementary School Mathematics Education," *Arithmetic Teacher*, XIII (May, 1966), 263–368.
[4]William A. Brownell, "Psychological Considerations in the Learning and the Teaching of Arithmetic," *Instruction in Arithmetic, Tenth Yearbook* (Washington, D.C.: National Council of Teachers of Mathematics, 1935), p. 2.

The main thrust of the drill theory in teaching arithmetic occurred during the period 1920 to 1935. These theories of teaching and learning were challenged by those who had participated in the child-study movement, by leading educators working with progressive education, and by psychologists. McConnell, Morton, Wheat, Brownell, and Thiele played important roles in demonstrating the importance of meaningful learning and the directing of learning experiences so that the exercise and development of ingenuity and resourcefulness became the main goal of teaching.[5] Thiele showed that when pupils were taught addition facts by the generalization and meaningful method, they learned the facts quickly and retained them. In his studies approximately 50 per cent more time was required for the drill-method pupils to equal the achievement of the generalization-method group.

Incidental and *social approaches* were theories of teaching arithmetic developed by those educators who were vigorously reacting against the formalism of traditional teaching. The two theories were popular from about 1930 to 1940. The *incidental approach* assumed that children, after entering school, would continue to find number a part of their daily activities. Informal, unplanned contacts with arithmetic would be adequate for later systematic teaching.

The *social approach* was similar to the incidental approach in that arithmetic was to be learned through school activities. The social approach, however, was based upon planned experiences centering around activities in the social studies such as studying the grocery store or post office, or learning about community activities. This program tried to make arithmetic functional in the lives of children.

Both programs were found inadequate by two leading educators. Paul Hanna found that the *social approach* used in the *activity programs* of leading experimental schools did not provide for effective and continuous learning of arithmetic skills and abilities.[6] William Brownell exploded the *incidental theory* in his monumental research study dealing with *Arithmetic in Grades I and II*. His findings demonstrated that primary-age children could learn arithmetic and that they came to school knowing a great deal about arithmetic. He recommended a sequential, systematic arithmetic program for primary-age children. He stated:

> If we want primary pupils to live fully and richly and if we want them to ground their later learning of arithmetic on meanings and basic understandings, systematic instruction in grades I and II is justified. More than that—it is demanded.[7]

[5]See the selected bibliography at the close of the chapter for specific references.
[6]Paul R. Hanna, "Opportunities For the Use of Arithmetic in An Activity Program," *The Teaching of Arithmetic, Tenth Yearbook* (Washington, D.C.: The National Council of Teachers of Mathematics, 1935), pp. 85–120.
[7]William A. Brownell, *Arithmetic in Grades I and II* (Durham, N.C.: Duke University Press, 1941), p. 169.

Meaning theory began about 1930 and is still an important part of modern mathematical teaching theory. Advocates of this approach stressed learning with understanding as contrasted to learning by drill or by the use of meaningless examples found in arithmetic textbooks. Arithmetic was viewed as a system of understandable ideas, principles, and processes. The basic idea in this approach was to help children develop the ability to do quantitative thinking and to understand the mathematical and practical aspects of arithmetic.

The meaningful approach to teaching arithmetic received its original impetus from psychologists who were proving the advantages of learning with understanding instead of learning by isolated drill. William A. Brownell, one of the outstanding advocates of meaningful teaching, identified four aspects of meaningful arithmetic: (1) basic number concepts, (2) fundamental operations, (3) important principles, relationships, and generalizations, and (4) the understanding of our decimal number system.[8]

From the standpoint of the teacher, meaningful arithmetic is interesting to teach. The need to develop understanding is a stimulating experience compared to teaching arithmetic by requiring children to listen, to memorize facts, and to participate in mechanical drill exercises.

The advantages of meaningful arithmetic to the pupil, according to Brownell are:

1. Gives assurance of retention.
2. Equips the pupil with the means to rehabilitate quickly skills that are temporarily weak.
3. Increases the likelihood that arithmetic ideas and skills will be used.
4. Contributes to ease of learning by providing a sound foundation and transferable understandings.
5. Reduces the amount of repetitive practice necessary to complete learning.
6. Safeguards the pupil from answers that are mathematically absurd.
7. Encourages learning by problem solving in place of unintelligent memorization and practice.
8. Provides the pupil with a versatility of attack which enables him to substitute equally effective procedures for procedures normally used but not available at the time.
9. Makes the pupil relatively independent so that he faces new quantitative situations with confidence.
10. Presents the subject in a way which makes it worthy of respect.

Discovery theory (modern mathematics) had its beginning about 1951. This current theory for teaching elementary school mathematics is undergoing continuous change, as psychologists try to define the method and as teachers interpret and use the method in their classrooms.

[8]William A. Brownell, "The Place of Meaning in the Teaching of Arithmetic," *Elementary School Journal*, XLVII (January, 1947), 257–58.

To understand the discovery theory of teaching, one should know the major causes of the mathematical revolution. Four of these causes will be discussed.

1. The first reason for change has been the new discoveries in mathematics and science. Research mathematicians in the past thirty years have developed more new mathematics than has been developed in the rest of the history of mathematics. Some of the new fields include: linear programming, theory of games, application of probability theory, and mathematics needed for the exploration of space and push-button warfare. Theoretical mathematicians are making tremendous advancements in pure mathematics.
2. The second cause for the new mathematics has been the demands from all aspects of American life for professional mathematicians, mathematically trained scientists, and mathematically skilled personnel in hundreds of occupations. The launching of the Russian satellite in the fall of 1957 brought much discussion about the effectiveness of American educational programs in mathematics and the physical sciences.
3. The industrial revolution, caused by discoveries in mathematics and science, is the third reason for the new mathematics. Automation demands that many thousands of mathematically trained men and women use digital computers. As machines take over the work done by unskilled labor, the demand for mathematically educated personnel increases.
4. Finally, vast sums of money have been spent on experimental mathematics programs. Projects have been financed with funds from the United States government, private foundations, and the publishing industry. Agencies and organizations giving financial assistance include: The Fund for the Advancement of Education; Carnegie Corporation; National Science Foundation; Department of Health, Education and Welfare; and research branches of military and industrial organizations.

Little would be gained by presenting a detailed description of the main curriculum projects in mathematics. The projects include such groups as the School Mathematics Study Group, the University of Illinois Committee on School Mathematics, the University of Illinois Arithmetic Project, the Greater Cleveland Mathematics Project, the Minnesota School Mathematics Center, the University of Maryland Mathematics Program, the Madison Project, the Suppes Experimental Project in the Teaching of Elementary School Mathematics, and many others. The influence of these projects upon teaching theory, however, is important.

According to John Goodlad, the aims and objectives of nearly all curriculum projects are strikingly similar.[9] These projects stress the importance

[9]John I. Goodlad, *School Curriculum Reform in the United States* (New York: The Fund for the Advancement of Education, 1964), p. 54.

of understanding the structure of the discipline, the purposes and methods of the field, and the part that creative leaders play in developing mathematics. The major aim has been to challenge students to explore, invent, and *discover* mathematical principles. The literature dealing with the new mathematics is full of references to *discovery*. Textbook publishers have used the term to title new textbook series and to help them sell books. Mathematicians use the word *discovery* for discussions of method ranging from "pure discovery" (little if any teacher guidance) to "guided discovery" (acknowledging the important role of the well-informed teacher and the well-written textbook).

Conclusions on Teaching Theories.   The most impressive fact apparent in reviewing the history of theories for teaching arithmetic is that each theory has left an important deposit of ideas. Drill theory has important contributions to make to certain aspects of learning, particularly after a child understands a new step and needs to make this work habitual. Incidental and social theories of teaching point out the importance of relating mathematics to the rest of the school program in order to make teaching vital and relevant. The meaningful teaching of arithmetic is basic to any modern method. Pupil understanding is the central aspect of desirable learning. Finally, the discovery theory has brought us back to some of John Dewey's theories of instruction. To him, thinking and intellectual development were research activities as well as the resolution of problems:

> . . . to say that thinking occurs with reference to situations which are still going on, and incomplete, is to say that thinking occurs when things are uncertain or doubtful or problematic. . . . Since the situation in which thinking occurs is a doubtful one, thinking is a process of inquiry. . . . Acquiring is always secondary, and instrumental to the act of inquiring. . . . All thinking is research, and all research is native, original, with him who carries it on, even if everybody else in the world already is sure of what he is still looking for.[10]

Dewey believed education was a reconstruction or reorganization of experience which adds to the meaning of experience and increases the ability to direct the course of subsequent experiences. Education thus conceived involves *growth* and the *changing of behavior* of individuals. Education must assist individuals in acquiring new experiences in order to direct subsequent experiences. Individuals must control their environment rather than merely adjust to it. Thus Dewey was not only interested in the capacity of the individual for setting and solving his own problems, he was interested in the freeing of intelligence for creative activity.

In studying the discovery approach, David P. Ausubel found that research literature supportive of learning by discovery is virtually nonexistent. He points out these three facts: (1) articles cited in the literature reporting results

---

[10]John Dewey, *Democracy and Education* (New York: The Macmillan Company, 1922), pp. 173f.

supportive of discovery techniques actually report no research findings what-soever; (2) most reasonably well-controlled studies report negative findings; and (3) studies reporting positive findings either fail to control other signif-icant variables or employ questionable techniques of statistical analysis.[11]

Teachers and administrators in America's elementary schools should be eclectic in their approach to a theory of instruction. This will mean selecting new content and methods whenever appropriate for a school system or for children. What is needed is the development of a sound, widely accepted theory of instruction. Glennon has discussed the dimensions, the metes and bounds, of two major ingredients of a theory of instruction—theories of content and theories of method—and proposed a model.[12]

In another article, Glennon recommends the development and acceptance of a theory of instruction to serve as the skeleton for structuring research programs that will put flesh on the bones. He believes that numerous pro-posed theories of instruction should be made available to the community of mathematics educators. Then from these efforts and from a reservoir of position papers to be used as guidelines for extensive and intensive dialogue, there should come a theory of instruction usable today and viable for the future.[13] This search for a viable theory of instruction, which is well under way at the present time, may be the fifth era in the teaching of elementary school mathematics. Little doubt exists that such a theory will be eclectic in nature and will include theories of "meaningful teaching" and "discovery methods."

We shall now turn to a consideration of the aims of modern mathematics.

1.3 Establishing Appropriate Aims and Objectives

Aims, used in this book, refer to the purposes stated for elementary schools or elementary teachers. The term *objectives* is used to designate the purposes stated specifically for pupils. We now turn our attention to aims for the elementary school mathematics program.

The preparation of clearly defined aims for the new mathematics has not been an outcome of the revolution in mathematics. Goodlad points out the fact that we should probably not expect such an outcome when the aims for America's schools have not been clearly stated.[14] Each curriculum project in mathematics has been free to formulate objectives for its own particular

[11]David P. Ausubel, "Learning by Discovery: Rationale and Mystique," *National Associa-tion of Secondary School Principals Bulletin,* XLV, No. 269 (December, 1961), 18–58.

[12]Vincent J. Glennon, ". . . And Now Synthesis: A Theoretical Model for Mathematics Education," *The Arithmetic Teacher,* XII (February, 1965), 134–41.

[13]Vincent J. Glennon, "Research Needs in Elementary School Mathematics Education," *The Arithmetic Teacher,* XIII (May, 1966), 366.

[14]John I. Goodlad, *op. cit.,* p. 11.

program. These aims have been poorly stated and are not adequate for evaluating the success of any given project.

As for objectives of the programs, Goodlad points out:

> ... the objectives of the new curriculum programs including mathematics appear to rest on the assumption that any significant behavior which can be derived from analysis of an academic discipline can be learned by students of a given age and is, therefore, worth learning. Those subjects already well established in the curriculum determine what the schools ought to teach. The school's curriculum is closed to new subjects, and to old subjects that have been poorly represented in the political market place.[15]

Guidelines for Statement of Objectives. In the *Twenty-sixth Yearbook* of the National Council of Teachers of Mathematics, a statement of objectives for mathematics has been given. Importance is attached to the objectives as a guide for the total educational program and to the evaluation process.

> ... Many sets of objectives may be developed; there is no commonly accepted list. We hope that the reporting of our list ... will not suggest that these objectives are official or complete or the best or the final ones. ... in order to have a framework or reference, a sample list of objectives is presented. ...[16]

The writers have restated these objectives in terms of student behaviors. The student should:

1. Have a knowledge and understanding of mathematical processes, facts, concepts.
2. Have skill in computing with understanding, accuracy, and efficiency.
3. Recognize and appreciate the role of mathematics in society.
4. Understand the logical structure of mathematics and the nature of proof.
5. Have the ability to use a general problem-solving technique.
6. Develop reading skill and vocabulary essential for progress in mathematics.
7. Use mathematical concepts and processes to discover new generalizations and applications.
8. Develop study habits for independent progress in mathematics.
9. Demonstrate such mental traits as creativity, imagination, curiosity, and visualization.
10. Develop attitudes that lead to appreciation, confidence, respect, initiative, and independence.[17]

This list of objectives represents a practical starting point for teacher planning or for long-range planning for instruction in elementary school mathe-

---

[15] *Ibid.*, p. 54.

[16] *Evaluation in Mathematics, Twenty-sixth Yearbook* (Washington, D.C.: The Council, 1961), p. 72.

[17] *Ibid.*, p. 73.

matics. There are three sources of these objectives: (1) the learner, (2) society, and (3) the discipline of mathematics. Through continuing study the teacher will have to determine whether the suggested list is appropriate for his particular children, for the community in which the children live, and for the new mathematics.

Teachers must make at least five important curriculum decisions. They must decide:

1. How to know children and thereby how to organize the classroom environment so as to promote optimum learning.
2. How to define objectives in behavioral terms to determine the scope and direction of children's learning experiences.
3. How to select and organize learning experiences so that children will achieve desirable educational aims.
4. How to guide the learning process so that experiences are most effectively used by children to achieve educational goals.
5. How to evaluate so as to determine the extent and quality of children's progress toward achievement of the established goals.

Each learning experience provided by the elementary school should involve these elements in some degree.

1.4   Guiding Effective Learning

While each of the curriculum decisions mentioned in the last section is important, the role of the teacher in guiding learning activities needs special emphasis. The principles which follow constitute some of the important learning theories needed for a good foundation for teaching.

The best kind of learning of mathematics takes place when children are actively working on new experiences.

This principle involves having children in classrooms where they solve interesting problems and have many opportunities to make discoveries about mathematics. The work should be exciting and should provide for many opportunities to find out, to experiment, and to feel the reward of successful accomplishment.

Children need freedom to work and to develop an interest in self-education.

Freedom to work means that each child can make mistakes and can try a variety of approaches to solve a problem. When mistakes are made, the teacher helps the child find ways to succeed and to learn from his mistakes. Security rather than punishment for mistakes or ridicule is always present in the classroom. Gradually the teacher helps each child discover the thrill of learning for himself through appropriate pacing of the child's learning activities. The teacher becomes an interested adult who is ever ready to guide the child to higher levels of achievement.

The teacher and the children gain an advantage when arithmetic is taught in a meaningful way.

When arithmetic is made meaningful to children, the subject is interesting to teach. When children understand arithmetic, they will retain, use, and like the subject more than they will when they have been required to memorize facts and to participate in mechanical drill work.

Concept development is the central and most important aspect of directing children's understanding of arithmetic and mathematics.

Concepts represent the whole class or set of things, and help to economize our intellectual efforts. The concept shows that a meaning has been clearly established. When concepts have been carefully taught, children can use these concepts to help them think, generalize, or apply mathematical ideas. Sound concepts can be extended and enlarged to keep pace with a child's new learnings in mathematics.

Many opportunities must be provided for children to work with objects and materials so that correct language and symbols will be learned.

The appropriateness of activities and instructional materials must be considered in teaching. Through the choice of activities children can be guided in their discussion of problems so that correct language will be learned. For example, measuring the classroom so that paint could be ordered, or so that floor covering could be purchased would necessitate a pupil's learning the units used in square measurement. The teacher must have measuring tapes and yard sticks available for children to use in actual measurement. In order to record the data from such measurements, the pupils next need to be familiar with the appropriate language and symbols. Learning the language and symbols of mathematics or arithmetic in this way is based upon understanding and meaningful activity.

Children need to know that number systems have been developed from simple experiences with number.

This approach enables children to gain an understanding of the way arithmetic and mathematics have been used, expanded, and revised to meet man's needs. Any good number system will be continuously changed to keep pace with modern technology and scientific developments.

Work with formalized methods for calculating with numbers should grow out of children's needs for these processes and should be based upon meaningful instruction.

The need for calculating occurs when a child advances beyond the counting of fingers and begins to use mathematical symbols. Later he must learn the four fundamental processes for calculating. These processes are all based upon counting and involve short cuts and abstract thinking. When these processes are learned through meaningful experiences and a discovery approach, children will probably use a variety of methods in solving problems and will experience successful achievement in mathematics.

Readiness for learning to use numbers must be developed at each learning level.

Readiness involves past experiences, mental maturity, appropriate vocabulary, and use of a wide variety of skills. These factors must be considered and appropriate instruction provided at each learning level. This involves provision for individual differences and direct instruction in order to enable readiness to take place. We cannot wait for readiness to occur by itself and without some teacher guidance. Knowing the appropriate time to present a new topic is an important aspect of readiness.

Evaluation is an integral part of learning and teaching.

Evaluation is centered around valid objectives. Children must be involved in the setting of clearly defined purposes—purposes meaningful to them and their community. Individual and group achievement should be measured in terms of these objectives. For the teacher, success should likewise be determined by the amount of progress pupils make toward the achievement of these valid objectives. The child and teacher must continuously evaluate their work in mathematics to see if meaningful learning and achievement have taken place.

1.5   Determining the Content for Elementary School Mathematics

The curriculum reform movement in mathematics covered a wide range of projects and extended to elementary as well as secondary education. Two important factors make the effectiveness of these projects impossible to assess: (1) the failure of each project to establish clearly defined goals, and (2) absence of criteria for comparing programs. Four major considerations are important in making judgments about required content in mathematics:

1. The broad aims of education
2. The demands of our present and emerging society
3. The kinds of learning opportunities needed by children in terms of their growth and development
4. The contribution of the subject field including basic concepts, generalizations, principles, and techniques of study.

Of these four, the curriculum revolution has made its greatest contributions in the areas of social need and identification of mathematical content. The effective development of broad aims of education and the selection of desirable learning experiences for children are now becoming major issues as both educators and subject matter specialists are confronted with the preparation of appropriate instructional materials and the using of efficient methods of instruction.

During the past five years considerable agreement has been reached among mathematicians and curriculum workers on the unifying themes or strands involved in teaching the new mathematics. The fact that textbooks had to be prepared necessitated developing criteria for determining the content and the selection of textbooks.

Statements of strands, to identify the content of the mathematics curriculum in grades K-8, take different forms depending upon the purposes established for their use. Strands may be stated in general form to identify a broad outline of content, or they may be stated as specific recommendations for a particular school system. For example, the State of California has recently issued a Strands Report for use in the selection of instructional materials.[18] The authors will identify and describe the strands essential to a modern mathematics program. Considerations of specific content will be given in the next section which deals with sequence of mathematical topics.

Number Systems. The teaching of modern arithmetic is based upon understanding the structure of number systems and appreciating the relationships between arithmetic and mathematics. Studying whole numbers involves learning an accurate vocabulary, working with the order property, understanding operations on the set of whole numbers, and learning important properties of whole numbers which are related to simple algebra. Once these properties and relationships are learned, they can be used in extending children's understanding of rational numbers and later irrational numbers.

Numeration Systems. A numeration system is the means used to denote or name numbers. Two factors are involved: (1) a set of symbols, and (2) rules for combining the symbols to denote other numbers. Studying the development and use of numeration systems used by the Egyptians, Babylo-

[18]California Statewide Mathematics Advisory Committee, "Mathematics Program, K-8, 1967–1968 Strands Report," *California Mathematics Council Conference Bulletin*, XXV, No. 1 (October, 1967), 5–17.

nians, and Romans may enable children to gain a deeper understanding and appreciation of the system they use. All systems of numeration have some characteristics in common. Children need to discover the importance of symbols, place value, base, and value of zero. Exploring the use of systems of numeration with base two, five, or eight may help children appreciate our base ten and prepare them for applications of these bases to computations with digital computers.

Operations with Whole Numbers. This strand constitutes the heart of a traditional program of mathematics and remains the central aspect of the work for elementary school pupils. Properties of order and relation should be studied on the number line. By using the number line, these concepts can be related to other strands such as geometry. The four fundamental *binary operations* include addition and subtraction, multiplication, and division. Commutative, associative, and distributive properties (as well as identity elements 0 and 1) are given attention.

Operations with Rational Numbers. The content included under this heading is usually developed as part of a large strand on numbers and operations. For clarity of presentation, we have made a separate strand.

Whole numbers (0, 1, 2, 3, 4, . . .) are used to describe sets of whole objects. New numbers (fractions) are used to describe parts of an object or part of a group of objects. The symbols used ($\frac{1}{2}$, $\frac{1}{4}$, and the like) are pairs of counting numerals. In the new mathematics, the arithmetic of fractions includes the arithmetic of whole numbers. Addition and multiplication of fractions have the same properties as whole numbers. Each whole number is a fraction ($3 = \frac{3}{1}$). The set of fractions includes all the whole numbers. Other important aspects include properties of order, betweenness, and density as applied in geometric interpretations. Not all points on a number line can be shown by rational numbers.

Measurement. Measurement is not a new topic. But many new applications of measurement and many new instruments for measuring are being invented. In a strict sense, measurement is largely an applied aspect of mathematics. Because of this fact, measurement provides a way to use mathematical concepts in several other strands. Measurement provides excellent motivation for introducing new mathematical concepts. The traditional English system of measurement is rapidly being replaced by the metric system. Other aspects of modern measurement include new instruments for measuring, indirect measurement, errors of measurement, estimation, and simple charts and graphs. The implications for using measurement in a space age are many and varied.

Applications and Problem Solving. Most mathematicians make a sharp distinction between process of applying mathematics and problem solving. As long as we deal with such applications as the applying of mathematical models and showing the significance of mathematics, this distinction holds.

But applications of mathematics can and should involve the use of mathematical models and problem solving in a variety of school situations and in work with other subjects such as science. The aspects stressed should include: construction of diagrams, guessing reasonable answers, translating the conditions of a problem into mathematical sentences, performing mathematical analysis and interpreting of answers, and building new methods or formulas growing out of adequate evaluation of processes used.

Geometry. The general intent of this strand is to provide for a wide assortment of informal geometric experiences at each learning level. The program should provide for a strong intuitive grasp of basic geometric concepts such as point, line, angle, plane, three dimensional space, congruence and similarity, and coordinate geometry. There should be many ways to use geometric experiences in connection with the strands of number, measurement, applications, problem solving, and logical thinking.

Algebra. While all modern mathematics programs include the provision for considerable work in algebra, algebra is not usually listed as a strand. We choose to do so because of the importance of the topic and thereby to stress the interrelationships with other strands. These aspects of algebra should be included in a modern mathematics program for elementary schools: numbers and operations with numbers, conventional algorithms, sets and functions, mathematical sentences, linear functions in a single variable, solution of linear equations and inequalities, quadratic equations, quadratic formula, and the role of the discriminant. Early use of algebraic forms and concepts should help children with advanced work in algebra. Algebraic principles are introduced and taught throughout the elementary school program.

Functions and Graphs. Functions and their graphs are important tools for studying mathematics and the applications of mathematics. The area of a rectangle is a function of the length of its sides or the volume of a cone is a function of the radius of its base and its height. Other experiences which contribute to the development of abstract mathematical concepts of function include the pairing of numbers with objects such as counting, lengths, formulas, tabular and graphical data, and operations.

Sets. The language of sets should be used to clarify and make precise the concepts and applications of mathematics. Thus the use of the set concept to express one-to-one correspondence and number should be introduced early. A universal rationale can be given for the properties of the integers. The language of sets is continued in studying geometry, functions, solutions of equations, inequalities, number theory, and graphing. The operations required are union, intersection, complementation, and Cartesian product. The properties of the set operations of union and intersection required are commutativity, associativity, and distributivity.

Mathematical Sentences. The language of mathematics has symbols which can be thought of as nouns, verbs, and phrases. Certain symbols are used as punctuation marks to clarify the meaning of a mathematical phrase or sentence. For example, a simple sentence might read: the sum of five and six is eleven. Another sentence might be: $7 = 4 + 3$. This would read: seven equals four plus three. Symbols are used for verb phrases: $=$ is equal to; $>$ is greater than; $<$ is less than; or $\neq$ is not equal to. An open sentence might be $\square + 3 = 10$. There are many uses for number sentences. They are helpful in finding solutions to word problems. Children can make up their own sentences to show understanding of a new process or to provide practice for newly learned skills. Many new textbooks in arithmetic use number sentences to provide a variety of lessons for practice and for drill.

Logic. Both inductive and deductive aspects of mathematics should be presented in a good elementary school program. Much stress is placed upon the inductive approach. However, mathematicians feel that the strength of mathematics comes from its deductive aspect. From certain assumptions they deduce and infer other properties and behaviors. Children should learn: logical connectives (and, or); the meaning of (if A, then B) and the rule of inference which yields ("B" if both) ("if A, then B" and "A" have been established); the role of negation; the role and scope of quantifiers (for all . . . there exists a . . . etc.); the notion of a proof as distinct from a check; and the use of equality in mathematics to mean two different names for the same object or number.

1.6   Determining an Appropriate Sequence for Mathematical Strands

In the last section we presented a description of the mathematical strands which determine to a large extent what will be taught in elementary school mathematics. These strands determine the scope of the curriculum. The next important curriculum problem has to do with sequence—the order or continuity of learning. We are interested in sequence because of possibilities involved in arranging children's learning experiences so that they will learn, reorganize, retain, and transfer what is learned to other learning activities. The sequence followed by a pupil or presented to the pupil may hinder or help him in learning mathematics.

We should take time at this point to identify sequences used in traditional curriculum work. The oldest sequence is *time* or *chronological order*. Events and subject matter were studied in terms of the time or order in which they occurred. The next plan for the sequencing of learning experiences was the *logical order*. This order has been used extensively in mathematics. An empirical decision of primacy is established by an "authority" and then principles and concepts are developed as they grow out of this basic assumption. Lastly, *difficulty* has been used as a basis for sequencing mathematical content. One starts with the simple and goes to the complex. Or, in methods of presentation, one may start with the concrete object and move through the semi-concrete to the abstract idea or symbol.

With these three traditional sequences, the difficulties center around the adult classification of mathematical knowledge and the assumption that this information has been organized in the order children will and should learn it. A premium is placed upon children adjusting to the sequences rather than upon pupils seeking new, creative organizations of their own.

During the last two decades emphasis has been placed upon determining the appropriate sequence for learning in mathematics based upon at least three factors:

1. The individual's pattern of growth and level of achievement influence the acquiring of new knowledge, skills, abilities.
2. The school, through the classroom environment, should stress the worth of each individual and provide for optimum growth through a variety of learning activities.
3. The teacher is the one responsible for guiding learning and providing for continuity of learning through the use of appropriate instructional procedures.

Bruner, in his recent writings on instructional theory, points out that there are various sequences in any instructional program. No unique sequence occurs for all learners. The optimum sequence will depend upon the child's previous learning, the child's stage of development, the nature of the material being learned, and individual differences. The optimum sequence is further influenced by: speed of learning and resistance to forgetting; transferability of old learning to new learning; economy in terms of the cognitive strain imposed; and effectiveness of the learning is generating new learning.[19]

1.7 Organizing the Classroom for Learning

The organizational structure of the modern elementary school, through which teachers guide children's learning experiences, has been undergoing considerable change during the past decade. These changes have been directed toward the improvement of instructional practices as well as greater involvement of the learner. While some instruction has been centered around group learning, the trend is increasingly in the direction of individualized instruction.

Experimentation with several kinds of classroom organization should continue during the next decade. Hopefully, as a new theory of instruction

[19]Jerome S. Bruner, *Toward a Theory of Instruction* (Cambridge, Mass.: Harvard University Press, 1967), pp. 49f.

is developed, we can expect improvement in the preparation of teachers and in the provision for good instructional materials. The self-contained classroom, team teaching, homeroom teachers working with specialists, exchange of classes so that an expert can teach mathematics, and the use of mathematics laboratories will form the nucleus for this experimentation. Each organization should be improved, extended, and evaluated.

Improvements within Self-contained Classroom. Experimentation should be encouraged in the self-contained classroom. Grouping should be used so that instruction can be made appropriate for at least three learning levels and so that considerable individualization will take place. Many teachers have found that two groups, supplemented by individual guidance during study periods, are practical for instruction in grades three through six. Two charts are shown to illustrate organizations of class time for a 45-minute period: (1) an arithmetic period for teaching a basic step or concept, and (2) a lesson growing out of a class problem in social studies or science.

I. TEACHING A BASIC STEP OR CONCEPT: 40–45 MINUTES DAILY

Time	*Group A*	*Group B*
Period I 5–10 min.	Discuss assignment.	1. Give diagnostic test or review. 2. Work on individual needs.
Period II 15–20 min.	Work on assignment. Work on individual needs.	Lesson directed by teacher.
Period III 15–20 min.	Check assignment done in Period II. Have directed lesson with teacher.	Follow-up assignment on skills growing out of directed lesson. Check work at close.

II. ARITHMETIC LESSON GROWING OUT OF SOCIAL STUDIES OR SCIENCE: FLEXIBLE TIME ARRANGEMENT

Period I 20–25 min.	The whole class discusses a common experience and seeks solutions to a problem. Teacher guides and helps with solutions.	
Period II 20–25 min.	Work on individual or group assignment suitable to ability level.	Work with teacher to develop understanding of process or concept presented.

Using Mathematics Specialists. Numerous cooperative teaching procedures have appeared during the last decade. These ventures will probably make important contributions to classroom organization and to teaching. *Team teaching* provides an organizational structure wherein teacher specialists work together with a group of pupils. Four or five teachers, each contributing his specialized abilities, may work cooperatively with 120–130 pupils.

A specialist in mathematics can be assigned to work with the teacher in a self-contained classroom either teaching selected lessons or advising and assisting the regular teacher.

Departmentalized teaching is being tried in some elementary schools in grades five and six. While this type of teaching does not further the goals of relating subjects and encouraging general education, the plan may have many advantages over present practices wherein state law requires teachers to attempt instruction in ten or more subjects daily.

Specialists are used in some schools on an exchange basis—teaching one or two periods of mathematics in classes where the teachers exchange with the specialist. For in-service instruction with teachers and for the preparation of instructional materials to complete a program, the specialist can be used.

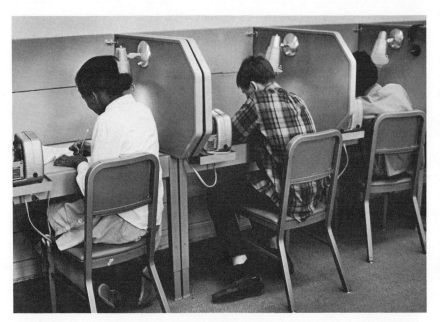

Individual booths provide space for viewing or listening and enable the child to review or move ahead at his own rate on new mathematical work. Photograph by Earl W. Dible, Santa Monica Public Schools.

Coordinator of Instructional Resources. Under this type of organization, the elementary school teacher coordinates the use of instructional resources. Basic skills and knowledge are built into the instructional units or packages. The teacher would be supplied with textbooks, programmed books, films, tapes, records, and instructional aids to use in guiding children's learning in mathematics. The teacher would administer pretests, give diagnostic tests, guide the use of instructional materials, help pupils record results of their work or evaluate their progress, and act as instructional director for the class.

Considerable attention is being given to the preparation of curriculum materials and instructional packages which support team teaching, teacher coordinators, and a mathematics laboratory.

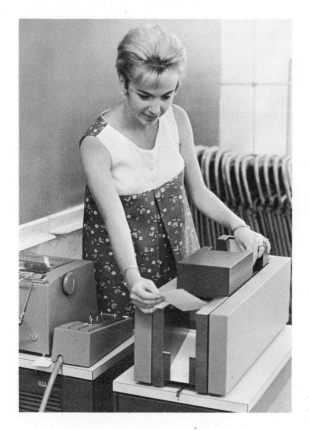

This Project PLAN teacher is sending individual test and status information to the computer. The return information will allow her to make judgments in regard to programs for individuals that will be based on the student's long-range educational effort as well as on recent productivity. San Carlos school district, California; Project PLAN Classrooms, Brittan Acres.

1.8 Learning the Concept of Number

Generally speaking the basic foundation of a subject is at the same time both the easiest part to understand and the most difficult part to discuss.

What is 3? Everyone knows that 3 means, but to discuss its meaning fully leads to philosophical, psychological, and abstract mathematical considerations. The mark that we make to indicate 3 is a symbol that stands for an idea. Thus III, three, and the French *trois* are other symbols for the concept of 3. Number is an abstract concept. Thus 3 apples and 3 oranges are not identical in nature, but they share a property of threeness which is in itself an abstraction.

Two approaches have been used in introducing the young child to mathematics. In England particularly, stress is placed upon the development of language to express mathematical ideas. Children are provided with a variety of instructional aids such as rods, disks, tiles, and counters. The teacher arranges learning activities which help children talk about size, shape, relationships, and counting. After an appropriate amount of time, children then develop the need to use cardinal numbers to quantify their experiences. In the United States we have introduced basic ideas about sets to provide the context within which the mathematical experiences of children can be unified. So children handle a variety of concrete objects much as children in England do. The major difference, however, lies in the emphasis upon sets and the development of the language of sets as the first step in the development of mathematical ideas. Sets and the language of sets will be discussed in the chapter on addition.

Number has two basic aspects—*cardinal* and *ordinal*. The cardinal aspect has to do with quantity, but the ordinal aspect introduces the idea of order. Therefore, in a row of chairs there is one chair that is the third chair from one end of the row; it is chair number three.

Number is a generic term, such as *man*, which is easy to understand and difficult to discuss precisely. Number is a product of the mind, and thus is of interest to psychologists.

From a mathematical point of view one can place the natural numbers 1, 2, 3, . . . on an abstract postulational basis. This was done by Peano, an Italian mathematician, who was able to construct the arithmetic of the natural numbers from five postulates:

1. 1 is a number.
2. The successor of any number is a number.
3. No two numbers have the same successor.
4. 1 is not the successor of any number.
5. Principle of mathematical induction.

In the new mathematics, attention is given to correct and precise mathematical terminology. A distinction is made between *number* and *numeral*. *Number*, as shown in the next chapter, is a property of a set. Number represents quantity, the number of things in a set (called elements in a set). We think with numbers. We cannot see numbers.

Numerals are names for numbers. We can see numerals because we write them. We use marks or symbols for the cardinal numbers. We may write 6 as six, 4 + 2, or VI, or we may punch a hole in an IBM card or tape to represent six in order to feed this data into a computer. Numeral is a communication device. So in elementary school mathematics we help children reach agreement on a variety of ways to write symbols for a number. *A number has many names.*

When the usual form for numerals is wanted, we ask children to write *standard numerals*. While 5 + 5, 6 + 4, or 8 + 2 are names for the same number, to find the sum of five and five, the child should be expected to write 10 as the standard numeral.

A system of numeration is used to communicate basic mathematical concepts. We shall turn our attention to the Hindu-Arabic system of numeration and basic concept of *place value* of numerals.

1.9   Hindu-Arabic Numeration System

The numeration system we use was invented by the Hindus. They developed the decimal place-value system for whole numbers. Probably during the second century, the numerals 1 2 3 4 5 6 7 8 9 were developed first. The symbol for zero was developed near A.D. 876. Then Arab traders carried the system to the Western world. For these reasons we say that the numeration system used in the United States is the Hindu-Arabic system.

Each of the first nine numerals can be written with a single symbol. To write the numeral following 9, two symbols must be used; 1 and 0 to make 10. Because we use the ten numerals in a place-value scheme based on the powers of ten, we call the system a decimal numeration system. The base of our number system is ten.

To see how the idea of place value works we will write the numeral 444. The numerals stand for 4 hundreds, 4 tens, and 4 ones. Shown on a place-value chart we see:

HUNDREDS	TENS	ONES
🗊🗊🗊🗊	🗊🗊🗊🗊	📄📄📄📄

the actual physical location of each numeral relative to the ones position. There are 4 pieces of paper in the ones place (4 × 1 = 4), 4 bundles of ten papers in the tens place (4 × 10 = 40), and 4 bundles of 100 pieces of paper in the hundreds place (4 × 100 = 400). Thus 400 + 40 + 4 = 444. Using educational toy money, the example could be shown as 4 $1 bills, 4 $10 bills, and 4 $100 bills. This provides a compact and efficient system of notation. In base ten, each numeral shown (such as 153) has a cardinal value (how many) and a positional or place value. The numeral 1 shows one and holds the hundreds position. The numeral 5 shows five and holds the tens place. The numeral 3 shows 3 in the ones place. Beginning with the ones place, each order to the left of the ones is ten times greater than the last order (see p. 24).

The concept of zero is not difficult to understand if place value is carefully taught at each new learning level. The primary-age child must first learn to use cardinal numbers to tell how many objects are in a set. When he reaches

10^2	10^1	10^0 *
Hundreds	Tens	Ones
1	5	3

* Shows no tens. The position shows units or ones.

ten, he discovers how to write the new numeral 10. Zero means no ones and is written as a place holder. The one shows 1 group of ten. This same type of meaningful teaching should take place when one hundred or one thousand is written.

Certain properties of zero are discovered as children use the fundamental operations. These will be discussed in detail in connection with the chapters on the four fundamental operations.

$$6 + 0 = 6$$
$$6 - 0 = 6$$
$$6 \times 0 = 0$$
$$0 \div 6 = 0$$
$$6 \div 0 \text{ is undefined.}$$

The applications of zero include: the beginning of a number line, zero on a thermometer scale, zero on a chart, and recording no score (0) for dart throwing or similar contests. The invention of zero and the idea of place value are two characteristics of our number system that set it apart from earlier systems used by the Greeks, Romans, and Egyptians. These two characteristics make our number system superior to these earlier systems.

One of the jobs of the elementary teacher is to provide instruction in reading numbers correctly. This is related to the task of writing numbers in words. For example, in writing 36 a hyphen is used: thirty-six. Also, 102 is read one hundred two, omitting the "and" that is sometimes erroneously used.

The names of the first ten orders in our place-value scheme are: ones, tens, hundreds, thousands, ten-thousands, hundred-thousands, millions, ten-millions, hundred-millions, and billions.

Each successive group of three orders is called a period. The first eleven periods are: thousands, millions, billions, trillions, quadrillions, quintillions, sectillions, septillions, octillions, nonillions, and decillions. Periods may be skipped, as shown in the table, and read sixty-four million, two hundred thirty-seven.

10^{18}	10^{17}	10^{16}	10^{15}	10^{14}	10^{13}	10^{12}	10^{11}	10^{10}	10^9	10^8	10^7	10^6	10^5	10^4	10^3	10^2	10^1	10^0
Quintillions	Hundred-quadrillions	Ten-quadrillions	Quadrillions	Hundred-trillions	Ten-trillions	Trillions	Hundred-billions	Ten-billions	Billions	Hundred-millions	Ten-millions	Millions	Hundred-thousands	Ten-thousands	Thousands	Hundreds	Tens	Ones
											6	4	0	0	0	2	3	7

The decimal system, with its ideas of place-value and notation, provides the rationale for the fundamental operations of arithmetic.

An interesting history is involved in the establishment of these basic operations.

An Arab mathematician, Mohammed ibu Musa al-Khowarizmi, wrote a book describing the Hindu system about A.D. 825. This textbook was translated and used in Europe during the twelfth century. The followers of al-Khowarizmi used his systems of computation and were called algorists. The name algorism grew out of the name of this mathematician. So today we use the word algorithm to describe an operation such as addition or subtraction.

Two methods of computation were used during this early period: the use of an abacus, and the algorithm system. Gradually the algorithm method (by about 1500) became the predominate way of computing in the Western world. The abacus is still widely used in the Far East. At the Tokyo airport recently, two cashiers were seen working—one using a modern calculator to do his computing and the other relying on the abacus. The abacist quickly aided his colleague in checking a computation involving exchange of United States and Japanese currency.

1.10 Learning Other Bases

Why should we teach number bases other than base ten used in our number system? The answer is rather clear. We want to provide an approach to review basic number relationships and the place-value structure. Children need to see that computation can be performed in bases other than ten. Furthermore some other number bases can be used more easily in electronic computers.

Difficulties have arisen concerning the use of other bases in modern elementary school textbooks. Because work with other bases has been included, some teachers feel compelled to make computation in other bases one of their main objectives. There is no sound justification for trying to develop computational proficiency in a base other than ten or to spend large amounts of class time on other bases. Priorities must be established for the essentials of modern mathematics which should be presented to elementary school children.[20]

Some of the essential aspects of other bases will now be presented. In any place-value system of numeration, symbols are chosen for the numbers zero, one, two, three, etc., up to but not including the base. For example, in base four, the symbols include:

$$0 \text{ zero}$$

X	1
XX	2
XXX	3

To write a symbol for XXXX, we would have to use the place-value system and write 10 four. Another way to designate the base is to use a subscript such as 10_4 or 13_5 (read: one zero base four and one three base five). We now will apply these principles using base eight.

The first seven numerals in base eight are: 1 2 3 4 5 6 7. The next numeral after seven is written 10_8 or 10_{eight}. This means 1 eight and no ones. Then 11_8 means 1 eight and 1 one; so 11_8 is equivalent to 9 in base ten. Can you continue writing the numerals in base eight up to 16 in base ten?

In base eight, the place values are:

PLACE VALUE IN BASE EIGHT			
Position 3	*Position 2*	*Position 1*	*Position 0*
Five hundred twelve	Sixty-four	eight	one
$8 \times 8 \times 8$	8×8	8	1
8^3	8^2	8^1	8^0

While the place values have position 0, 1, 2, 3 as in base ten, the place value for each position is different from that in the base-ten system. Position 0 has place value one, or 8^0. After that, each place value is eight times the place value of the next position *to the right*. Position 1 has a place value of the base, in this case eight (8×1). Position 2 has place value (8×8) or sixty-four. The place value of position 3 is $(8 \times 8 \times 8)$ or five hundred-twelve.

Now study the following example which uses expanded notation to express the number named by 132_{eight} or (132_8).

---

[20]Jesse A. Rudnick, "Numeration Systems and Their Classroom Roles," *The Arithmetic Teacher*, XV (February, 1968), 138–47.

Position 2   Position 1   Position 0

$$132_8 = (1 \times 64) \; + \; (3 \times 8) \; + \; (2 \times 1)$$

What would 132_8 be in base ten? Another name for base eight is *octal system*. Some numerals expressed in base ten, two, and eight are:

Base ten	Base two	Base eight
1	1	1
2	10	2
3	11	3
4	100	4
5	101	5
6	110	6
7	111	7
8	1000	10
9	1001	11
10	1010	12
11	1011	13
12	1100	14
13	1101	15
14	1110	16
15	1111	17
16	10000	20

Base two, called *binary system* of numeration, is important because the modern electronic computer is based on binary notation for numbers. Note the following features:

1. Every place-value system of numeration has a base which may be any whole number greater than one.
2. The number of different symbols used is the same number as the base.
3. Each position in a numeral has an assigned place value. This value is a power of the base.

PLACE VALUE IN BASE TWO (BINARY)					
Position 5	*Position 4*	*Position 3*	*Position 2*	*Position 1*	*Position 0*
thirty-two	sixteen	eight	four	two	one
$2 \times 2 \times 2 \times 2 \times 2$	$2 \times 2 \times 2 \times 2$	$2 \times 2 \times 2$	2×2	2	1
2^5	2^4	2^3	2^2	2^1	2^0

Study the binary numerals:

$$101_{two} = (1 \times two^2) + (0 \times two^1) + (1 \times two^0)$$
$$= (1 \times four) + (0 \times two) + (1 \times one)$$
$$= (1 \times 4_{ten}) + (0 \times 2_{ten}) + (1 \times 1_{ten})$$
$$= 4_{ten} + 0_{ten} + 1_{ten}$$
$$= 5_{ten}$$

How would you show the expanded notation for 11011? Can you extend the chart to include positions 6 and 7?

1.11   Learning about Other Numeration Systems

The newer mathematical programs expose children to nonpositional or semi-positional systems such as the Egyptian, Babylonian, or Roman. In nonpositional systems each symbol represents a quantity. Then the value of a number being represented is found by adding the values assigned to each symbol. For positional systems, the number value of a given set of symbols is shown by the order in which the symbols appear.

The main reason for including ancient numeration systems in the elementary school mathematics program is to provide background for studying our decimal system and for understanding its unique property—place value.[21] Studying ancient systems can be a very interesting and challenging experience for gifted children and for related study in social studies. Properly taught, without emphasis upon computation, other numeration systems can provide an enjoyable support for our decimal system. Let us turn our attention to one of the ancient systems of numeration, Roman numerals. The basic Roman numerals and their values are:

I = 1	C = 100
V = 5	D = 500
X = 10	M = 1,000
L = 50	

The numbers from 1 to 20 written in the Roman numeral system show some of the rules used in writing numbers in Roman numerals. They are: I, II, III, IV, V, VI, VII, VIII, IX, X, XI, XII, XIII, XIV, XV, XVI, XVII, XVIII, XIX, XX.

To express the number two use two ones, II, and to express three use three ones, III. Repeating a symbol repeats its value.

To express the number four one could use four ones, but a certain economy of symbols is attained by introducing a new rule: If a symbol is placed at the left of a symbol of greater value, then the combined value of the two symbols is the difference of their values. Thus, IV means to subtract one from five,

---

[21] *Ibid.*, p. 144.

so it represents four. Likewise, IX means to subtract one from ten, so IX represents nine.

If a symbol is placed at the right of a symbol of greater value, the combined value of the two symbols is the sum of their values. Thus, VI means to add five and one, so it represents six. Similarly, XI means to add ten and one, so it represents eleven.

If a symbol is placed between two symbols of greater value, the combined value of the three symbols is the sum of the two greater minus the smallest. For example, in XIX, the one is placed between two tens, so the combined value is:

$$(10 + 10) - 1 = 19$$

In writing numbers in Roman numerals, the symbols are written from left to right in the order of decreasing value, and the symbols are added, with the exception that I before V, I before X, X before L, X before C, C before D, and C before M, each indicates a subtraction.

Placing a horizontal line over a symbol multiplies its value by one thousand. Thus, $\overline{V}$ means five thousand.

In a certain sense, there is no place-value idea in the Roman numeral system. In our Hindu-Arabic system each of the sixes in 666 has a different value, but in XXX each of the tens has the same value. In another sense, there is a type of place value in the Roman system, since IV and VI do not stand for the same number, that is, the order of the symbols is significant.

Roman numerals are taught in the elementary school; they are introduced early and the topic is developed gradually through the grades. This is done for several reasons. Roman numerals are used on some clocks. They are sometimes used in numbering the chapters of a book and in the major subdivisions of an outline. Also, they are frequently used in stating the dates in years on cornerstones of buildings and in copyright notes.

The Roman system of numeration was used primarily for recording quantitative data. As we stated earlier in this chapter, mechanical devices such as the abacus were used to perform computations. All one has to do is attempt ordinary computations with Roman numerals to appreciate the fact that the Romans did not contribute much to arithmetic.

1.12   Chapter Summary

Mathematics and numerical operations are indispensable in our scientific space age. Because of this fact, America's elementary schools are responsible for the kind of mathematics needed for social competence as well as individual efficiency.

Theories for the teaching of elementary school mathematics have undergone several major changes during the last 50 years. Each change has left a residue which continues to influence current teaching theories. Teachers are urged to be eclectic in their approach to teaching—accepting those theories which seem to produce the best results in terms of well-defined goals and specific groups of children. A combination of teaching procedures, stressing meaningful learning through guided discovery, is in vogue. The search for a viable theory of instruction continues and points the way toward extensive use of modern instructional media and learning laboratories.

The need for establishing valid objectives for elementary school mathematics, growing out of clearly defined goals for elementary education, has been identified. At present, there is no external criterion for comparing the effectiveness of the old with the new mathematics.

A heavy burden has been placed upon the elementary school teacher to coordinate the use of a variety of instructional materials particularly appropriate for the children being taught. The selection of content, determination of learning activities, and provision for continuity in learning are major teacher responsibilities. Becoming expert in these aspects of teaching requires careful preparation and continuing in-service improvement.

Basic principles and terminology required for effective teaching of elementary school mathematics have been identified. The characteristics of our Hindu-Arabic numeration system and the use of base ten have been discussed and related to the fundamental operations which constitute the central core of the mathematics program.

Stress has been placed upon the establishment of priorities for determining the amount of mathematical theory and the selection of essential content to be presented to elementary school children. Tribute should be paid to the skill of elementary school teachers in their accomplishments in teaching the new mathematics. We express our confidence in their ability to acquire new teaching skills and to participate in cooperative curriculum improvement projects.

QUESTIONS AND EXERCISES

1. Prepare a list of arguments *for* and *against* social usage as the one most important criterion for selecting the content to be taught in elementary school mathematics.

2. When arithmetic is taught to the entire class, what may happen to: **(a)** the gifted child **(b)** the average child **(c)** the slow learner

3. Read one of these references (Ausubel, Hendrix, or Riedesel) to gain background on the discovery method of teaching. Then make a list of criteria for evaluating a lesson taught by this method.

4. Use the statement of aims given in this chapter for an elementary school mathematics program to evaluate a course of study for some school system (New York State, California, Illinois, or a single school system such as Boston).

5. Use the strands given in this chapter to evaluate (for coverage of basic mathematical topics) one of the modern mathematics books written after 1964 for elementary schools.

6. Write a brief position paper (refuting or substantiating) Bruner's hypothesis that "any idea, problem, or body of knowledge can be presented in a form simple enough so that any particular learner can understand it in a recognizable form."

7. What does the following statement mean? The number of different symbols used in a particular numeration system is the same number as the base.

8. Show that a place value is a number which is a power of the base used.

9. Give five different names for any one of the following:
   (a) six   (b) ten   (c) zero

10. Complete these two statements.
    (a) In the numeral 2503, the place value of the position of "5" is _____ times as great as the place value of the position "0."
    (b) In the numeral 2503, the place value of the position of "2" is _____ times as great as the place value of the position "0." .

11. Write the base four numerals for numbers from one to twenty used in base ten.

12. What is the greatest number that can be represented by a two-digit numeral in base five?

13. Write the decimal numerals for the following:
    (a) $3T_{twelve}$ (b) $T0_{twelve}$ (c) $1TT_{twelve}$

14. Use expanded notation to show the value of each example.
    (a) 325_{six} (b) 875_{ten} (c) 11011_{two}

15. Write these numerals in the decimal system:
    (a) CMXLVII   (b) MCIV   (c) LXII   (d) MCMXIX

16. What are the three main advantages of the Hindu-Arabic numeration system?

17. Identify three applications of zero in everyday usage.

SELECTED REFERENCES

Ausubel, David P., "Learning by Discovery: Rationale and Mystique," *National Association of Secondary School Principals Bulletin*, XLV (December, 1961).

Brownell, William A., *Arithmetic in Grades I and II*. Durham, N. C.: Duke University Press, 1941.

———, *The Development of Children's Number Ideas in Primary Grades*. Chicago: University of Chicago Press, 1928.

———, "The Place of Meaning in the Teaching of Arithmetic," *Elementary School Journal*, XLVII (January, 1947).

———, "Psychological Considerations in the Learning and Teaching of Arithmetic,"

Instruction in Arithmetic, Tenth Yearbook. Washington, D.C.: National Council of Teachers of Mathematics, 1935.

Bruner, Jerome S., *Toward a Theory of Instruction.* Cambridge, Mass.: Harvard University Press, 1967.

California Statewide Mathematics Advisory Committee, "Mathematics Program K-8, 1967–68 Strands Report," *California Mathematics Council Conference Bulletin* (October, 1967).

Dewey, John, *Democracy and Education.* New York: The Macmillan Company, 1922.

Glennon, Vincent J., ". . . And Now Synthesis: A Theoretical Model for Mathematics Education." *The Arithmetic Teacher,* XII (February, 1965), 134–40.

————, "Research Needs in Elementary School Mathematics Education," *The Arithmetic Teacher,* XIII (May, 1966), 363–67.

Goodlad, John I., *School Curriculum Reform in the United States.* New York: The Fund for the Advancement of Education, 1964.

Karpinski, Louis, *The History of Mathematics.* New York: Russell and Russell, 1965.

Hanna, Paul R., "Opportunities for the Use of Arithmetic in An Activity Program," *The Teaching of Arithmetic.* Washington, D.C.: The National Council of Teachers of Mathematics, 1935, pp. 85–120.

Hendrix, Gertrude, "Learning by Discovery," *The Mathematics Teacher,* LIV (May 1961), 290–99.

McConnell, T. R., "Discovery vs. Authoritative Identification in the Learning of Children," *Studies in the Psychology of Learning, II,* IX, No. 5. Iowa City: University of Iowa, 1934, pp. 13–62.

Morton, R. L., *Teaching Arithmetic in the Elementary School,* Vol. I. New York: Silver Burdett Co., 1937.

Riedesel, C. Alan, *Guiding Discovery in Elementary School Mathematics.* New York: Appleton-Century-Crofts, 1967.

Rudnick, Jesse A., "Numeration Systems and Their Classroom Roles." *The Arithmetic Teacher,* XV (February, 1968).

Smith, David E., *History of Mathematics,* Vol. II. New York: Dover Publications, 1953.

Swain, Robert L., "Modern Mathematics and School Arithmetic," *Instruction in Arithmetic, Twenty-fifth Yearbook.* Washington, D.C.: The National Council of Teachers of Mathematics, 1960.

Thiele, C. L., *The Contribution of Generalization to the Learning of the Addition Facts.* New York: Bureau of Publications, Teachers College, Columbia University, 1938.

Welmers, Everet T., "Arithmetic in Today's Culture," *Instruction in Arithmetic, Twenty-fifth Yearbook.* Washington, D.C.: The National Council of Teachers of Mathematics, 1960.

Wheat, H. G., *The Psychology and Teaching of Arithmetic.* Boston: D. C. Heath, 1937.

▲▲▲▲▲▲▲

2

▼▼▼▼▼▼▼

Language and Operations
Used in Addition

2.1 Developing a Need for Calculating

The need for arithmetic begins early in a child's life. Our highly industrialized society provides the setting for many varied experiences with arithmetic beginning in early childhood and continuing throughout adult life. Research studies, beginning with Brownell's classical study of 1928, have shown that children possess many number concepts before entering first grade.[1] Sussman, in a recent study, has shown that today's kindergartners know as much about arithmetic at the beginning of kindergarten as first-grade children did a few decades ago.[2] These important facts provide the foundation for instruction in mathematics in the elementary school:

1. Instruction must provide for the extension of children's arithmetic concepts.
2. The language arts aspects of mathematics must be provided for because the out-of-school language development of children will influence the way they express mathematical ideas as well as the way they condition their ability to understand the oral expression of others.

[1] William A. Brownell, "The Development of Children's Number Ideas in Primary Grades," *Supplementary Educational Monograph*, *No. 35* (Chicago: University of Chicago Press, 1928).
[2] David Sussman, *Number Readiness of Kindergarten Children* (unpublished doctoral dissertation, University of California, Los Angeles, 1962).

3. A child's experiences with mathematics in and out of school should lead to the discovery of certain operations which are based upon the structure of our number system.

Considerable evidence exists to show that these important foundation factors just mentioned are not being considered or adequately provided for in either the beginning instructional programs in mathematics or in the preparation of instructional materials based upon modern mathematical investigations. For example, Dutton found that kindergarten mathematics programs in a major city school system were not systematically providing for the top one-third of the children entering the program mature enough and ready for counting, enumerating, grouping, reproducing numerals, and extending mathematical concepts of size, shape, form, and measurement.[3] The study showed that the average and near-average children gained the most from the informal mathematics program. The lowest one-third of the children enrolled in kindergarten were seriously handicapped by informal and incidental teaching which did not meet their needs or provide readiness experiences for later learning. Likewise, the highest one-third were not challenged or provided with a program to extend their knowledge in mathematics.

Through a variety of classroom activities young children must be guided in their use of number to count objects, number collections, identify size or weight, and arrange things in some order. Along with these manipulative experiences with concrete objects, children should learn the names of numbers and the language needed to express their ideas clearly. Left on their own, children will learn very little about our mathematical system. So at the appropriate time, after rich experiences with mathematics and when children are mature enough for the advanced learning step, the classroom teacher guides each child in acquiring a way to calculate and use our number system. This process, according to Piaget, a noted authority on concept development, cannot be hurried.[4] Rich experiences, guidance, time, and maturity are needed.

The preparation of appropriate instructional materials for a mathematics program based upon the foundation factors just discussed is a cooperative undertaking. The writing team should include the skilled classroom teacher, the curriculum expert, the mathematician, the psychologist, and the linguistic specialist. The work should begin with the careful preparation of behavioral objectives to define the pupil achievement desired and to guide the evaluation of each aspect of the instructional program. The work should not be considered finished after the book or course of study has been printed. *Con-*

[3]Wilbur H. Dutton, "Growth in Number Readiness in Kindergarten Children," *The Arithmetic Teacher*, X (May, 1963), 252–54.
[4]Jean Piaget, *The Child's Conception of Number* (London: Routledge & Kegan Paul, Ltd., 1952).

tinuous try-out, evaluation, and *revision* should become accepted aspects of modern curriculum improvement work in mathematics.

2.2   Language and Mathematics

Learning mathematics involves the use of two different but related language systems: (1) the common English language needed for communication, and (2) the language used in the development of mathematical ideas and concepts. These two language systems function differently for children who are bi-lingual or who have their own well-developed language style which has resulted from their living in certain socio-economic groups or regions.

Considerable attention should be given to the input and the output aspects of mathematics. In working with young children, the teacher must be concerned with listening (hearing the child's spoken language), with using concrete objects to build the child's background and meaning, and with demonstrating by means of the use of simple written symbols—*all intake* aspects. Gradually the teacher helps the young child use the *output aspects* of language —*to speak* about mathematical experiences, *to demonstrate* understanding by the use of objects and simple symbols, and *to write* numerals or use mathematical symbols.

Learning the language of mathematics is important at each learning level. New vocabulary must be learned regularly. Pupils should be able to illustrate ideas with drawings. They must be able to describe new mathematical concepts in words and to relate one idea to another. The ability to have a clear mental picture of ideas or drawings is needed for recalling ideas, for understanding spoken or written mathematical work, and for writing one's mathematical ideas.

To aid in the learning of the language of mathematics, modern scholars in mathematics have introduced several methods and techniques: (1) the use of simple language from set theory; (2) the use of mathematical sentences and appropriate symbols; and (3) the use of the number line. While other aids to language development are also used in elementary school mathematics, these three have been stressed in all modern textbooks. Each will be discussed in the sections which follow.

2.3   Using the Language of Sets

Elementary school teachers are confronted with the teaching of new topics in mathematics, working with variations of old topics, and using a precise language for describing mathematical ideas or concepts. Difficulties are encountered when these teachers are introduced to a new topic, such as set theory, and expected to understand more about the topic than they will teach. Teachers should take background courses which will enable them to understand mathematical concepts beyond their teaching level. This preparation is especially necessary with the use of set-theory language in mathematics. The use of the set concept in elementary mathematics has the advantages of helping with clarity and precision in communicating mathematical ideas. In addition to this, many mathematical disciplines are regarded as branches of set theory. Set theory provides a means for unifying and simplifying many aspects of mathematics. For later work in algebra and elementary geometry, the simple set concepts presented in elementary mathematics are necessary. Teachers should know what pupils will study later in order that they can provide sound foundation work and direct the capable students into advanced work in mathematics.

The ideas of sets and relationships among sets will be described so that elementary school teachers will understand the use of these ideas in the mathematics program. The vocabulary and language of sets will be presented first. Applications of sets will be made throughout this book whenever appropriate to the discussion, as, for example, during discussions of basic operations, simple algebra, or geometry.

DEFINITION AND ELEMENTS

A *set* is a collection of objects. The exact nature of the objects depends upon the thought process or problem situation. One can think of a set of blocks, numerals, people, books, or any other group of objects. Sets have two important characteristics: (1) an object can be identified as a member of the set; and (2) an object can be identified as not a member of the set. An example of this definition could be: the set of all red-haired girls in your school. Members of the set of red-haired girls can be identified easily. Likewise, girls who are not a member of this set can be clearly identified.

The elements of a set name the things included in each set. These include providing a general description of a set, naming elements of a set, and showing set membership. The definition and language for each of these elements is shown below:

Description
   A set of fractional numbers used on a ruler $A = \{\frac{1}{2}, \frac{1}{4}, \frac{1}{8}\}$

Naming elements of a set
   The digits used in decimal notation $B = \{0, 1, 2, 3, 4, 5, 6, 7, 8, 9\}$

Showing set membership
   Identifying a specific element $5 \in B$

The Greek letter Epsilon " $\in$ " means the element belongs to set B. The language of sets in this section (capital letters A or B, braces { } and an element of ∈) along with other symbols will be used in connection with beginning work in addition later in this chapter.

KINDS OF SETS

In this section four kinds of sets will be discussed: (1) equal sets, (2) equivalent sets, (3) nonequivalent sets, and (4) null or empty sets.

Equal sets

Two or more sets with the same or identical members.

$A = \{1, 2, 3, 4, 5\}$
$B = \{5, 4, 3, 2, 1\}$

Equivalent sets

Set A is equal to Set B—numerically equivalent
Using the symbol ≠ shows not equal
Two or more sets with one-to-one correspondence of the members.

$A = B$
$C \neq D$
$A = \{\square, \square, \square.\}$
$B = \{\bigcirc, \bigcirc, \bigcirc\}$

Since the elements in Set A match the elements in Set B, Set A is numerically equivalent to Set B.
The symbols ↔ or ~ indicate equivalence—A ↔ B or A ~ B.

Nonequivalent sets

Members cannot be matched in one-to-one correspondence.

$C = \{\bigcirc, \bigcirc\}$
$D = \{\square, \square, \square\}$

Empty set or null set

Not any members, an empty set. In advanced work with set theory, the symbol ∅ is used to denote the empty set. The word null (derived from French *nul*, not any) may also be used to describe no elements in a set.

$A = \{\ \}$
or
$A = ∅$

Creative thinking, involving solving problems with larger numbers or very large sets, has an important place in elementary school mathematics. The teacher may wish to have children think about "all points on a line (geometry)" or "all whole numbers." This type of work necessitates using other kinds of sets than those just described. These useful sets include *unit set, finite set, infinite set, universal set,* and *complementary set.*

Unit set

A set with one element
The one continent could be named, the continent of South America.

$A = \{\text{one continent}\}$
$A = \begin{Bmatrix} \text{continent of} \\ \text{South America} \end{Bmatrix}$

Finite set

A set with a given number of elements

$$A = \begin{cases} \text{Countries in the} \\ \text{Eastern} \\ \text{Hemisphere} \end{cases}$$

Naming the countries we have

$$A = \begin{cases} \text{Europe, Asia} \\ \text{Africa, Australia} \end{cases}$$

Infinite set

A set with unlimited elements

$$A = \{\text{All whole numbers}\}$$

How far could one go when counting whole numbers? There is no logical stopping point. This is shown as

$$A = \{1, 2, 3, 4, 5, \ldots\}$$

The dots (leaders) direct the reader to continue on indefinitely. Another example could be "points on a line."

$$A = \{ \longleftrightarrow \}$$

There is an infinite number of points on the line, extending in both directions.

Universal set

All members of a specific set

$$U = \begin{cases} \text{All citizens of the} \\ \text{United States} \end{cases}$$

The capital letter U stands for universal set.

Complementary set

Elements of a set in a universal set other than the elements in a given set

$$A = \begin{cases} \text{All male citizens in} \\ \text{the United States} \end{cases}$$

If $A =$ the given set, then $A' =$ the complementary set.

$$A' = \begin{cases} \text{All citizens of the} \\ \text{United States} \\ \text{other than male} \\ \text{citizens} \end{cases}$$

RELATIONSHIPS AMONG SETS

When considering relationships between or among sets, we use specific language. We speak of *disjoint sets*, *intersection of sets*, and *subsets*. Numerals and Venn[5] diagrams will be used to show certain set operations.

$$A = \{0, 1, 2, 3, 4, 5, 6, 7, 8, 9\}$$
$$B = \{2, 4, 6, 8\}$$
$$C = \{1, 3, 5, 7\}$$
$$D = \{1, 2, 3, 4\}$$
$$E = \{ \ \}$$
$$F = \{1, 2, 3\}$$

[5]Venn is the name of a mathematician who used diagrams to show relationships.

Disjoint sets

Two or more sets with no common elements

Using Venn diagrams, sets A and B have no common elements. Thus the two are disjoint sets.

$A = \{\square, \square, \square\}$
$B = \{\bigcirc, \bigcirc\}$

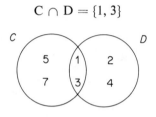

Intersection or overlapping sets

The set of all elements common to two or more sets

Using the sets shown above with numerals C ∩ D (read set C intersection D).

The symbol ∩ may be called cap.

Using diagrams, we see that sets C and D intersect or overlap at 1 and 3. Numerals showing common elements in a set are not repeated. So the common elements (1, 3) found in both sets shown only once in the diagram and in the brackets.

$C \cap D = \{1, 3\}$

Subset

A collection of elements all of which are members of a given universal set

We could describe a subset as *a set within a set*. If D = {1, 2, 3, 4} and F = {1, 2, 3}, then F is a subset of D. This relationship is written F ⊂ D. The symbol (⊂) indicates "a proper subset of." The open side *faces the larger set*.

A proper subset is a given set containing only the elements of the given set.

The original set (in the above example D) and the null set are counted as improper subsets.

Using a diagram, we see the proper set and subset B ⊂ A. B is a subset of A and the symbol (⊂) is opened toward A, the larger set.

$D = \{1, 2, 3, 4\}$

$F = \{1, 2, 3\}$

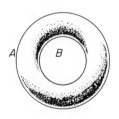

OPERATIONS WITH SETS

Since the language of sets will be used later in the chapter when the addition algorism is introduced and in subsequent chapters with other operations, only the binary set operation of *union* will be discussed at this time. Other set operations include intersection, set difference, set product, and partition.

Addition is the process of finding the sum of two or more numbers. This is a *binary operation*, using exactly two numbers at a time. Applying binary set operation of union to two sets, a single set results. The new set contains all the elements of the first set and the second set.

If set C = {1, 3, 5, 7} and set F = {1, 2, 3}, then the union of these two sets would be C ∪ F = {1, 2, 3, 5, 7}. Note that the symbol (∪) indicates *union* and common elements (1 and 3) are not repeated.

Study the following examples:

with the universe (U) = {all whole numbers}

and Set A = {1, 3, 5, 7}

Set B = {1, 2, 4, 6, 8}

Set C = {1, 3, 4, 9}

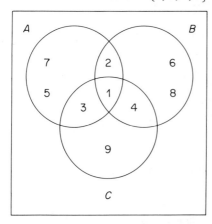
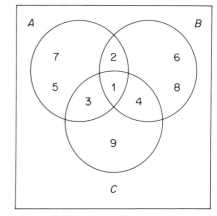

A ∪ B = {1, 2, 3, 4, 5, 6, 7, 8}   B ∪ C = {1, 2, 3, 4, 6, 8, 9}

You may wish to try other unions of these three sets. For example, what would C ∪ A or C ∪ B be? Could you have (A ∪ B) ∪ C or A ∪ (B ∪ C)?

Your attention is now directed to the use of mathematical sentences and the symbols used for expressing mathematical ideas.

2.4 Mathematical Sentences

Learning to use language to express ideas easily and correctly is an important aspect of any subject. The language used to express mathematical ideas has been carefully developed by mathematicians. The process of helping children learn the subject matter of mathematics involves a language function. Thus, one of the most important aspects of the teacher's job is to provide experiences which will enable pupils to express mathematical ideas accurately and clearly. This process takes careful planning and appropriate appraisal to make certain that pupils learn and understand the language of mathematics.

The unit of thought in any language form is the sentence. So when expressing mathematical ideas, *sentences* are used. These sentences, however, are usually concise and involve special number language. Children must be taught to translate ideas from the vernacular language into succinct mathematical language. New mathematical programs emphasize the language of mathematics and use appropriate symbols to provide a variety of practice exercises for mathematical ideas and concepts.

One of the first steps in learning a mathematical sentence involves using a *statement*. In English, we call this a declarative sentence. For example, we say the sum of four and one is five, or four and one are five. To write this sentence in mathematical symbols we use: $4 + 1 = 5$. Other symbols are used to write mathematical statements in textbooks: $(>)$ greater than, $(<)$ less than, $(=)$ equal, or $(\neq)$ not equal. Study the symbols used in these sentences:

$$5 < 4 \qquad \text{Five is less than four. (false)}$$
$$6 > 5 \qquad \text{Six is greater than five. (true)}$$
$$11 \neq 4 + 7 \qquad \text{Eleven is not equal to four plus seven. (false)}$$
$$3 + 2 = 4 + 1 \qquad \text{Three plus two is equal to four plus one. (true)}$$

In writing mathematical sentences, the *statements* may be true or false. Pupils are encouraged to study each example and to determine whether it is true or false. For variety, pupils may be asked to change statements so that they are true or false. For example:

Change the statements so that they are true.

$$6 < 4$$
$$5 \neq 3 + 2$$
$$7 > 4 + 4$$

Or, change the statements so that they are false.

$$6 = 3 + 3$$
$$10 < 6 + 5$$
$$15 \neq 7 + 7$$

In the examples just shown, the nouns are the numbers. The verb forms are symbols $(=)$, $(<)$, $(>)$, and $(\neq)$. Conjunctions include $(+)$, $(-)$, $(\times)$, or $\div)$.

When communicating mathematical ideas that are neither true nor false, a *variable* is used. In algebra the letter X can be used to show a variable or an unknown. In the sentence $15 \neq 10 + X$, there are several replacements for X. If 5 is used to replace X, the sentence is false. But the sentence will be true if any number other than 5 is used. Textbook writers have used a variety of symbols to show a variable. Study these examples:

$$7 + 7 = 10 + \blacksquare$$
$$8 + 4 = \square$$
$$? \times 5 = 25$$
$$8 + 9 = \triangle. \text{ So, } \triangle = \underline{\quad ? \quad}$$
$$\text{If } 7 + \square = 16, \text{ does } \square = 7, 8, \text{ or } 9?$$
$$4 - \bigcirc = 2$$

$$\overset{a}{} \quad \overset{b}{}$$
$$a + b = \square \quad ///// \quad /////// \quad 5 + \bigcirc = \square$$

Number sentences using a variable may be *open sentences* if several answers are acceptable. For example: $\square + \triangle + 4 = 16$. This sentence is read, a number plus a different number plus four equals sixteen. Several numbers can be substituted for the box and triangle to make a true sentence: $10 + 2 + 4 = 16$, $2 + 10 + 4 = 16$, $8 + 4 + 4 = 16$, etc. Note that two unknowns have been used, constituting a difficult example for some children. In most practice examples for young children, one variable is used. The symbols $\square$, $\bigcirc$, $\triangle$ or a shaded space ▓ are also used as placeholders.

$$
\begin{array}{ccc}
4▓ & \text{or} & 42 \\
+\,35 & \text{or} & +\,35 \\
\hline
77 & & 7▓
\end{array}
$$

A compound mathematical sentence (two sentences) may be needed to express a mathematical idea. For example, in studying multiplication facts, one can also learn division facts (inverse process). If $7 \times 8 = 56$, then $56 \div 8 = 7$. The first sentence (*the antecedent*) follows the word "if" and the other sentence (*consequent*) follows the word "then." Two types of sentences are used to relate multiplication and division facts:

1. If $6 \times 8 = 48$, then $48 \div 8 = 6$.
2. If $6 \times 8 = 48$ and $8 \times 6 = 48$, then $48 \div 6 = 8$ and $48 \div 8 = 6$.

Number sentences, when properly used, will help children express mathematical ideas accurately and clearly. Children will be able to discover numerous ways to express mathematical relationships with the use of number sentences. Number sentences, as we will show later, contribute to problem solving, motivate pupil work, and strengthen pupils' understanding of mathematics.

Teachers should be cautious in the use of number sentences. Improper use, such as pages of repetitious work or inappropriate applications, will cause pupils to dislike mathematics and to acquire poor work habits. Number sentences must be more than a substitute for the meaningless drill and boring work which are characteristic of traditional work in arithmetic.

2.5 The Number Line

The number line is a pictorial representation of some aspect of a number system. By using a variety of simple symbols, one can show number sequence, direction, operations, values of a rational numbers, decimal fractions, measurement, algebraic relationships, and geometric principles. Because the number line is so useful and easy to construct, modern textbooks have made widespread use of it. The number line will be used throughout this book as one important teaching aid to show the structure of our number system and to encourage meaningful interpretation of basic principles and operations. The number line, like set theory and number sentences, is extremely useful in

communicating mathematical ideas and providing a means for pupil exploration and demonstration of mathematical concepts.

Uses of the number line in addition and subtraction are shown here.

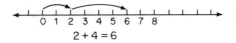

$$2 + 4 = 6$$

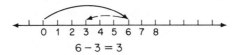

$$6 - 3 = 3$$

Note that the points are arbitrarily set. One may decide to use any unit of
measure as long as the unit is systematically used after being established.
Arrows ($\leftarrow \rightarrow$) are used to show that line continuing in either direction. A
starting point or reference point (zero) is established.

Relating addition and subtraction on a
number line to the number sentence helps
the learner move from a picture stage
(semi-concrete) to the abstract stage. For
example, a number sentence may be written
for each number-line picture as in the
illustration here.

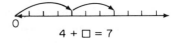

$$4 + \square = 7$$

Opportunities to explore important uses
of the number line will be provided in most
chapters of this book. The good teacher will

$$8 - \square = 5$$

search for the appropriate time to use the number line to help children
understand each new mathematical concept and to discover the mathematical
relationships existing between basic operations and systems.

2.6   The Addition Algorithm

An algorithm is a special computational system or process. We use a
particular process appropriate for working with a base of ten for finding
the sum of two or more numbers—addition. This procedure is based on
counting. To add 3 and 2:   0 0 0
                               0 0
Count the objects: 1, 2, 3, then 4, 5. Experiences in counting lead to addition.
After many experiences with counting and combining sets of objects and
pictures of objects, the child is ready to memorize the addition fact, such as:

$$
\begin{array}{r}
3 \\
+ \ 2 \\
\hline
5
\end{array}
$$

Eventually the child is taught to look at the combination of number symbols:

$$\begin{array}{r} 3 \\ + 2 \\ \hline \end{array}$$

and give an automatic response "5." The child must be taught to write the symbols and the facts in vertical $\left(\begin{array}{r} 3 \\ + 2 \\ \hline 5 \end{array} \right)$ and horizontal $(3 + 2 = 5)$ forms.

We say that addition is the process of finding the sum of two or more numbers without counting. This definition emphasizes the idea that the child must memorize the basic addition facts, give their sums, and use them in difficult problems without counting. The process (addition of whole numbers) is, however, based on counting. Using a number line, to add $3 + 2 = 5$ we count to 3 on the line and then count 2 more.

All numbers are abstract, but for convenience we refer to a number with a name attached to it as concrete, for example, 2 houses or 2 cars. When no name is attached, the number is referred to as an abstract number. This distinction proves useful in talking about numbers.

In the case of concrete numbers, only like numbers can be added. That is, 2 apples and 3 apples make 5 apples. Two apples and 3 oranges give neither 5 apples nor 5 oranges. We can emphasize the fact that oranges and apples are pieces of fruit, then 2 apples (fruit) combine with 3 oranges (fruit) to give 5 pieces of fruit.

Mathematically, there are three fundamental postulates (assumptions) that apply to addition:

The commutative law

$a + b = b + a$

The associative law

$(a + b) + c = a + (b + c)$

The law of closure

For every pair of numbers, a and b, there exists a unique number $(a + b)$ which is called the sum of a and b.

Through teacher guidance and pupil discovery, the child learns the many short cuts involved in the addition process as well as the fundamental postulates just enumerated. These assumptions will be identified and discussed in connection with particular steps of the addition process in the following sections.

2.7 Adding with One-digit Numerals

The ten one-digit numerals in our number system are 0, 1, 2, 3, 4, 5, 6, 7, 8, and 9. Young children come to school having had a variety of experiences with counting, ordering, buying, and combining sets of different objects.

One of the first instructional jobs is to help children become aware of sets of objects and to develop the need for putting sets together. Experiences are provided which will enable children to understand how to think with the use of numbers and to use symbols for recording these ideas. This beginning work centers around using and understanding the one-digit numerals through 9.

Using the language of sets, described in section 2.3, the teacher provides opportunities for children to feel and work with a variety of concrete objects to form different sets of objects. The child discovers that a set may have one element or object. Then he discovers one more than one is two. But three is one more than two.

Sets are compared by matching the elements of one set with the elements in another set. This is called a one-to-one relationship and helps children determine whether one set has the exact number of elements as does another set.

In joining (union) sets, the child learns that a set is made up of a number of elements and the number of elements in one set is being added to the number of elements in another set.

Gradually the meaning of each number (0 through 9) is developed. Children

Team learning and self-checking devices allow students to learn appropriate information without the necessity of continuous teacher direction. The student takes responsibility for what he learns. He is able to work at the level that is truly appropriate to his skills. San Carlos School district, California; Project PLAN classrooms, Brittan Acres.

put sets together and take them apart. For this reason, addition and subtraction are usually taught together in primary grades. We separate the two processes for the sake of convenience when discussing addition concepts and skills.

When does a child know a number, such as 5? When he can: recognize a set of five objects; read the numeral; know the serial order of the counting number; write the numeral; show one more than five and one less than five; and give several names for five (3 and 2, 2 and 3, 4 and 1, 1 and 4).

Children must learn the 100 primary facts in addition. These are learned in random order as children learn to visualize sets of objects and to put them together. The discovering of other names for a number (6 as $4 + 2$ or $3 + 3$) extends children's understanding of basic addition facts and aids in retention of these facts. In logical order the facts can be arranged as follows:

$$
\begin{array}{cccccccccc}
0 & 0 & 0 & 0 & 0 & 0 & 0 & 0 & 0 & 0 \\
\underline{0} & \underline{1} & \underline{2} & \underline{3} & \underline{4} & \underline{5} & \underline{6} & \underline{7} & \underline{8} & \underline{9} \\
\\
1 & 1 & 1 & 1 & 1 & 1 & 1 & 1 & 1 & 1 \\
\underline{0} & \underline{1} & \underline{2} & \underline{3} & \underline{4} & \underline{5} & \underline{6} & \underline{7} & \underline{8} & \underline{9} \\
\\
2 & 2 & 2 & 2 & 2 & 2 & 2 & 2 & 2 & 2 \\
\underline{0} & \underline{1} & \underline{2} & \underline{3} & \underline{4} & \underline{5} & \underline{6} & \underline{7} & \underline{8} & \underline{9} \\
\\
9 & 9 & 9 & 9 & 9 & 9 & 9 & 9 & 9 & 9 \\
\underline{0} & \underline{1} & \underline{2} & \underline{3} & \underline{4} & \underline{5} & \underline{6} & \underline{7} & \underline{8} & \underline{9}
\end{array}
$$

The ten rows (rows 3–8 are omitted), with ten facts in each row, make a total of 100 facts. Zero facts are taught when needed, as a place holder or to show "not any."

The development of English language and mathematical language needed for adding with one-digit numerals can be accomplished with Cuisenaire rods, Stern's materials, or other manipulative aids. Cuisenaire materials consist of rods which the child can use, each with a definite length and size. One can join a three rod ▭▭▭ with a two rod ▭▭ to get a five rod ▭▭▭▭▭. Likewise, the child can take away subsets of the original set.

Whatever materials are used, the teacher acts as a model to help children use appropriate language to describe the addition process: "I have one and one more, two; one and one are two; I can write 1 and 1 are 2 or $1 + 1 = 2$." Considerable evidence is available which suggests that the skill and enthusiasm of the teacher are the main contributing factors in using various manipulative materials. Brownell, who studied the use of Cuisenaire rods and other instructional materials in Scotland and England, showed that the significant variable was the *quality of teaching*. He stated that "an instructional program is one thing in the hands of expert, interested teachers, and another thing in the hands of teachers not possessed of these characteristics."[6]

[6]William A. Brownell, "Arithmetical Abstractions—Progress Toward Maturity of Concepts Under Differing Programs of Instruction," *The Arithmetic Teacher*, X (October, 1963), 329.

The commutative postulate can be identified while children work with sets of objects or sets of pictures. A child may make a set of four and a set of two. Combining these he gets a set of six. By reversing the procedure, first a set of two and then a set of four, he gets the same number six. This process is also useful in finding several names for the same numeral. But as Vincent Glennon suggests in his *Elementary School Mathematics: A Guide to Current Research*[7] these basic laws should emerge as useful structures for learning. We would not call this the "commutative property" at this time.

When the child understands the number 9, he is ready to discover one more than 9 and a way to write the numeral 10. This is the beginning of addition with two-digit numerals. Before discussing this new aspect, we should show the importance of zero in addition.

2.8   Zero in Addition

Building a concept of zero, as it is used in addition and in counting, requires patience and numerous experiences with sets and problem situations. A child may be given three balls. Then he is requested to put the balls in a box and is asked, "how many balls do you have now?" The child may say "none" or "I do not have any balls." The teacher records a zero (0) on the chalkboard to show "not any" or "none." Other examples should be used to show "none" or "not any." A child may be scorekeeper for a game of throwing darts at a target. One child throws three times and misses the target each time. What is his score? The child records a zero (0). If a boy throws a basketball at the goal two times and does not make any baskets, what is his score? After children understand this use of zero, the teacher can extend the concept to include zero as a beginning point.

A number line may be used to show zero as the beginning point. This shows that we start at zero and begin counting to three. A thermometer may show zero as the beginning point for reading room temperatures. Zero is used on a variety of gauges in a car to show amount of gasoline, oil pressure, or speed.

Learning to use the zero as a place holder is essential if the child is going to add numbers beyond 9. The game situation which requires recording of scores is a good starting point. Scores for hitting a target can be shown as:

Turns	Bill	Mary	Joe
1	1	1	1
2	0	1	1
3	1	0	1

[7]Vincent J. Glennon and Leroy G. Callahan, *Elementary School Mathematics: A Guide to Current Research* (Washington, D.C.: Association for Supervision and Curriculum Development, 1968), pp. 25f.

Then ask children to tell the scores for each thrower. Zero must be written to show that Bill did not hit the target on his second throw and that Mary missed the target on her last throw. The first real test of place value will come when introducing the number ten.

When children have learned "9" and know how to put nine together and take nine apart, they learn that ten comes after nine and is one more than nine. First grade teachers use a variety of aids and problem situations to teach the meaning of 10. Ten pennies can be arranged so that children see them on the table. The teacher asks, "Can I use these pennies to get another coin?" Children respond that one dime could be used to represent or name ten pennies. The teacher writes 10¢ on the chalkboard and reads ten cents—one ten and no ones. Some teachers use tongue depressors or sticks to show tens and ones. A place-value holder is used to show one bundle of ten and no ones.

TENS	ONES

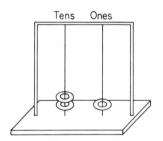

A simple abacus or counting frame may be used to show numbers whose sums are more than ten. The abacus or counting frame necessitates using positional value and a different colored bead or counter to show place value. This work is similar to the example using a dime to represent one ten-cent piece.

Children have learned how to rename a number such as "6": $3 + 3 = 6$; $2 + 4$, $4 + 2 = 6$; $5 + 1$, $1 + 5 = 6$. The concept should be extended and strengthened when adding numbers whose sums are larger than ten. For example: 11 may be renamed $10 + 1$ or one ten and a one; or 14 may be renamed $10 + 4$. Many experiences with the place-value holder will help to maintain this skill and encourage children to think of the place value of numbers larger than ten.

Through actual experiences with addition problems children should be taught that zero in addition results in the given number and identifies the number. In column addition (recording scores) we see that the zero is a place holder for one addend or set of scores. In adding down we think $4 + 3 = 7$, $7 + 0 = 7$, and $7 + 2 = 9$. Thus, the sum of any whole number and zero is that number. Since the sum of any whole number and zero is that whole number, we say that 0 is the *identity element* for addition. This principle holds true for the set of whole numbers.

4
3
0
2
___
9

2.9   Column Addition: Two or More Digits

Column addition should be developed gradually, from the simple to the complex in easy stages.

Consider these examples and the skills involved:

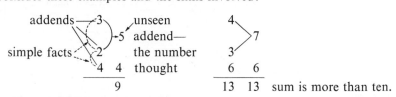

Children may add upward or downward. Adding from the top, we discover (first example) that three and two are five. The five must be thought or remembered and then added to four to get a sum of nine. Practice can be given to develop proficiency in remembering the unseen addend by writing an example on the chalkboard and then covering it with a piece of cardboard. Have children do the adding orally. Then uncover the example and check the answer. In oral work of this type, give the addends from the top and then check the answer by adding from the bottom of the column.

When children understand simple column addition with one-digit numerals, the process can be extended to include *adding by endings.*

$$
\begin{array}{ccc}
(1) & (2) & (3) \\
12 & 24 & 36 \\
\underline{3} & \underline{3} & \underline{2}
\end{array}
$$

In these examples a two-digit number is added to a one-digit number. The sum is in the same decade, the groups 0–9, 10–19, 20–29, 30–39. Children should be encouraged to think 12 and 3 are 15. This is done with one mental operation rather than $3 + 2 = 5$ ones, then bring down the one ten to make 15. The ending in each example should help the child think the total sum $(24 + 3 = 27$ and $36 + 2 = 38)$. Adding by endings is especially useful in column addition. Without developing this skill, children will count on their fingers or use a pencil to help count the next addend to be added in a column.

Bridging the tens is similar to adding by endings, except that the sum is in the next decade. Study the examples.

$$
\begin{array}{ccc}
(1) & (2) & (3) \\
18 & 27 & 36 \\
\underline{6} & \underline{5} & \underline{8}
\end{array}
$$

Note that in (1) the two-digit number 18 is in the second decade, while the sum (24) is in the third decade. This is called bridging the tens. The process is more difficult than addition by endings.

The place-value chart is useful in introducing the concept.

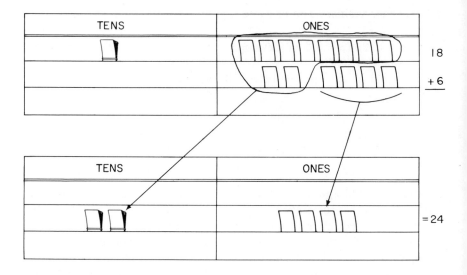

The regrouping or carrying concept must be carefully taught. Study the example.

$$
\begin{array}{r}
1 \\
37 \\
+\ 45 \\
\hline
82
\end{array}
$$

The child should think $7 + 5 = 12$; 12 is 1 ten and 2 ones; put the 2 ones in the ones' column; carry 1 ten to the tens' column; 1 ten and 3 tens are 4 tens; 4 tens and 4 tens are 8 tens; place the 8 tens in the tens' column. The work is shown with a place-value chart.

TENS	ONES	
		37
		+45

TENS	ONES	
		=82

Using expanded notation, the same example can be taught as follows:

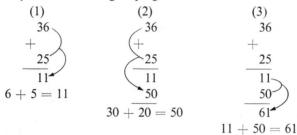

$$37 = 3 \text{ tens and } 7 \text{ ones} \qquad\qquad 37$$
$$+\, 45 = 4 \text{ tens and } 5 \text{ ones } \text{ Then, } +\, 45$$
$$7 \text{ tens and } 12 \text{ ones } = \qquad\quad 82$$
$$7 \text{ tens } + 1 \text{ ten and } 2 \text{ ones } = 82$$

Another way to show the regrouping is as follows:

(1)	(2)	(3)
36	36	36
+	+	+
25	25	25
11	11	11
$6 + 5 = 11$	50	50
	$30 + 20 = 50$	61
		$11 + 50 = 61$

A shorter method, showing the "short cut," is:

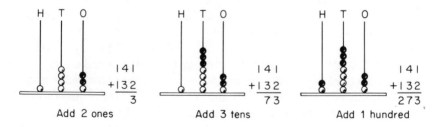

(1)	(2)
	1
36	36
+	+
25	25
1	61

$6 + 5 = 11$ (1 ten and 1 one)   1 ten + 3 tens + 2 tens = 6 tens (60)

Adding three-digit numbers without regrouping can be taught with the use of place-value charts or a simple abacus. Study the example illustrated here.

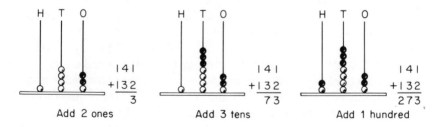

Carrying (or regrouping) when adding three-digit numbers involves a thorough understanding of place value and requires considerable practice for each new step. Note the carrying required in each of the examples.

(1)	(2)	(3)
1	1	11
264	232	834
+	+	+
127	271	276
1	03	1,110

Opinions differ concerning the use of the "crutch," the showing of the amount carried with a mark above the next position ([1] above the 6 in example [1]). Most teachers allow the crutch in the beginning stages of learning and encourage pupils to discard the practice when it is no longer needed. By stressing place value and using place-value charts of holders, pupils may be able to think the amount carried without using the crutch.

2.10   Using Basic Skills and Principles

After pupils understand carrying in the positions shown by the three examples, they are ready for all types of work in addition. Column addition involving several addends will necessitate concentration, adding by endings, skill in grouping pairs of numbers, carrying, and place value. For example, pairs of numbers may be added in any order. Picking pairs whose sum is 10 will help the pupil secure an accurate sum easily. Thus, $(4 + 6) = 10$, $(7 + 3) = 10$, then $10 + 10 + 2 = 22$ ones. In the tens column $(2 + 8) = 10$, $(6 + 4) = 10$, then $10 + 10 + 7 = 27$ tens, etc.

```
  2
3284
1907
1176
4262
9843
―――
  2
```

Changing the order of two addends does not change the sum. This is the *commutative principle* of addition presented earlier in this chapter. We may change the grouping of the addends and the sum will be the same. This grouping is called the *associative principle* of addition. By using the commutative and associative principles in addition, we can add any two addends to get a partial sum and then add another addend to get the same sum for the numbers being added. Thus, in adding $3 + 2 + 6 + 7 + 4$, we think $10 + 10 + 2 = 22$. We could use other groupings such as: $(3 + 2) + 6 + (7 + 4) = 22$ or $(4 + 7) + 6 + (3 + 2) = 22$. Since grouping tens is probably easier and quicker, we have stressed using this particular method.

Two other variations of grouping tens in addition will be helpful to some pupils. When adding two-digit numbers and one-digit numbers $(30 + 20 + 5)$, we can think $30 + 20 = 50$, and $50 + 5 = 55$. We know that three tens plus two tens equal five tens (50) and $50 + 5 = 55$. The other variation involves adding a number to one addend and subtracting the same amount from another addend. Thus in adding $8 + 7 + 6 + 4$, we can take 2 from 7 and add this to 8 (making $10 + 5$). Then $15 + (6 + 4) = 25$. This type of thinking involves the *principle of compensation*—subtracting from one number and adding the same amount to another number does not change the sum. Applying this principle to adding two-digit numbers: We would think, take 1 from 31 and add this to 59; that is, $(31 - 1) = 30 + (59 + 1) = 60$, and, therefore, $30 + 60 = 90$.

```
 0
3ｊ
60
59
――
```

These three principles (*commutative, associative, compensation*) have many applications to operations with whole numbers. Watch for these applications as you read other chapters in this book.

2.11   Errors in Addition

The common errors in addition are:

1. Lack of knowledge of primary facts
2. Lack of ability to add by endings
3. Lack of ability to bridge the tens
4. Copying the example incorrectly
5. Not writing the number symbols clearly
6. Incorrect placing of number symbols in column addition (place value)
7. Forgetting to carry
8. Errors in carrying
9. Lack of concentration

In diagnosing difficulties of specific pupils one may have to have the pupils narrate their thought processes orally in order to discover the sources of error.

2.12   Checking Addition

An addition example may be checked in several ways. The pupil may add the numbers again, in the same way. He may add up the column first, and then down the column, or vice versa.

A more elaborate process of checking an addition example is that of casting out nines.

$$
\begin{array}{cc}
3256 & 7 \\
4195 & 1 \\
3147 & 6 \\
8265 & 3 \\
\hline
18863 & 8
\end{array}
$$

Adding horizontally in 3256,

$$3 + 2 + 5 + 6 = 16;$$

casting out nine,

$$16 - 9 = 7.$$

Next,

$$4 + 1 + 9 + 5 = 19;$$

casting out nines,

$$19 - 18 = 1.$$

In 4195 one can disregard the 9; then:

$$4 + 1 + 5 = 10, \text{ so } 10 - 9 = 1.$$

In 3147,
$$3 + 1 + 4 + 7 = 15, \text{ and } 15 - 9 = 6.$$
In 8265,
$$8 + 2 + 6 + 5 = 21, \text{ and } 21 - 18 = 3.$$
Adding the remainders,
$$7 + 1 + 6 + 3 = 17; 17 - 9 = 8.$$
Casting out nines in the sum 18863,
$$1 + 8 + 8 + 6 + 3 = 26, \text{ and } 26 - 18 = 8.$$
Here 8 checks with 8, so we are reasonably certain that the addition is correct.

A slight variation can be used in 8265, as follows:
$$8 + 2 + 6 + 5 = 21, \text{ and in } 21, 2 + 1 = 3$$
which is the same remainder obtained by using $21 - 18 = 3$.

We are only reasonably certain that the sum is correct because an error of transposition in the sum is not disclosed by this method. Thus, a sum of 18836 would check as well as 18863. Also, an error of 9 or a multiple of 9 will not be disclosed.

The method is based on the fact that the base of our number system is ten, so the excess of nines in a given number is equal to the excess of nines in the sum of its digits. For example:
$$48 = 4(10) + 8$$
$$= 4(9 + 1) + 8$$
$$= 4(9) + 4 + 8$$

Since $4(9)$ represents nines cast out, the remainder on the left equals the remainder on the right, or the remainder in 48 equals the remainder in $4 + 8$. The method of casting out nines is usually taught in the seventh and eighth grades, if at all. "It is worth adding to the arithmetic repertory. But do not accept it as another mechanical device."[8]

Another method of checking an addition example is to add the columns separately and stagger the totals as in this illustration:

3256	25	(ones)
4128	21	(tens)
3164	13	(hundreds)
2987	12	(thousands)
13535	13535	

This is sometimes called the accountants' method of checking an example in addition.

To check pupils' understanding of place value, have them show the answer by adding partial sums, For example:

[8]Tabbie Mae Moore, "More About Casting Out Nines," *The Arithmetic Teacher*, III (November, 1956), 204–6.

$$379 = 300 + 70 + 9$$
$$+$$
$$\underline{756 = 700 + 50 + 6}$$
$$1000 + 120 + 15$$
$$1000 + 100 + 20 + 10 + 5$$
$$1100 + 30 + 5 = 1135$$

2.13   Speed and Accuracy

Accuracy is more important than speed in addition or any process in arithmetic. The teacher should not assign grades by merely marking the examples that have incorrect results. The act of teaching is not complete until the specific error or errors have been located, and some effort has been made to avoid their occurrence in future examples, such as by the assignment of remedial work.

Emphasis on speed can be overdone. Continual time drills in addition can cause formation of undesirable attitudes, neglect of accuracy, and even unwanted nervous tensions on the part of some pupils. On the other hand, some emphasis on speed is desirable, at least to the extent that it develops reasonably quick, correct results in addition examples.

After accuracy in primary facts and the other phases of addition have reached a desired perfection, speed can be developed in several ways. Practice leads to speed, in most cases. To develop speed in addition one should think as few words as possible. Thus, in adding "6 + 8 = 14," we can think "6 and 8 are 14," but the words "and" and "make" are really unnecessary, so it saves time if we think 6, 8, 14 in that order, without thinking the connecting words. Grouping combinations that give ten, adding by endings, and using the principle of compensation should increase speed and improve accuracy.

2.14   Chapter Summary

Children's preschool experiences are usually highly motivated and appropriate for the immediate needs of each child. Instruction at school must strive to continue this interesting, practical type of learning and at the same time develop a concise language which will enable children to understand the structure of our number system.

Through numerous classroom activities children must be guided in discovering the use of number to count objects, in numbering collections, in identifying size or weight, and in arranging things in some order. At the appropriate time, after rich experiences with mathematics and when children are mature enough for the new learning step, children should be introduced to basic operations used with our number system.

Language development is the central and most important aspect of instruction in mathematics for young children. They must be able to communicate their ideas with the use of the common English language and the language used in the development of mathematical ideas and concepts. The teacher must act as a model and patiently guide children's language development throughout elementary school work. To aid in learning the language of modern mathematics, three approaches have been recommended: (1) the use of simple language from set theory; (2) the use of mathematical sentences and appropriate symbols; and (3) the use of the number line.

The addition algorithm was presented in a discussion which stressed the development of basic skills, the understanding of place value, the development of appropriate language, and a thorough grasp of the short cuts used in the system.

QUESTIONS AND EXERCISES

1. We have a common verbal language appropriate for everyday use. Do we have a single, common number language?
2. In column addition, children may add numbers out of order. What would be some of the reasons for this type of work? What should you probably know about the child's method?
3. Study the two exercises and then describe how you think they could be used in teaching addition:
   (a) Since $30 + 20 = 50$, we know that $2 + 30 + 7 + 20 = \square$
   (b) Since $2 + 5 = 7$, we know that $20 + 50 = \square$
4. Prepare a set of six addition examples beginning with a simple fact and moving toward a complex type.
5. Define and give an example for each of these concepts:
   (a) addition by combining groups
   (b) the commutative law in addition
   (c) the associative law in addition
   (d) the principle of compensation
   (e) the law of closure
6. Find the sum for the example and identify the skills and understandings which the child should know in order to understand the work.

$$245$$
$$832$$
$$788$$
$$365$$

7. When, if at all, should a child find a sum by counting?
8. Find the sum for each example, then show the place value for each partial sum. Example (a) is done.

(a) $462 = 400 + 60 + 2$
$543 = 500 + 40 + 3$
$900 + 100 + 5$
$1000 + 5 = 1005$

(b) 375
$+ 628$

(c) 758
$+ 563$

(d) 4362
$+$
1658

(e) 7234
$+$
4686

9. Make number lines to show correct answers for each example.
   (a) How many whole numbers are *between* 0 and 11?
   (b) How many whole numbers are *between* 2 and 15?
   (c) How many whole numbers are *between* 0 and 40?

10. Complete these number sentences by writing T (true), F (false), or O (open—neither true nor false). Then make five new number sentences.
    (a) $5 > 7$
    (b) $8 > 8$
    (c) $4 + 2 < 3 + 2$
    (d) $\triangle = \triangle$
    (e) $16 = 14 + 2$

11. Make each example true. Then make three similar examples of your own.
    (a) $(4 + 2) + 8 = 4 + (2 + \square)$
    (b) $(\square + 10) + 4 = \square + (10 + 4)$
    (c) $(\square + \triangle) + 6 = \square + (\triangle + 6)$

12. Give four examples of a description of a set (see example (a) below) and then express the set.
    (a) Five numerals between 8 and 14. $A = \{9, 10, 11, 12, 13\}$
    (b) A set of all coins used in . . . .

13. Complete the union of the three pairs of sets. Then make three similar examples of your own.
    (a) $\{3, 4, 5\} \cup \{5, 8, 9\} = \{3, 4, 5, 8, 9\}$
    (b) $\{3, 2, 1\} \cup \{2, 3, 4, 5\}$
    (c) $\{a, b\} \cup \{a, b, c, d\} =$

14. Show the intersection for each set. Then prepare three similar examples of your own.
    (a) $\{3, 4, 5\} \cap \{4, 6, 8\} = \{ \ \}$
    (b) $\{1, 2, 3\} \cap \{2, 3, 4, 5\} =$
    (c) $\{2, 3, 4\} \cap \{5, 6, 7\} =$

15. Show (by examples) how joining sets is an operation on sets and addition is an operation on numbers.

16. What are the main short cuts in addition that children should understand?

SELECTED REFERENCES

Brownell, William A., "Arithmetical Abstractions—Progress Toward Maturity of Concepts Under Differing Programs of Instruction," *The Arithmetic Teacher*, X (October, 1963), 310–29.

Churchill, Eileen M., *Counting and Measuring*. Toronto: University of Toronto Press, 1961.

Dutton, Wilbur H., "Growth in Number Readiness in Kindergarten Children," *The Arithmetic Teacher*, X (May, 1963), 252–54.

Flournoy, Frances, "A Consideration of the Ways Children Think When Performing Higher-Decade Addition." *Elementary School Journal*, LVII (January, 1957), 204–8.

Gagne, Robert, *The Conditions of Learning*. New York: Holt, Rinehart, & Winston, Inc., 1965.

Glennon, Vincent J., and Leroy G. Callahan, *Elementary School Mathematics: A Guide to Current Research*. Washington, D.C.: Association for Supervision and Curriculum Development, 1968.

Lovell, K., *The Growth of Basic Mathematical and Scientific Concepts in Children*. London: University of London Press, 1962.

National Council of Teachers of Mathematics, *Sets* (Booklet 1). Washington, D.C.: The Council, 1964.

Piaget, Jean, *The Child's Conception of Number*. London: Routledge & Kegan Paul, Ltd., 1952.

Spencer, Peter L., and Marguerite Brydegaard, *Building Mathematical Competence in Elementary School*. New York: Holt, Rinehart & Winston, Inc., 1966.

Sussman, David, *Number Readiness of Kindergarten Children* (unpublished doctoral dissertation, University of California, Los Angeles, 1962).

3

Language and Operations Used in Subtraction

3.1 Definition of Subtraction

Subtraction is the process of finding one of two numbers when their sum and the other number are given. Thus, $8 - 2$ indicates that 8 is the sum of two numbers, 2 is one of the numbers, and we are attempting to find the other number.

Eight minus two means: what must be added to 2 to give 8? In this sense subtraction is the inverse of addition. Inverse processes are usually more difficult to understand than direct processes. Also, subtraction can arise in three slightly different ways:

1. Finding the remainder.
   Example. If there are 8 children in a room and 2 children leave the room, how many children remain in the room?
2. Finding the missing addend.
   Example. If John saved $2 and desires to save a total of $8, how much more must he save? Find how many dollars must be added to $2 to give $8.
3. Finding the difference between two numbers.
   Example. If there are 8 boys and 2 girls in a room, how many more boys are there than girls? Find the difference between the number of girls and the number of boys.

The fact that subtraction is an inverse process, together with the fact that subtraction can arise in three similar, although slightly different, ways implies that subtraction must be taught very carefully if understanding is to be achieved.

3.2 Subtraction Facts

As soon as the addition process has been introduced, work with subtraction should be started. Children put two sets together to form a new set. Then the new set may be taken apart and subsets formed. When children know "6," they should be able to show (by grouping of sets and by writing) how to put 6 together and how to take 6 apart. This should be done so that relationships can be discovered. Learning the basic facts in this way is called working with groups or "number families." For example, the "six family" consists of all combinations which have a sum of six and all subsets of six.

$$
\begin{array}{ll}
3 + 3 = 6 & 6 - 6 = 0 \\
2 + 4 = 6 & 6 - 5 = 1 \\
4 + 2 = 6 & 6 - 4 = 2 \\
1 + 5 = 6 & 6 - 3 = 3 \\
5 + 1 = 6 & 6 - 2 = 4 \\
0 + 6 = 6 & 6 - 1 = 5 \\
6 + 0 = 6 & 6 - 0 = 6
\end{array}
$$

While there seems to be no one best order for teaching basic number facts in addition or subtraction, considerable evidence is available to indicate that facts should be presented so that pupils will discover relationships among them. Thiele found that children who learned number facts and generalized with them made superior progress in comparison with pupils who learned these facts in a routine, drill manner.[1]

Like addition, there are 100 subtraction facts. Arranged in logical order there would be 10 rows of 10 examples each. Only three of the ten rows are shown here.

0	1	2	3	4	5	6	7	8	9	
0	0	0	0	0	0	0	0	0	0	
0	1	2	3	4	5	6	7	8	9	
	1	2	3	4	5	6	7	8	9	10
	1	1	1	1	1	1	1	1	1	1
	0	1	2	3	4	5	6	7	8	9
		2	3	4	5	6	7	8	9	10	11
		2	2	2	2	2	2	2	2	2	2
		0	1	2	3	4	5	6	7	8	9

[1] C. L., Thiele, *The Contribution of Generalization to Learning Addition Facts*, Contributions to Education, No. 763 (New York: Bureau of Publications, Teachers College, Columbia University, 1938).

Charts may be used to encourage children to discover relationships between addition and subtraction or to strengthen their understanding of basic facts.

+	0	1	2	3	4	5	6	7	8	9
0	0	1	2	3	4	5	6	7	8	9
1	1	2	3	4	5	6	7	8	9	10
2	2	3	4	5	6	7	8	9	10	11
3	?	?	?	?	?	?	?	?	?	?
4										
5										
6										
7										
8										
9										

1. 6

IN	OUT
2	8
6	?
4	
8	
5	
3	

2. 8

IN	OUT
8	16
7	?
4	
5	
6	
9	

3. 5

IN	OUT
9	4
11	?
13	
14	
12	
10	

4. 7

IN	OUT
18	11
16	?
14	
13	
15	
17	

A two-column function machine using input ("in") and output ("out") with a rule or number to apply will help children think about addition and subtraction facts. In example 1, the child puts in 2, "thinks 6," and gets an output of 8. Think what should go in the empty spaces?

Counting with the use of number lines as in the example will also strengthen the concept that addition and subtraction are related.

$$2 + 3 = ? \text{ or } \begin{array}{r} 2 \\ + 3 \\ \hline ? \end{array}$$

$$6 - 3 = ? \text{ or } \begin{array}{r} 6 \\ - 3 \\ \hline ? \end{array}$$

Children discover that they can count to find a sum and that they can count to find a missing addend. There are many different ways to count numbers. For example, counting by 2's from 0 to 12:

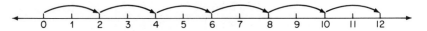

Or, counting backward by 3's from 12 to 0:

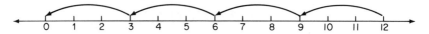

3.3 Using Number Sentences

The number sentence should be used as a natural part of each basic process. When children subtract elements from a set to make a new set, they should be directed toward thinking the abstract fact. After working with concrete objects, they should move to the semi-concrete or picture stage. Finally, they write the abstract fact such as $4 - 2 = 2$. These steps can be reversed if the teacher wishes to check a child's understanding of a new fact or step. For example, the child may write $5 - 3 = 2$. The teacher can then ask: "Show me how you found the answer by drawing pictures or using the flannel board." The child demonstrates his understanding by making five circles or symbols and taking away three. When concrete objects are used, the child forms a set of five objects and takes away three to show two as the remainder.

To show "greater than" and "lesser than" relationships between sets, the same procedure is used. First have children show which set of objects is "greater than" or "lesser than" another set. This is followed by pictures so

that children can check or point to the set with the greater number of marks. Finally, the sentence should be written $6 > 5$ or $5 < 6$. Discovering that a set is one more or one less than another set strengthens the child's understanding of addition and subtraction as related processes based upon counting. The serial order of counting numbers should also be discovered. This can be accomplished by number sentences such as: $4 + \square = 5, 5 + \square = 6,$ $6 + \square = 7$, or $4 < 5, 5 < 6, 6 < 7$, and $4 > 3, 5 > 4, 6 > 5$. The subtraction symbol can be used to show the serial order ($7 - 1 = 6, 6 - 1 = 5,$ $5 - 1 = 4$) for counting backwards.

Numerous practice examples can be provided by using number sentences. For example:

Show that subtracting a number *undoes* the addition of the same number.

To undo $5 + 4 = 9$, we subtract $\square$ from 9 and get 5.

To undo $6 + 4 = 10$, $\underline{\ ?\ }$ $-$ $\underline{\ ?\ }$ $=$ $\underline{\ ?\ }$

Undo $8 + 7 = 15$.

Add a number, then subtract a number

$6 + 3 = 9$ $\qquad\qquad$ $6 - 3 = 3$

$10 + 5 = 15$ $\qquad\quad$ $10 - 5 = \underline{\ ?\ }$

$12 + 6 = \underline{\ ?\ }$ $\qquad\quad$ $\underline{\ ?\ } - 6 = \overline{12}$

Work these.

If $6 + 8 = 14$, $14 - \square = 8$ or $14 - \square = 6$

If $10 + 6 = 16$, $16 - \square = 6$ or $16 - \square = 10$

If $10 + 2 = 12$, $12 - \square = 2$ or $12 - \square = 10$

3.4 Subtraction without Regrouping

After the primary facts of subtraction have been learned very thoroughly through meaning, drill, and activity, the next step is to present subtraction in columns, without regrouping, such as:

$$\begin{array}{ccccc} 68 & 465 & 8263 & 78 & 32 \\ -\,42 & -\,123 & -\,4121 & -\,23 & -\,12 \end{array}$$

Here each digit in the subtrahend is less than (or possibly equal to) the digit above it in the minuend.

In the first example, the thought process is: "8 ones take away 2 ones are 6 ones," or "2 ones from 8 ones leaves 6 ones"; and "6 tens take away 4 tens are 2 tens," or "4 tens from 6 tens leaves 2 tens." In one case, the direction is downward, and in the other case it is upward. There is some difference of opinion as to which of these is better.

Examples such as these may be made meaningful with objects and with place-value charts. When a pupil does not understand the total number involved in either the minuend or the subtrahend, he should not be working the problem.

In this example: 68

————

42

place 6 bundles of ten slips in each bundle in the tens' column, and 8 slips in the ones' column. Then, looking at the example as it is written, the child may take 2 slips away from the ones' column and set them aside. Finally, he removes 4 bundles from the tens' column and sets them aside. The result, 26, is left in the place-value chart shown below the chart on p. 64.

We can also explain the meaning of an example such as this with money. The example becomes:

$$\begin{array}{r} 68¢ \\ -\,42¢ \\ \hline 26¢ \end{array}$$

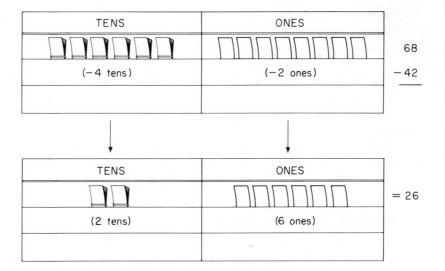

The thought process becomes: 2 cents from 8 cents leaves 6 cents; place the 6 cents in the cents' column; 4 dimes from 6 dimes leaves 2 dimes; place the 2 dimes in the dimes' column.

Place 6 dimes and 8 pennies on a table. Take 2 pennies from the 8 pennies; that leaves 6 pennies. Take 4 dimes from the 6 dimes; that leaves 2 dimes.

In writing these examples the pupils must be taught to write their numbers clearly and to arrange them carefully in columns. Providing practice with examples having missing numerals in subtraction may be used to help children understand the algorithm and to strengthen their concept of place value. Use examples like these:

$$\begin{array}{cccc}
24 & 7\square & 88 & 85 \\
-\square2 & -\square2 & -\square5 & -\square1 \\
\hline
12 & 57 & 63 & 24
\end{array}$$

3.5 Using Zero in Subtraction

Zero may cause difficulty in subtraction if pupils do not understand the use of zero as a numeral and as a place holder. The teacher should build an understanding of the use of zero as a place holder in subtraction when working with the numeral 10 in addition. At this time the child is guided toward discovery of the numeral coming after 9 (one more than nine). Before this work, the child has learned that zero is a starting point on a number line and is used to show "not any" for keeping a record of chances taken in a contest or score made during a game. Now the child must be shown how to subtract from 10. The child at this point should know that the numeral 10 shows one ten and no ones.

Concrete objects should be used to show a set of ten. Subsets can be taken away from ten. Thus, in these examples:

$$\begin{array}{cc} 10 & 10 \\ -\ 2 & -\ 4 \end{array}$$

the child learns by actual experiences with objects that two ones cannot be taken from zero. By having 10 ones, however, he can subtract 2 ones and have 8 ones left.

Following these experiences the child should learn that when a number is subtracted from itself, the result is $0 \, (10 - 10 = 0)$. When 0 is subtracted from a number, the result is the given number $(10 - 0 = 10)$. Then the role of zero in addition and subtraction can be summarized.

$$\begin{array}{ll} 0 + N = N & N - N = 0 \\ N + 0 = N & N - 0 = N \\ 0 + 1 = 1 & 1 - 1 = 0 \\ 1 + 0 = 1 & 1 - 0 = 1 \end{array}$$

The concept of zero as a place holder will be strengthened when children advance in subtraction work which requires regrouping in an example such as this:

$$\begin{array}{c} 20 \\ -\ 6 \end{array}$$

Then, using concrete objects, they can regroup to get one group of 10 and 10 ones. Six ones can be taken from 10 ones, leaving 4 ones, the one 10 and 4 ones $(10 + 4 = 14)$ remain.

A place-value chart should be used to present the semi-concrete situation.

Using expanded notation, the example is then written,

$$
\begin{array}{rcccl}
 & \text{tens} & & \text{ones} \\
20 = & 1 & + & 10 \\
- \; 6 = & & - & 6 \\
\hline
 & 1 & + & 4 \;\; = 10 + 4 = 14.
\end{array}
$$

This type of work in subtraction is usually presented in third grade. When children can master the concept of grouping and regrouping by tens, they are probably ready for work with hundreds and thousands. First children must understand place value in ten, then place value in other two-digit numerals. This work underlies the numeration system as a whole. To understand the subtraction algorithm (which is based upon our base ten system) the child must understand the grouping and regrouping process based upon groups of tens. Advanced work in subtraction, including the use of zero in a variety of positions, will now be presented.

3.6 Subtraction with Regrouping

In this example:
$$
\begin{array}{r}
93 \\
- 26 \\
\hline
67
\end{array}
$$

a process called "borrowing," "decomposition," or "regrouping" is required. Two methods may be used to complete the example:

1. *Borrowing*, *decomposition*, or *regrouping* using these steps. We cannot take 6 ones from 3 ones, so borrow 1 ten from the 9 tens. Then 1 ten and 3 ones make 13 ones. Now 6 ones from 13 ones leaves 7 ones. Write 7 in the ones' column, and change the 9 in the tens' column to an 8. Next, 2 tens from 8 tens leaves 6 tens. Write 6 in the tens' column. The answer (difference) is 67.

2. *Equal additions* or *additive method* using these steps. We cannot take 6 ones from 3 ones, so add 1 ten to 3 ones; this gives 13 ones. Now 6 ones from 13 ones leaves 7 ones. Write 7 in the ones' column. We added 1 ten to the minuend (93), so add 1 ten to the subtrahend (26) to keep the difference the same (law of compensation discussed earlier in the chapter). Thus, 2 tens in the subtrahend becomes 3 tens. Next, 3 tens from 9 tens leaves 6 tens. Write 6 in the tens' column. The answer is 67.
Another variation of this work is:
$$
\begin{array}{r}
93 \\
-26
\end{array}
$$
What must I add to 6 to make 13? (7). Write the 7 in the ones' column. Since this involved borrowing 1 ten from the 9 tens, think 3 tens from 9 tens leaves 6 tens. Write the 6 tens in the tens' column. The answer is 67.

The first method is used more widely than the second mainly because it is easier to rationalize. However, these two methods have alternated in popularity during the course of the history of teaching arithmetic. Thus, in Ray's *Arithmetic* in 1845, these two methods are described in approximately the same way as above, and the remark is made that "the second method of proceeding is the one generally used in practice; it is more convenient, and less liable to error, especially when the upper number contains one or more zeros."

Research by Brownell and Moser,[2] comparing the effectiveness of decomposition and equal addition methods, showed that: the decomposition method when taught meaningfully was the more successful method; the equal additions method was difficult to rationalize; the use of the crutch facilitated the teaching and learning of the decomposition method; and children discarded the crutch when encouraged to do so by teachers.

Some educators object to the use of the word "borrow" in the first method on the grounds that the number borrowed is not paid back. Because of this, the word "regroup" is preferred as an accurate description of the process used.

The second method is based on the principle that in a subtraction example the same number (1 ten or 10 ones) may be added to both minuend and subtrahend, and the difference will remain the same. Since the advent of the meaning theory of teaching arithmetic, this method has fallen into some disrepute because it is more difficult to explain in a meaningful way than the first method.

Using the first method, we can explain the example $93-26$ logically with a place-value chart (see p. 68). We proceed thus: We cannot take 6 ones from 3 ones. Regroup by taking one group of 10 from the tens' column. Remove the rubber band and place them in the ones' column. There are then 13 ones in the ones' column and 8 tens in the tens' column. Take 6 ones from the 13 ones. That leaves 7 ones in the ones' column. Take 2 tens from the 8 tens. That leaves 6 tens in the tens' column. The remainder is 6 tens and 7 ones, or, 67.

Having introduced the idea of subtracting with regrouping by using objects and pictures of objects, we then proceed to teach the operation with abstract symbols. In doing this, most teachers use a "crutch":

$$
\begin{array}{r}
\overset{8}{\cancel{9}}\ {}^{1}3 \\
-2\ \ 6 \\
\hline
6\ \ 7
\end{array}
$$

[2]William A. Brownell and H. E. Moser, *Meaningful vs. Mechanical Learning: Study in Grade III Subtraction* (Durham, N.C.: Duke University Press, 1949), pp. 207f.

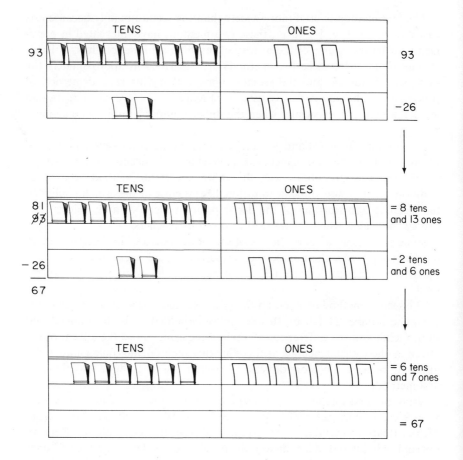

The 9 is changed to an 8, and a one is placed near the 3 to indicate 13.

Some educators advocate the use of a crutch, some recommend that its use be discontinued after the process is clearly understood, and others oppose it on the basis that it is poor procedure psychologically to teach a method with the idea of discarding it later, since this means teaching the process twice. The proponents seem to be in the majority at the present time.

Another point of view is often expressed in connection with the use of crutches in general. Introduce a concept without using a crutch, and some of the pupils will be able to perform the operation without it. If some pupils do not seem to be able to do the work, *then* show the crutch to them. This point of view is quite sound.

Subtracting with two- and three-digit numbers should include using a place-value holder and expanded notation. For example:

$$\begin{array}{r} 302 \\ -3 \\ \hline \end{array}$$

can be rationalized by using a simple place-value rack.

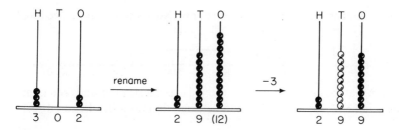

Check 299 + 3 = 302
The work shown by expanded notation includes:

$$\begin{array}{cccccc} & H & T & O & H & T & O \\ 302 = & 300 + & 0 + & 2 = & 290 + & 0 + & 12 \\ - \quad 3 = & & & - \, 3 & & & - \, 3 \\ \hline & & & & 290 + & 0 + & 9 = 299 \end{array}$$

For the example: 255
                    − 135

rename and subtract this way:

$$\begin{array}{l} 252 = 200 + (50 + 2) = 200 + 40 + 12 \\ - 135 = 100 + 30 + 5 = 100 + 30 + \ 5 \\ \hline \qquad\qquad\qquad\qquad\quad 100 + 10 + \ 7 \end{array}$$

For the example: 305
                    − 124

rename and subtract like this:

$$\begin{array}{l} 305 = 300 + \ 0 + 5 = 200 + 100 + 5 \\ - 124 = 100 + 20 + 4 = 100 + \ 20 + 4 \\ \hline \qquad\qquad\qquad\qquad\quad 100 + \ 80 + 1 \end{array}$$

$$\begin{array}{llcccc} & & H & T & O & H & T & O \\ \text{or} \quad 305 = & 3 + & 0 + 5 = & 2 + & 10 + 5 \\ - 124 = & 1 + & 2 + 4 = & 1 + & \ 2 + 4 \\ \hline & & & & 1 + & \ 8 + 1 = 181 \end{array}$$

Using tens, hundreds, and thousands in subtraction may be presented so
that the zero actually makes the work easy to rationalize. For example:

40	40	40	40
− 10	− 20	− 30	− 40
30	20	10	0

400	400	400	400
− 100	− 200	− 300	− 400

4,000	4,000	4,000	4,000
− 1,000	− 2,000	− 3,000	− 4,000

Children can "think" the answer and gain a clear understanding of place
values.

The number line can be used to supply assistance for those needing help.
4,000 — 3,000 = ?

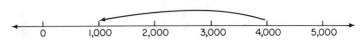

Note that the comma has been inserted to separate thousands and hundreds. The number 3,540 would be read as three thousand five hundred forty.

3.7   Making Change

A commonly used application of subtraction is in making change. If a $1 bill is offered in payment for a purchase of a 17¢ item, the clerk must find the amount of change to give the customer. That is, he must find the remainder when 17 is subtracted from 100.

One way to do this would be to subtract 17 from 100, either mentally or with paper and pencil. A better way is to use the second method in section 3.4, finding what must be added. The thought process is as follows: 17 cents and 3 cents make 20 cents; give the customer 3 cents. Now, 20 cents and 1 nickel make 25 cents, give the customer 1 nickel. Twenty-five cents and 1 quarter make 50 cents; give the customer 1 quarter. Fifty cents and 1 half-dollar make 1 dollar; give the customer 1 half-dollar. The clerk has given the customer 3 cents, 1 nickel, 1 quarter, and 1 half-dollar. This is an additive process; 17 cents and what makes 1 dollar?

This is by far the best method of making change. Storekeepers must educate their clerks in this process if they do not already know it. In the illustrative example, the clerk is also instructed to place the $1 bill in full view on or near the cash register until the entire transaction has been completed.

Teachers should help elementary school pupils in making change. The usual rule of proceeding from the simple to the complex in easy stages should be followed. Experiences with actual money should be provided, so that the situation will be as realistic as possible. Follow this work with practice examples like this:

Show how you would make change for each example.

Spend	Amount given	Change
$4.50	$ 5.00	
1.65	3.00	
5.00	10.00	
1.30	2.00	

3.8   Errors in Subtraction

In the very early stages of subtraction, primary-age children may try to subtract the smaller number from the larger number, regardless of whether the smaller number is the minuend or subtrahend. For example: 32
— 18

some pupils may think, "I cannot take 8 ones from 2 ones, so I will take 2 ones from 8 ones." This error will disappear quickly when children understand place value and when they are able to relate subtraction to addition. The pupils should relate the two operations by showing the different numbers in each process, as shown.

$$
\begin{array}{ll}
14 & \text{addend} \\
+\ 18 & \text{addend} \\
\hline
32 & \text{sum}
\end{array}
\qquad
\begin{array}{ll}
32 & \text{sum} \\
-\ 18 & \text{addend} \\
\hline
14 & \text{addend}
\end{array}
$$

The terms "minuend" and "subtrahend" have little meaning for children and are not significant for later work in mathematics. In subtraction examples we refer to the sum, one addend, and the unknown or missing addend in this manner:

$$
\begin{array}{ll}
324 & \text{sum} \\
-\ 133 & \text{addend} \\
\hline
& \text{unknown addend or difference}
\end{array}
$$

Other errors made in subtraction are similar to those found in addition:

1. Not knowing primary facts
2. Not being able to subtract by endings
3. Errors in regrouping
4. Copying examples incorrectly
5. Not writing numerals clearly
6. Problems with place value in writing numerals
7. Difficulties with zero.

Careful teaching, based on pupil understanding, will reduce errors. In correcting papers (teacher or pupil), the corrector must locate the particular error which makes the example incorrect. Then the teacher must give the individual pupil guidance in removing the difficulty.

Children should be encouraged to strive for accuracy in all work with mathematics. In checking subtraction, several methods should be used. For example:

$$
\begin{array}{ll}
36 & \text{Check by adding} \\
-\ 24 & \text{(subtract 24, then} \\
\hline
12 & \text{add 24)}
\end{array}
\qquad
\begin{array}{l}
12 \\
+\ 24 \\
\hline
36
\end{array}
$$

or

$$
\begin{array}{ll}
36 & \text{taking 24 from 36} \\
-\ 24 & \text{is 12, then} \\
\hline
12 &
\end{array}
\qquad
\begin{array}{l}
24 \\
+\ 12 \\
\hline
36
\end{array}
$$

A child may rework or "rethink" the example or add the difference to the subtrahend like this:

$$
\begin{array}{c}
3\ 6 \\
-\ 2\ 4 \\
\hline
3\ 1\ 2\ 6
\end{array}
$$

Encourage and motivate children to work accurately rather than penalize them by requiring a formal check for practice sets involving a large number of examples.

Estimating an approximate answer will encourage pupils to think of place value. For example:

$$
\begin{array}{ccc}
350 & 300 & 50 \\
-\,125 & -\,100 \quad \text{and} & -\,25 \\
\hline
225 & 200 \qquad + & 25 \\
& \searrow\; 225 \;\swarrow &
\end{array}
$$

$$
\text{or} \quad
\begin{array}{cccc}
687 & 600 & 80 & 7 \\
-\,217 & -\,200 \quad \text{and} & -\,10 & -\,7 \\
\hline
470 & 400 \qquad + & 70\,+ & 0 = 470
\end{array}
$$

Using an additive method to check answers by estimation will be equally effective for most children.

In the example:
$$
\begin{array}{r}
719 \\
-\,296 \\
\hline
423
\end{array}
$$
a pupil may quickly think 690 (400 + 290) + 6 + 23 = 719 or 700 (690 and 10 from 23) + 13 + 6 = 719.

3.9 Chapter Summary

The two major meanings of subtraction, "borrowing" and "additive," have been presented. Both have distinct contributions to make to the instructional program as well as to methods used by children. The teaching of the "borrowing" or "decomposition" methods must be accomplished through meaningful presentations. The authors have recommended using concrete objects to introduce the subtraction algorithm. Then gradually pupils are guided toward the discovery of the abstract work.

Three slightly different ways to use subtraction were introduced and suggestions given for their presentation to children.

Subtraction is an inverse process and should be taught along with addition. When a child "puts together," he should then be able to "take apart." Since the "additive" method is based upon a particular thought process stressing combining addends to find a third number, showing the meaning of an inverse process is highly essential.

The authors have recommended teaching basic subtraction facts as "number families" so that pupils will discover relationships as well as patterns among the facts. The use of charts, function machines, number lines, number sentences, and place-value charts should help to make the discovery process meaningful to children.

Children must understand the place value of numbers used in each aspect of subtraction. The meaningful introduction of each new step must be based upon a thorough understanding of renaming or regrouping without changing the value of the original number—the subtrahend.

QUESTIONS AND EXERCISES

1. What is the additive method used in subtraction? Ask several of your friends or classmates to "say out loud" what they actually think as they work this example: 745
                                                                 — 356
2. Why do some teachers object to the term "borrowing" in compound subtraction?
3. In subtracting: 254
                       — 147

   what is the number used to change or regroup when 7 can not be taken from 4?
4. What does the word *decomposition* mean when used in subtraction?
5. What do we mean when we say a child uses a *crutch* in subtraction?
6. Make three or four rules for checking subtraction problems.
7. How can a pupil demonstrate that he knows an arithmetic fact?
8. What is the value in having a pupil generalize about subtraction?
9. A teacher assigns 50 subtraction problems and then asks pupils to check each one by adding the answer to the subtrahend. Do you think this is a good policy?
10. What is meant by equal-additions as a method in subtraction?
11. Research seems to indicate that pupils should be taught to use a teaching aid (pocket chart or place-value box) in the first stages of learning compound subtraction. Why is this so?
12. List examples of three or four structural types of compound subtraction. Identify the skills involved in each.
13. Look at this example: 7004
                             — 3425

   What difficulties might a fourth-grade pupil have with this problem?
14. Locate the probable errors made in each of the following examples. How would you help children overcome these difficulties?

   (a)   200   (b)   562   (c)   42   (d)   66
         — 42   — 293   — 20   — 3
         ———————   ———————   ———————   ———————
           168   271   20   33

15. The cashier is given a five-dollar bill to pay for a dinner costing \$3.82. She returns with two one-dollar bills and eight cents. What are some possible mental processes used in arriving at this amount?
16. Can pupils be taught to subtract by endings? How?

17. Name at least ten words that should be taught as vocabulary related to subtraction; for example, remaining, no more, take away.
18. How would you explain to a fourth grade pupil that each figure in subtraction must be written in its proper place or column?
19. Is regrouping the opposite of carrying?
20. Subtraction examples used for teaching or for practice should not be larger than a pupil's understanding of place value. True? False? Explain your choice of answers.

SELECTED REFERENCES

Brownell, William A., and H. E. Moser, *Meaningful vs. Mechanical Learning: Study in Grade III Subtraction.* Durham, N. C.: Duke University Press, 1949.

Cronbach, Lee J., "Issues Current in Educational Psychology." *Monograph of the Society for Research in Child Development*, XXX, No. 1 (1965).

Crumley, Richard D., "A Comparison of Different Methods of Teaching Subtraction in the Third Grade" (unpublished doctoral dissertation, University of Chicago, 1956).

Gibb, E. Glenadine, "Children's Thinking in the Process of Subtraction," *Journal of Experimental Education*, XXV, (September, 1965), 71–80.

Glennon, Vincent J., and Leroy G. Callahan, *A Guide to Current Research in Elementary School Mathematics.* Washington, D. C.: Association for Supervision and Curriculum Development, 1968, pp. 85–87.

Mueller, Francis J., *Arithmetic: Its Structure and Concepts.* Englewood Cliffs, N.J.: Prentice-Hall, Inc., 1964, Unit 6.

Reckzeh, John, "Addition and Subtraction Situations," *The Arithmetic Teacher*, III (April, 1956), 94–97.

Ruck, G. M., and Cyrus D. Mean, "A Review of Experiments on Subtraction," *Committee on Arithmetic, the Twenty-Ninth Yearbook*, National Society for Study of Education. Bloomington, Ind.: Public School Publishing Co., 1930, pp. 671–78.

Schell, L. M., and P. C. Burns, "Pupil Performance with Three Types of Subtraction Situations," *School Science and Mathematics*, LXII (March, 1962), 208–14.

Van Engen, Henry, M. L. Hartung, and J. E. Stochl, *Foundations of Elementary School Arithmetic.* Chicago: Scott Foresman and Company, 1965, Chap. vii.

Weaver, J. Fred, "Whither Research on Compound Subtraction?" *The Arithmetic Teacher*, III (February, 1956), 320–24.

4

Multiplication

4.1 Definitions and Interpretations

The fundamental operation of multiplication is based on addition. In addition, addends may be unequal, as in $2 + 3 + 5 = 10$. In multiplication, addends must be equal. For example, 3×2 means three twos:

$$
\begin{array}{r} 2 \\ \times 3 \\ \hline 6 \end{array}
\qquad
\begin{array}{r} 2 \\ + 2 \\ 2 \\ \hline 6 \end{array}
$$

The reverse fact is 2×3 and means two threes:

$$
\begin{array}{r} 3 \\ \times 2 \\ \hline 6 \end{array}
\qquad
\begin{array}{r} 3 \\ + 3 \\ \hline 6 \end{array}
$$

Since multiplication is based on addition, and addition is based on counting, it follows that multiplication is based indirectly on counting.

Multiplication and addition are direct processes (putting together), while division and subtraction are inverse processes (taking apart). Subtraction as the inverse of addition is explained in the previous chapter. Division as the inverse of multiplication is explained in the next chapter. While multiplication and division are related, we have chosen to discuss them in separate chapters in order to identify basic concepts and skills for each process.

The terms in multiplication are: 5   factor (multiplicand)
                                    × 2   factor (multiplier)
                                    ——
                                     10   product

Multiplication assigns a third number (the product) to a pair of numbers (factors). For example, 2 × 5 = 10. The factors are 2 and 5. The product is 10. The product is a multiple of 2 and a multiple of 5. The signs used for multiplication include: ×, ·, ( ). If only letters are used, no symbol is needed (*ab* indicates *a* × *b*). The introduction and use of these signs in elementary school classrooms will depend upon the maturity of the pupils and the mathematical experiences provided by the teachers.

Three interpretations of multiplication should be developed with elementary school children: (1) repeated additions of equivalent sets; (2) the ratio-comparison of number pairs; and (3) the Cartesian product of two sets. The basic concepts involved in understanding and using these interpretations will be given at this time. Applications of the three interpretations of multiplication to other aspects of mathematics will be made in subsequent chapters.

Multiplication as repeated additions of equivalent sets provides for a natural, meaningful extension of addition. These two operations (addition and multiplication) are combining operations. The work is introduced in a manner such as this: (••••)   (••••)   (••••)

                            3 sets
                            4 dots in each set
                            12 dots in all

The child thinks 4 + 4 + 4 = 12, or three times four equals 12 (3 × 4 = 12). This process is continued, first with concrete objects, then semi-concrete, and finally the abstract multiplication fact. Several practice exercises should follow the work with concrete objects. For example:

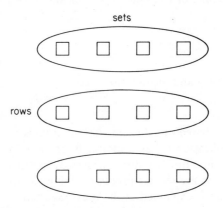

This is called an *array*. The child is directed to identify the number of rows or sets and the number of squares in each row or set.

Then a series of questions should be asked.

1. How many sets? (3)
2. How many squares in each set? (4)
3. How many squares in all? (12)
4. Can you write a number sentence about the sets?
   $(4 + 4 + 4 = 12)$ or $(3 \times 4 = 12)$

Another exercise which will test pupils' understanding of the process is:
Draw the sets for each example. Write an addition sentense and then a multiplication sentence for each. Example 1 is done.

1. 2 sets of 5 $5 + 5 = 10$ and $2 \times 5 = 10$
2. 4 sets of 2
3. 5 sets of 3
4. 6 sets of 4

Thus pupils are guided to learn that one factor names the number of sets. A second factor names the members in each set. The product is a new set resulting from the combining action.

The ratio-comparison of number pairs is used to find a number that is so many times greater than a given number. For example, Karen has 3 balloons. Debbie has 2 times as many balloons as Karen. How many balloons does Debbie have? To find the number 2 times greater than 3, multiply $2 \times 3 = 6$. The product is related to 3 as 2 is related to 1. So, 2 is 2 times greater than 1 and 6 is 2 times greater than 3. This constant relationship may be expressed as a proportion: $\frac{2}{1}$ or $\frac{6}{3}$, etc. This interpretation of multiplication is known as the ratio-comparison. In this example the numbers (2 and 1 or 6 and 3) are an *ordered pair* of numbers. A special meaning has been given to each number of the pair. The order of the numbers (the ratio-comparison) used indicates first the "greater than" (2 times as many) and the given number 3. As long as this type of problem is used and we agree upon this type of ordered pairs, the numbers in all of the ordered pairs should be given in this order. The symbolism used to name the ordered pairs is usually the pair of numerals separated by a comma and enclosed by parentheses (2, 1) or (6, 3).

The Cartesian product of two sets is another way to interpret multiplication. Study these sets: $A = \{2, 4, 6, 8\}$
$B = \{3, 5, 7, 9\}$
A new set may be made with pairs of numbers. Each pair must contain one number from each of the two sets. The new set will be:
$$C = \{(2, 3), (2, 5), (2, 7), (2, 9),$$
$$(4, 3), (4, 5), (4, 7), (4, 9),$$
$$(6, 3), (6, 5), (6, 7), (6, 9),$$
$$(8, 3), (8, 5), (8, 7), (8, 9)\}.$$
The new set C is called the Cartesian products of sets A and B. Set C contains all possible pairs.

The word Cartesian comes from the name of a French mathematician, Rene Descartes. Children can make Cartesian products with sets of objects or pictures. Suppose there are two sets:

A = {red, green, blue}

B = {brown, orange, white}

How many pairs of colors could be formed?

C = {(red, brown), (red, orange), (red, white), (green, brown), (green, orange), (green, white), (blue, brown), (blue, orange), (blue, white)}.

Children match the colors in set A with the colors in set B and discover that there are 9 different pairs. The total 3 × 3 = 9 different pairs of colors. One factor is the number of members in set A. The other factor indicates the number of members in set B. The product (set C) is the Cartesian Product of set A and set B (A × B). This is read A across B. There were 9 ordered pairs in the Cartesian Product set A across set B.

4.2 Using Basic Facts

There are 100 primary facts in multiplication, just as there were 100 primary facts in addition and in subtraction. The facts can be listed in ten rows of ten facts each or in chart form.

0	1	2	3	4	5	6	7	8	9
× 0	× 0	× 0	× 0	× 0	× 0	× 0	× 0	× 0	× 0
0	0	0	0	0	0	0	0	0	0

0	1	2	3	4	5	6	7	8	9
× 1	× 1	× 1	× 1	× 1	× 1	× 1	× 1	× 1	× 1
0	1	2	3	4	5	6	7	8	9

0	1	2	3	4	5	6	7	8	9
× 2	× 2	× 2	× 2	× 2	× 2	× 2	× 2	× 2	× 2
0	2	4	6	8	10	12	14	16	18

These three rows of ten facts each are followed by seven more rows of ten facts each, making 10 × 10 or 100 facts.

The first row shows that zero × any number = zero. Children do not need to memorize the individual zero facts. By demonstration and generalization children are taught that 0 × any number = 0. The second row shows that 1 × any number = the number. One is called the identity element with respect to multiplication, since $a \times 1 = a$ for all numbers a.

The beginning work in multiplication should probably consist of the joining of equal sets. By using objects and pictures of objects children should gain an understanding of the meaning of multiplication. In learning 3 × 4 = 12, the child could be introduced to three sets of four objects (discs, balls, or counters). Next, pictures of three sets of four should be used. Finally, the abstract symbols are used: $3 \times 4 = 12$ and   4

$$\begin{array}{r} \times\ 3 \\ \hline 12 \end{array}$$

The array is useful in teaching multiplication facts after children have been introduced to the multiplication concept. In learning $4 \times 5 = 20$, the child can be guided toward learning the meaning of the factor which multiples. There are four rows of five X's each.

in rows

4 x 5 = 20

and   5

$$\begin{array}{r} x\ 4 \\ \hline 2\ 0 \end{array}$$

The reverse fact (completing the commutative property) should be learned too:

in columns

5 x 4 = 20   and   4

$$\begin{array}{r} x\ 5 \\ \hline 20 \end{array}$$

There are two ways to think about the 20 X's: 4 sets of $5 = 20$ or 5 sets of $4 = 20$. Then $4 \times 5 = 20$ and $5 \times 4 = 20$. *In multiplication we can change the order of the factors and get the same product.*

Children can make charts to show the 100 multiplication facts and to aid them in generalizing about these facts. For example, they can discover the commutative property of multiplication by finding $3 \times 5 = 15$ and $5 \times 3 = 15$ on the chart. As pupils continue learning the basic multiplication facts they can concentrate on the difficult facts or the new facts for each line. In the 5's, for example, children will have learned the facts through 4×5 while mastering the 4's. The new 5's facts will include $5 \times 5, 5 \times 6, 5 \times 7, 5 \times 8$, and 5×9. As the child masters the facts for each row after the 5's, he will have to learn fewer facts in each row but these facts may be more difficult to learn. There are only 15 new facts for the 5's, 6's, 7's, 8's, and 9's.

Factor **I**

		0	1	2	3	4	5	6	7	8	9
	0	0	0	0	0	0	0	0	0	0	0
	1	0	1	2	3	4	5	6	7	8	9
	2	0	2	4	6	8	10	12	14	16	18
	3	0	3	6	9	12	15	18	21	24	27
Factor II	4	0	4	8	12	16	20	24	28	32	36
	5	0	5	10	15	20	25	30	35	40	45
	6	0	6	12	18	24	30	36	42	48	54
	7	0	7	14	21	28	35	42	49	56	63
	8	0	8	16	24	32	40	48	56	64	72
	9	0	9	18	27	36	45	54	63	72	81

4.3   Commutative, Associative, and Distributive Properties of Multiplication

Five properties (laws or principles) apply to the multiplication operation: (1) closure, (2) identity element, (3) commutative law, (4) associative law, and (5) distributive law.

LAW OF CLOSURE

The product of two natural numbers is a natural number. This is the law of closure for multiplication. Thus, $2 \times 3 = 6$. The product 6 is a natural number. We say that the set of natural numbers is closed with respect to multiplication. This law applies to addition also: The sum of two natural numbers is a natural number.

IDENTITY ELEMENT

While this property has been discussed in the section on basic facts, a review and restatement may be helpful to some readers. The law is: the product of any whole number and one is that whole number ($2 \times 1 = 2$, $10 \times 1 = 10$, etc.); and the product of one and any whole number is that whole number ($1 \times 3 = 3$, $1 \times 23 = 23$, etc.). Thus, $a \times 1 = a$ and $1 \times a = a$ for all numbers a.

COMMUTATIVE LAW

The product of two numbers is the same for either order of multiplication: $a \times b = b \times a$, or $2 \times 5 = 10$ and $5 \times 2 = 10$. The facts have different meanings but the product is the same.

As suggested in the last section (4.2), children can use the chart or table to look for and discover patterns with numbers. In learning the 3's table, the children should discover that $3 \times 4 = 12$. Later they learn the 4's table and discover the $4 \times 3 = 12$. Encourage them to discover other applications of the commutative law. Perhaps the number line will be useful to some children in discovering the meaning of the commutative law.

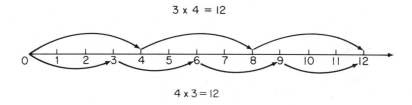

$3 \times 4 = 12$

$4 \times 3 = 12$

ASSOCIATIVE LAW

This law states that the product of three numbers is the same no matter how the numbers are grouped:
$$(4 \times 5) \times 3 = 4 \times (5 \times 3)$$
$$20 \times 3 = 4 \times 15$$
$$60 = 60$$
This idea may be generalized by letting a, b, and c represent whole numbers:
$$(a \times b) \times c = a \times (b \times c)$$

DISTRIBUTIVE LAW

Multiplication has a distributive property which is the basis for the algorithm. Distributing the multiplier over the terms of the other factor (multiplicand) is called the distributive property of multiplication with respect to addition. For example, in multiplying 2×123, the operations include multiplying to find the product of the units, the tens, and the hundreds. Then the separate products are added to find the sum.
$$2[(100) + (20) + (3)] = 200 + 40 + 6 = 246$$
Generalizing the idea with the use of letters we see that:
$$a(b + c + d) = (a \times b) + (a \times c) + (a \times d)$$
The common multiplier "2" is used for each of the values of the digits in the multiplicand: 2×3 ones; 2×2 tens; 2×1 hundred. Another way to show the law and operation is:

$$\begin{array}{r} 123 \\ \times\ \ 2 \\ \hline \end{array} = \times \begin{array}{r} 100 + 20 + 3 \\ 2 \\ \hline 200 + 40 + 6 = 246 \end{array}$$

Multiplication of whole numbers can be defined as an operation that begins with two numbers and produces a unique number called the product. The work is characterized completely by the commutative law, associative law, law of closure, distributive law, and identity number (one).

4.4 Relating Multiplication to Division

Division and multiplication are related operations. For example:

$$18 \div 3 = \square \qquad \square \times 3 = 18$$

We can divide to find a missing factor. The two boxes represent the same number. We can think "18 ÷ 3 = 6" or "what number multiplied by 3 = 18?"

Division is the process used to determine the amount of one factor when when the amounts of the product (dividend) and the other factor (divisor) are given. For example, $6 \times 3 = 18$ and $3 \times 6 = 18$. Then $18 \div 6 = 3$ and $18 \div 3 = 6$. As children learn the multiplication facts, they should also learn the related division facts. As shown above, there are four related sentences for each basic multiplication fact. Exercises stressing these relationships could include:

If $6 \times 8 = 48$ and $8 \times 6 = 48$, then $48 \div 6 = \boxed{8}$ and $48 \div 8 = \boxed{6}$
or

$$\square \times 5 = 15$$
$$5 \times \square = 15$$
$$15 \div 3 = \square$$
$$15 \div \square = 5$$

4.5 Multiplication of a Two-digit Number by a One-digit Number; No Regrouping (Carrying)

Multiplication of a two-digit number by a one-digit number without regrouping may be introduced in several ways. One way is by using multiplying by tens and another is by using the distributive law.

Pupils are usually familiar with counting by 10's. This type of counting is used in games and in repeated additions. United States currency (dimes) can be used to show this. Children can easily think, three dimes make 30¢. The zero should not cause any difficulty if children understand the place value involved and the rule that any number times zero = 0. After ample work with concrete objects and United States money, children can write the

(10 ¢) (10 ¢) (10 ¢) = 3 × 10 = 30

$$\text{or} \quad \begin{array}{r} 10 \\ \times\ 3 \\ \hline 30 \end{array}$$

products for examples such as these:

$$\begin{array}{cccc} 10 & 10 & 10 & 10 \\ \times\ 3 & \times\ 5 & \times\ 2 & \times\ 6 \\ \hline \end{array}$$

and $10 \times 2 = \square$, $10 \times 3 = \square$, $5 \times 10 = \square$.

The distributive law is useful in extending the multiplication of a two-digit number by a one-digit number. In teaching $\begin{array}{r} 13 \\ \times\ 2 \\ \hline \end{array}$ concrete objects or pictures can be used:

$$\begin{array}{ccc} 0000000000 & 000 & 10 + 3 \\ & = & \\ 0000000000 & 000 & \underline{\times\quad\ \ 2} \\ & & 20 + 6 = 26 \end{array}$$

The child is directed to think: 2×3 ones $= 6$ ones, place the 6 in the ones' column. Then 2×1 ten $= 2$ tens. Place the 2 in the tens' column.

A place-value chart can also be used:

see	*think*		*write*	
	TENS	ONES	TENS	ONES
13	1	3	1	3
$\times\ 2$	$\times$	2	$\times$	2
		6	$\square$	6
	2	0		
	2	$\square$		

Observe that one factor (multiplier) is an abstract number. In 2×13 the multiplier is 2. The multiplier tells "how many" and is an abstract number without an attached name.

4.6 Multiplication of a Two-digit Number by a One-digit Number with Regrouping (Carrying)

A combination of concrete objects and a place-value chart should probably be used in introducing multiplication involving regrouping. For example, in multiplying 3×14, dimes and pennies could be used:

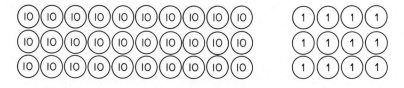

$$
\begin{array}{cc}
14 & 10 + 4 \\
\times\ 3 & \times\quad 3 \\
\hline
& 30 + 12 = 42
\end{array}
$$

TENS	ONES		TENS	ONES
1	4		1	4
×	3		×	3
1	2	3×4 ones $= 12$	4	2
3	0	3×1 ten $= 30$		
4	2			

Children should first be shown the concrete objects (dimes and pennies) and the combining of three groups of 4 pennies to make 12 pennies. This partial sum is written as 1 ten and 2 ones. Then 3 times 1 ten (10) = 3 tens or 30. Write the 3 tens in the tens column. Adding partial products, 2 ones + 4 tens = 42.

$$
\begin{array}{r}
1 \\
14 \\
3 \\
\hline
2
\end{array}
$$

In the abstract stage, children may need to write the carried number if they cannot remember to add the 1 ten after multiplying 3 × 1 ten. Some teachers call this process a "crutch" because it helps pupils remember the number carried when multiplying. After careful work with concrete objects, using expanded notation of the multiplicand, and identifying place value, many children will not need to write the carried number in multiplication.

The process just described may be thought of as two ways to find the product; a long way and a short way.

Long way   *Short way*

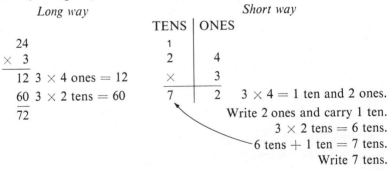

$$
\begin{array}{l}
24 \\
\times\ 3 \\
\hline
12\quad 3 \times 4 \text{ ones} = 12 \\
60\quad 3 \times 2 \text{ tens} = 60 \\
\hline
72
\end{array}
$$

TENS	ONES
1	
2	4
×	3
7	2

$3 \times 4 = 1$ ten and 2 ones. Write 2 ones and carry 1 ten. 3×2 tens $= 6$ tens. 6 tens + 1 ten = 7 tens. Write 7 tens.

In finding each partial product in multiplication, pupils must learn to keep an "unseen" number in mind or think the number. For example:

$$
\begin{array}{r}
746 \\
\times\quad 6 \\
\hline
\end{array}
$$

the pupil thinks 6 × 6 = 36, he writes the 6 ones and remembers the 3 tens to be carried. Then 6 × 4 = 24 tens and 24 tens + 3 tens carried = 27 tens. The 7 tens is written in the tens place and the operation continues. Finally, 6 × 7 hundreds = 42 hundreds + the 2 hundreds carried

= 4400. Then 4400 + 76 = 4476, the final product. This addition involves adding by endings (thinking 24 + 3 = 27, 42 + 2 = 44 with one mental operation). Since children need practice with this skill, some teachers encourage the use of the visual aid showing the carried numbers:

$$
\begin{array}{r}
2\,3 \\
746 \\
\times\quad 6 \\
\hline
76
\end{array}
$$

The authors recommend that the process be taught so that most pupils will not have to use this *crutch*.

4.7   Rationalizing the Use of Zero in Multiplying

The use of zero in multiplication has been discussed in section 4.2 in connection with basic multiplication facts. Additional attention should be given to rationalizing the use of zero.

Any number × zero = zero. This may be rationalized on the basis of interpreting multiplication as cumulative addition. For example, $6 \times 0 = 0$ can be explained by saying that 6×0 means six zeros, or

$$6 \times 0 = 0 + 0 + 0 + 0 + 0 + 0$$

Rationalizing the fact that $0 \times 6 = 0$, we say that 0×6 means not any sixes, which is zero. The commutative law may be used thus, $0 \times 6 = 6 \times 0$ and since $6 \times 0 = 0$ then $0 \times 6 = 0$.

Practical applications may be used to help children rationalize the process. If a pupil throws a dart at a target three times and misses the target each time, his score will be zero ($3 \times 0 = 0$). Or, a pupil may have three chances but does not choose to throw. His score would be $0 \times 3 = 0$.

4.8   Multiplying a Two-digit Number by a Two-digit Number

When children understand how to multiply a two-digit number by a one-digit number, they are probably ready to extend their concept of multiplication to include two-digits in the multiplier. This extension can be introduced with examples which do not include carrying. For example:

$$
\begin{array}{r}
23 \\
\times\ 12 \\
\hline
\end{array}
$$

no carrying is involved and children apply previously learned skills.

Long way

HUNDREDS	TENS	ONES	
	2	3	
	× 1	2	
		6	2 × 3 = 6
	4	0	2 × 20 = 40
	3	0	10 × 3 = 30
2	0	0	10 × 20 = 200
2	7	6	

Short way

HUNDREDS	TENS	ONES	
	2	3	
	× 1	2	
	4	6	2 × 3 = 6
			2 × 20 = 40
2	3		10 × 3 = 30
			10 × 20 = 200
2	7	6	

Another variation which may help pupils understand the place values and partial products is:

$$
\begin{array}{llll}
23 & 20+3 & 20+3 & 20+\;3 \\
\times 12 = & \times 10+2 = & \times \quad 2\,+ & \times \quad\quad 10 \\
\hline
46 & & 40+6=46 & 200+30=230 \\
23 & & & \\
\hline
276 & & 46+230=276 &
\end{array}
$$

The 23 (rewritten as 20 + 3) is multipled by 12 (rewritten as 10 + 2). First multiply by 2—(2 × 3) + (2 × 20), then multiply by 10—(10 × 3) + (10 × 20). Each factor in the multiplier is used to multiply each factor is the multiplicand. Note that the distributive law in multiplication have been used twice in the example.

Multiplying a two-digit number by a two-digit number with carrying (or regrouping) would be the next type to study. For example, $\begin{array}{r}25\\ \times 23\end{array}$. The carrying involved is similar to that used with a one-digit multiplier and extended to carrying in the tens' position of the multiplier. Both long and short forms should be used, supported by expanded notation to show factors being multiplied to get partial products.

$$23 \times 25 = (20 + 3)(25) = 20(25) + 3(25)$$

Long

$$
\begin{array}{r}
25 \\
\times\ 23 \\
\hline
15 \\
60 \\
100 \\
400 \\
\hline
575
\end{array}
\qquad
\begin{array}{l}
3 \times 5 = 15 \\
3 \times 20 = 60 \\
20 \times 5 = 100 \\
20 \times 20 = 400
\end{array}
$$

Short

HUNDREDS	TENS	ONES
1	1	
	2	5
	× 2	3
	7	5
5	0	
5	7	5

$3 \times 5 = 15$. Write 5 ones, carry 1 ten.
$3 \times 20 = 60 + 1$ ten $= 70$. Write 7 tens.
$20 \times 5 = 100$. Write 0 in tens' place as place holder. Carry 1 hundred.
$20 \times 20 = 400$
$400 + 100 = 500$. Write 5 in hundreds' place.

Identifying the multiplication of the multiplicand by each number in the multiplier may also be shown like this:

$$
\begin{array}{ccccc}
 & & 1 & & \\
25 & & 25 & & 25 \\
\times\ 23 & \neq & \times\ 20 & + & \times\ 3 \\
\hline
 & & 00 & & 15 \\
 & & 500 & & 60 \\
\cline{3-3}\cline{5-5}
 & & 500 & + & 75 = 575
\end{array}
$$

Pupils should be encouraged to experiment to find different solutions for problems in multiplication. Here are examples of methods used by children.

(1)

$$
\begin{array}{rl}
14 & \\
\times\ 12 & \\
\hline
28 & 2 \times 14 = 28 \\
 & \text{and} \\
140 & 10 \times 14 = 140 \\
\hline
168 &
\end{array}
$$

(2) *Multiplying from left to right*

$$
\begin{array}{rl}
56 & \\
\times\ 12 & \\
\hline
500 & (50 \times 10) \\
60 & (6 \times 10) \\
100 & (50 \times 2) \\
12 & (6 \times 2) \\
\hline
672 &
\end{array}
\qquad
\text{or}
\qquad
\begin{array}{rl}
56 & \\
\times\ 12 & \\
\hline
560 & (56 \times 10 = 560) \\
100 & (50 \times 2 = 100) \\
12 & (6 \times 2 = 12) \\
\hline
672 &
\end{array}
$$

(3)

43	43	43		43	43	43
× 24 =	× 10 +	× 4	or	× 24 = ×	20 +	× 4
172	430	172			860	172
86	× 2				860 + 172 = 1032	
1032	860					
	860 + 172 = 1032					

Multiplying with three or more digits in the multiplicand and multiplier requires careful attention to place value. To insure proper placement of partial products, use the long form before introducing short cuts and dropping of zeros.

For example:

$$
\begin{array}{r}
262 \\
\times\ 123 \\
\hline
\end{array}
$$

6	$3 \times 2 = 6$
180	$3 \times 60 = 180$
600	$3 \times 200 = 600$
40	$20 \times 2 = 40$
1,200	$20 \times 60 = 1,200$
4,000	$20 \times 200 = 4,000$
200	$100 \times 2 = 200$
6,000	$100 \times 60 = 6,000$
20,000	$100 \times 200 = 20,000$
32,226	

Short method

$$
\begin{array}{r}
262 \\
\times\ 123 \\
\hline
786 \\
5\ 24 \\
26\ 2 \\
\hline
32,226 \\
\end{array}
$$

Note the short cuts involved in working this example: 3 times 2 = 6, write 6 ones. 3 times 60 = 180, write 8 tens (drop the zero) and carry 1 hundred. Three times 200 = 600, and 1 hundred carried, write 7 in the hundreds' column. The next two steps (multiplying by 20 and by 100) are similar and involve complicated short cuts, combining of partial products, dropping the zeros, and understanding place values.

The antiquated method used by some teachers, having pupils draw lines to keep numbers in correct position without understanding place values, cannot be defended and should not be perpetuated. Pupils must understand place values and must be able to demonstrate the values of partial products. When pupils have difficulty with multiplication examples, work on their mastery of multiplication facts and encourage them to work examples simple enough to demonstrate the place values of each partial product. After mastery of simple forms, move ahead gradually and with confidence to more difficult examples.

Keep in mind the fact that in this modern age we should not expect children to compete with adding machines or computers. Thus, there must be some work with long multiplication examples but not continued and laborious assignments of this unpleasant work.

4.9 Three- and Four-digit Multiplication with Examples Involving Zeros

Zeros may cause difficulty in complex multiplication problems if children do not understand place values of partial products. To help pupils avoid these difficulties, the authors recommend using expanded notation and the long form of multiplication before introducing short cuts.

For example:

$$
\begin{array}{r} 207 \\ \times\ \ 2 \\ \hline \end{array}
=
\begin{array}{r} 200 \\ \times\ \ 2 \\ \hline 400 \end{array}
+
\begin{array}{r} 7 \\ \times\ 2 \\ \hline 14 \end{array}
$$

$$
\begin{array}{r} 3004 \\ \times\ \ \ 2 \\ \hline \end{array}
=
\begin{array}{r} 3000 \\ \times\ \ \ \ 2 \\ \hline 6000 \end{array}
+
\begin{array}{r} 4 \\ \times 2 \\ \hline 8 \end{array}
\quad \text{and} \quad
\begin{array}{r} 3004 \\ \times\ \ \ 2 \\ \hline 8 \\ 00 \\ 000 \\ 6000 \end{array}
\quad
\begin{array}{l} \\ \\ \text{no tens} \\ \text{no hundreds} \\ 2 \times 3000 \end{array}
$$

Consider the case of zeros in the multiplier:

$$
\begin{array}{r} 322 \\ \times\ 203 \\ \hline 966 \\ 0,000 \\ 64,400 \\ \hline 65,366 \end{array}
=
\begin{array}{r} 300 + 20 + 2 \\ \times\ 200 + \ \ 0 + 3 \\ \hline \end{array}
$$

0,000 Show the zeros (no ones, tens, hundreds).
64,400 $(200 \times 322 = 64400)$

The advanced pupil will probably be able to multiply 200×322 and 3×322 using the distributive law. He would think 3×322 to get a partial product of 966. Then $2 \times 322 = 644$ (affixing 2 zeros to make hundreds), the second partial product would be 64,400. Combining partial products, the pupil would have $64,400 + 966 = 65,366$.

4.10 Using Calculating Machines

We should emphasize that the multiplication process is a shortened form of addition. If it were not for this shortened process, one would have to write 16,298 a total of 3,428 times and then add to find the product of large numbers such as $3,248 \times 16,298$.

In connection with multiplication by a two-digit multiplier, it is instructive to study the operation of a hand-operated calculating machine. To multiply 32 × 28, the multiplicand, 28, is entered on the keyboard. Next, the hand crank is turned forward through two complete revolutions. This is equivalent to adding two 28's. Now the carriage is moved one place to the right. This movement changes the next digit from 3 to 30, making direct use of the idea of place value. Now the hand crank is turned forward through three complete revolutions. Since the carriage has been moved one place, this is equivalent to adding 280 three times, or adding 28 thirty times. The final result is now on the dials, since the previous product has been automatically increased by the second product.

Electrically operated calculators work on the same principle, except that the revolutions are performed electrically rather than by hand.

4.11   Short Cuts and Interesting Products

After pupils attain some proficiency in multiplication, they become interested in short cuts and unusual products. This is especially true of the more gifted pupils.

Short cuts for multiplying by a number ending in zeros are shown below:

36	36	36	36
× 10	× 20	× 100	× 200
360	720	3,600	7,200

The short cuts consist simply of writing the multiplier in such a way that the terminal zero or zeros are carried down into the product.

A short cut for multiplying a two-digit number ending in 5 by itself is as follows:

$$\begin{array}{r} 75 \\ \times \quad 75 \\ \hline 5,625 \end{array}$$

The rule is: first write 25 in the product. These will always be the two digits in the product on the right. Next, add 1 to the tens' digit and multiply this by the tens' digit. In this example:

$$7 + 1 = 8 \quad \text{and} \quad 8 \times 7 = 56$$

This gives the remaining digits of the product.

Another example of this short cut is:

$$\begin{array}{r} 65 \\ \times \quad 65 \\ \hline 4,225 \end{array}$$

First, write 25. Then:

$$6 + 1 = 7 \quad \text{and} \quad 7 \times 6 = 42$$

The algebraic proof of this short cut is:
$$(10a + 5)(10a + 5) = 100a^2 + 100a + 25$$
$$= 100a(a + 1) + 25$$
This short cut can be extended to the case of multiplying two two-digit numbers if the tens' digits are the same and the sum of the units' digits is 10.

$$\begin{array}{r} 72 \\ \times \quad 78 \\ \hline 5,616 \end{array}$$

First, write $8 \times 2 = 16$ for the two right digits of the product. Then:
$$7 + 1 = 8 \quad \text{and} \quad 8 \times 7 = 56$$
Another example is:

$$\begin{array}{r} 63 \\ \times \quad 67 \\ \hline 4,221 \end{array}$$

Here $7 \times 3 = 21$. Then:
$$6 + 1 = 7 \quad \text{and} \quad 7 + 6 = 42$$
In both of these examples the sum of the units' digits is 10. In the first example, $2 + 8 = 10$, and in the second example $3 + 7 = 10$.

The better pupils like short cuts such as these. It would be good teaching to show the pupils a few examples and let them discover the rule for themselves. This procedure encourages the spirit of looking for patterns and allows the pupils to have the rewarding feeling that accompanies discovery.

Another short cut is:

$$\begin{array}{r} 326 \\ \times \quad 84 \\ \hline 1\ 304 \\ 26\ 08 \\ \hline 27,384 \end{array}$$

Multiply by 4. Next, instead of multiplying the multiplicand by 8, multiply 1304 by 2. This is permissible because 8 is twice 4. This idea can be used with multipliers such as 63 and 41.

Some interesting products are:

$$\begin{array}{r} 12{,}345{,}679 \\ \times \quad\quad 9 \\ \hline 111{,}111{,}111 \end{array} \qquad \begin{array}{r} 12{,}345{,}679 \\ \times \quad\quad 18 \\ \hline 222{,}222{,}222 \end{array}$$

What would be the product of $12{,}345{,}679 \times 27$, or $12{,}345{,}679 \times 36$?

Some other short cuts are:

1. To multiply a number by 25, annex two zeros to the number and divide the result by 4.
$$328 \times 25 = 32{,}800 \div 4 = 8{,}200$$

2. To multiply a number by 5, annex a zero to the number and divide by 2.
$$328 \times 5 = 3280 \div 2 = 1{,}640$$

An arithmetic teacher would do well to keep a notebook for short cuts, interesting products, number tricks, and so forth, recording them from sources such as newspapers, magazines, and mathematical journals.

Consider multiplication of 9:

1	2	3	4	5	6	7	8	9
$\times 9$	$\times 9$	$\times 9$	$\times 9$	$\times 9$	$\times 9$	$\times 9$	$\times 9$	$\times 9$
9	18	27	36	45	54	63	72	81

In every case the sum of the digits in the product is 9. This may aid some pupils in remembering the primary facts for 9. With larger numbers, the sum of the digits in the product is a 9 or a multiple of 9: thus,

$$9 \times 2684 = 24{,}156, \quad \text{and} \quad 2 + 4 + 1 + 5 + 6 = 18$$

which is a multiple of 9.

To multiply a number by 99, annex two zeros to the number, and subtract the number from this result. For instance:

$$\begin{array}{r} 326 \\ \times\ 99 \\ \hline \end{array} \qquad \begin{array}{r} 32{,}600 \\ -\ 326 \\ \hline 32{,}274 \end{array}$$

The proof of this rule lies in the fact that $99 = 100 - 1$. Then:

$$326 \times 99 = 326 \times (100 - 1) = 32{,}600 - 326 = 32{,}274$$

Can you devise a rule for multiplying a number by 999?

4.12 Using the Law of Compensation

This law involves changing one factor and then compensating for the change with the other factor so that the product will be the same as it would have been when both factors were multiplied without any change. For example, one can *half one factor* then *double the other factor* without changing the product:

$$12 \times 35 = 6 \times 70 = 420$$
$$18 \times 25 = 9 \times 50 = 450$$
$$16 \times 50 = 8 \times 100 = 800$$

In the example 15×14, one can multiply 15 by 10 twice and then divide one of these partial products by 2:

$$15 \times 14 = (10 \times 14) + \frac{(10 \times 14)}{2}$$

$$= 140 + \frac{140}{2} = 140 + 70 = 210$$

Multiplying by 25, one can multiply by 100 and then divide by 4:

$$12 \times 25 = \frac{12 \times 100}{4} = \frac{1200}{4} = 300$$

Factoring may be used to simplify the multiplication operation.

$$18 \times 35 = 9 \times 2 \times 35 = 9 \times \quad 70 = 630$$
$$15 \times 30 = 3 \times 5 \times 30 = 3 \times 150 = 450$$

or

$$15 \times 10 \times 3 = 150 \times 3 = 450$$

These applications of the law of compensation may be introduced with mature pupils in fifth or sixth grade after they have explored some of the methods suggested in section 4.8.

4.13   Using Other Bases

The complete multiplication tables for base 2 are:

$$0 \times 0 = 0$$
$$1 \times 0 = 0$$
$$0 \times 1 = 0$$
$$1 \times 1 = 1$$

Multiplication in base 2 is very simple. For example:

$$
\begin{array}{ll}
101 & = (1 + 0 + 4 = 5) \text{ base } 10 \\
\times \quad 11 & = (1 + 2 = 3) \text{ base } 10 \\
\hline
101 & = 1 + 0 + 4 = 5) \\
101 & = (2 + 0 + 8 = 10) \\
\hline
1111 & = (1 + 2 + 4 + 8 = 15)
\end{array}
$$

Notice that $101 = 5$ in base 10, $11 = 3$ in base 10, and the product $1111 = 15$ in base 10, so this example in base 10 is $3 \times 5 = 15$.

A more difficult example is

$$
\begin{array}{r}
111 \\
\times \quad 11 \\
\hline
111 \\
111 \\
\hline
10101
\end{array}
$$

The difficulty here is in the carrying in the addition. Recall that $1 + 1 = 10$. Write 0 and carry 1. Then:

$$1 + 1 + 1 = 10 + 1 = 11$$

so write 1 and carry 1. Finally $1 + 1 = 10$. Write 0 and carry 1.

Multiplication in base 8 is more difficult than multiplication in base 2. Here there are 64 primary facts to memorize, rather than 100 as in base 10. An example is this row of eight facts.

0	1	2	3	4	5	6	7
$\times 4$	$\times 4$	$\times 4$	$\times 4$	$\times 4$	$\times 4$	$\times 4$	$\times 4$
0	4	10	14	20	24	30	34

Observe that $4 \times 2 = 8$ in base 10, but 8 in base 8 is written 10, which means 1 eight and not any ones. Next $4 \times 3 = 12$ in base 10, but 12 is 14 in base 8, since 14 in base 8 means 1 eight and 4 ones. Next, $4 \times 4 = 16$ in base 10, but $16 = 20$ in base 8 since 20 means 2 eights and not any ones.

The complete multiplication tables for base 8 would include 8 rows of 8 examples each, or 64 primary facts. These facts would have to be memorized, just as they must be memorized in our base 10.

The study of other bases contributes to the understanding of base 10. Some of the difficulties that pupils in elementary school have with processes in base 10 are made apparent when one attempts to do these same processes in other bases. Because at the present time base 2 and base 8 are used in electronic digital computers, we believe that we can justify the study by teachers of other bases than that of base 10.

4.14   Chapter Summary

Multiplication assigns a third number, the product, to a pair of numbers called factors. While multiplicand and multiplier are still commonly used terms in multiplication, the use of "factor" provides flexibility and relates to modern mathematical work.

The three interpretations of multiplication used in the chapter are: (1) repeated addition, (2) a ratio or comparison of number pairs, and (3) the Cartesian product of two sets. Basic concepts involved in understanding and using these interpretations were given.

Emphasis was placed upon learning the basic multiplication facts, including the reverse facts, in a meaningful way. As pupils work on these facts, they should concentrate on the new facts rather than upon "table form" and routine repeating of answers. Building times tables and using charts, such as the one shown in section 4.2, should be used to discover relationships and patterns among the tables.

The properties of multiplication were used to justify the algorithm and to identify the difficult "short cuts" used in working examples. Expanded notation was also used to help pupils identify basic concepts and skills.

The relationships between multiplication and division were stressed, especially the importance of learning the multiplication and division facts. For example:

If $\quad\quad\quad\quad 5 \times 6 = 30 \quad$ and $\quad 6 \times 5 = 30,$

then $\quad\quad\quad 30 \div 5 = 6 \quad$ and $\quad 30 \div 6 = 5.$

Both long and short multiplication processes were presented so that teachers could clearly identify the difficult steps involved in working examples with two- and three-digit numbers.

The use of calculating machines, working to find interesting products, and using the "law of compensation" were included in the chapter to suggest the importance of motivating pupils to use discovery techniques and to develop efficient methods in their work.

The chapter closed with a brief presentation of multiplying with bases other than base 10.

QUESTIONS AND EXERCISES

1. Make a list of basic vocabulary used in multiplication.
2. Explain why multiplication may be thought of as cumulative addition.
3. What is the difference in meaning of these two facts?

$$\textbf{(a)} \quad \begin{array}{r} 8 \\ \times\ 3 \\ \hline \end{array} \qquad \textbf{(b)} \quad \begin{array}{r} 3 \\ \times\ 8 \\ \hline \end{array}$$

4. Illustrate with examples: the commutative law, the associative law, the distributive law, and the law of closure.
5. Make a list of reasons for not having pupils learn their multiplication facts in table form.
6. When, if at all, should children learn multiplication facts through the 12's?
7. What are acceptable ways to check an answer in multiplication?
8. Why must the multiplier be an abstract number?
9. Rationalize the meaning of each example.

(a) 8×0 (b) 0×8
$$\textbf{(c)} \quad \begin{array}{r} 12 \\ \times\ 4 \\ \hline \end{array} \qquad \textbf{(d)} \quad \begin{array}{r} 18 \\ \times\ 4 \\ \hline \end{array}$$

$$\textbf{(e)} \quad \begin{array}{r} 122 \\ \times\ \ \ 4 \\ \hline \end{array} \qquad \textbf{(f)} \quad \begin{array}{r} 182 \\ \times\ \ \ 4 \\ \hline \end{array} \qquad \textbf{(g)} \quad \begin{array}{r} 22 \\ \times\ 12 \\ \hline \end{array} \qquad \textbf{(h)} \quad \begin{array}{r} 28 \\ \times\ 12 \\ \hline \end{array}$$

10. What are some difficulties children may have with the use of zero in multiplication? What could be done to overcome or to avoid these difficulties?
11. What would you do to help a pupil who was confusing the answer to 6×9 with the answer to 7×8?
12. Make a list of multiplication examples beginning with a simple fact (2×3) and continuing through difficult problems with three-place multiplication.
13. Identify the skills and concepts necessary for working and for understanding each example shown in the above exercise.
14. How does mental higher decade addition help students in working multiplication problems?
15. Work the example 450×15 by multiplying by 10 and then by 5 to show the meaning of partial products and the place values of each.
16. What value do you see in using the zero as shown in these examples?

$$\textbf{(a)} \quad \begin{array}{r} 42 \\ \times\ 12 \\ \hline 84 \\ 420 \\ \hline 504 \end{array} \qquad \textbf{(b)} \quad \begin{array}{r} 34 \\ \times\ 75 \\ \hline 170 \\ 2380 \\ \hline 2,550 \end{array}$$

17. How would you explain these short cuts?

(a) 60	**(b)** 332	**(c)** 670
× 20	× 10	× 40
1,200	3,320	26,800

18. What value, if any, do you see in this problem for sixth-grade pupils? A farmer owns a ranch 4,750 feet long and 1,250 feet wide. What is the area in square feet?

19. Use short cuts to complete these examples.

(a) 85	**(b)** 82	**(c)** 325
× 85	× 88	× 99

20. Use *base two* and complete the examples.

(a) 10	**(b)** 101
× 11	× 11

21. Mr. Gates averages 18 miles per day driving to and from work. How far does he travel in four weeks of five days each?

22. Which is larger, 32 × 465 or 31 × 466? How much larger?

23. Below are sample exercises for pupils. What values do you see in assigning each type?

(a) Solve the equations.

$16 \times 10 = (10 \times 10) + (6 \times n) = 160$
$56 \times 10 + (50 \times 10) + (6 \times n) = 560$

(b) Since $4 \times 60 = 240$, we know that $4 \times 61 = n$
(c) Since $5 \times 50 = 250$, we know that $5 \times 51 = n$
(d) $(3 \times 10) + (3 \times 4) = n$
(e) Find the missing numbers.

$4 \times 22 = (4 \times 20) + (4 \times 2) = n + 8 = 88$
$3 \times 12 = (3 \times 10) + (3 \times n) = 30 + 6 = 36$

24. On a test one point is given for each correct answer, and two points are deducted for each incorrect answer. On a test containing 100 items, a student answered 83 correctly. What is his score?

25. A brick wall is 2 bricks wide, 10 bricks high, and 58 bricks long. How many bricks are there in the wall?

26. A golfer scored four 78's, three 80's, two 81's, and one 85 in his latest ten rounds of play. What was his total for these ten rounds? What was his average score?

27. A television dealer purchased 18 sets at $216 each, and 14 sets at $135 each. He sold the higher-priced sets for $299 each, and the others for $178 each. How much profit did he make?

28. An orchard has 28 rows of trees and there are 36 trees in each row. How many trees are there in the orchard?

SELECTED REFERENCES

Christofferson, H. C. "Meanings in Multiplication " *The Arithmetic Teacher*, VI (April, 1959), 148–51.

Fejfar, James L., "A Teaching Program for Experimentation with Computer-Assisted Instruction," *The Arithmetic Teacher*, XVI (March, 1969), 184–88.

Gray, Roland F., "An Experiment in the Teaching of Introductory Multiplication," *The Arithmetic Teacher*, XII (March, 1965), 199–203.

Grossnickle, Foster E., "Discovering the Multiplication Facts," *The Arithmetic Teacher*, VI (October, 1959), 195–98.

Hannon, Herbert, "A New Look at the Basic Principles of Multiplication with Whole Numbers," *The Arithmetic Teacher*, VII (November, 1960), 357–61.

Harvey, Lois F., and George C. Kyte, "Zero Difficulties in Multiplication," *The Arithmetic Teacher*, XII (January, 1965), 45–50.

Higgins, Conwell, and R. R. Rusch, "Remedial Teaching of Multiplication and Division: Programmed Textbook versus Workbook," *The Arithmetic Teacher*. XII (January, 1965), 32–38.

Lowrey, Charlotte, "Making Sense of the Nines Check," *The Arithmetic Teacher*, XIV (March, 1967), 222–24.

National Council of Teachers of Mathematics, *Topics in Mathematics, Twenty-ninth Yearbook*. Washington D. C.: The Council, 1964, pp. 153–57.

Schell, Leo M., "Two Aspects of Introductory Multiplication: The Array and the Distributive Property," *Dissertation Abstracts*, XXV (March-April, 1965), 5,161f.

Williams, Catherine M., "The Function of Charts in the Arithmetic Program." *The Arithmetic Teacher*, II (October, 1955), 72–76.

5

Division

5.1 Interpretations of Division

Division may be interpreted in four ways. Each interpretation will be described and an example given.

DIVISION AS THE INVERSE OF MULTIPLICATION

In the example $8 \div 4 = ?$, the 8 is the product of two numbers, 4 is one of the two numbers, and we seek to find the other of the two numbers.

If a man works five days and earns a total of $60, what is his daily wage? $5 \times$ daily wage $= \$60$. The \$60 is the product of two numbers, and one of the numbers is 5. What is the other number? $\$60 \div 5 = \$12$.

Division is the inverse of multiplication.

DIVISION AS A PROCESS OF MEASUREMENT

In working the example $10 \div 2$, we may wish to find "how many 2's are in 10?" This is the measurement interpretation of division. We could actually measure the 10 (using feet as the unit) by 2.

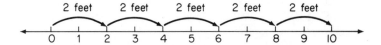

There would be 5 two-foot groups or units in 10 feet. An example could involve the use of streamers for decorating a float. How many streamers can be made from 60 feet of paper, if each streamer is 10 feet long? How many ten-foot pieces are contained in 60 feet? $60 \div 10 = 6$

Division may be interpreted as a process of measurement—showing how many parts.

DIVISION AS A PROCESS OF PARTITION

In this interpretation of division, one seeks to find the "size of each part." For example, if we had 60 feet of ribbon and needed 4 streamers, how long would each streamer be?

The 60 feet is to be divided into 4 equal parts. What is the *size* of each part? 60 feet $\div$ 4 = 15 feet

Division may be interpreted as partition—showing the size of each part.

DIVISION AS SUCCESSIVE SUBTRACTION

Division is the inverse of multiplication, and subtraction is the inverse of addition. Multiplication is successive addition, so it is logical that division is successive subtraction. Calculators divide by treating division as successive subtractions. One can enter a number such as 20 on the calculator and then divide by 4 by making repeated subtractions. As each subtraction is made, the turn of the crank is recorded. Thus there would be 5 subtractions (backward turns) and this numeral would be shown on a lower set of dials.

Some authors of textbooks believe children should use a procedure emphasizing the meaning of division and reducing the necessity for estimating and adjusting partial quotients in the first stages of instruction.[1] This procedure begins with repeated subtractions such as how many fives are there in 35?

[1] See Maurice L. Hartung *et al.*, *Teacher's Edition, Book 4, Seeing Through Arithmetic* (Glenwood, Ill.: Scott Foresman and Company, 1967), pp. 402f.

```
5 )   35
  −  5   1
    ───
    30
  −  5   1
    ───
    25
  −  5   1
    ───
    20
  −  5   1
    ───
    15
  −  5   1
    ───
    10
  −  5   1
    ───
     5
  −  5   1
    ───
         7
```

or shortening the process by using multiples of 5 (5, 10, 15, etc.)

```
5 ) 35
    15   3
    ──
    20
    20   4
    ──
     0   7
```

There are 7 fives in 35

Using the repeated subtraction form of division, children are encouraged to use any combination of partial quotients if the sum is equal to the total quotient.

The authors of this book believe that this interpretation of division should be one of several approaches used to encourage children to discover meaningful ways to divide. Children should be introduced to numerous measurement and partition situations requiring meaningful and appropriate learning experiences. Thus, the type of problem and the gradual development of concepts should enable children to learn the division process easily.

Division can be expressed in any of these ways:

$$8 \div 2 = 4 \qquad \frac{8}{2} = 4 \qquad 2 \overline{\smash{)}\,8}^{\,4}$$

The fraction line indicates division.

Division exercises may be written in two ways:

2 quotient 4)8 dividend divisor		divisor 8 ÷ 4 = 2 dividend quotient
	or	

5.2 One-digit Divisors and Quotients

There are 90 primary facts in division. This is because *division by zero* is not allowed.

Helping children understand the use of zero facts in division requires special time and thought. Since we know that for each number sentence involving division, there is a related sentence for multiplication, the role of zero in division can be taught by using this relationship. For example:

$$0 \div 3 = n \text{ means that } n \times 3 = 0$$

If the product of two numbers is 0, then one of the numbers must be zero. Replacing n in $0 \div 3 = n$ and $n \times 3 = 0$, we secure 0. The sentences $0 \div 3 = n$ and $n \times 3 = 0$ are true statements. Dividing 0 by any number greater than zero $= 0$. Thus the sentence $0 \div b = 0$, when b is any number greater than zero, is true.

Now let us try dividing a number by zero.

$$6 \div 0 = a \text{ means that } a \times 0 = 6$$

The product of any number and 0 is always 0. So there is no replacement for a that will make $a \times 0 = 6$ a true statement.

Try dividing 0 by 0. $0 \div 0 = b$ means that $b \times 0 = 0$.

When b is replaced by any number, we secure a true statement for $b \times 0 = 0$. Mathematically $0 \div 0$ is equal to any number. So, $0 \div 0$ is indeterminate. There is no one number that is equal to $0 \div 0$.

So excluding division by zero, the 90 facts can be listed as follows:

$$
\begin{array}{ccccccccc}
0 & 0 & 0 & 0 & 0 & 0 & 0 & 0 & 0 \\
1\overline{)0} & 2\overline{)0} & 3\overline{)0} & 4\overline{)0} & 5\overline{)0} & 6\overline{)0} & 7\overline{)0} & 8\overline{)0} & 9\overline{)0} \\
1 & 1 & 1 & 1 & 1 & 1 & 1 & 1 & 1 \\
1\overline{)1} & 2\overline{)2} & 3\overline{)3} & 4\overline{)4} & 5\overline{)5} & 6\overline{)6} & 7\overline{)7} & 8\overline{)8} & 9\overline{)9} \\
2 & 2 & 2 & 2 & 2 & 2 & 2 & 2 & 2 \\
1\overline{)2} & 2\overline{)4} & 3\overline{)6} & 4\overline{)8} & 5\overline{)10} & 6\overline{)12} & 7\overline{)14} & 8\overline{)16} & 9\overline{)18} \\
3 & 3 & 3 & 3 & 3 & 3 & 3 & 3 & 3 \\
1\overline{)3} & 2\overline{)6} & 3\overline{)9} & 4\overline{)12} & 5\overline{)15} & 6\overline{)18} & 7\overline{)21} & 8\overline{)24} & 9\overline{)27}
\end{array}
$$

If continued, there would be 10 rows of 9 facts each. The last fact would be $9\overline{)81}$, with quotient 9. Note that at the beginning of each row, the divisor is 1. Children can be directed to discover that since $1 \times 2 = 2$, then $2 \div 1 = 2$ or $1 \times 15 = 15$, then $15 \div 1 = 15$. Also, they should discover that $2 \div 2 = 1$ and $15 \div 15 = 1$.

While division facts may be developed along with the multiplication facts, the authors recommend a systematic attack using ample concrete materials and story problems to help children master the division facts. The two ways of thinking about division (measurement and partition) should be stressed. For example, working with 2 as the divisor the teacher could use 10 blocks to show the measurement concept of division. If Joe has a set of 10 blocks, how many sets of 2 can he make? Through demonstration, he shows 5 sets with 2 blocks in each set.

Children could continue the work by showing how many sets of 2 blocks in 12 blocks, in 14, in 16, and 18. This could be followed by short story problems such as:

8 balls, 2 to a box

How many boxes?

$$2\overline{)8} \quad \text{quotient } 4$$

Then exercises leading to abstract work could include:

Write the quotient.

$$10 \div 2 = \square \quad \text{and} \quad 2\,\overline{)\,10}$$
$$12 \div 2 = \square \quad \text{and} \quad \overline{)}$$
$$14 \div 2 = \square \quad \text{and} \quad \overline{)}$$
$$16 \div 2 = \square \quad \text{and} \quad \overline{)}$$

The partition concept of division should be introduced with concrete objects. Bill's dad wanted him to put the pile of 10 bricks in 2 equal piles. How many bricks will be in each pile?

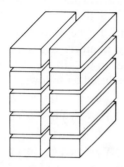

There will be 2 piles with 5 bricks in each pile.

This work could be followed by an exercise such as this. How many bricks in each pile?

3 piles: $12 \div 3 = \square$
4 piles: $12 \div 4 = \square$
6 piles: $12 \div 6 = \square$

In continuing division work with one-digit divisors and one-digit quotients, children must understand that division depends upon their ability to use multiplication. While repeated subtractions may have been used for introductory work, now we want children to search for the "missing factor." For example, have pupils think the multiplication fact and write the quotient:

$$4\,\overline{)\,4} \qquad 4\,\overline{)\,12} \qquad 4\,\overline{)\,20} \qquad 4\,\overline{)\,16}$$

	2	4	?	?	?	?	?	?
4	$\overline{)\,8}$	$\overline{)\,16}$	$\overline{)\,24}$	$\overline{)\,20}$	$\overline{)\,36}$	$\overline{)\,12}$	$\overline{)\,28}$	$\overline{)\,32}$

Complete the table by thinking "what must I multiply 4 by to get the quotient?"

5.3 Division with Remainders

Children are familiar with dividing candy among several friends. For example: Jane has 13 pieces of candy and wishes to divide the candy equally with 2 friends (counting Jane there will be 3 to receive candy).

13 pieces in all ⟨/ / / / / / / / / / / / /⟩   4

3 sets of 4 ⟨/ / / /⟩ ⟨/ / / /⟩ ⟨/ / / /⟩ /   3 ⟩ 13

3 fours in 13 and 1 left   12

13 divided by 3 equals 4 and 1 remaining   1

This example introduces the problem of what should be done with the remainder. Children make the decision (relating to candy) in numerous ways: Jane keeps the extra piece; they match for the extra piece; they break the one piece into 3 small pieces. *Thus the problem or situation determines the way the remainder will be used or shown.*

Study these uses of a remainder in division:

Discard the Remainder.   Mary has one piece of cloth 34 inches long and 2 inches wide. How many 8″ pieces can she cut from the cloth?

$$4 \text{ pieces}$$
$$8 \,\overline{\smash{)}\, 34}$$
$$\underline{32}$$
$$2 \text{ remainder of } 2''$$

She will probably throw the 2″ piece away.

Round the Quotient Upward.   Mrs. Smith has invited 23 people for dinner. How many tables, four to a table, will she need?

$$5 \text{ tables}$$
$$4 \,\overline{\smash{)}\, 23}$$
$$\underline{20}$$
$$3 \text{ remainder of three people}$$

Obviously, Mrs. Smith will need another table. So the quotient must be rounded upward to 6 instead of 5 tables.

Express the Remainder as a Fraction.   In the game of horseshoes, 4 horseshoes are needed. How many sets of 4 would there be in 26 shoes?

$$6 \text{ sets}$$
$$4 \,\overline{\smash{)}\, 26}$$
$$\underline{24}$$
$$2 \text{ remainder of two horseshoes}$$

There would be 6 sets of 4 shoes and 2 remaining. This could be expressed as 6 and $\frac{2}{4}$ or 6 and $\frac{1}{2}$ sets. Two more horseshoes would be needed to make another set of 4.

Thus there are four ways to express a remainder in division:

1. Make a decision to use the remainder (piece of candy shared).
2. Throw away or not use the remainder (piece of cloth).
3. Round the quotient upward and make another group or division.
4. Show the remainder as a fraction.

Unfortunately, some teachers have required children to record all remainders as fractions, and in some cases considered the answer incorrect if the fraction is not reduced to lowest terms. Obviously, then, *the problem being solved should determine how the remainder is to be expressed.* In drill exercises, the authors recommend leaving the remainder after the last division step or using the letter R if the remainder is shown with the quotient.

$$
\begin{array}{r}
62 \\
5\ )\overline{\ 313\ } \\
30 \\ \hline
13 \\
10 \\ \hline
3
\end{array}
\qquad \text{or} \qquad
\begin{array}{r}
62 \quad \text{R3} \\
5\ )\overline{}
\end{array}
$$

5.4 Extending Division

Prior to working with two-digit numbers in the divisor and dividend, children will have had experiences such as these:

$$
\begin{array}{r}
34 \\
-\ 20 \\ \hline
14
\end{array}
\qquad
\begin{array}{r}
60 \\
-\ 40 \\ \hline
20
\end{array}
\qquad
\begin{array}{r}
45 \\
-\ 30 \\ \hline
15
\end{array}
$$

$$
\begin{array}{r}
30 \\
\times\ 2 \\ \hline
60
\end{array}
\qquad
\begin{array}{r}
40 \\
\times\ 2 \\ \hline
80
\end{array}
\qquad
\begin{array}{r}
50 \\
\times\ 3 \\ \hline
150
\end{array}
$$

Then with the use of concrete materials and place-value holders, the division process including work with two-digit numbers can be meaningfully presented.

First use examples related to previous work in multiplication—$3 \times 10 = 30$, then $30 \div 10 = \square$. $(10¢)\ (10¢)\ (10¢) \div 10 = 3$. There are 3 tens in 30. Then $30 \div 3 = \square$ (if $3 \times 10 = 30$, then $\square \times 3 = 30$). Show the standard division form.

$$
\begin{array}{r}
10 \\
3\ )\overline{\ 30\ } \\
30 \\ \hline
0
\end{array}
\qquad \text{and} \qquad
\begin{array}{r}
3 \\
10\ )\overline{\ 30\ } \\
30 \\ \hline
0
\end{array}
$$

$$
\begin{array}{r}
3 \\
10\ )\overline{\ 30\ } \\
30 \\ \hline
0
\end{array}
$$

Helping children understand the place values represented by quotient numbers is very important. Stress place value for each new extension of the division process. For example: the 3 is placed over the 0 in the quotient because there are *three* groups of 10 in 30 (units). Then the 1 is placed over the tens' place and 0 shows no ones. There are 10 groups of 3 in 30.

$$
\begin{array}{r}
10 \\
3\ )\overline{\ 30\ } \\
30 \\ \hline
0
\end{array}
$$

This type of example can be used to test pupils' understanding of place value:

$$
\begin{array}{r}
2 \\
14\ )\overline{\ 297\ } \\
28 \\ \hline
1
\end{array}
$$

Ask pupils to tell why the 2 is placed over the 9. What does the 2 mean? After the first division, there is 1 left over. What is the value of the 1? What is the next step? (Bring down the 7.) What does the 17 show?

Using expanded notation, children can discover how to divide and then add the quotient numbers. In the example $36 \div 3$, this process is used: $36 \div 3 = (30 + 6) \div 3$ or $3 \overline{\smash{)}\,30 + 6}$. This work encourages children to look for a common factor. They must think of renaming 36 as the sum of two addends which have a common factor.

$$(30 \div 3) \qquad + \qquad (6 \div 3)$$

$$= \quad 3 \overline{\smash{)}\begin{array}{l} 10 + 2 \\ 30 + 6 \\ \underline{30 + 6} \\ 0 \quad 0 \end{array}} \begin{array}{l} = \ 12 \end{array} \qquad = \quad 3 \overline{\smash{)}\,36}^{\,12}$$

There are (by measurement) 12 groups of 3 in 36.

Next, leading to the abstract work, children should be shown the long form of the division algorithm:

$$\begin{array}{r} 2 \\ 10 \\ 3 \overline{\smash{)}\ 36} \\ -30 \\ \hline 6 \\ 6 \\ \hline \end{array}$$

Finally, the short cuts are discovered:

$$\begin{array}{r} 2 \\ 10 \longrightarrow \\ 3 \overline{\smash{)}\ 36} \\ -30 \\ \hline 6 \\ -6 \\ \hline 0 \end{array} \qquad \begin{array}{r} 12 \longrightarrow \\ 3 \overline{\smash{)}\ 36} \\ -30 \\ \hline 6 \\ -6 \\ \hline 0 \end{array} \qquad \begin{array}{r} 12 \\ 3 \overline{\smash{)}\ 36} \\ -3 \\ \hline 6 \\ -6 \\ \hline 0 \end{array}$$

Using groups of ten and building upon the concept of base ten, division work can be extended to include three-digit numbers in the dividend. For example:

$$\begin{array}{lll} 6 \times 4 = 24 & \text{then} & 24 \div 4 = 6 \\ 60 \times 4 = 240 & \text{then} & 240 \div 4 = 60 \\ 4 \times 6 = 24 & \text{then} & 24 \div 6 = 4 \\ 4 \times 60 = 240 & \text{then} & 240 \div 60 = 4 \end{array}$$

The computation would include:

$$
\begin{array}{r}
6 \\
4\,\overline{)\ 24} \\
-\,24 \\
\hline
0
\end{array}
\quad\text{and}\quad
2\,\overline{)\,240} = 4\,\overline{)
\begin{array}{c}
50 + 10 \\
200 + 40 \\
-\,20 \ -\,40 \\
\hline
00 \quad\ 0 \\
-\,00
\end{array}}
= 4\,\overline{)
\begin{array}{c}
60 \\
240 \\
24 \\
\hline
00 \\
-\,00
\end{array}}
$$

The child should be able to reason: since $24 \div 4 = 6$, then $240 \div 4$ will be 60 because 240 is 10 times larger than 24.

5.5 Estimating Quotient Numbers

Division with two-digit divisors can be introduced next. One way to begin is with easy divisors such as: How many bundles of 10 tickets each can be made of 40 tickets? The child is encouraged to think, "how many 10's are in 40?" $10 \times \square = 40$. If he cannot do this example, back up to "how many 10's are in 20?" Gradually increase the size of the divisor: 30, 32, 42, 53. Use dividends where no trial and error is necessary in the first step. For example, $32\,\overline{)\,864}$. Either say, "How many 30's are there in 80?" or "How many 3's are in 8?"

Next, present an example such as:

$$
\begin{array}{r}
19 \\
32\,\overline{)\,625} \\
32 \\
\hline
305 \\
288 \\
\hline
17
\end{array}
$$

where the first division seems to indicate 2, but the trial of 2 and comparison of 64 and 62 shows that 2 is too large and must be revised to 1. Emphasize the fact that mature workers in mathematics have to make adjustments in estimating choices for partial quotients. Because of this fact pupils should estimate a trial quotient number, multiply, and then compare to see if a good choice has been made.

Three methods are used to estimate quotient figures when dividing with divisors of two or more digits: (1) the first digit method, (2) increase-by-one method, and (3) subtracting partial quotient estimates.

FIRST DIGIT METHOD

The first digit method requires the pupil to estimate the first quotient figure (in $31\,\overline{)\,96}$) by thinking "how many three's in nine." The first digit of the divisor is used for estimating.

INCREASE-BY-ONE METHOD

Applying the increase-by-one method, the pupil uses a rule: if the ones' digit is less than 5, use the tens' digit as a trial divisor the same way as in the apparent method. If the ones' digit is more than 5, use the next higher *tens'* digit as a trial divisor. For the divisors: 60, 61, 62, 63, 64 use 6 as a trial divisor. For example, $62\overline{\smash{\big)}\,3256}$: try $32 \div 6 = 5$ as the first digit for the quotient; $68\overline{\smash{\big)}\,3256}$: try $32 \div 7 = 4$ as the first digit of the quotient; or $36\overline{\smash{\big)}\,1475}$: try $14 \div 4 = 3$ as the first digit of the quotient. In this last example *the rule fails*. The first digit must be 4.

Studies show that the main value of the increase-by-one method is that it produces true quotient figures more often than the apparent method does. For two-place division, excluding multiples of 10, the apparent method gives true quotient figures in about 64 per cent of the cases, while the increase-by-one method gives the true quotient in about 78 per cent of the estimates.

The three disadvantages of the increase-by-one method are: (1) two methods of estimation must be used; (2) corrections for mistakes in estimates are difficult to see; and (3) corrections when needed may be one above or one below the estimated quotient number.

SUBTRACTION METHOD

This method encourages the child to make efficient choices for partial quotients in division by using a factor (usually 10 or multiples of 10) which seems best for him. For example:

$$
\begin{array}{rl}
13\,\overline{\smash{\big)}\,182} & \text{multiply 13 by 10}\\[2pt]
10 & \\[2pt]
-\,130 & 10 \times 13 = 130\\[-2pt]
\overline{52} & \text{multiply 13 by 4}\\[2pt]
4 & \\[2pt]
-\,52 & 4 \times 13 = 52\\[-2pt]
\overline{14} & \text{add partial products}\\[2pt]
14 \times 13 = 182 &
\end{array}
$$

or

$$
\begin{array}{rl}
50\,\overline{\smash{\big)}\,4500} & \text{multiply 50 by 50}\\[2pt]
50 & \\[2pt]
-\,2500 & 50 \times 50 = 2500\\[-2pt]
\overline{2000} & \text{then multiply by less than 50 (say, 30)}\\[2pt]
30 & \\[2pt]
-\,1500 & 30 \times 50 = 1{,}500\\[-2pt]
\overline{500} & \\[2pt]
10 & \text{now multiply by 10}\\[2pt]
-\,500 & 10 \times 50 = 500\\[-2pt]
\overline{090} & \\[2pt]
90 \times 50 = 4500 &
\end{array}
$$

The authors consider this procedure useful as introductory work in division to help children understand the process and to encourage them to search for a more efficient method.

Children should use the first digit method for estimating quotients as soon as they understand division with two-digit divisors and are mature enough for advanced work in division.

5.6 Short Division

When pupils thoroughly understand long division, they should be taught short division. This is so because short division is difficult. Pupils must understand place value, be able to regroup, and be able to work problems by thinking the computations rather than thinking and the writing each step. For example:

$$\begin{array}{r} 1\ 6\ 8\ 8 \\ 3\ \overline{)\ 5\,^2 0\,^2 6\,^2 4} \end{array}$$

involves regrouping to divide so that 2 thousands are taken from 5 thousand to make 20 hundred; 2 hundreds are taken from 20 hundred to make 26 tens; 2 tens are taken from 26 tens to make 24 ones.

Teaching short division follows the same general procedures used with long division using one-digit divisors. Teach the easy forms first. For example:

$$\begin{array}{ccc} 2 & 12 & 122 \\ 3\,\overline{)\,6} & 3\,\overline{)\,36} & 3\,\overline{)\,366} \end{array}$$

Help children identify the place value of each quotient figure by rationalizing the work. In the example $6 \div 3$, units are being divided into units. Then in $36 \div 3$, tens and units are being divided by 3. In the problem $366 \div 3$, the pupil must understand that the quotient means 1 hundred, 2 tens, and 2 ones, or $100 + 20 + 2$. There are 122 groups of 3 contained in 366.

The preceding work should then be followed by examples involving regrouping, such as:

$$\begin{array}{ccc} 1\ 7 & 7\ 8 & 2\ 4\ 9 \\ 2\,\overline{)\,3\,^1 4} & 2\,\overline{)\,1\ 5\,^1 6} & 3\,\overline{)\,7\,^1 4\,^2 7} \end{array}$$

and later by examples having remainders, such as:

$$\begin{array}{ccc} 11 & 204 & 1170 \\ 4\,\overline{)\,47} & 3\,\overline{)\,614} & 7\,\overline{)\,8192} \\ \text{R3} & \text{R2} & \text{R2} \end{array}$$

To check the work, use the usual procedure: factor $\times$ quotient = factor or divisor $\times$ quotient = dividend.

$$\begin{array}{r} 17 \\ 2\ \overline{)\ 34} \end{array} \qquad 17 \times 2 = 34$$

and

$$\begin{array}{r} 11 \\ 4\ \overline{)\ 47} \\ \text{R3} \end{array} \qquad \begin{array}{l} 11 \times 4 = 44 \\ 44 + 3 = 47 \end{array}$$

5.7   Rules of Divisibility

Certain rules of divisibility are useful to the elementary teacher:

1. A number is divisible by 2 if and only if it ends in 0, 2, 4, 6, 8.
   Examples. The following numbers are divisible by 2:
   $$34; 168; 5526; 99{,}992; 340$$
   The following numbers are not divisible by 2:
   $$13; 467; 3289; 46{,}425; 111$$
   Discussion. Any number of two or more digits can expressed as number of tens + its last digit. Thus,
   $$9824 = 982 + 4$$
   Since any number of tens is divisible by 2, it follows that the entire number is divisible by 2 if and only if its last digit is divisible by 2, or if it ends in 0.
2. A number is divisible by 4 if and only if its last two digits form a number that is divisible by 4, or if it ends in two zeros.
   Examples. The following numbers are divisible by 4:
   $$384; 2916; 13{,}764; 1700$$
   The following numbers are not divisible by 4:
   $$379; 2457; 83; 101; 1234; 2258$$
   Discussion. Any number of three or more digits can be expressed as a number of hundreds + its last two digits. Since any number of hundreds is divisible by 4, it follows that the entire number is divisible by 4 if and only if the last two digits form a number that is divisible by 4, or if it ends in two zeros. Thus,
   $$89{,}248 = 892 \text{ hundreds} + 48 = 89{,}200 + 48$$
3. A number is divisible by 8 if and only if its last three digits form a number that is divisible by 8, or if it ends in three zeros.
   Examples. These numbers are divisible by 8:
   $$4{,}864; 2{,}009{,}488; 35{,}000$$
   These numbers are not divisible by 8:
   $$6{,}109; 23{,}017; 415{,}183; 1258; 3462$$

Discussion. Any number of four of more digits can be expressed as number of thousands + its last three digits. Since any number of thousands is divisible by 8, it follows that the entire number is divisible by 8 if and only if the last three digits form a number that is divisible by 8, or if it ends in three zeros. Thus,

$$17,168 = 17 \text{ thousands} + 168 = 17,000 + 168$$

4. A number is divisible by 5 if and only if it ends in 0 or 5.

Examples. These numbers are divisible by 5:

$$75; \ 13,965; \ 7820$$

These numbers are not divisible by 5:

$$23; \ 467; \ 8,917, \ 102$$

Discussion. Any number of two or more digits can be expressed as a number of tens + the last digit. Thus,

$$845 = 84 \text{ tens} + 5 = 840 + 5$$

Since any number of tens is divisible by 5, then the entire number is divisible by 5 if and only if it ends in 5 or 0.

5. A number is divisible by 9 if and only if the sum of its digits is divisible by 9.

Examples. These numbers are divisible by 9:

$$32,472; \ 639; \ 5148$$

These numbers are not divisible by 9:

$$32; \ 634; \ 245,372$$

Discussion. Consider a special case, the number 3528.

$$3528 = 3000 + 500 + 20 + 8$$
$$= 3(1000) + 5(100) + 2(10) + 8$$
$$= 3(999 + 1) + 5(99 + 1) + 2(9 + 1) + 8$$
$$= 3(999) + 3 + 5(99) + 5 + 2(9) + 2 + 8$$

Now 999 is divisible by 9, so 3(999) is divisible by 9; 99 is divisible by 9, so 5(99) is divisible by 9; 9 is divisible by 9, so 2(9) is divisible. Therefore:

$$3(999) + 5(99) + 2(9)$$

is divisible by 9. The remainder of the number is $3 + 5 + 2 + 8$, which is the sum of the digits of the original number. The entire number is, therefore, divisible by 9 if and only if the sum of its digits is divisible 9.

6. A number is divisible by 3 if and only if the sum of its digits is divisible by 3.

Examples. These numbers are divisible by 3:

$$453; \ 2,121,633; \ 1011$$

These numbers are not divisble by 3:

$$217; \ 13,402; \ 2000$$

Discussion. The discussion follows the same lines as the discussion for 9. At the end:

$$3(999) + 5(99) + 2(9)$$
is divisible by 3, so the entire number is divisible by 3 if $3 + 5 + 2 + 8$ (the sum of the digits) is divisible by 3.

7. A number is divisible by 6 if it is divisible by both 2 and 3.

   Examples. These numbers are divisible by 6:
$$36; 126; 612; 2142$$
   Discussion. The rule follows immediately from the fact that $2 \times 3 = 6$.

8. There is a rule for divisibility by 7, but it is not very practical. An example shows how it works.

   Example. To test 2492 for divisibility by 7, first strike out the last digit. The remaining digits are 249. Double the digit struck out, and subtract the result from 249. Here:
$$2 \times 2 = 4 \quad \text{and} \quad 249 - 4 = 245$$
   If this is divisible by 7, then the original number is divisible by 7. Here 245 is divisible by 7, so the original number is divisible by 7.

These rules for divisibility can be very useful. If a teacher wants to devise some division examples with a divisor of 4, and wants them to be exactly divisible, with no remainder, then she can use the rule for 4. Thus:
$$4\,\overline{)\,3{,}259{,}348}$$
will be exact, with no remainder, since the last two digits form the number 48, which is divisible by 4. Or, if the teacher desires an example with a remainder of 1, she can change the last digit in this example to 9:
$$4\,\overline{)\,3{,}259{,}349}$$
Since $49 = 48 + 1$, this example will have a remainder of 1.

Also, these rules are useful in finding least common multiples and least common denominators, which will be shown later.

5.8   Chapter Summary

Several interpretations of division have been presented: division as the inverse of multiplication; division as a process of measurement; division as partition; and division as successive subtraction. Each of these interpretations extends pupils' understanding of the division process and adds to their repertoire of skills needed to solve a variety of practical problems.

The introduction of the division processes should be accomplished by using the measurement concept which relates to familiar work with sets in addition and multiplication. Pupils seek to discover "how many sets" of the divisor are contained in the dividend.

The extension of the division algorithm is made possible by the use of concrete materials, a variety of manipulative materials, and the use of place-value holders. Each new step should be introduced with the use of practical word problems related to children's experiences in and out of school.

When children thoroughly understand the division process, they are ready for experimenting with short division, for estimating quotients with new methods, and for relating the distributive principle to division.

QUESTIONS AND EXERCISES

1. Study this example $4\overline{)4536}$. Then answer the following questions:
   (a) What is the place value of each digit in the dividend?
   (b) Where will the first quotient figure be placed? What is its value?
   (c) How many places will the quotient have?
   (d) Why do we divide from left to right?
   (e) After the second step in the division, there will be a number left after subtracting. What is the value of this number?
2. Write a word problem for each of the division concepts (measurement, partition, and so forth) discussed in the chapter.
3. Arrange these examples in order of difficulty.
   (a) $22\overline{)132}$ (b) $23\overline{)74}$ (c) $22\overline{)66}$ (d) $34\overline{)142}$
4. Study the examples.

   (a)   31   (b)   2   (c)   41
       $?\overline{)124}$ $?\overline{)124}$ $?\overline{)124}$

   (d)   21   (e)   64   (f)   18
       $?\overline{)147}$ $?\overline{)144}$ $?\overline{)144}$

   With one factor given, estimate the missing factor. Then complete the division work to check your estimates.
5. Apply the distributive property for each example.
   (a) $2\overline{)72}$ (b) $12\overline{)84}$
6. How could these questions help children with multiplication or division work?
   (a) 48 is how many times greater than 8?
   (b) What number is 7 times greater than 6?
   (c) What number when increased 4 times equals 36?
   (d) What number when divided into 3 parts equals 9?
7. Find the numbers between 20 and 40 that have only two divisors, the odd number itself and 1. What are these numbers called?
8. Complete the example by showing the meaning of each partial quotient.

$$
\begin{array}{r}
13? \\
32\overline{)4384} \\
-\ 3200 = 32 \times 100 \\
\hline
1184 \\
\underline{} \\
=
\end{array}
$$

9. Complete the blanks in the table.

ordered pairs (a, b)	$a = (b \times q) + r$	"q" quotient	"r" remainder
1. (16, 6)	$16 = (6 \times 2) + 4$	2	4
2. (18, 7)			
3. (58, 12)			
4. (150, 25)			
5. (125, 22)			

10. Complete the family of facts for each set of factors and product. Example **(a)** is done.

    (a) $\{3, 7, 21\} = 3 \times 7 = 21 \qquad 21 \div 7 = 3$
                               $7 \times 3 = 21 \qquad 21 \div 3 = 7$
    (b) $\{9, 6, 54\}$
    (c) $\{7, 6, 42\}$
    (d) $\{3, 8, 24\}$
    (e) $\{7, 8, 56\}$

11. Study the examples. Then write the advantages of each example for helping children understand naming the quotient.

    (a)   **(b)**   135

```
                                      135
            5                     5 ) 679
           30                         500    5 × 100 = 500
          100                         179
        5 ) 679                       150    5 × 30 = 150
          500                          29
          179                          25    5 × 5 = 25
          150                           4  R
           29
           25                        5 × 135 = 675
            4  R                     675 + 4 = 679
```

12. Write a list of basic vocabulary necessary for understanding the division algorithm.

13. Identify the skills and understandings needed for working these examples:

    (a) $25 \overline{)\ 475}$ **(b)** $47 \overline{)\ 2768}$ **(c)** $59 \overline{)\ 2945}$ **(d)** $77 \overline{)\ 6086}$
    (e) $16 \overline{)\ 912}$ **(f)** $36 \overline{)\ 1476}$ **(g)** $56 \overline{)\ 50400}$ **(h)** $94 \overline{)\ 64760}$

14. List the advantages and difficulties involved when introducing division with a two-place divisor such as this: $20 \overline{)\ 400}$.

15. Study the examples used for naming the quotient in the example $56 \div 4$.

(a) $56 \div 4 = (40 + 16) \div 4$ **(b)** $4\overline{)56}$

$= (40 \div 4) + (16 \div 4)$ -40 10 $10 \times 4 = 40$

$= 10 + 4$ 16

$= 14$ -16 4 $4 \times 4 = 16$

0 14

$14 \times 4 = 56$

How could you use these examples to help pupils understand the division algorithm?

16. Illustrate these key mathematical ideas applied to division. Example **(a)** is complete.

   (a) Division is distributive over addition.

      $572 \div 4 = (400 \div 4) + (160 \div 4) + (12 \div 4)$

      $ = 100 + 40 + 3$

      $ = 143$

   (b) Multiplication is distributive over addition.

   (c) Multiplication and division are inverse operations and may be used to check each other.

17. Complete the divisions.

   (a) $6\overline{)68} = 6\overline{)60 + 8}$ **(b)** $9\overline{)108} = \overline{)}$

   (c) $6\overline{)65} = \overline{)}$ **(d)** $8\overline{)96} = \overline{)}$

SELECTED REFERENCES

Brownell, William A., "The Effects of Practicing a Complex Arithmetic Skill upon Proficiency in Its Constituent Skills," *Journal of Educational Psychology*, XLIV (February, 1953), 65–81.

Grossnickle, Foster E., Leo J. Brueckner, and John Reckzeh, *Discovering Meanings in Elementary School Mathematics*, 5th ed. New York: Holt, Rinehart & Winston, Inc., 1968, pp., 182–204.

Gunderson, Agnes G., "Thought-patterns of Young Children in Learning Multiplication and Division," *Elementary School Journal*, LV (April, 1953), 453–61.

Hartung, Maurice L., "Estimating the Quotient in Division," *The Arithmetic Teacher*, IV (April, 1957) 100–111.

Hill, Edwin H., "A Study of Preferences and Performance on Partition and Measurement Division Problems" (unpublished doctoral dissertation, State University of Iowa, Iowa City, 1952).

National Council of Teachers of Mathematics, *Topics in Mathematics*. Washington, D. C.: The Council, 1964, pp. 157–66.

Scott, Lloyd, "A Study of Teaching Division Through the Use of Two Algorithms," *School Science and Mathematics*, LXIII (1963), 739–52.

Spencer, Peter L., and Marguerite Brydegaard, *Building Mathematical Competence in the Elementary School*. New York: Holt, Rinehart & Winston, Inc., 1966, pp. 162–69.

Spitzer, Herbert F., "Measurement or Partition Division for Introducing Study of the Division Operation," *The Arithmetic Teacher*, XIV (May, 1967), 369–72.

Stephens, Lois, "An Adventure in Division," *The Arithmetic Teacher*, XV (May, 1968), 427–29.

Van Engen, Henry, and E. Glendadine Gibb, *General Mental Functions Associated With Division*, Educational Service Studies, No. 2. Cedar Falls: Iowa State Teachers College, 1956, p. 181.

Zweng, Marilyn J., "Division Problems and the Concept of Rate," *The Arithmetic Teacher*, VIII (December, 1964), 547–56.

6

Measurement

Measurement is a topic emphasized in the mathematics revolution now underway. Exciting scientific discoveries are being made in the exploration of space beyond the earth, in studying the oceans' depths, and in experimenting with minute particles of living tissue such as the meristem of a plant. Each of these discoveries necessitates the use of some aspect of measurement and perhaps a new form of mathematics. The electronic computers and systems needed in modern industry require new mathematics and intensive research work. Likewise, professional educators are becoming increasingly aware of the need for experimental programs and research work concerned with the learning of new mathematical concepts. The pioneering work done by Jean Piaget points out the importance of cognitive and developmental processes in mastering concepts of number and measurement.[1]

This chapter provides an overview of the main aspects of measurement needed by children and introduces some scientific applications of measurement which should be included in the improvement of the elementary school mathematics curriculum. The approximate nature of measurement is presented. No matter what unit is chosen to use in measuring some object, smaller and smaller units may be used to provide for greater accuracy.

[1] See the selected references at the end of the chapter, especially the work of Daiyo Sawada.

6.1   Standard Units of Measurement

Measurement in mathematics describes a *way of measuring* and indicates *the result of this process.* In the measurement of a play area, one may use a tape measure marked off into one-foot segments to measure and to record the length and width of the area. In this example measurement involves using a tape measure and recording the result as the number of feet for the length and width. We have described the *way to measure* and *the result of measuring.*

All measurement necessitates using some unit for comparison or for applying mathematical operations on measures. Our forefathers might have compared the height of a horse to the height of a man or measured the horse as so many "hands high." They may have used the outstretched hand (span) to estimate one-half foot, the length of one's shoe for one foot, and the distance from one's nose to the end of an extended arm for one yard. Experience with these nonstandard units motivated people to find better, more accurate ways to measure. So Englishmen established the units for linear measure as:

$$12 \text{ inches} = 1 \text{ foot}$$
$$3 \text{ feet} = 1 \text{ yard}$$
$$5\tfrac{1}{2} \text{ yards} = 1 \text{ rod}$$
$$320 \text{ rods} = 1 \text{ mile}$$

These units have been carefully defined and recorded in the United States Bureau of Standards. But European countries discovered that the English system was not accurate enough for them and the system was very difficult to use. They called upon scientists in Europe to prepare another system. The metric system was created with the following units:

$$10 \text{ millimeters} = 1 \text{ centimeter}$$
$$10 \text{ centimeters} = 1 \text{ decimeter}$$
$$10 \text{ decimeters} = 1 \text{ meter}$$
$$10 \text{ meters} = 1 \text{ decameter}$$
$$10 \text{ decameters} = 1 \text{ hectameter}$$
$$10 \text{ hectameters} = 1 \text{ kilometer}$$

The history of measurement involves a fascinating story of attempts to find accurate units for measurement and to standardize them. This process continues today as scientists and mathematicians strive to discover new units for measurement of speed, sound, light, heat, reaction of atoms, and numerous other aspects of scientific work. When successful, new mathematical systems are invented and the discipline continues its healthy growth.

One of the important contributions of the "new mathematics" is the introduction of nonstandard units in order to help children understand that units of measurement need to be standardized. After experimenting with a stick, a piece of string, or a block of wood to measure the length of a book or distance around a ball, pupils readily see the need for standardized units.

In this process pupils discover that the unit of measurement must be the same kind as the object being measured. The chart illustrates this important concept for measurement of length, area, and volume.

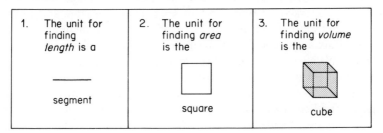

1. The unit for finding *length* is a ————— segment	2. The unit for finding *area* is the □ square	3. The unit for finding *volume* is the cube

Segments, squares, and cubes used for measuring are called *units*. Measurement is not a number. It does not belong to a set of numbers such as counting numbers. *Operations are made on measures.* To find the length of a segment as long as a segment 4 inches long and a segment 5 inches long when placed end to end, the operation 4 + 5 is made. The answer is recorded as 9 inches. The expression 4 inches + 5 inches is not meaningful or appropriate, since addition is an operation on numbers rather than on measurements.

A variety of units for measurement will be presented in this chapter. Particular attention will be given to the metric system. Unquestionably the United States should be using the metric system now. The longer we delay this important change from English measurement to the use of the metric system, the more expensive the process will be. Elementary school children should have a working knowledge of the metric system in order to be ready for the changeover and to introduce them to the system now being universally used in scientific measurement.

6.2 Measuring with Unit Segments

We begin this discussion of measuring with unit segments by presenting the concept of a *mathematical model of space*. This concept is basic to an understanding of the mathematics of measurement.

The mathematician describes space as being made up of definite, precise locations. Space, according to mathematicians, consists of a set of points, each designating one exact location. A point is *an idea* and has no dimensions or size. A point describes one location in space. So *mathematical space* is a creation of the mind which provides a model for *ordinary space* without having a physical existence. Think about the differences between ordinary space and a mathematical model as you read the chart showing ordinary space as compared to a mathematical model (see the next page).

The discussion of measuring with unit segments is a study of subsets of the set of points in space. The idea of space is a mathematical model set up

ORDINARY SPACE	MATHEMATICAL MODEL
1. ▰▰▰▶ Pencil	X •———————• Y Line segment ($\overline{XY}$)
2. Circular shape (ball)	(•) A set of points the same distance from a fixed point — the center
3. 🔦 Beam of light	•——————▶ Ray: part of a line with an endpoint and another point along the ray

to interpret (theoretically) the world of experience. So the theory of measurement, developed within the mathematical model, is applied to physical measurements.

Within the mathematical model of sets of points, the concept of *congruence* is the basis for the theory of measurement. Congruence means the same shape and size if placed one upon another. This concept is used to answer the question of how a number can be applied to a segment, when the segment is a set of points. Applying this to measurement of a line segment $\overline{CE}$, with the unit segment given as $\overline{AB}$:

$$\begin{array}{ccc} A & & B \\ \llcorner\!\!\rule{2cm}{0pt}\!\!\lrcorner & & \\ C & D & E \\ \llcorner\!\!\rule{2cm}{0pt}\!\!\rule{2cm}{0pt}\!\!\lrcorner \end{array}$$

we see that $\overline{CD}$ and $\overline{DE}$ are each congruent to segment $\overline{AB}$. If $\overline{AB}$, the arbitrary unit segment, has a measure of 1, then $\overline{CE}$ has a measure of 2. So the measure of line segment ($\overline{CE}$) is the number of times the unit segment ($\overline{AB}$) can be placed end to end along the segment ($\overline{CE}$) from one endpoint to the other.

Using the model just presented, we can now turn our attention to linear measurement.

6.3 Linear Measurement: Length

Linear measurements are made with two systems (1) English (inch, foot, yard, mile); and (2) metric (centimeter, decimeter, meter, kilometer). Several factors are important in making a choice of which system to use. For illustration, let us start with three objects to be measured, a fish, a glass tube, and a spark plug gap.

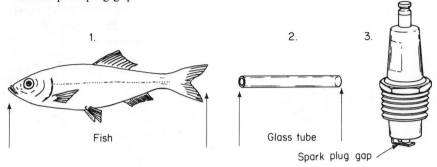

Before measuring these objects, one must decide upon the unit, the measuring instrument, and the accuracy expected. Study the two rulers and the metal gauge to decide upon the instrument and unit for measuring each object.

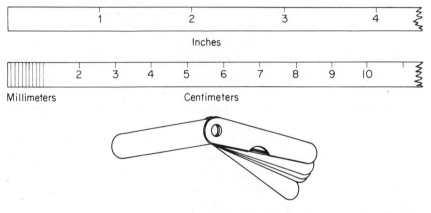

One could use either inches or centimeters to measure the length of a fish. In the United States, we would probably use inches as the unit of measure, and say "the fish is 7 or 8 inches long." Perhaps one might measure to the nearest one-half inch and say "$7\frac{1}{2}$ inches long."

The glass tube may be used in a chemistry class and inches might not be the appropriate unit for measurement. So we could use the centimeter as the unit of measure, and say "the tube is $3\frac{1}{2}$ centimeters long."

Spark plugs used in cars need to be cleaned regularly and the electrode gap checked and adjusted. This requires greater accuracy in measurement than we used with the fish or glass tube. The wire gauge has several thicknesses of metal which may be used. Since instructions in the maintenance book (Volvo) call for using a wire gauge with a diameter of 0.7–0.8 mm. (or 0.028–0.032″), we would have to use this type of gauge to see if the gap was too wide or too narrow.

Measuring the length of these objects illustrates some of the problems encountered when one has to use two systems. Obviously the metric system could be used to measure all three objects. The work would be easier because the ratio between consecutive linear units in the metric system is the same as the decimal ratio of consecutive places in our numeration system.

To teach the measurement of length in the elementary school, we recommend having pupils make measurements of lengths of objects using a foot ruler, yardstick, and tape measure. Children can discover how to measure the length of the teacher's desk, the length of the chalkboard, and the length of the classroom. When pupils record the measurement, they name the unit and tell the number of units. In making these measurements, pupils will discover that measurement is not exact. So they must learn to measure to the nearest inch and the nearest half inch. *Measurement is always approximate.*

When pupils begin work with fractions (usually 9 to 10 years of age), there will be the need for combining units such as $1\frac{1}{2}$ ft. and $1\frac{1}{2}$ ft. As the need arises, teach the relations between units:

If there are 12 inches in one foot, how many inches are there in 3 feet?

If there are 12 inches in one foot, how many feet are there in 60 inches?

This may be called converting feet to inches and inches to feet.

This introduction and use of the centimeter ruler and the meterstick should parallel the work just described. Comparisons should be made between English and metric systems. When one inch is broken into fourths and halves, the centimeter can be shown as 10 millimeters and 5 millimeters as one-half centimeter, $\frac{5}{10}$. Children should be encouraged to discover how to measure with the centimeter ruler and to appreciate the degree of accuracy achieved when measuring. The metric system is used in the Olympic games to determine distances for races and swimming events. The distances established for different events will provide interesting data for comparing English and metric systems of measurement.

6.4 Measuring Perimeter

Finding the perimeter of various geometric shapes should provide a variety of rich learning experiences for children. Examples of uses for perimeter should be identified as: fencing for the school grounds or a home near the school; plants or hedge to make a border for a garden or yard; border design for a page or cover for a book; molding used to frame a picture or to provide a door-stop in a doorway; and facing for the edge of a table top.

Have pupils measure the distance around a picture frame or the distance around the edges of a piece of paper. By direct measurement with a ruler, children discover that perimeter is equal to the sum of the measure of the four sides.

Next, have children review the meaning of a polygon—a closed curve made up of line segments. Then identify several kinds of polygons.

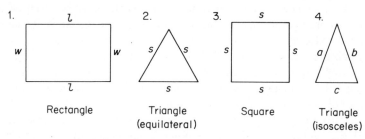

| Rectangle | Triangle (equilateral) | Square | Triangle (isosceles) |

From previous work, children should be able to state that the perimeter of a polygon is the sum of the measures of the sides of the figure. By using a ruler and a compass, the length of a side can be found by direct measurement. Use the compass to measure the length of one side of a polygon (for example, the rectangle illustrated in example 1) and then lay off a segment having the same measure on a ray. Continue this measurement for the other three sides.

Using a ruler to measure the segments on the ray, pupils find the sum of these measures to be 5 inches—the perimeter of the rectangle. For variety, the ruler can be used to measure the sides of the polygons. Using this procedure, children may discover that a compass will be more accurate for finding the measure of a segment than the ruler.

After finding the perimeter for the four examples, children should be ready to build the rule and formula for each polygon shown in the examples.

1. The perimeter of a rectangle is defined to be the sum of the four sides.
$$P = l + w + l + w$$
$$P = 2l + 2w$$
$$P = 2(l + w)$$
This is an application of the distributive property of multiplication over addition.

2. The perimeter of an equilateral triangle is defined to be the sum of the three sides (or is equal to three times the measure of one side).
$$P = s + s + s$$
$$P = 3s$$

3. The perimeter of a square is defined to be the sum of the four sides.
$$P = s + s + s + s$$
$$P = 4s$$

4. The perimeter of an isosceles triangle is defined to be the sum of the three sides (or equal to $2a + b$).
$$P = a + a + b$$
$$P = 2a + b$$

6.5   Measuring Area

The concept of congruence, which we applied to measurement of line segments, applies in the measurement of area. For example, consider measuring a region ABCD using region NLOM as a unit of measure and then region EFGH as the unit.

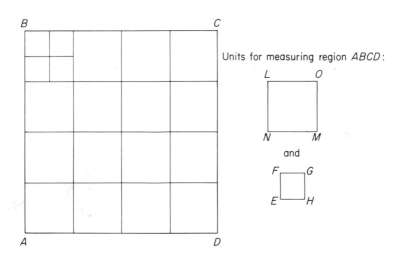

Using unit NLOM to measure region ABCD, one finds there are 16 of these units. When one uses unit EFGH to measure the same region, there are 64 units because there are 4 of the EFGH units in each NLOM unit (4 × 16 = 64). We may conclude that *square units* of area can be any size. The measure of a region such as ABCD involves using a square unit and finding the number of times the unit can be laid within the region covering only one square region at a time.

To help pupils grasp the concept of area as the number of square units for a region, examples such as the six shaded areas illustrated here could be used.

Find the area (the number of square units, ☐'s) for each shaded region.

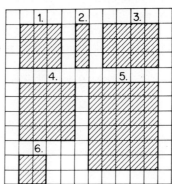

Estimating the area of regions expands the pupils' concept of area and introduces the use of real numbers (fractions). While considerable attention will be given to measurement in the chapter on fractions, four examples to show the importance of estimation are illustrated here.

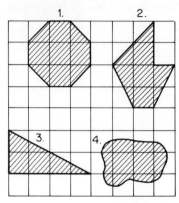

Find the area (the number of square units, 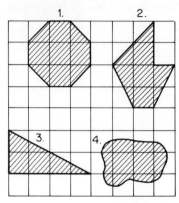 s) for each shaded region.

Using the irregular shaded shapes shown on the graph paper, pupils should discover that: every region has an area; not every region has the shape of a rectangle; the square unit may not fit the region exactly—one must estimate with the use of fractional parts of the square unit. In the example just used, for region (3) one estimates the area by counting each square unit, then count each part of a square unit in the region as $\frac{1}{2}$. Then $(1 + 1 = 2) + (\frac{1}{2} + \frac{1}{2} + \frac{1}{2} + \frac{1}{2} = 2) = 2 + 2 = 4$.

Square measure (area) is used in many ways, each requiring a specific square unit. For example, one buys floor covering by the square foot (tile or linoleum squares) or by the square yard (carpets and linoleum). Paint is sold by the gallon, and each gallon will cover a number of square feet (244 or 300 sq. feet). Remnants of carpeting or linoleum should be secured so that square units (1 sq. ft. and 1 sq. yard) may be cut and used in the classroom to measure the area of the floor or the area of the walls. Before abstract work is assigned for finding area of these large regions, an intermediate step should be taken. For example, use the type of exercise illustrated here.

Find the number of square units, ☐'s for each example. The size of each unit () is shown for each example.

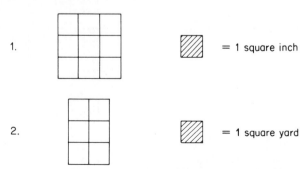

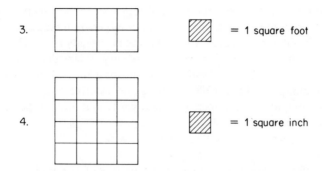

3.   = 1 square foot

4.   = 1 square inch

The area (for examples 1–4) can be found by counting the squares. Children can then discover that there are *n* rows with *n* squares in each row. Still later, the area of these rectangles can be expressed algebraically as: $A = lw$.

This formula should be read: the *number* of square units in the area of a rectangle is equal to the *number* of units in the length times the *number* of units in the width. The multiplication operation is completed with abstract numbers. In each example (1 through 4), pupils are required to think the unit of measurement (as they do in using a scale drawing) as square inches, square feet, and square yards. The unit ☐ is shown and named, similar to using $1'' = 1$ ft. in scale drawings or $\frac{3}{8}'' = 1$ ft.

Commonly used units in area are: square inch, square foot, square rod, acre, and square mile. Some of the relations between pairs of these units are:

144 square inches = 1 square foot
9 square feet   = 1 square yard
160 square rods = 1 acre

One way to teach 144 square inches = 1 square foot is to use a diagram such as the one shown here.

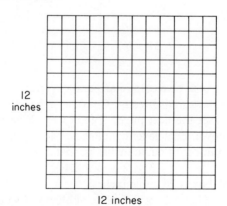

12
inches

12 inches

The diagram shows 12 rows with 12 square inches in each row. There are 144 square inches in one square foot.

A similar diagram or model could be used to show 9 square feet = 1 square yard.

Sites for homes may be expressed in feet (80′ × 150′) or by part of an acre. Suburban homesites may be one-half acre or larger. You may ask, "How large is an acre?" One might say, "About the size of five city lots." This would not give us enough accurate data because lots vary in size depending upon the land development. An acre is about the size of a football field (the lined or marked region). The field is 300 feet long and 145 feet wide. We will ask the reader to compute the number of square yards in a football field. Using the following relations:

$$160 \text{ sq. rods} = 1 \text{ acre}$$
$$5\tfrac{1}{2} \text{ yards} = 1 \text{ rod}$$

is a football field about the same size as an acre of ground?

6.6 Measuring Volume

To measure the volume of a geometric solid means to find how many times it contains a unit of volume measure.

Consider the cubic inch: A cubic inch is a cube that is one inch on each side. It is said to have a volume of one cubic inch.

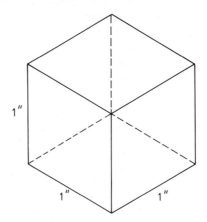

The volume of a box, or rectangular parallelepiped, as it is called in solid geometry, can be measured directly. Consider a box that is 2 inches by 3 inches by 4 inches (see the next page). The box can be separated into 3 horizontal layers, as shown. Each layer contains 2 × 4 = 8 cubic inches, by actual count. The total number of cubic inches is, therefore:

$$3 \times 2 \times 4 = 24$$

The volume of the box is 24 cubic inches.

A model of a box (4″ × 2″ × 3″) made of blocks of wood makes an excellent teaching device to introduce the idea of volume. The volume of the box can be obtained by actually counting the blocks. The idea of separating

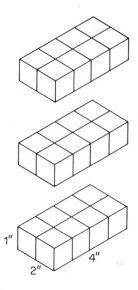

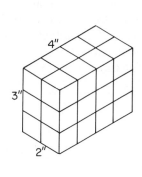

the interior regions of the box into layers leads to the discovery of a formula:

$$V = lwh$$

This formula can be read: The number of cubic inches in a box is equal to the number of inches in the length × the number of inches in the width × the number of inches in the height. Emphasis is placed on the word number. Later, the formula can be described as:

volume = length × width × height.

The commonly used units of volume measure are: cubic inch, cubic foot, and cubic yard. They are related as follows:

1728 cubic inches = 1 cubic foot
27 cubic feet   = 1 cubic yard

A working model of the relation 1728 cubic inches = 1 cubic foot is difficult to construct. A picture, however, conveys the idea.

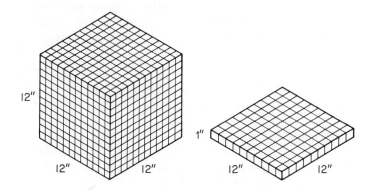

The idea of layers is useful. By actual count there are $12 \times 12 = 144$ cubic inches in the top layer, and there are 12 such layers, so there are $12 \times 12 \times 12 = 12 \times 144 = 1728$ cubic inches in one cubic foot. If a pupil forgets the number 1728, he should be able to reason its value by thinking in terms of this separation of the cubic foot into layers. Developing a visual understanding of the relationship 1728 cubic inches = 1 cubic foot is better than asking children to memorize an isolated, unrelated fact.

The relation 27 cubic feet = 1 cubic yard can be shown by a working model, but the model is rather large.

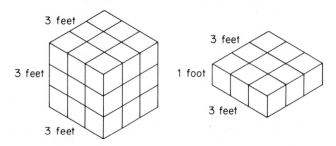

The top layer contains $3 \times 3 = 9$ cubic feet, and there are three such layers, so there are $3 \times 3 \times 3 = 27$ cubic feet in one cubic yard.

A good test of spatial visualization can be based on this diagram: if the entire *outside* surface of the cubic yard shown above were painted, how many of the cubic foot blocks would have

3 faces painted?

2 faces painted?

1 face painted?

0 face painted?

The sum of the answers should be 27.

6.7 Measuring Lumber

Many opportunities to measure lumber arise at home and at school. The unit of measure used is a board foot. A board one foot wide, one foot long, and one inch thick would be a board foot. This is expressed as one $1'' \times 12'' \times 12''$ or a foot of lumber.

Finished lumber used by children or adults has been run through a planer to smooth the surfaces. The finished piece of lumber will be much less than the measures used to describe the lumber or to compute the cost of the lumber. For example, a $1'' \times 4''$ piece of lumber is actually $\frac{3}{4}'' \times 3\frac{3}{4}''$. A $2'' \times 4''$ piece will measure $1\frac{5}{8}'' \times 3\frac{5}{8}''$ after planing.

The length of a board is usually expressed in feet, and the width and thickness in inches. Thus, one piece of wood one inch thick, four inches wide, and six feet long would be written $1'' \times 4'' \times 6'$.

To compute the board feet for a piece of lumber, divide the product of the number of feet in length, the number of inches in width, and the number of inches in thickness by 12. The board just described would have 2 board feet.

$$\frac{1 \times \overset{2}{\cancel{4}} \times \overset{1}{\cancel{6}}}{\underset{\underset{1}{\cancel{2}}}{\cancel{12}}} = 2 \text{ (board feet)}$$

Children first encounter problems involving thickness, width, and length of wood in construction work in primary grades. They should learn the correct terms to describe the type of board needed in their project. The concept of board feet used in figuring cost of lumber should be developed when children are learning how to work volume.

6.8   Denominate Numbers

In mathematics certain specific words and terms are used in connection with measurement. All numbers are *abstract*. If a name is attached to a number (2 apples, 4 oranges, or 5 cows), the result is called a *concrete* number. When the name attached to a number is a unit of measure (2 inches, 8 pounds, 6 minutes), the result is called a *denominate* number. Denominate is derived from the Latin word *denominare*, meaning "to call by name." Thus a denominate number is always a concrete number. A concrete number is not always a denominate number.

Named categories, such as denominate numbers, have many uses in mathematics. For example, we use place value in decimal notation, categories of size in common fraction notation, and measurement categories in denominate numbers. Note that the methods used in regrouping into categories of related values are similar for these numbers. In each category listed, there is a grouping of values into higher forms—tenths, hundredths, thousandths; fourths, eighths, sixteenths; or inches, feet, yards. Procedures used to regroup or change the scale value from a higher to a lower category are the same—like terms (within the same categories) may be added or subtracted. If we used the metric system of measurement, working with denominate numbers would be greatly simplified. This would be so because all measures are calibrated in the decimal scale. Metric measures of length are related to the meter. Metric measures of weight are related to the gram. Metric measures of capacity are related to the later. Thus it is easy to see the interrelationships between and among these measures. Real hardships are encountered in working with denominate numbers because the English measures we use are arbitrary and there are irregular relationships among the groupings and scales.

6.9 Tables Used with Denominate Numbers

The following tables illustrate some of the more common denominate numbers, and some of the relations among them.

Length

12 inches (in.) = 1 foot (ft.)
3 feet (ft.) = 1 yard (yd.)
$5\frac{1}{2}$ yards (yd.) = 1 rod
5280 ft. = 1 mile
1760 yards = 1 mile

Area

144 square inches (sq. in.) = 1 square foot (sq. ft.)
9 square feet (sq. ft.) = 1 square yard (sq. yd.)
30.25 square yards (sq. yd.) = 1 square rod (sq. rd.)
4840 square yards = 1 acre (A.)
160 square rods = 1 acre
640 acres = 1 square mile (sq. mi.)

Volume

1728 cubic inches (cu. in.) = 1 cubic foot (cu. ft.)
27 cubic feet (cu. ft.) = 1 cubic yard (cu. yd.)
231 cubic inches (cu. in.) = 1 gallon (gal.)

Avoirdupois Weight

16 drams (dr.) = 1 ounce (oz.)
16 ounces (oz.) = 1 pound (lb.)
2000 pounds (lb.) = 1 ton (T.)

Dry Measure

2 pints (pt.) = 1 quart (qt.)
8 quarts (qt.) = 1 peck (pk.)
4 pecks (pk.) = 1 bushel (bu.)

Liquid Measure

4 gills = 1 pint (pt.)
2 pints (pt.) = 1 quart (qt.)
4 quarts (qt.) = 1 gallon (gal.)

Time Measure

60 seconds (sec.) = 1 minute (min.)
60 minutes (min.) = 1 hour (hr.)
24 hours (hr.) = 1 day (da.)
7 days (da.) = 1 week (wk.)
365 days (da.) = 1 year (yr.)
360 days (da.) = 1 commercial year

52 weeks (wk.) = 1 year (yr.)
366 days (da.) = 1 leap year
10 years (yr.) = 1 decade
100 years (yr.) = 1 century

Paper
24 sheets = 1 quire
20 quires = 1 ream
480 sheets = 1 ream

Miscellaneous
6 feet = 1 fathom
1 nautical mile = 6080.27 feet
1 knot = 1 nautical mile per hour
1 hand = 4 inches
1 furlong = 220 yards
12 dozen = 1 gross

6.10   Computations with Denominate Numbers

Three factors cause pupils and adults difficulty in computing with denominate numbers: (1) learning and being able to recall the tables presented in the last section (6.9); (2) regrouping or changing a scale value from a higher to a lower category; and (3) failing to change terms correctly (regrouping or carrying a whole number instead of the scale value).

Probably the best way to help pupils understand their work with denominate numbers is to help them make actual measurements in the classroom. A variety of units of measure and models should be available for pupils to use: pint, quart, gallon, ruler, yardstick, scales for weighing, and models for work with area and volume.

A large number of regroupings of scale values take place in working with denominate numbers. A few of the basic computations will be illustrated by examples.

Example 1. Changing feet to inches in subtraction.

Whole numbers

$$24 = 10 + 14 \qquad \text{or} \qquad \overset{\overset{1}{\underset{}{\scriptstyle 1}}}{2}\,\cancel{4}$$
$$\begin{array}{r} -\ 6 \\ \hline \end{array} \qquad \begin{array}{r} -\ 6 \\ \hline 10 + 8 = 18 \end{array} \qquad \begin{array}{r} -\ 6 \\ \hline 1\ 8 \end{array}$$

Denominate numbers

2 feet 4 inches = 1 ft. + (12 + 4 in.) =   16 in.
  −6 inches   − 6
  ─────────────   ─────────────────────   ──────
                   1 ft. +   10 in. or 1′–10″

In example 1, work with whole numbers involves regrouping or borrowing one ten (to make $10 + 14 = 24$) and then subtracting 6 units. With denominate numbers one must always use the values or measurement units specified in the example. So 2 feet 4 inches must be regrouped to 1 foot 16 inches in order to subtract 6 inches.

Example 2. Change 60 inches to feet.

Solution. There are 12 inches in 1 foot, so:

$$\frac{60}{12} = 5 = \text{number of feet in 60 inches}$$

Example 3. Find the number of acres in a rectangular plot of ground that is 600 feet long and 400 feet wide.

Solution. $A = lw$

$A = 600 \times 400$

$A = 240,000$ number of square feet in the plot of ground

There are 9 sq. ft. in 1 sq. yd., so:

$$\frac{240,000}{9} = 26,666\tfrac{2}{3} \quad \text{number of square yards in the plot of ground.}$$

There are 4840 sq. yd. in 1 acre, so:

$$\frac{26,666.7}{4840} = 5.5 \quad \text{number of acres, correct to the nearest tenth of an acre.}$$

Alternate solution. There are 3 ft. in 1 yd., so the plot is $\dfrac{6000}{3} = 200$ yd.

long and $\dfrac{4000}{3} = 133\tfrac{1}{3}$ yd. wide.

There are 4840 sq. yd. in 1 acre, so:

$$\frac{200 \times 133\tfrac{1}{3}}{4840} = 5.5 \quad \text{number of acres, correct to the nearest tenth of an acre.}$$

Example 4. A rectangular tank is 8 ft. 9 in. long, 16 ft. 3 in. wide, and 25 ft. 2 in. deep. Find the number of gallons of water that it will hold.

Solution. 8 ft. 9 in. = 96 in. + 9 in. = 105 in.

16 ft. 3 in. = 192 in. + 3 in. = 195 in.

25 ft. 2 in. = 300 in. + 2 in. = 302 in.

The volume of the tank is:

$$105 \times 195 \times 302 = 6,183,450 \text{ cu. in.}$$

There are 231 cu. in. in 1 gallon, so:

$$\frac{6,183,450}{231} = 26,768 \text{ gal. correct to the nearest gallon.}$$

Example 5. Find the number of tons in 12,867 lb., correct to the nearest tenth of a ton.

Solution. There are 2000 lb. in 1 ton, so:

$$\frac{12,867}{2,000} = 6.4 \quad \text{number of tons, correct to the nearest tenth of a ton.}$$

Example 6. Find the number of seconds in 1 day.

Solution. There are 60 seconds in 1 minute, and there are 60 minutes in

1 hour, so there are $60 \times 60 = 3600$ seconds in 1 hour. There are 24 hours in 1 day, so there are:

$$24 \times 3600 \text{ secs.} = 86,400 \text{ secs. in 1 day}$$

Example 7. Find the number of pints in 6 gallons.

Solution. There are 2 pints in 1 quart, and there are 4 quarts in 1 gallon, so there are $2 \times 4 = 8$ pints in 1 gallon. In 6 gallons there are:

$$6 \times 8 \text{ pints} = 48 \text{ pints}$$

The addition and subtraction of denominate numbers may involve reduction, or regrouping.

Example 8. Add:

$$
\begin{array}{r}
5 \text{ ft. } 8 \text{ in.} \\
+ \, 2 \text{ ft. } 10 \text{ in.} \\
\hline
7 \text{ ft. } 18 \text{ in.} = 8 \text{ ft. } 6 \text{ in.}
\end{array}
$$

Example 9. Add:

$$
\begin{array}{r}
6 \text{ lb. } 9 \text{ oz.} \\
+ \, 2 \text{ lb. } 8 \text{ oz.} \\
\hline
8 \text{ lb. } 17 \text{ oz.} = 9 \text{ lb. } 1 \text{ oz.}
\end{array}
$$

Example 10. Add:

$$
\begin{array}{r}
5 \text{ gal. } 3 \text{ qt.} \\
2 \text{ gal. } 2 \text{ qt.} \\
+ \, 6 \text{ gal. } 3 \text{ qt.} \\
\hline
13 \text{ gal. } 8 \text{ qt.} = 15 \text{ gal.}
\end{array}
$$

Example 11. Subtract:

$$
\begin{array}{r}
5 \text{ yd. } 1 \text{ ft.} \\
- \, 2 \text{ yd. } 2 \text{ ft.} \\
\hline
\end{array}
\qquad
\begin{array}{r}
4 \text{ yd. } 4 \text{ ft.} \\
- \, 2 \text{ yd. } 2 \text{ ft.} \\
\hline
2 \text{ yd. } 2 \text{ ft.}
\end{array}
$$

Example 12. Subtract:

$$
\begin{array}{r}
9 \text{ lb. } 2 \text{ oz.} \\
- \, 3 \text{ lb. } 12 \text{ oz.} \\
\hline
\end{array}
\qquad
\begin{array}{r}
8 \text{ lb. } 18 \text{ oz.} \\
- \, 3 \text{ lb. } 12 \text{ oz.} \\
\hline
5 \text{ lb. } 6 \text{ oz.}
\end{array}
$$

Multiplying denominate numbers by abstract numbers may involve reduction, or regrouping:

Example 13. Multiply:

$$
\begin{array}{r}
30 \text{ min. } 20 \text{ sec.} \\
\times \, 5 \\
\hline
150 \text{ min. } 100 \text{ sec.} = 151 \text{ min. } 40 \text{ sec.}
\end{array}
$$

Example 14. Multiply:

$$
\begin{array}{r}
5 \text{ gal. } 3 \text{ qt.} \\
\times \, 8 \\
\hline
40 \text{ gal. } 24 \text{ qt.} = 46 \text{ gal.}
\end{array}
$$

Many lessons can be planned that use the units of measure in meaningful, interesting projects. Some of the difficulties in computation with denominate numbers stem from a lack of experience with the units of measure.

6.11   Metric System

The metric system was devised and adopted in France in 1791. The system is used in scientific work throughout the world. All major countries of the world now use the metric system in measurement except England and the United States. Recently England began activities leading to moving from the English system to the metric system. So our nation will be the last to give up the antiquated English system!

Elementary school children can be assisted in learning the metric system by stressing three basic words and three prefixes. The three words are: (1) meter (a unit of length), (2) liter ("lee-tar," a unit of volume), and (3) gram (a unit of weight). The prefixes used as common subdivisions of each unit are: (1) deci- $(\frac{1}{10})$ (2) centi- $(\frac{1}{100})$, and (3) milli- $(\frac{1}{1000})$. Prefixes for whole numbers include: (1) deka- (tens), (2) hecto- (hundreds), and (3) kilo- (thousands).

Units used in the metric system were intended to be based upon natural standards. The meter was to be $\frac{1}{10,000,000}$ of the distance from the earth's equator to either pole. The founders of the system made a slight mistake, so the meter only approximates the unit intended! In spite of this, the meter was standardized. The standard meter is the distance measured at 0°C, between two parallel lines marked on a platinum-iridium bar kept at the International Bureau of Weights and Measures at Sèvres, France. Copies are made from this standard. We have a standard meter bar in the Bureau of Standards, Washington, D.C.

The basic simplicity of the metric system lies in the conversion factors, which are powers of ten. For instance, 10 millimeters = 1 centimeter, 10 centimeters = 1 decimeter, and 10 decimeters = 1 meter. These simple relations among units make the system very easy to learn and use. The metric system is studied in elementary school arithmetic. Some of the relations are listed in the following tables.

Length
10 millimeters (mm.) = 1 centimeter (cm.)
10 centimeters (cm.) = 1 decimeter (dm.)
10 decimeters (dm.) = 1 meter (m.)
1000 meters (m.) = 1 kilometer (km.)

Weight
10 milligrams (mg.) = 1 centigram (cg.)
100 centigrams (cg.) = 1 gram (gm.)
1000 grams (gm.) = 1 kilogram (kg.)

Liquid Measure
1000 cubic centimeters (c.c.) = 1 liter (1.)

One of the problems that arises in connection with the metric system is the matter of converting from the English system to the metric system, and vice versa. Two useful conversion factors in length units are:

$$39.37 \text{ in.} = 1 \text{ meter}$$
$$2.54 \text{ cm.} = 1 \text{ in.}$$

Example 1. Which is longer, 100 meters or 100 yards? How much longer?

Solution. 100×39.37 in. $= 3937$ in., in 100 meters

100×36 in. $= 3600$ in., in 100 yards

Therefore, 100 meters are 3937 in. $-$ 3600 in. $=$ 337 in. longer than 100 yards. This difference can be reduced to 28 ft. 1 in. That is, the 100-meter dash as run in the Olympic games track meets is 28 ft. 1 in. longer than the 100 yard dash, as run in the American track meets.

Example 2. (a) How many centimeters are there in 1 foot? (b) How many inches are there in 50 centimeters?

Solution. (a) There are 2.54 cm. in 1 inch, and there are 12 in. in 1 ft., so there are:

$$12 \times 2.54 \text{ cm.} = 30.48 \text{ cm. in 1 foot}$$

(b) There are 2.54 cm. in 1 inch, so there are:

$$\frac{50}{2.54} = 19.685 \text{ in. in 50 cm.}$$

A number of meter sticks should be available for use in the classroom. Models of the sizes of the metric units as compared with English units should also be available.

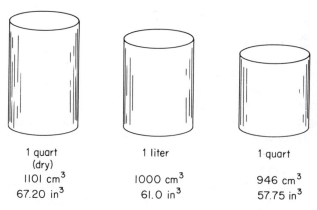

1 quart (dry)	1 liter	1 quart
1101 cm^3	1000 cm^3	946 cm^3
67.20 in^3	61.0 in^3	57.75 in^3

Note that in the United States dry measure, the quart is larger than the liter. The liquid quart, however, is slightly smaller.

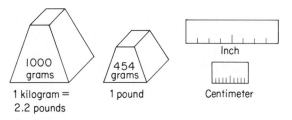

1 kilogram = 2.2 pounds   1 pound   Centimeter

A useful weight conversion factor is:

1 kg. = 2.2 lb. correct to the nearest tenth of a pound.

Example 3. A man weighs 70 kg. What is his weight in pounds?

Solution. There are 2.2 lb. in 1 kg., so there are:

70 × 2.2 = 154 lb. in 70 kg.

Example 4. A man weighs 180 lb. What is his weight in kg., correct to the nearest tenth of kg.?

Solution. There are 2.2 lb. in 1 kg., so there are: $\frac{180}{2.2} = 81.8$ kg. in 180 lb. correct to the nearest tenth of a kilogram.

In solving problems such as these, keep in mind the relative sizes of the units. Thus, 1 kg. is heavier than 1 lb. This may help decide the basic matter of whether to multiply or divide in changing from one system to the other.

A useful conversion factor for volume is:

1 liter = 1 quart approximately

This relation is of interest in purchasing gasoline, which is sold by the gallon in the United States and by the liter in most European countries.

Example 5. If gasoline (petrol in Europe) costs 15 cents a liter, what is the equivalent cost per gallon?

Solution. There are approximately 4 liters in 1 gallon, so:

4 × 15¢ = 60¢, cost per gallon.

Another useful conversion factor for length, in addition to those given previously, is:

1 kilometer = $\frac{5}{8}$ mile approximately.

6.12   Precision and Accuracy

As we have already stated in this chapter, measurement is never exact. This being so, we need to discuss ways to work with this condition and to develop the vocabulary needed for discussing the topic.

Finding or stating the closeness to a true measurement is called *precision.* The ordinary ruler used in the elementary school classroom has eights marked as the smallest subdivision of inches. The measurement of $1\frac{1}{8}''$ is precise to the nearest one-eighth inch. If the ruler were constructed to show sixteenths of an inch, then a measurement of $2\frac{3}{16}$ inches would be precise to the nearest $\frac{1}{16}$ inch. Some steel tape measures used in machine shops or in carpentry work marked off to 32 of an inch. *The smaller the unit of measure, the more precise is the measurement.*

The precision called for in a measurement may be stated in several ways: (1) writing out in the instructions that measurement is to be made to the nearest inch, half inch, or smaller unit; (2) showing by an underlined zero the precision desired (150̲0 miles to the nearest mile, 150̲00 miles to the nearest 100 miles); and (3) using decimal fractions (rounding off to hundredths or thousandths or to the nearest tenth of a measurement). These measurements are not exact, so the true measurement lies between any measurements made. For example, the true measurement for a line segment $3\frac{3}{8}$ inches long would be between $3\frac{5}{16}$ and $3\frac{7}{16}$ inches (one sixteenth of an inch either side of $3\frac{3}{8}''$). *The greatest possible error* between the measurement $3\frac{3}{8}''$ and the true measurement can only be $\frac{1}{16}$ inch. So we say that *the greatest possible error is one-half the unit used to measure.*

Accuracy of a measurement is determined by the *relative error*. The relative error is the ratio of the greatest possible error to the measurement.

$$R\ E = G\ P\ E: \text{measurement}$$

The smaller the relative error, the more accurate the measurement is.

In measurement, a *tolerance* may be called for. This is an allowance made to cover or to adjust for the error in measurement. The measurement of a steel rod of 6.3 inches with a tolerance of .05 inches in both directions is indicated as $6.3'' \pm .05''$. So the rod could represent measurement from 6.25 inches to 6.35 inches. In the manufacture of machinery or parts for machines, the workmen have definite tolerances stated for the production of each part. These tolerances are usually expressed with decimal fractions such as $\pm .005''$. Accuracy involving thousandths or ten-thousandths is not uncommon for precision work.

6.13 Chapter Summary

The topic of measurement has been expanded and emphasized in the new mathematics curriculum for elementary schools. There is new content to teach and many new applications of theories of measurement to learn. The search for new, accurate units of measurement and procedures for measuring continues as it has in the past, stimulating the healthy growth of mathematics.

QUESTIONS AND EXERCISES

1. In section 6.11 (metric system) reference is made to measurement under conditions expressed as 0°C. What does this mean?
2. The problem to be solved will usually determine the type of measurement used and the precision needed. Apply this principle to the following:
   (a) Ordering wire fence for an enclosure such as a play area
   (b) Estimating the length of a football field
   (c) Checking the odometer in a car
   (d) Cutting glass for a window
   (e) Measuring a room for purchasing a new carpet
   (f) Checking the thickness of sheet metal used in the production of airplanes

3. List the degree of accuracy for these measuring instruments:
   (a) Odometer   (b) Pedometer   (c) Tape measure
   (d) Surveyor's tape measure (e) Instrument for measuring cloth in a store
   (f) Meterstick
4. What are some practical uses for finding the perimeter of a rectangle?
5. Two corner posts are 100 feet apart. How many posts 10 feet apart can be placed between these two posts?
6. How many tiles 8 inches square will be needed to cover a hall 40 feet long and 4 feet wide?
7. A local newspaper carried an advertisement for rugs. The selling price was $8.85 per square yard. Padding to be placed under the rug was priced at $1.25 per square yard. The charge for laying the carpet was $1.25 per square yard. How much money would be needed to carpet a room 12′ × 20′?
8. A rectangular solid is 6 in. wide and 10 in. long and contains 480 cu. in. Find the height. Make a drawing showing the solution.
9. Find the cost of digging a basement 30 ft. long, 20 ft. wide, and 7 ft. deep, at $2.75 per cubic yard.
10. How may board feet are in a piece of lumber 2″ × 4″ × 12′?
11. How would you find the area of irregular-shaped floor surfaces such as an "L"-shaped hallway?
12. Space measurement includes linear, surface, solid, and angular. List examples of how these measures are used in the home or classroom.
13. Make five examples showing how to find area by counting squares. One example is complete.

   (a) The area of this figure is (▨) units.

14. A driveway is 10 feet wide, 4 inches thick, 100 feet long. How much concrete is in the driveway? At $10 per cu. yd., what would the cement cost?

SELECTED REFERENCES

Bendick, Jeanne, *How Much and How Many: The Study of Weights and Measures.* New York: McGraw-Hill Book Company, 1960.

Bourne, H. N., "The Concept of Area," *The Arithmetic Teacher*, XV (March, 1968), 233–43.

Bradley, Duane, *Time for You.* Philadelphia: L. B. Lippincott, 1960.

Brindze, Ruth, *The Story of Our Calendar.* New York: The Vanguard Press, 1949.

Churchill, Eileen M., *Counting and Measuring.* Toronto: University of Toronto Press, 1961.

Daiyo, Sawada, and Doyal Nelson, "Conservation of Length and the Teaching of Linear Measurement: A Methodological Critique," *The Arithmetic Teacher,* XIV (May, 1967), 345–48.

Dutton, Wilbur H., "Teaching Time Concepts to Culturally Disadvantaged Primary-age Children," *The Arithmetic Teacher,* XIV (May, 1967), 358–64.

McClintic, Joan, "The Kindergarten Child Measures Up," *The Arithmetic Teacher,* XV (January, 1968), 26–29.

Murray, F. B., "Conservation of Illusion-distorted Lengths and Areas by Primary School Children," *Journal of Educational* Psychology, LVI (1965), 62–66.

Parker, Helen C., "Teaching Measurement in a Meaningful Way." *The Arithmetic Teacher,* IV (April, 1960), 194–98.

Piaget, Jean, *The Child's Conception of Number.* London: Routledge & Kegan Paul, Ltd., 1952.

——, "Number and Measurement," *The Arithmetic Teacher,* X (November, 1963), 428–34.

Smart, James R., and J. L. Marks, "The Mathematics of Measurement," *The Arithmetic Teacher,* XIII (April, 1966), 283–87.

Smedslund, J., "Development of Concrete Transitivity of Length in Children," *Child Development,* XXXIV (1963), 389–405.

Swart, William L., "A Laboratory Plan for Teaching Measurement in Grades 1–8," *The Aritmetic Teacher,* XIV (December, 1967), 652–53.

7

Problem Solving

A major contribution of the continuing curriculum revolution in mathematics and science has been the emphasis placed upon new methods of learning, especially the use of problem solving and discovery techniques. However, while considerable progress has been made in learning theory pertaining to concept development and processes used in thinking, these theories have not been implemented in the elementary school classroom. Instructional materials, likewise, are inadequate in the way problem-solving exercises are presented.

This chapter introduces some of the major aspects of problem solving and suggests ways to direct pupil growth in problem-solving abilities. The topics included are: (1) types of problems; (2) children's thinking; (3) concept formation; and (4) strategies for solving problems.

7.1 Types of Problems

Considerable progress has been made in the development of a rationale for the selecting and stating of educational objectives.[1] Applications of this

[1]D. R. Krathwohl, B. S. Bloom, and B. B. Masia, *Taxonomy of Educational Objectives* (New York: David McKay Co., 1964), Appendix B, pp. 186–93.

140

rationale have been made in suggestions for lesson planning in several chapters in the first part of this book. The importance of this rationale is twofold: (1) the specifying of cognitive problems to be used (process), and (2) the mathematical topics (content) to be presented.

Study of *The Taxonomy of Educational Objectives* for the cognitive domain suggests the following types of learning abilities:

1. Knowledge, requiring recall of specific facts, trends and sequences, classifications, criteria, theories, and structures
2. Comprehension, requiring understanding, translation, interpretation, and extrapolation
3. Application, requiring the use of abstractions in particular and concrete situations
4. Analysis, requiring a breakdown of communication into its constituent elements such that the relative hierarchy of ideas is made clear or the relations between the ideas made explicit
5. Synthesis, requiring the putting together of elements so as to form a whole
6. Evaluation, requiring judgments about the value of material and methods for given purposes

This classification enables the curriculum developer and the teacher to select the level of cognition intended for a particular unit or lesson. Careful study of the classification should help you appreciate the difficulties involved in directing cognitive development from level one, recall situations, to increasingly higher levels involving analysis, synthesis, and evaluation. The implications for teaching problem solving are likewise important. To these aspects we now turn our attention.

The classification just identified provides a guide for *presenting* problems. The teacher, by selecting and stating an objective in the cognitive domain, specifies the content and thought process which will be used in an instructional period. According to Getzels, this procedure omits from our consideration the problems which an individual could discover. So a classification for including *presented* and *discovered* problems needs to be used. Getzels suggests this kind of classification based upon what is known and what is unknown in a problem situation. He identifies eight types of problems:

1. Problem is *given* (is known) and there is a standard method for solving it known to the problem-solver and to others. The solution is guaranteed in a finite number of steps.
2. Problem is *given* (is known) but no standard method for solution is known by problem-solver, although known to others.
3. Problem is *given* (is known) but no standard method for solving is known to the problem-solver or to others.

4. Problem *exists* but remains to be identified (become known) by the problem-solver, although known to others.
5. Problem *exists* but remains to be identified (become known) by the problem-solver and by the others.
6. Problem *exists* but remains to be identified (as in 4 and 5) and there is a standard for solving it (once the problem is discovered) known to the problem-solver and to the others.
7. Problem *exists* but remains to be identified or discovered and no standard for solution is known to the problem-solver, although known to the others.
8. Problem *exists* but remains to be identified or discovered and no standard method for solving it is known to the problem-solver or to the others.[2]

While other possibilities exist for listing types of problems, one should not escape the implications of this approach for discussing problem solving and for teaching. When problem solving is broken down into this type of pattern, one can readily see that at present neither textbooks nor teachers cover the important categories shown. Closer study of the list would also reveal that the full range of problems could not be easily presented in a textbook. A skillful teacher would be required to guide pupil growth in identifying problems, discovering possible solutions, and finding accurate answers. The list, as it is organized, suggests that there are various degrees of what is *known* and *unknown*. This being so, consideration should be given to the way children acquire the skills and abilities necessary for advancing from one level of problem solving to the next. Apparently, considerable study needs to be made to determine the level appropriate for the learner at any given stage of school work and to encourage innovation and creativeness in finding solutions to problems.

In planning lessons to enable pupils to make growth in problem solving, the teacher must select his objectives carefully. What level of cognition and what aspect of problem solving is to be taught? What kind of outcomes will be acceptable as evidence that the pupil has achieved the objectives established for the lesson?

This kind of planning, which involves the use of behavioral objectives, helps the teacher guide pupil growth in problem solving. Furthermore, there should be some continuity and sequencing of learning experiences dealing with problem solving.

The consideration of continuity in learning involves the discussion of children's thinking as an important aspect of learning to solve problems.

---

[2]J. W. Getzels, "Creative Thinking, Problem-Solving, and Instruction," *Theories of Learning and Instruction, Sixty-third Yearbook of the National Society for the Study of Education,* Part I (Chicago: The University of Chicago Press, 1964), p. 241.

7.2   Children's Thinking

Child psychologists and writers dealing with children's thinking[3] generally agree that the infant and young child first learn to perceive accurately and to judge in terms of immediate physical environment. However, evidence from research on the child's ability to reason about problems is not so definite or conclusive. The reasoning ability grows gradually, has some irregular advances in certain aspects, and probably grows rather continuously. In discussing these developmental aspects of children's thinking, we must turn to the work of Piaget, a student of the genesis of mental operations for over 40 years.[4]

Piaget provides us with an insight into the logical organization of different kinds of thinking. He presents data relating to different stages in the child's development of mental processes.

Piaget believes that thought processes may be analyzed in terms of groups or systems of operations. These groupings are relational systems with three defining properties: (1) *composition*—any two-unit operations can be combined to produce a new unit; (2) *reversibility*—any two units which are combined can be separated again; (3) *associativity*—the same result may be obtained by combining units in different ways. Each system is connected to actions which can be internalized, reversed, or coordinated into patterns of thought. The structures used by a child early in life are different from those constructed and used later. Maturity is shown in the way a pupil demonstrates the use of the three properties listed.

Three stages of mental structuring correspond to the thought processes just discussed: (1) sensori-motor group structures; (2) concrete-operation group structures; and (3) formal mental structures. Each will be described.[5]

Sensori-motor Structures.   During this first stage the child can only perform actions. At first there are no operations because the child cannot internalize activities. But gradually notions of objects are formed, and he learns to construct the idea of an object lying beyond the field of vision. Piaget used a watch to demonstrate this type of mental structure. A watch, with which he and a child had been playing, was hidden. At first the child lost interest if the watch was covered completely. Later the child learned to search for a hidden object. By the age of two the child had formed certain behavioral concepts of a permanent object. This development was made possible because of the organization of the child's perceptual experience and his increasingly effective coordination of bodily movements. The child at this stage coordinated sensory data and movement information into *sensori-motor group structures*. This

[3]See David H. Russell, *Children's Thinking* (New York: Ginn and Company, 1956).
[4]J. Piaget, *The Child's Conception of Number* (London: Routledge & Kegan Paul, 1952).
[5]For this section materials have been taken from Wilbur H. Dutton, *Evaluating Pupils' Understanding of Arithmetic* (Englewood Cliffs, N.J.: Prentice-Hall Inc., 1964), pp. 35–43.

represents, to Piaget, the beginnings of intelligence because: (1) the child acted in a certain way in response to a sensory impression—demonstrating *properties of composition*; (2) he looked for an object which he had seen hidden, going back the starting point of the activity—demonstrating *reversibility*; (3) he changed his movement response to a known object—demonstrating *associativity*.

Concrete-operation Group Structures. This represents Piaget's second stage. The stage is much longer than the sensori-motor group and has three phases: (1) "preoperational thought," (2) "intuitive thought," and (3) the "concept of conservation."

Preoperational thought is found from about two to four years of age. The child's actions are internalized and he uses imagery to imitate an action. The beginning of symbolic behavior is noted, and the child learns to use language. Piaget stresses the egocentric attitude which the child has during this period. The small child has difficulty distinguishing between inner experiences and external reality. Thinking has started because the child uses symbols to represent objects and experiences. Piaget believes, however, that this thinking is preoperational because the internalized actions are not reversible, and conservation is only understood at the sensori-motor level.

The next phase, according to Piaget, is *intuitive thought*. This develops in children between four and seven years of age. While concrete-operation group structures are slowly becoming organized, the child's thinking is still tied to perceptual factors. The child's structures are rigid and irreversible. Piaget demonstrated this stage with the use of a set of beads. First the child was asked to put out a set of beads corresponding to a model set. He was asked to say how many beads were in each set and agreed that the sets were the same. Then the arrangement of the model set was changed so that it occupied more space. The child was then asked whether the sets were still the same in number of beads. A child with irreversible mental structures will say that the set spread out is more than the other set because it is wider—the usual response of a five-year-old child. The child's judgment is based on immediate, intuitive perception rather than upon what has been done with the beads.

The *concept of conservation* is achieved when the child becomes capable of moving in reverse. The child sees that moving a number of beads to make a longer line or to occupy more space than an equal number of beads does not change the number or value of the beads. He understands the numerical value of the set. The child now has the concept of conservation of a sum.

Piaget believes that when a child has the concept of conservation of a sum, the concrete operation groupment structures are becoming organized. The chiid's actions are internalized, and this enables him to work with concrete operations, classification, and seriation. By age seven, Piaget believes that children can work with concepts of number as equivalent and orderable and with concepts of time and space. Inhelder,[6] however, has shown that a child must be ten or eleven years of age before he is capable of reversible reasoning in connection with weight and volume.

Formal Mental Structures. Earlier operations involved reasoning about things and events. Now, in formal mental structures, the pupil is capable of reasoning about these concrete operations themselves. This period is reached, according to Piaget, in early adolescence. The adolescent is able to form hypotheses, make assumptions, and draw conclusions.

In conclusion, Piaget shows that children's basic cognitive categories for interpreting physical reality (thinking, reasoning, understanding) are the product of slow, painstaking construction. The development of mental processes proceeds through a series of clearly defined stages, each having its own particular type of mental operation. While recent research shows that the general rate of progress through the stages may be accelerated or retarded (owing experience, culture, or other factors) the sequence of stages will be invariant.[7] Piaget's work suggests that the teacher must provide children with experiences which will enable them to operate constructively and gradually to become aware of the relationship between things defined in the language of mathematics. He directs our attention to individual differences in growth, development, and concept formation.

Considerable research has been done on concept development. Our attention will now be turned to a discussion of mathematical concepts.

7.3 Concept Formation

John Dewey has shown the importance of concepts by pointing out the fact that they enable one to generalize, that is, to extend and carry over our understanding from one thing to another. In his early work on thinking he stated: "Since concepts represent the whole class or set of things, they economize our intellectual efforts. The concept shows that a meaning has been clearly established and will remain the same in different contexts."[8]

A British research worker, Lovell, identifies the sequence in concept development as perception, abstraction, and generalization.[9] He believes a concept enables one to make generalizations about data which are related; it enables one to respond to, or think about, specific stimuli or percepts in a particular way. Hence a concept is exercised as an act of judgment.

[6] J. Piaget and B. Inhelder, *The Growth of Logical Thinking from Childhood to Adolescence* (New York: Basic Books, Inc., 1958).

[7] See P. C. Beard, "An Investigation of Concept Formation among Infant School Children," *British Public School Bulletin*, No. 41 (1960). pp. 55f.

[8] John Dewey, *How We Think* (New York: D.C. Heath and Co., 1933), pp. 150f.

[9] K. Lovell, *The Growth of Basic Mathematical and Scientific Concepts in Children* (London: University of London Press, 1961).

Children must be taught the language and symbols of mathematics. This should be done gradually and systematically. The language of mathematics enables children to communicate in a particular way with their peers and their teacher. Mathematical concepts, when properly taught and when thoroughly understood, may be used to solve new problems, or they may be combined with other concepts and used to solve problems. Individual differences in learning and in using concepts should be expected. A brief review of individual differences is important at this point because of the implications for problem solving.

Individual Differences in Concept Development. Considerable work has been done in this aspect of learning. Two research workers have made major contributions. Bruner investigated the attainment of two kinds of concepts, conjunction and disjunction. Subjects were given cards which could vary in four possible ways: color, type of figure, number of figures, and border. By varying these attributes consistently, he showed how different individuals made widely differing uses of the cues, or adopted different methods in attaining specific kinds of concepts.[10]

Dienes points out in his research that there are many polarities in thinking. He claims, however, that the most fundamental aspects of thinking are to be found in the analytic-constructive dimension. He defines *constructive thinking* as the tendency to attain a goal by having an overall idea of the ultimate shape or structure of the goal and working towards this in some intuitive way. He feels that the details and their interrelationships will take care of themselves as the individual works on a problem. The steps in a problem, which appear to be logically required, are somehow passed over. The analytic thinker progresses toward a goal by going from one step to the next, as required by the logical steps within the system. The analytical thinker may not be aware of the pattern or structure until he completes the problem.

According to Dienes, constructive thought is typical of the thinking children do while working at the concrete stage. On the other hand, analytical thinking is characteristic of the reasoning which appears at adolescence. His thinking, however, is based upon the concepts of abstraction and generalization. Dienes draws heavily upon the work of Piaget and links these ideas with his own views on the analytical-constructive approach.

Dienes views abstraction as a drawing-out process. The learner is given experience of a wide variety of situations, differing in detail but having one property which is to be abstracted. In mathematical situations the property to be abstracted is their common logical structure. When the individual sees the irrelevance of the details and discovers the single class property which unites the exemplars, he has abstracted it and has formed a concept. If the

[10]J. S. Bruner, J. J. Goodnow, and G. A. Austin, *A Study for Thinking* (New York: John Wiley & Sons, Inc., 1956).

concept is to become operational, the individual must be able to reapply it. The new concept thus formed, together with other concepts, can become exemplars for further abstraction.

A mathematical meaning for generalization is adopted by Dienes. A generalization refers to the passage from a limited set of data to a more extended set. Judgments made about the truth of a relationship as being applicable to a set of data are mathematical generalizations. For example, the commutative law is true for specific multiplication facts ($4 \times 3 = 12$ and $3 \times 4 = 12$) and for all numbers of a certain kind ($a \times b = b \times a$ when a and b are natural numbers). Generalizations are based upon higher order abstractions, and some analytic awareness (knowledge of its structure) is needed.

Finally, Dienes establishes a series of stages in the concept-forming process. First is the apparently purposeless play stage which consists of getting to know the particulars. Second is an awareness stage when the learner sees something about the particulars which makes them the same in some respect. Third is an insight stage when all the consitutent parts fall into place and the child sees what the common structure is. Later the child may be able to verbalize the concept. A cautionary note should be sounded at this point pertaining to verbalization of the newly learned concept. Considerable evidence exists to show that premature verbalization of generalizations may be harmful to some children.[11]

Dienes has formulated four principles of conceptual learning. These will be used to summarize his work.

1. *The Dynamic Principle.* This refers to the stages in the abstraction of a concept, for example, the play stage when the individual becomes aware of particulars.
2. *The Perceptual Variability Principle.* The principle states that the more varied individual experiences are, as long as the structure is the same, the more likely that efficient abstracting will take place.
3. *The Mathematical Variability Principle.* The point of this principle is that since certain mathematical concepts depend upon the notion of a variable, the successful attainment of these concepts will depend upon the variation of their values, as well as upon perceptual or qualitative variations, in the exemplars.
4. *The Constructivity Principle.* This principle draws attention to the fact that the analysis of a concept cannot occur without preceding construction. Unless the pupil has built up a concept out of his own experience, subsequent logical analysis is impossible.

Conclusions on Concept Formation. From the abundance of research evidence now available on the development of children's mathematical

[11]See Gertrude Hendrix, "A New Clue to Transfer of Training," *Elementary School Journal*, XLVIII (December, 1947), 197–208.

concepts, several principles have been formulated to guide instruction in problem solving as well as to guide general instructional practices:

1. Concept development is the most important aspect of guiding pupils' understanding of elementary school mathematics. When concepts have been carefully learned, pupils can generalize and extend their understanding of mathematics from one aspect to another.
2. Carefully and gradually children must be taught the language and symbols of mathematics. This mathematical language enables them to communicate in a particular, exact way and to develop concepts necessary for successful problem solving.
3. For each child and for each stage of development, the teacher must create an appropriate environment which will evoke discovery, impel thinking, and extend mathematical experiences.
4. Children go through similar sequences in the development of mathematical ideas although wide differences exist at each age level.
5. The development of mathematical understanding and skill at each successive level of pupil progress in school is dependent upon the principles of concept development just presented.

So far we have identified the basic factors necessary for pupil growth in their ability to solve problems. In order to solve problems, pupils will need: (1) specific computational skills; (2) understanding of basic vocabulary and appropriate language; (3) the ability to think and reason, which involves the gradual development of their cognitive powers; and (4) basic mathematical concepts and generalizations, which help to aid pupils in finding solutions to problems. In addition to these fundamental factors, a variety of other strategies for solving problems can help many pupils when properly used. To these strategies we now turn.

7.4 Strategies for Solving Problems

An important consideration needs to be expressed at the beginning of this section: Strategies or techniques for helping children solve problems must supply careful guidance while at the same time assuring that careful consideration is given to the basic factors discussed in section 7.3. The art of teaching problem solving will be revealed in the way teachers can anticipate individual needs and can determine when to give guidance or when to encourage increased pupil discovery. The procedures presented in this section should *facilitate problem solving* when properly used. When these procedures are used incorrectly (without regard to pupils' ability, development, or experience with mathematics), they will probably hinder pupils' growth in problem solving or limit pupils to the working of the dull, routine examples found in some textbooks.

Some procedures which facilitate problem solving are: (1) using visual and manipulative materials; (2) using a variety of techniques for presenting problems; (3) using mathematical sentences; (4) using mathematical models; (5) formulating word problems; and (6) stimulating experimentation. Each of these procedures will now be discussed.

USING VISUAL AND MANIPULATIVE MATERIALS

Objects, pictures, mathematical aids, and models have been widely used in the teaching of elementary school mathematics. When one searches for evidence indicating the value of these aids and specific outcomes achieved, relatively little data are available on these issues; quite obviously criteria are needed for directing the use of visual and manipulative materials in the teaching of mathematics. These criteria may also be used to evaluate the effectiveness of these instructional materials.

Criteria for selecting and using visual and manipulative instructional materials:

1. A specific purpose should be established for the use of visual and manipulative materials.
2. The aids used should fit the mathematical concept which the pupils are working with and attempting to structure: (1) a physical structure (the sequence of events and arrangement of objects) and (2) the psychical structure (that which causes a given situation to make sense so that everything fits).[12]
3. Mathematical concepts are not derived from materials themselves, but from an appreciation of the significance of operations performed with the materials. The concepts and the ability to maneuver them in the mind are built up from using the concrete materials.[13]
4. Using a variety of instructional aids can be justified only if these materials are suitable for the learner's level of development and extends or enrichens mathematical concepts and background.
5. Careful attention must be given to the understanding of and use of instructional materials constructed to elicit specific mathematical thinking (Stern's materials emphasizing measuring rather than counting; Cuisenaire rods for discovering mathematical relationships; and Dienes multibase arithmetic blocks and algebraical experience materials).[14]

The specific applications of these visual and manipulative materials to

[12]H. van Engen and E. Glenadine Gibb, "Structuring Arithmetic," *Instruction in Arithmetic, Twenty-fifth Yearbook* (Washington, D. C.: National Council of Teachers of Mathematics, 1960), pp. 33–61.

[13]K. Lovell, *The Growth of Basic Mathematical and Scientific Concepts in Children* (London: University of London Press, 1961), Piaget's views.

[14]See C. Stern, *Children Discover Arithmetic* (New York: Harper & Row, Publishers, 1953); and Z. P. Dienes, "The Growth of Mathematical Concepts in Children through Experience," *Educational Research*, II, No. 1 (1959), 9–28.

problem solving are important and numerous. The materials, when carefully selected and used, should motivate the lesson. The experiences children have with aural, tactile, kinesthetic, visual, or thermal stimuli can be quantified. Children can be assisted in understanding a mathematical concept in order to be prepared to solve problems involving the concept. For example, pupils can use a wheel (bicycle or small wagon wheels) to determine the circumference-diameter relationship. Before working problems involving area, children should discover the meaning of square measure. Once having grasped the meaning of this concept, problem-solving experiences involving area should be interesting and successful.

We have suggested the importance of using visual and manipulative materials to assist pupils in their understanding of abstract mathematical ideas and concepts. We seek to enable children to think mathematically and use the abstract symbols and language as soon as possible. When these visual and manipulative materials are not needed, withdraw them. Overuse of instructional aids could hinder some pupils from thinking with abstractions or from solving problems using abstract ideas. On the other hand, these instructional materials should be used when the teacher recognizes that certain children need more work with concrete or visual materials before moving to the abstract stage. Finally, the visual and manipulative aids can be reintroduced in a problem-solving situation to enable the child to demonstrate his solution to a problem or his understanding of a problem. In this instance, the instructional materials are being used for evaluation purposes.

Visual and manipulative materials may be used as part of a specific technique for presenting problems.

TECHNIQUES FOR PRESENTING PROBLEMS

The Discovery Approach. This method for solving problems is based upon the principle that children learn best from doing, exploring, and discovering mathematical ideas as they work on a variety of interesting problems. The method has been popularized by leaders of the mathematical revolution now underway.

Children cannot discover without adequate background work in the specific aspects of mathematics being studied. They will need to have those "entrance skills" needed for solving particular problems. Along with these prerequisites, pupils cannot go very far with the discovery approach without considerable teacher guidance. "Guidance discovery" in problem solving seems to express the modern view toward this aspect of elementary school mathematics.

A variety of procedures are used to lead children toward discovering mathematical ideas and concepts. For example, one textbook series uses these steps:

1. Using objects and pictures to begin instruction on a topic or problem,
2. Relating the new work to meaningful, everyday experiences,
3. Presenting and developing mathematical ideas and concepts before introducing abstract symbols or other formalizations,
4. Developing effective study procedures,
5. Varying teaching procedures to meet individual differences.

Some teachers establish a set of rules to direct children in solving problems. For example:

1. Read the problem.
2. Decide what was given.
3. Decide what is to be found.
4. Decide which operations are necessary to take what is given and use it to find what is to be found.
5. Solve the problem.
6. Check the result.

This set of rules might be used in connection with the development of effective study procedures for word problems found in most elementary school textbooks.

The authors of this series recommend that problem-solving work should be organized around the abilities and experiences of children. For each type of problem (types 1 through 8 presented in section 7.1), the teacher should use appropriate instructional materials to make the work meaningful to children. He should use "guided discovery" techniques in the establishment of procedures needed for solving problems.

Most mathematicians agree that the procedures used in solving problems should include the development of children's ability to translate a given situation into mathematical symbolism. To this aspect we now turn.

Using Mathematical Sentences.   In modern mathematics programs the analogy between a *number sentence* and a *word sentence* is intentional and useful. Children are guided to discover that ideas are expressed as sentences. However, when wishing to provide experiences in computing and using numbers, another language (mathematical) is needed. So the teacher helps children translate, from one language (vernacular) to another (mathematical). In the vernacular, a "set of words" is used to express a thought (the boy's name is Joe). In mathematics, a number sentence is a "set of numerals" that expresses a mathematical thought ($4 + 2 = 6$).

Sentences (vernacular or mathematical) may be true or false. For example:

1. Los Angeles is the largest city in the United States. (F)
2. Los Angeles is the largest city on the West Coast of the United States. (T)
3. $15 \times 11 = 155$ (F)
4. $6 + 8 = 14$ (T)

Discovering whether a sentence is true or false requires certain thought processes and computations. So this form of mathematical sentence (presented by the teacher or prepared by pupils) has certain values in studying the four fundamental operations in arithmetic. A variety of these sentences has already been used in previous chapters.

Another form of the mathematical sentence is the *open sentence*. For example:

$$\square + 5 = 12 \text{ (Read a number plus five equals twelve.)}$$

In examples of this type, several symbols are used in textbooks ($\square$, 0, $\triangle$, X, N) as *place holders* for potential numerals. Some textbooks use *variable* to express the idea of *number*.

You may think that this is the beginning of algebra. You are right. Algebra uses letters and symbols to express and analyze relationships between concepts of quantity in terms of formulas. Algebra is a generalized form of arithmetic. By beginning with simple mathematical sentences and gradually introducing different forms, we can help children solve a variety of problems. In addition to this, we will guide pupils toward meaningful use of numerous algebraic formulas.

An extension of the number sentence from the true or false to a higher level is accomplished by the use of two place holders expressed as symbols in a sentence. For example:

$$\square + \triangle = 10$$

Children are asked to discover possible pairs of numbers which make the sentence true (6 + 4, 4 + 6; 8 + 2, 2 + 8; 7 + 3, 3 + 7; 9 + 1, 1 + 9; 0 + 10, 10 + 0). These are ordered pairs of numbers used to replace the symbols $\square$ and $\triangle$. These may also be called the solution set numbers that make the sentence true.

From this developmental stage, children can move to a higher level requiring the making of word problems.[15] For example:

In the sentence 5 $\times$ $\square$ = 25, pupils could be asked to construct a variety of word problems, each a true solution for the statement. Answers which could be given are:

If the product is 25 and one factor is 5, what will the other factor be?

What is the cost of 1 candy bar if 5 bars cost 25 cents?

Inequalities. Inequalities have many uses in daily living and in mathematics. We can ask questions involving inequality. Do we weigh more or less than the average for our sex and age? Have I enough money to pay for the dinner (more than or less than)? Is the statistical measurement significant $(.01 < P < .05)$?

Inequalities can be easily introduced within the framework of number sentences. For example, $\square + 3 = 5$ is interpreted to mean "what number

---

[15]Textbooks have many names for written (vernacular) problems: thought problems, story problems, reading problems, stated problems, word problems, verbal problems!

(replacing the box) will equal five?" Then changing the example to $\square + 3$ < 5, can be interpreted as "what number replacing the box can make the statement true?" The answer could be either 0 or 1.

Inequalities can be used in the daily mathematics program in numerous ways: as oral exercises with whole numbers, $34 > 31, 23 < 33, 4000 > 3999$; as written exercises with rational numbers (use $<$, $=$, or $>$), $\frac{1}{2}$ $\frac{1}{3}$, $\frac{2}{3}$ $\frac{3}{4}$, $\frac{1}{4}$ $\frac{2}{12}$; or in problem solving. A man wants to make a 120 mile trip. Driving at a speed not less than 30 miles per hour or more than 60 miles per hour, how long will the trip take?

$$+ = \leq 4 \text{ hrs. and } + = \geq 2 \text{ hrs.}$$

The last example is read + (time) is equal to or less than 4 hours and + is equal to or greater than 2 hours.

We have shown two basic types of number sentences: (1) *equations* for which the *verb* is "$=$"; and (2) *inequalities* for which the *verb* may be $\neq$, $<, >, \geq$, or $\leq$ (read as not equal to, less than, greater than, is greater than or equal to, and is less than or equal to).

When carefully used, both types of number sentences are useful in problem solving. The teacher's role is to guide children in the development of the ability to analyze a mathematical problem and to write the mathematical sentence describing the problem

USING MATHEMATICAL MODELS

The word model, as used in the discussion which follows, has two meanings: (1) a small copy or imitation of an existing object; and (2) a representation of something, serving as the plan from which other objects can be constructed. Both meanings are useful in problem solving.

The small copy or imitation of an existing object is needed to lead children's thinking from the physical world to the mathematical world. In guiding this important developmental aspect of children's thinking, the teacher should have two major objectives to direct his teaching: (1) helping children use the model to gain an understanding of mathematical concepts and relationships when the actual object cannot be used in the classroom; and (2) enabling children to move from thinking with objects to abstract, mathematical thinking.

Numerous models have been suggested for use in developing concepts of measurement in the last chapter (cubical counting blocks for understanding volume and solids; pieces of linoleum for understanding square measure; or a variety of objects to help understand geometric figures). Children can use these models as they solve problems in the classroom. Then an intermediate stage can be reached by encouraging pupils to make a sketch or line drawing. Finally, children should be guided toward thinking with abstractions.

The second use of a model, the representation or plan for constructing and thinking, is very important in mathematics. Engineers, architects, design experts, scientists, and others use models to study problems encountered in their work. The model can be modified and fashioned to fit the conditions of the problem. Pupils, too, can write a mathematical model or equation using symbolic materials. This is the type of mental work done in developing a mathematic model for the study of geometry in elementary schools (which was discussed in Chapter 6). A mathematical idea of space (a model) is used to interpret in a theoretical way everyday experiences.

With teacher guidance, pupils should be encouraged to develop models for a variety of mathematical experiences. For example, in business operations one model might be: price-cost = overhead and profit. Then after using the model, other models for determining profit, or "rate pairs" for ordered pairs of numbers used in telling about a price $(10, 15, \frac{10}{15}$, or $10:15)$ could be discovered and used. These models will be referred to again in chapters of this book concerned with decimal fractions and per cent.

FORMULATING WORD PROBLEMS

Solving word problems represents the most disliked aspect of the total elementary school arithmetic program. Adults and children seem to share in their dislike for this aspect of arithmetic. Over one-third of the children tested by one of the authors[16] disliked word problems. These dislikes were developed over a period of years, mainly in grades three through eight, and were fairly permanent. In some instances, extreme dislike for this aspect of arithmetic influenced pupils' total dislike for any kind of mathematics. There are two identifiable reasons for pupils learning these undesirable attitudes toward word problems.

First, throughout the history of writing arithmetic textbooks for elementary schools, word problems have been inadequately prepared and poorly conceived. Most of the examples used were not "real problems" because real problems exist in the experiences of individual learners. Second, many exercises were prepared to trick students, to be difficult so that they would "challenge" pupils, or to provide routine practice in problem solving. Fortunately, modern mathematics programs are emphasizing the importance of word problems that are needed by the learner and that challenge him to discover possible solutions.

Teachers should be encouraged to use textbooks as sources which can be used when pupils understand new processes and when appropriate practice exercises are needed.

Esther Swenson,[17] in a stimulating article on problem solving, stresses the

---

[16]Wilbur H. Dutton, "Another Look at Attitudes of Junior High School Pupils Toward Arithmetic," *Elementary School Journal*, LXVIII (February, 1968), 265–68.
[17]Esther J. Swenson, "How Much Real Problem Solving?" *The Arithmetic Teacher*, XII, No. 6 (October, 1965), 426–30.

importance of having rich *problem-solving* experiences rather than numerous formal exercises or routine word problems. She identifies the characteristics of a real problem-solving situation as one which: encourages children to face a difficulty which is real to them; stimulates inquiry into the circumstances of the problem; directs pupils toward selecting relevant data; encourages a variety of strategies; and enables children to make their own judgments about various solutions.

The authors recommend that four procedures be introduced immediately in the directing of pupils' growth in their ability to solve word problems: (1) begin work with problems growing out of children's experiences in their particular community; (2) gradually introduce word problems appropriate for pupils' mathematical ability; (3) provide many opportunities for pupils to make their own word problems and to write mathematical sentences for these problems; and (4) use the textbook and other resource materials carefully, adjusting the examples to fit individual pupils' abilities and deleting examples which are inappropriate.

Examples of word problems showing several levels of difficulty are:

1. One-step Word Problems. One-step word problems found in textbooks involve the use of the four fundamental operations. In solving one-step word problems, pupils can be guided toward the acceptance of a method which will help them find solutions.

a. Read the problem to see what is given. What sets are used?
b. Decide upon the "action" required (join sets, remove or compare sets, join equivalent sets, separate equivalent sets).
c. Write a number sentence for the problem.
d. Solve the number sentence.
e. Check the result.

The following example illustrates the method:

Our reading book has 264 pages. We have read 160 pages. How many more pages must we read to finish the book?

1. Given 264-page book and 160 pages read.
2. Action required removing a set of 160 pages from a set of 264 pages.
3. Equation: $264 - 160 = \Box$.
4. Solve: $264 - 160 = 104$.
5. Check pages read $160 +$ pages to read $104 = 264$ pages in book. Question is answered (104 pages to read).

Some types of one-step problems involving the four fundamental operations are:

Finding the total when combining sets $5 + 4 = \Box$
How many more must be added? $12 + \Box = 28$
Removing a set $25 - 15 = \Box$

Think a number to complete the $\square - 6 = 20$ sentence or make a set.
Find the missing factor: $7 \times \square = 35$ or $\square \times 6 = 30$
Find the number of equivalent sets: $30 \div 5 = \square$
Find the divisor (factor): $24 \div \square = 6$
The authors recommend using concrete objects and social experiences to
introduce word problems for each type of one-step problem suggested above.
Then move to pictures, and finally to the abstract. Pictures and miniprob-
lems are useful to provide opportunities for quick review and for the evalua-
tion of pupils' understanding of the process. For example, see the illustration
of the balls in the boxes.

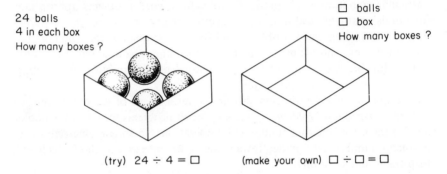

24 balls
4 in each box
How many boxes ?

□ balls
□ box
How many boxes ?

(try) $24 \div 4 = \square$ (make your own) $\square \div \square = \square$

Pupils should have many opportunities to make their own word problems.
If writing and reading are difficult, the teacher can record pupils' word
problems and then ask them to write the equation or number sentence. The
procedure can then be reversed. The child or teacher can write a number
sentence on the chalkboard and ask another pupil to make a word problem
for the sentence.

   2. Two- or Three-step Word Problems.   The new skills and abilities required
for working two-step word problems center around the child's knowledge of
relationships between operations and writing number sentences to describe
the problem. Difficulties may be encountered when a decision must be made
concerning the operation to use and the sequence of steps to take. To avoid
these difficulties, the authors suggest beginning with concrete objects and
helping children make two-step and three-step problems. For example:

   June spent $5.50 for three gifts. She spent $1.50 for one gift and $1.75
for another gift. How much did she spend for the other gift?

   Using United States currency, the teacher could help children discover the
correct answer and write the number sentence:

$1.50 + $1.75 + \square = $5.50 $5.50
                                        or $- 3.25$ ($1.50 + $1.75)
$3.25 + $2.25 = $5.50 $\overline{\$2.25}$

Other word problems could then be made and the United States currency used to show the steps of the problem and to evaluate pupils' understanding of the new work.

Extension of problem solving to provide for other situations would involve similar processes. Start with a social problem.

> Jane earned money working on Saturday. She earned $1.50 baby-sitting, $1.00 washing dishes, and $1.25 helping her Dad trim the flower beds. How much did she earn? She spent $2.65 the next day. How much did she have left?

> Step one: $1.50 + $1.00 + $1.25 = □
> Step two: $3.75 − $2.65 = □ .
> The whole number sentence is:
> ($1.50 + $1.00 + $1.25) − $2.65 = □

Parentheses have been introduced to separate the addends from the amount spent.

To avoid reading difficulties, the problem could be given orally first. Then the written work could be shown on the chalkboard. Presentation of examples that are not within the child's experience containing difficult reading should be deleted from the program or introduced as work for the intellectually gifted. Charles Schulz, in one of his delightful cartoons, has captured the significance of this aspect of problem solving.

© 1968 United Feature Syndicate, Inc.

STIMULATING EXPERIMENTATION

Pupil experimentation in mathematics has at least three important implications for problem solving and for teaching: (1) the mathematical experiences children have in elementary school may determine their potential mathematical development; (2) since mathematics is man-made and exists only in their minds, children remake (possibly create) the mathematics they use; and (3) experimentation and creation take place in a particular social environment.

The authors have already commented upon the negative attitudes learned by children as they encounter difficult word problems. The experiences children have with mathematics during the years they are in elementary school provide the skills and abilities needed for later successes. Any failures they encounter while working with mathematics will probably determine how much they like the subject and how interested they will be in continued study of mathematics. Emphasis upon "mastery of content" and upon "routine computational skill," while important, are really secondary in importance to flexibility, generating of creative ways to work problems, and the learning of ways to create new mathematics.

Piaget has contributed to the belief that the individual learner must "internalize" new mathematical concepts. Each child must "remake" his mathematics as he learns it. We know that each child has different resources and experiences which are used by him as he solves word problems. This personal creation of mathematics must be understood by the teacher and used to direct pupil growth in mathematical thinking through a wide variety of novel problems, games with numbers, and operations that can be performed with numbers. The English Association of Teachers of Mathematics[18] has prepared an excellent source book to stimulate experimentation in elementary school mathematics. Topics presented are: number patterns, inventions with induction, place value, tessellations, classification of shapes, playing of games, and use of numerous devices.

Children learn mathematics in a particular way in our society, just as they learn our language. Teachers, parents, and friends influence this learning through the kinds of reinforcement and rejection given to the individual as he learns his mathematics. So in problem solving, if teachers and parents are content with rigid, teacher or parent-dominated mathematical experiences, children will not be creative or invent new mathematics. Modern mathematics necessitates the use of word problems covering a wide range of application and teaching procedures encouraging experimentation and discovery.

[18]Association of Teachers of Mathematics, *Notes on Mathematics in Primary Schools* (London: Percy Lund, Humphries and Co., 1967).

7.5   The Importance of Reading Skills and Abilities

Reading word problems involves several factors. Each factor is difficult to control and is influenced by the individual learner. For example, the type of reading used will depend upon: (1) the way the problem is written; (2) the readiness of the individual; (3) the methods known by the individual; and (4) the type of content being used. We will discuss each of these variables.

STATEMENT OF PROBLEMS

The way a word problem is written has a great deal to do with its reading difficulty. A word problem may contain certain mathematical symbols and terms. The concepts involved may be omitted. Because of these factors, pupils will need guidance in "adjusting the meaning" of sentences or the whole problem. This may be done by simplifying the problem. For example:

The normal annual rainfall in a certain city is $23\frac{7}{8}$ inches. Last week it rained $1\frac{3}{16}$ inches. That is what part of the normal annual rainfall?

When simplified, the problem would be: The normal annual rainfall in a certain city is 20 inches. Last week it rained 2 inches. Last week's rain is what part of the normal annual rainfall?

The essential idea is: 2 is what part of 20? The answer is $\frac{2}{20}$ which may be reduced to $\frac{1}{10}$ or 10 per cent.

The answer to the original problem is: $\dfrac{1\frac{3}{16}}{23\frac{7}{8}}$ which reduces to $\frac{19}{382}$. While this type of problem could occur in actual daily life, it certainly is not recommended for regular work in elementary schools.

READINESS OF THE LEARNER

Readiness is an important factor in solving problems. This is accomplished by making sure that the learner sees the importance of the problem and has a purpose for learning. The attitude of the pupil will probably have much to do with the way he attacks the problem and persists in trying to read or solve the problem. The learner should know the new mathematical terms and understand the mathematical concept involved in the problem. The introduction of new ideas should be accomplished with simple reading materials; then gradually increase the reading difficulty. In general, however, simplified reading vocabulary and clear sentence structure should be used in most word problems. Careful, precise oral and written statements are the precursors of clear, accurate use of mathematical sentences.

METHODS KNOWN BY THE PUPIL

Problem solving proceeds best when the learner is introduced to new exercises which require the application of previously learned skills or extension of these skills. The teacher should know if the learner has the "entrance skills and abilities" required for successful reading and solving of the word problems being studied.

CONTENT OF WORD PROBLEMS

While much study has been given to the preparation of word problems found in modern mathematics textbooks, the content may not be appropriate for the individual reader. For this reason, the authors have recommended using learning activities which are meaningful to children and which encourage them to find solutions to problems encountered. Certain reading-thinking abilities are involved in solving word problems. These abilities are: applying past experiences to new situations; reading for specific purposes; restructuring a problem to analyze the facts given or the process required; sequencing of steps or subordinate problems; and making critical evaluations of the solution secured in relation to the problem being studied. The mathematical content used in word problems must be selected with due consideration to the way children learn and apply these reading abilities.

The authors recommend the presentation of directed reading lessons using specific mathematical content to develop the abilities and skills needed for the effective reading of word problems. This should include lessons on how to read graphs, charts, and tables.

7.6 Chapter Summary

This chapter was organized around four aspects of problem solving: (1) types of problems; (2) children's thinking; (3) concept development; and (4) strategies for solving problems.

Emphasis was placed upon the use of a rationale for selecting and stating of objectives which would direct teachers toward the development of the cognitive domain—especially the application, analysis, synthesis, and evaluation aspects. By using Getzels' classification of eight types of problems, teachers should be able to help children acquire problem-solving skills and abilities in a developmental way.

Developing children's thinking and reasoning abilities requires time, guidance, and appropriate mathematical experiences. The work of Piaget was used because he has pointed out the importance of certain identifiable stages in the development of mental processes. Teachers must provide children with a variety of experiences which will enable children to proceed through these stages gradually and meaningfully.

Concept development has been stressed as one of the most important aspects of problem solving. One theoretical model (Dienes) of conceptual learning was presented to direct teachers' thinking on this topic. Carefully and gradually children must be taught the language and symbols of mathematics. This mathematical language enables them to communicate in a particular, exact way and to develop concepts necessary for successful problem solving.

Strategies for helping children solve problems were presented. Emphasis was placed upon teachers anticipating pupil needs and upon giving guidance to discovery techniques used by children. Numerous opportunities must be provided for children to study problems meaningful to them and useful in daily life. The classroom environment should permit pupils to formulate word problems useful in their study of mathematical concepts. Other techniques for directing pupil growth in problem solving included: use of mathematical sentences; construction of mathematical models; and stimulation of experimentation.

QUESTIONS AND EXERCISES

1. What are some of the main characteristics of a "good word problem"?
2. Take five word problems from an arithmetic textbook and rewrite them in a simpler form.
3. Prepare a list of arithmetic problems you or a friend have used during the past week (shopping, paying bills, etc.).
4. Select a few pages from a local newspaper (advertisement section) and analyze the mathematical processes involved in reading these ads. What age level would be required (elementary school level) to read the materials and solve problems using these materials?
5. Half-an-inch square

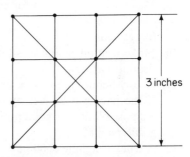

How many inch squares inside the three-inch square?
How many inch squares inside half the three-inch square?

What kinds of responses do you think fifth-grade pupils would make to these questions?
6. Pegboard or line squares

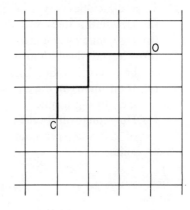

Suppose the drawing represents city streets marked off into blocks. One can travel only on the lines. How could you get from C to O? What is the best way go from C to O?

What kinds of investigation might sixth-grade pupils make?
7. Relative sizes of fractions

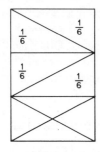 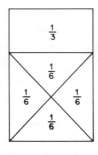

Can you show $\frac{1}{6} \div \frac{1}{12} = 2$?
Use the example first, then make another drawing of your own.
What does the drawing show?

8. For each problem make mathematical sentences. Make true statements and show the answer.
   (a) Joe bought 3 rolls of film for 95¢ per roll, and 2 sets of flashbulbs for 90¢ per package. How much money did he spend?
   (b) Mary mailed packages weighing 14 lbs., 18 lbs., and 15 lbs. What was the average weight of the packages?
   (c) Bill has 28 stamps and 7 coins. He has how many fewer coins than stamps?
9. Make a word problem for each sentence show below
   (a) $45 - n = 13$ (b) $32 \div n = 8$
   (c) $15 + n = 47$ (d) $180 = 4 \times 45$
10. Make a number line to show the answer to the problem shown in the Peanuts cartoon.
11. A Boy Scout swam twice the length of a pool to pass a swimming test. If the pool was 90 feet by 60 feet, how far did the boy swim? Do you see possibilities for good pupil discussion of this example by intermediate grade pupils?
12. A truck weighing 6600 pounds was carrying three horses weighing about one-half ton each. A sign read "Load Limit on Bridge 5 Tons." Should the driver try to cross the bridge?
13. What difficulties may arise in working these problems?
   (a) How tall a stack will 124 boards, each 1 inch thick, make?
   (b) How much will a gross of pencils cost, at two for 8¢?
   (c) A certain bacterium is 0.0001 inches long. How many bacteria can be placed in a line 1 inch long?
   (d) If one man can dig a post hole in one hour, how long will it take two men to dig a hole?
   (e) How long will it take an airplane to go around the earth at the rate of 250 miles per hour? The earth's circumference is about 25,000 miles.

SUGGESTED REFERENCES

Biggs, J. B., *Anxiety, Motivation and Primary School Mathematics*, Occasional Publication No. 9. London: The National Foundation for Educational Research in England and Wales, 1962.

Brownell, William A., "Problem-solving," in *The Psychology of Learning, Forty-first Yearbook of the National Society for the Study of Education*, Part II. Chicago: University of Chicago Press, 1942.

Churchill, E. M., "The Number Concepts of The Young Child," *Researcher and Studies*, University of Leeds, Nos. 17 and 18 (1958), 34–39, 28–46, respectively.

Cohen, Louis S., and David C. Johnson, "Some Thoughts about Problem Solving," *The Arithmetic Teacher*, XIV (April, 1967), 261–71.

Corle, Clyde G., "In Answer to Your Questions—Why Do Children Have Difficulty with Verbal Problems?" *The Arithmetic Teacher*, XII (January, 1965), 13, 18, 23.

Dutton, Wilbur H., *Evaluating Pupils' Understanding of Arithmetic*. Englewood Cliffs, N.J.: Prentice-Hall, Inc., 1964.

Getzels, J. W., "Creative Thinking, Problem-solving, and Instruction," in *Theories of Learning and Instruction, The Sixty-third Yearbook of the National Society for the Study of Education, Part I*. Chicago: University of Chicago Press, 1964.

Guilford, J. P., *et al.*, "A Revised Structure of Intellect," Reports from the *Psychological Laboratory*, No. 19. Los Angeles: University of Southern California, 1957.

MacKinnon, D. W., "The Nature and Nurture of Creative Talent," *American Psychologist*, VII (July, 1962), 488–95.

Mearns, Hughes, *Creative Power: The Education of Youth in the Creative Arts*. New York: Dover Publications, 1958.

Mueller, Francis J., *Understanding the New Elementary School Mathematics*. Belmont, Calif.: Dickenson Publishing Co., 1965.

Perkins, Ruth M., "Patterns and Creative Thinking," *The Arithmetic Teacher*, XIV (December, 1967), 668–70.

Riedesel, C. Alan, "Problem Solving: Some Suggestions for Research," *The Arithmetic Teacher*, XVI (January, 1969), 54–58.

Swenson, Esther J., "How Much Real Problem Solving?" *The Arithmetic Teacher*, XII (October, 1965), 426–30.

Torrance, E. Paul, "Priming Creative Thinking in the Primary Grades," *Elementary School Journal*, LXII (1961), 34–41.

Trueblood, Cecil R., "Promoting Problem-solving Skills through Nonverbal Problems," *The Arithmetic Teacher*, XVI (January, 1969), 7–10.

8

Rational Numbers

8.1 Meaning of Rational Numbers

Children have many uses for fractions in daily life. At an early age they learn to break a candy bar into halves. They see pies or cakes cut into fourths, fifths, or sixths. Gradually, through experience and guidance, they understand that fractions are needed for measurement and to make possible the division of any two whole numbers.

Modern mathematics programs provide for an intuitive approach to the teaching of fractions in the elementary school. Concrete objects, models such as line drawings or geometric figures, and pictures are used to build children's concepts of fractions and to help them perform the basic operations with fractions. The use of correct language and mathematical symbols is stressed. Children are guided toward discovering efficient ways to express numbers used to denote parts of a whole. These numbers are also discovered to be part of a large system and as special cases of numbers behaving according to basic laws.

Numbers shown by fractions such as $\frac{1}{2}$ or $\frac{1}{4}$ are called *rational numbers*. They are abstract mathematical ideas like the counting numbers. Rational numbers can be shown as points on a number line, such as those illustrated at the top of p. 165.

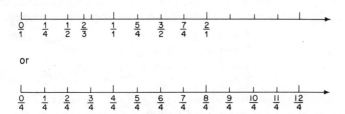

or

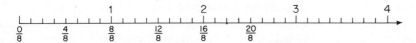

Fractions are the numerals (names for rational numbers).

In establishing a model for work with rational numbers, we will use three approaches: (1) congruent regions; (2) unit figures; and (3) linear representations. These approaches will be used extensively in connection with those sections covering operations on rational numbers. As you see, linear representation has already been used to introduce the concept of rational numbers. The language used in connection with each of these approaches is very specific and important to pupils' understanding of basic mathematical concepts.

Continuing, then, with the meaning of rational numbers, we will use a number line with *unit intervals* divided into the same number of subintervals or *congruent subintervals.*

The *unit intervals* are shown by counting numerals 1, 2, 3, . . . Each unit interval is divided into 8 *subintervals.* These subintervals are *congruent*— equal in length and the same size and shape. Starting at the left ($\frac{0}{8}$) and stopping at the last number (20) of congruent subintervals, we say that the right-hand endpoint of the last subinterval corresponds to a *rational number*. The rational number is represented by the fraction.

In this example the numerator (20) expresses the number of chosen subintervals. The denominator (8) denotes the number of congruent subintervals into which the unit intervals are divided. While we have shown $\frac{0}{8}$ (the numerator of 0 indicating no eighths), the denominator is never 0.

8.2   Fractions Which Name the Same Rational Number

The reader should be familiar with the concept of different names for the same whole number used in discussing number sentences earlier in this book. In the open number sentence $\square + \triangle = 10$, there are several names which can be used to make the sentence true ($8 + 2$, $9 + 1$, $5 + 5$, $6 + 4$, etc.).

Each of the number pairs names 10. So with rational numbers, different fractions may be used to name the same rational number. For example:

$$\frac{0}{1} = \frac{0}{2} = \frac{0}{3} = \frac{0}{4} = \frac{0}{5} \cdots$$
$$\frac{2}{1} = \frac{4}{2} = \frac{6}{3} = \frac{8}{4} = \frac{10}{5} \cdots$$
$$\frac{1}{2} = \frac{2}{4} = \frac{4}{8} = \frac{8}{16} \cdots$$
$$\frac{1}{3} = \frac{2}{6} = \frac{4}{12} = \frac{8}{24} \cdots$$

Pupils should understand the importance of this concept (different names for the same rational numbers) in working with operations on the rational numbers.

8.3   Equivalent Fractions

Using fractions in daily life requires renaming, the writing of a fraction $\frac{1}{2}$ as $\frac{2}{4}$ or the fraction $\frac{1}{3}$ as $\frac{2}{6}$. The same relationship between numerator and denominator (part-whole relationship) is maintained. Pairs of fractions ($\frac{2}{3}, \frac{4}{6}$) are called *equivalent fractions*. They are not the same, but they name the same amount of an object or unit.   *need to stress*

In adding two related fractions, $\frac{1}{2} + \frac{1}{4}$, the one-half must be renamed as $\frac{2}{4}$ so that the operation can be completed. Then $\frac{2}{4} + \frac{1}{4} = \frac{3}{4}$. Fractions may be changed to lower terms ($\frac{4}{16}$ as $\frac{1}{4}$) or to higher terms ($\frac{2}{3}$ as $\frac{6}{9}$). Gradually children must learn how to build sets of equivalent fractions such as: $\{\frac{1}{2}, \frac{2}{4}, \frac{3}{6}, \frac{4}{8}, \ldots\}$. This is accomplished by helping children discover a way to rename a fraction without changing the part-whole relationship. So for the set shown, pupils could be directed to try this procedure:

$$\frac{1 \times 1}{1 \times 2} = \frac{1}{2}, \ \frac{2 \times 1}{2 \times 2} = \frac{2}{4}, \ \frac{3 \times 1}{3 \times 2} = \frac{3}{6} \cdots$$

Once the pattern of work has been discovered, pupils can explore the making of other sets such as:

$$\frac{1 \times 1}{1 \times 3} = \frac{1}{3}, \ \frac{2 \times 1}{2 \times 3} = \frac{2}{6} \cdots$$

This work can be generalized, when pupils are ready, and a rule prepared. One can multiply the numerator and denominator of a fraction by the same number to express the fraction in higher terms without changing the (value) part-whole relationship of the fraction.

Later, when pupils need to reduce a fraction to lower terms, the inverse process can be discovered:

$$\left\{\frac{4}{8}, \frac{3}{6}, \frac{2}{4}, \frac{1}{2}\right\} \ \frac{4 \div 4}{8 \div 4} = \frac{1}{2}, \ \frac{3 \div 3}{6 \div 3} = \frac{1}{2} \cdots$$

After discovering the patterns and understanding the work, pupils should be ready to build a rule for this process.

A check for equivalent fractions can be introduced such as this:

multiply across terms to get 1 × 4 = 4

2 × 2 = 4

Another variation is: $\frac{2}{3}$ is equivalent to $\frac{6}{9}$.

Check by writing 2 × 9 = 18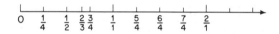

3 × 6 = 18

If the two products are the same, the fractions are equivalent.

8.4 Extending the Meaning of a Fraction

ORDERING RATIONAL NUMBERS

Rational numbers have been shown as points on a number line.

$$0 \quad \frac{1}{4} \quad \frac{1}{2} \quad \frac{2}{3} \frac{3}{4} \quad \frac{1}{1} \quad \frac{5}{4} \quad \frac{6}{4} \quad \frac{7}{4} \quad \frac{2}{1}$$

For any two rational numbers, the point corresponding to the first number which lies to the left of the point corresponding to the second number, coincides with it, or lies to the right of it. We say that for any two given rational numbers, the first is either less than, equal to, or greater than the second. The set of rational numbers is *ordered*. There is an *order relation* between pairs of its members.

The inequality symbols are used to express the order relation:

$$\frac{1}{4} < \frac{2}{3}, \quad \frac{5}{4} > \frac{3}{4}, \quad \frac{1}{1} < \frac{6}{4} \quad \text{or} \quad \frac{3}{4} = \frac{6}{8}.$$

COMMON MEANINGS OF FRACTIONS

A fraction may be used to show several mathematical concepts. For example, a fraction may be:

1. An ordered pair of numbers
2. One or more equal parts of a unit
3. One or more equal parts of a set
4. An indicated division
5. A ratio

Examples will be given for each of these concepts.

Look at the example. Think about a *numbered pair*.

2 parts shaded
4 parts in all

Write a fraction for the number pair. ($\frac{2}{4}$) two fourths.

Part of a unit may be shown like this: Karen gave her sister, Debbie, part
of a candy bar. Did Debbie get half of the bar?

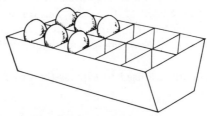

Or in this example: What part of the region is shaded?

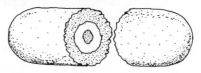

A fraction as part of a set may be demonstrated with an egg carton.

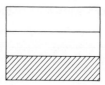

Six out of the dozen eggs are in the carton.

The idea of a *fraction as an indicated division* is shown this way: $\frac{2}{3}$ means
$2 \div 3$, the fraction line (bar) indicating division. So:

$$
\begin{array}{r}
.66 \\
3\,\overline{)\,2.00} \\
1\,8 \\
\hline
20 \\
18 \\
\hline
2
\end{array}
\qquad \text{and} \quad .66\tfrac{2}{3} = \tfrac{2}{3}.
$$

Ratio can be shown by this example:

One child has $2 and another child has $3. The ratio of their money is
2: 3 or $\frac{2}{3}$.

The topic of ratio and proportion will be presented later in the chapter.

WHOLE NUMBERS AND RATIONAL NUMBERS

There is a correspondence between the whole numbers and certain rational numbers. For example:

Whole number	0	1	2 ...
Rational number	$\frac{0}{1}$	$\frac{1}{1}$	$\frac{2}{1}$ ...

For each whole number there corresponds exactly one rational number. For each rational number in the set $\{\frac{0}{1}, \frac{1}{1}, \frac{2}{1} \ldots\}$ there corresponds exactly one whole number. The correspondence is one-to-one,[1] as shown in this example:

$$0, 1, 2, 3, 4, \ldots$$
$$\frac{0}{1}, \frac{1}{1}, \frac{2}{1}, \frac{3}{1}, \frac{4}{1}, \ldots$$

The operations on rational numbers are defined as they are for whole numbers, $1 + 2 = 3$, whether these symbols stand for whole numbers or for rational numbers. The basic principles and intuitive ideas used with whole numbers should serve as the model for performing basic operations on rational numbers. When this is done, teaching will be relatively easy, and pupils' new learnings will involve repeated use of previously acquired knowledge about whole numbers.

8.5   Addition of Rational Numbers

Two important concepts will be used to introduce the addition operation on rational numbers: (1) the concept of congruent regions in a plane or congruent segments on a number line; and (2) the unit fraction concept.

Look at example (a). Think of combining the shaded regions. Replacing the $\square$ with a natural number, the sentence would be $1 + 1 = 2$. The regions are considered congruent regions in the plane. Next identify the total number of congruent regions in the plane $3 \times 1 = 3$. So each congruent region is $\frac{1}{3}$. Then

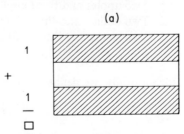

(a)

$$\begin{array}{c} 1 \\ + \\ \frac{1}{\square} \end{array}$$

---

[1] For additional discussion of this concept see: National Council of Teachers of Mathematics, *Topics in Mathematics, Twenty-Ninth Yearbook* (Washington, D.C.: The Council, 1964), pp. 215–35.

think of combining one third with another third. How many thirds will this make?

$$\tfrac{1}{3} + \tfrac{1}{3} = \tfrac{2}{3}$$

Discrete regions, such as the circles in example (b), may be used to extend the addition operation.

(b)

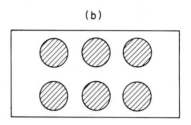

Pupils can observe that sentences such as:

$$\tfrac{1}{6} + \tfrac{1}{6} = \tfrac{2}{6}, \ \tfrac{1}{6} + \tfrac{2}{6} = \tfrac{3}{6}, \ \tfrac{2}{6} + \tfrac{3}{6} = \tfrac{5}{6}$$

express true statements.

(c)

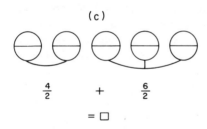

$$\tfrac{4}{2} \quad + \quad \tfrac{6}{2}$$

$$= \square$$

Pictures, such as example (c), can be used to help pupils discover that in addition on rational numbers, the combining of the numerators of two fractions with the same denominator produces the correct sum. Think of 4 halves added to 6 halves. Then the number sentence can be completed. There are $\tfrac{10}{2} =$ ten halves,

$$\tfrac{4}{2} + \tfrac{6}{2} = \tfrac{10}{2} = 5.$$

Another way to help pupils rationalize the work in example (b), the combining of the numerators, is to say:

1. Two apples and three apples are five apples.
2. Two dollars and three dollars are five dollars.
3. Two sixths and three sixths are five sixths.
4. $\tfrac{2}{6} + \tfrac{3}{6} = \tfrac{5}{6}$

Algebraically, we define the sum of rational numbers

$$\frac{a}{c} \text{ and } \frac{b}{c} \text{ as } \frac{a+b}{c},$$

no matter what whole numbers a and b represent or what counting number c represents.

Also,

$$\frac{a}{c} + \frac{b}{d} = \frac{ad + bc}{cd}$$

Applying the definition we have:

$$\frac{1}{2} + \frac{1}{3} = \frac{3 + 2}{6} = \frac{5}{6}$$

The next step, the addition of two rational numbers with unlike denominators, can be approached as follows:

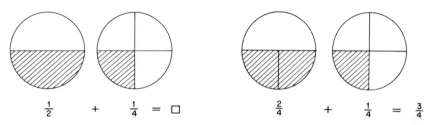

$$\frac{1}{2} \quad + \quad \frac{1}{4} \quad = \quad \square \qquad\qquad \frac{2}{4} \quad + \quad \frac{1}{4} \quad = \quad \frac{3}{4}$$

Only congruent regions can be combined. So rename $\frac{1}{2}$ as $\frac{2}{4}$.

This is similar to saying: you cannot add 1 apple and 1 dollar and get either apples or dollars.

Next in difficulty would be work with fractions having unrelated denominators, such as $\frac{1}{2} + \frac{1}{3}$. Concrete objects such as apples or candy could be used to demonstrate the operation.

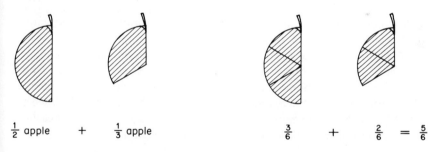

$$\frac{1}{2} \text{ apple} \quad + \quad \frac{1}{3} \text{ apple} \qquad\qquad \frac{3}{6} \quad + \quad \frac{2}{6} \quad = \quad \frac{5}{6}$$

Change to congruent regions by renaming $\frac{1}{2}$ as $\frac{3}{6}$ and $\frac{1}{3}$ as $\frac{2}{6}$.

For beginning work, a chart may be used to help children find a common denominator for examples such as

$$\frac{1}{2} + \frac{1}{3}, \quad \frac{1}{2} + \frac{1}{6} \quad \text{or} \quad \frac{1}{6} + \frac{1}{12}.$$

Gradually children must discover several ways to find a common denominator such as: by inspection $\frac{1}{2} + \frac{1}{6}$ (use the 6); or by multiplying denominators;

$$\frac{1}{4} + \frac{1}{6} \left(\frac{}{4 \times 6} = \frac{}{24}\right)$$

One		
$\frac{1}{2}$		$\frac{1}{2}$
$\frac{1}{3}$	$\frac{1}{3}$	$\frac{1}{3}$
$\frac{1}{6}$ $\frac{1}{6}$	$\frac{1}{6}$ $\frac{1}{6}$	$\frac{1}{6}$ $\frac{1}{6}$
$\frac{1}{12}$ $\frac{1}{12}$ $\frac{1}{12}$ $\frac{1}{12}$	$\frac{1}{12}$ $\frac{1}{12}$ $\frac{1}{12}$ $\frac{1}{12}$	$\frac{1}{12}$ $\frac{1}{12}$ $\frac{1}{12}$ $\frac{1}{12}$

or taking

$$\frac{1}{2} \text{ of } \frac{1}{24} = \frac{1}{12}.$$

Most of the examples presented in this chapter have been written horizontally. This arrangement is preferred in algebra. The vertical arrangement should also be used. In addition involving mixed numbers, the vertical arrangement seems best for children. Three examples will be given.

$$
\begin{array}{r}
3\frac{1}{4} \\
+\ 2\frac{2}{4} \\
\hline
5\frac{3}{4}
\end{array}
\quad \text{Like denominators, no reduction}
$$

$$
\begin{array}{r}
2\frac{1}{2} = 2\frac{3}{6} \\
+\ 5\frac{1}{3} = 5\frac{2}{6} \\
\hline
7\frac{5}{6}
\end{array}
\quad \text{Lowest common denominators, no reduction}
$$

$$
\begin{array}{r}
3\frac{3}{4} = 3\frac{9}{12} \\
+\ 4\frac{2}{3} = 4\frac{8}{12} \\
\hline
7\frac{17}{12} = 8\frac{5}{12}
\end{array}
$$

These examples show the importance of selecting an order of presentation which will introduce new skills gradually and meaningfully.

The addition of three or more fractions should be presented to children after they thoroughly understand examples involving two fractions. Begin the work with like denominators and then extend the operation to include unlike denominators and mixed numbers. A 12-inch ruler may be used to introduce this work and to relate the work to the number line or to measurement. For example, mark a ruler into fourths or eighths.

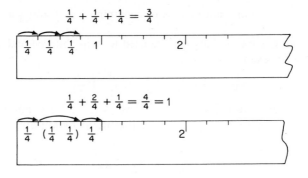

$$\frac{1}{4} + \frac{1}{4} + \frac{1}{4} = \frac{3}{4}$$

$$\frac{1}{4} + \frac{2}{4} + \frac{1}{4} = \frac{4}{4} = 1$$

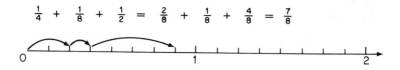

$$\tfrac{1}{8} + \tfrac{1}{4} + \tfrac{1}{8} = \tfrac{1}{8} + \tfrac{2}{8} + \tfrac{1}{8} = \tfrac{4}{8}$$

Then use the number line.

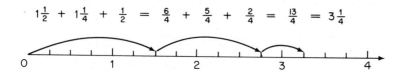

$$\tfrac{1}{4} + \tfrac{1}{8} + \tfrac{1}{2} = \tfrac{2}{8} + \tfrac{1}{8} + \tfrac{4}{8} = \tfrac{7}{8}$$

$$1\tfrac{1}{2} + 1\tfrac{1}{4} + \tfrac{1}{2} = \tfrac{6}{4} + \tfrac{5}{4} + \tfrac{2}{4} = \tfrac{13}{4} = 3\tfrac{1}{4}$$

8.6   Properties of Addition for Rational Numbers

The properties established for addition of whole numbers (discussed in Chapter 2) hold for addition of rational numbers.

Closure property

$$\frac{a}{b} + \frac{c}{b} = \frac{a+c}{b}$$

then

$$\frac{1}{4} + \frac{2}{4} = \frac{1+2}{4} = \frac{3}{4}$$

Note that a, b, and c are whole numbers $\neq$ to 0. The numerator of the right-hand member of the equation is a whole number, since the system of whole numbers is closed under addition and the denominator is also a nonzero whole number. The right-hand member names a rational number.

Commutative property

By definition, we have:

$$\frac{a}{b} + \frac{c}{b} = \frac{a+c}{b}, \quad \frac{c}{b} + \frac{a}{b} = \frac{c+a}{b}$$

Commutative property of addition of whole numbers $(a + c = c + a)$:

Then,

$$\frac{a}{b} + \frac{c}{b} = \frac{a+c}{b} = \frac{c+a}{b} = \frac{c}{b} + \frac{a}{b}$$

Example:

$$\frac{1}{4} + \frac{2}{4} = \frac{1+2}{4} = \frac{3}{4} \text{ and } \frac{2}{4} + \frac{1}{4} = \frac{2+1}{4} = \frac{3}{4}$$

Associative property

By definition, we have:

$$\frac{a}{b} + \left(\frac{c}{b} + \frac{d}{b}\right) = \frac{a}{b} + \frac{c+d}{b} = \frac{a+(c+d)}{b}$$

$$\left(\frac{a}{b} + \frac{c}{b}\right) + \frac{d}{b} = \frac{a+c}{b} + \frac{d}{b} = \frac{(a+c)+d}{b}$$

Associative property with whole numbers $[a+(c+d) = (a+c)+d]$:
Then,

$$\frac{a}{b} + \left(\frac{c}{b} + \frac{d}{b}\right) = \frac{a+(c+d)}{b} = \frac{(a+c)+d}{b} = \left(\frac{a}{b} + \frac{c}{b}\right) + \frac{d}{b}$$

Example:

$$\frac{1}{5} + \frac{2}{5} + \frac{3}{5} = \frac{1}{5} + \frac{2+3}{5} = \frac{1}{5} + \frac{5}{5} = \frac{6}{5}$$

and

$$\left(\frac{1}{5} + \frac{2}{5}\right) + \frac{3}{5} = \frac{1+2}{5} + \frac{3}{5} = \frac{3}{5} + \frac{3}{5} = \frac{6}{5}$$

Identity element

When $\frac{a}{b}$ is a rational number, then $\frac{0}{b} = 0$

We have:

$$\frac{a}{b} + 0 = \frac{a}{b} + \frac{0}{b}$$

$$= \frac{a+0}{b}$$

$$= \frac{a}{b}$$

Definition of addition and 0 is the identity element.
Similarly,

$$0 + \frac{a}{b} = \frac{0}{b} + \frac{a}{b}$$

$$= \frac{0+a}{b}$$

$$= \frac{a}{b}$$

8.7 Subtraction of Rational Numbers

When pupils understand the addition of rational numbers, subtraction is made relatively easy. Subtraction is the inverse of addition. To subtract $\frac{1}{5}$ from $\frac{4}{5}$ means to find a number (fraction) which when added to $\frac{1}{5}$, gives $\frac{4}{5}$. After pupils have learned to put two related fractions together, they can easily learn to take related fractions apart. Thus much of the work in subtraction of rational numbers parallels the work in addition, as in this example of adding or subtracting thirds.

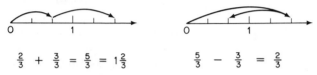

$$\frac{2}{3} + \frac{3}{3} = \frac{5}{3} = 1\frac{2}{3} \qquad \frac{5}{3} - \frac{3}{3} = \frac{2}{3}$$

Using pictures showing congruent regions, subtraction can proceed along the same lines as the teaching of addition of rational numbers.

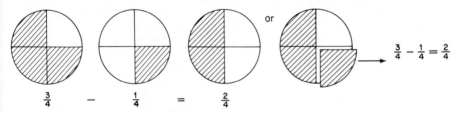

$$\frac{3}{4} \quad - \quad \frac{1}{4} \quad = \quad \frac{2}{4} \qquad\qquad \frac{3}{4} - \frac{1}{4} = \frac{2}{4}$$

Pupils' thinking can be directed along these lines:

1 apple from 3 apples leaves 2 apples.

1 fourth from 3 fourths leaves 2 fourths.

$$\frac{3}{4} - \frac{1}{4} = \frac{2}{4}$$

When a ruler is used to add rational numbers, the inverse process can be shown.

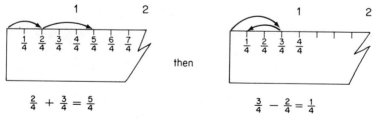

then

$$\frac{2}{4} + \frac{3}{4} = \frac{5}{4} \qquad\qquad \frac{3}{4} - \frac{2}{4} = \frac{1}{4}$$

The process can also be shown with a number line.

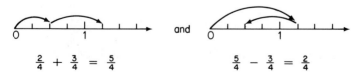

and

$$\frac{2}{4} + \frac{3}{4} = \frac{5}{4} \qquad\qquad \frac{5}{4} - \frac{3}{4} = \frac{2}{4}$$

Algebraically, the subtraction of fractions can be defined as:

$$\frac{a}{c} - \frac{b}{c} = \frac{a-b}{c}$$

$$\frac{a}{c} - \frac{b}{d} = \frac{ad-bc}{cd}$$

The order of presentation is similar to the order suggested for addition of rational numbers:

$\frac{3}{5} - \frac{2}{5} = \frac{1}{5}$	Like denominators, no reduction
$\frac{3}{6} - \frac{1}{6} = \frac{2}{6} = \frac{1}{3}$	Like denominators, with reduction
$\frac{1}{2} - \frac{1}{3} = \frac{3}{6} - \frac{2}{6} = \frac{1}{6}$	Common denominator, product of the denominators
$\frac{1}{4} - \frac{1}{6} = \frac{3}{12} - \frac{2}{12} = \frac{1}{12}$	L.C.D., not the product of the denominators
$4\frac{2}{3} - 1\frac{1}{3} = 3\frac{1}{3}$	Mixed numbers, no reduction
$4\frac{2}{3} - 2\frac{1}{4} = 4\frac{8}{12} - 2\frac{3}{12} = 2\frac{5}{12}$	Mixed numbers, common denominator, no reduction

Regrouping in the subtraction of mixed numbers requires special attention. Since pupils have learned to regroup in subtraction with whole numbers, this work should be related to fractions. For example:

(a)   (b)   (c)

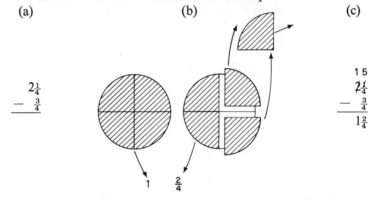

$$2\frac{1}{4}$$
$$-\ \frac{3}{4}$$

$$1 \qquad \frac{2}{4}$$

$$
\begin{array}{r}
1\ 5 \\
\cancel{2\frac{1}{4}} \\
-\ \frac{3}{4} \\
\hline
1\frac{2}{4}
\end{array}
$$

Using a fraction kit, the work shown in example (b) requires taking away the three fourths. This leaves a remainder of 1 and $\frac{2}{4}$. In example (c) 1 (whole number) is regrouped to make $\frac{4}{4}$. Then $\frac{4}{4} + \frac{1}{4} = \frac{5}{4}$. Then $\frac{3}{4}$ from 1 and $\frac{5}{4}$ leaves $1\frac{2}{4}$.

Work involving subtraction of mixed numbers with regrouping and unrelated fractions is very difficult. For example:

$$
\begin{array}{r}
3\frac{1}{2} \\
-\ 1\frac{2}{3} \\
\hline
\end{array}
\qquad\qquad
\begin{array}{r}
3\frac{3}{6} \\
-\ 1\frac{4}{6} \\
\hline
\end{array}
\qquad\qquad
\begin{array}{r}
2 \\
\cancel{3}\frac{9}{6} \\
-\ \frac{4}{6} \\
\hline
2\frac{5}{6}
\end{array}
$$

Rewriting the example, as shown above, will be helpful for many pupils during the introductory stages. Pupils should be encouraged to think the process as soon as possible and only make the regrouping with the use of a crutch when needed. For example:

$$
\begin{array}{r}
2 \\
\cancel{3}\cancel{\tfrac{1}{2}}\ \tfrac{9}{6} \\
-\ 1\cancel{\tfrac{7}{8}}\ \tfrac{4}{6} \\
\hline
1\ \tfrac{5}{6}
\end{array}
$$

Our attention is now directed to the statement of answers in subtraction with rational numbers. Should the answer always be reduced in examples like these?

$$
\begin{array}{cc}
\text{(a)} & \text{(b)} \\
4\tfrac{3}{4} & 6\tfrac{6}{8} \\
-\ 2\tfrac{1}{4} & -\ 2\tfrac{2}{8} \\
\hline
2\tfrac{2}{4} & 4\tfrac{4}{8}
\end{array}
$$

Obviously not. The examples are correct as they are written. The way the work is presented should determine whether the reduction of the answer to lowest terms is required. When practice is needed for finding lower or higher terms, assign specific exercises designed to help those pupils needing the work. For example:

1. Circle the fractions in set A with terms lower than $\frac{4}{8}$:
   A $\frac{1}{2}, \frac{2}{4}, \frac{3}{6}, \frac{4}{8}, \frac{5}{10}, \frac{6}{12}, \frac{7}{14}, \frac{8}{16}$
2. Check the fractions in set A with terms higher than $\frac{4}{8}$.
3. Write a number sentence for each example; a is done.
   (a) To work $\frac{1}{2} - \frac{1}{4}$, think $\{\frac{1}{2}, \frac{2}{4}, \frac{3}{6}, \frac{4}{8}, \frac{5}{10} \ldots\}$
   $$\frac{2}{4} - \frac{1}{4} = \frac{1}{4}$$
   (b) To work $\frac{3}{4} - \frac{1}{6}$, think $\{\frac{3}{4}, \frac{6}{8}, \frac{9}{12}, \frac{12}{16}, \frac{15}{20} \ldots\}$
   $$\square - \frac{1}{6} = \square$$
   (c) To work $\frac{1}{2} - \frac{1}{3}$, think $\{\frac{1}{2}, \frac{2}{4}, \frac{3}{6}, \frac{4}{8}, \frac{5}{10} \ldots\}$
   (d) Write the missing numerator or denominator for each example.
   (1) $\frac{4}{2} = \frac{8}{\square}$. (2) $\frac{2}{4} = \frac{\square}{2}$ (3) $\frac{5}{4} = \frac{10}{\square}$ (4) $\frac{3}{3} = \frac{\square}{9}$
   (e) Write T (true) or F (false) for each statement.
   (1) $\frac{2}{2} < \frac{3}{2}$ (2) $\frac{3}{4} > \frac{3}{2}$ (3) $\frac{6}{8} < \frac{3}{4}$ (4) $\frac{9}{4} < 2$

8.8 Multiplication of Rational Numbers

Just as we used the system of whole numbers as a model in determining the meaning of addition of rational numbers, we can use some of these same procedures for multiplication of rational numbers. Other aspects, however, must be taught as special operations. The six basic types of cases to consider in the multiplication of rational numbers are:

1. Integer × fraction
2. Fraction × integer
3. Fraction × fraction
4. Integer × mixed number
5. Mixed number × integer
6. Mixed number × mixed number

We will consider each of these cases as listed.

INTEGER TIMES FRACTION

Using a number line and the concept of repeated additions, we will consider the example:

$$3 \times \tfrac{1}{2}$$

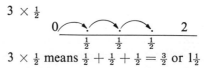

$3 \times \tfrac{1}{2}$ means $\tfrac{1}{2} + \tfrac{1}{2} + \tfrac{1}{2} = \tfrac{3}{2}$ or $1\tfrac{1}{2}$

Pupils can readily understand this process if they use concrete materials or a fraction kit to discover that multiplying a fraction by an integer is similar to repeated additions. For example, $3 \times \tfrac{3}{4}$ could be shown with a fraction kit.

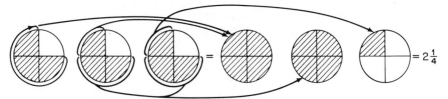

Or $3 \times \tfrac{3}{4}$ could be shown with a ruler.

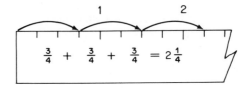

FRACTION TIMES INTEGER

How can we explain an example like $\tfrac{2}{3} \times 6$? One factor is a fraction and this creates some difficulties. The fraction $\tfrac{2}{3}$ means that something has been divided into three equal parts and then two parts are taken. So if 6 is divided into three equal parts, the size of each part is 2. Take two of these equal parts and the result is 4. Study this set of six circles.

Now divide the set of 6 into three equal parts.

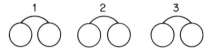

Take two of the equal parts.

The result is 4. So $\frac{2}{3} \times 6 = 4$.

With the use of fraction kits, children can observe that the fraction $\frac{2}{3}$ may be thought of as an operation: we operate in this way, divide by 3 and then multiply by 2. When we apply this operation to 6 the result is 4. Note that the order of operations is reversible: we could multiply by 2 and then divide by 3 and get the same product.

The product of $\frac{2}{3} \times 6 = 4$ is smaller than the 6, even though we are multiplying 6 by a number. If this causes difficulty for a pupil to understand, the commutative law ($ab = ba$) may be used.

$$\tfrac{2}{3} \times 6 = 6 \times \tfrac{2}{3}$$

so

$$\tfrac{2}{3} + \tfrac{2}{3} + \tfrac{2}{3} + \tfrac{2}{3} + \tfrac{2}{3} + \tfrac{2}{3} = \tfrac{12}{3} \text{ or } 4$$

This process may help to rationalize the result, but it circumvents the main idea, which is that multiplication by a fraction is essentially different from multiplying by an integer. We have redefined the multiplication operation for this type of example.

FRACTION TIMES FRACTION

When the preceding case (fraction times integer) has been taught carefully, the teaching of this new example should not be difficult for most pupils. Consider the example $\frac{1}{2} \times \frac{3}{4}$. Using line drawings, congruent regions can be shown for the vertical side of each unit as well as the horizontal side. In the example there are two rows (horizontal) and four columns (vertical). The cross-hatch shows the $\frac{3}{4}$. To

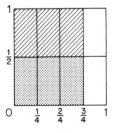

find the product of $\frac{1}{2} \times \frac{3}{4}$ take $\frac{1}{2}$ of the cross-hatched region (dark shaded region) which is $\frac{3}{8}$. Thus,

$$\frac{1}{2} \times \frac{3}{4} = \frac{1 \times 3}{2 \times 4} = \frac{3}{8}.$$

Another way to rationalize this example is to use a ruler.

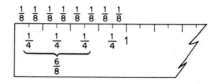

For example, we can rename $\frac{3}{4}$ as $\frac{6}{8}$ (equivalent fraction). Then one-half of $\frac{6}{8}$ is $\frac{3}{8}$. So

$$\frac{1}{2} \times \frac{3}{4} = \frac{1 \times 3}{2 \times 4} = \frac{3}{8}.$$

Fraction kits can also be used to help pupils rationalize an example such as $\frac{1}{2} \times \frac{1}{2}$.

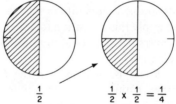

The multiplicand $\frac{1}{2}$ is shown. Applying the multiplier to this multiplicand (divide into two equal parts and take one of these equal parts), we obtain $\frac{1}{4}$. Thus $\frac{1}{2}$ of $\frac{1}{2}$ is $\frac{1}{4}$.

In the example, notice that:

$$\frac{2}{3} \times \frac{3}{4} = \frac{6}{12}$$
$$\frac{1}{2} \times \frac{1}{4} = \frac{1}{8}$$

The product of the denominators is the denominator of the product, and the product of the numerators is the numerator of the product.

$$\frac{\text{numerator} \times \text{numerator}}{\text{denominator} \times \text{denominator}}$$

One should ask the question, when do people use fractions such as those just described? Women use multiplication of fractions in cooking. For example: A recipe calls for $\frac{1}{2}$ cup of sugar, $\frac{1}{4}$ teaspoon salt and $\frac{3}{4}$ teaspoon baking soda. To cut the recipe in half, these examples occur.

$$\frac{1}{2} \times \frac{1}{2} = \frac{1}{4} \quad \text{cup sugar}$$
$$\frac{1}{2} \times \frac{1}{4} = \frac{1}{8} \quad \text{teaspoon salt}$$
$$\frac{1}{2} \times \frac{3}{4} = \frac{3}{8} \quad \text{teaspoon baking soda}$$

The common expression used is "take one-half of the recipe." If the division operation were used, the divisor would be 2, not $\frac{1}{2}$, and the examples would be written:

$$\frac{1}{2} \div \frac{2}{1} =$$
$$\frac{1}{2} \times \frac{1}{2} = \frac{1}{4}$$

Obviously, it is much simpler for women to use multiplication as the inverse process for dividing the recipe.

Men use similar processes in cutting wood, metal, or other shop materials which have dimensions expressed in inches. Examples might include: $\frac{1}{2}$ of $\frac{3}{4}''$ metal strip; $\frac{1}{4}$ of $\frac{3}{4}''$ piece of leather; or $\frac{1}{4}$ of $\frac{7}{8}''$ molding.

INTEGER TIMES MIXED NUMBER

Consider the example $3 \times 1\frac{1}{2}$. The multiplier is 3, a whole number indicating how many. Using repeated additions, we get:

$$3 \times 1\frac{1}{2} = 1\frac{1}{2} + 1\frac{1}{2} + 1\frac{1}{2} = 4\frac{1}{2}$$

This example can be rationalized with a fraction kit or with line drawings.

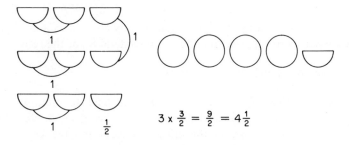

Another method is to change the mixed number $1\frac{1}{2}$ to an improper fraction, $\frac{3}{2}$. Then: $3 \times 1\frac{1}{2} = 3 \times \frac{3}{2}$ and the explanation is the same as an integer times a fraction. Thus:

$$3 \times \frac{3}{2} = \frac{3}{2} + \frac{3}{2} + \frac{3}{2} = \frac{9}{2} = 4\frac{1}{2}$$

Also, this can be shown as illustrated here.

$$3 \times \frac{3}{2} = \frac{9}{2} = 4\frac{1}{2}$$

MIXED NUMBER TIMES INTEGER

Consider the example $2\frac{1}{2} \times 3$. The multiplier is $2\frac{1}{2}$, the mixed number. Now:

$$2\frac{1}{2} = 2 + \frac{1}{2}$$

SO:
$$2\tfrac{1}{2} \times 3 = (2 + \tfrac{1}{2}) \times 3 = (2 \times 3) + (\tfrac{1}{2} \times 3)$$
The distributive law:
$$a \times (b + c) = (a \times b) + (a \times c)$$
and the commutative law:
$$a \times (b + c) = (b + c) \times a$$
may be used to explain the example. Multiplying by $2\tfrac{1}{2}$ consists of multiplication, first by 2 and then by $\tfrac{1}{2}$, then addition of the products. Thus:
$$2\tfrac{1}{2} \times 3 = (2 \times 3) + (\tfrac{1}{2} \times 3) = 6 + 1\tfrac{1}{2} = 7\tfrac{1}{2}$$
The work can also be shown as illustrated here.

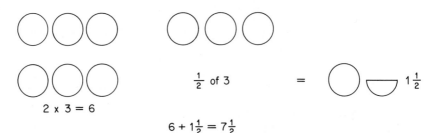

An alternative explanation is: change the multiplier ($2\tfrac{1}{2}$) into an improper fraction $\tfrac{5}{2}$. Then: $2\tfrac{1}{2} \times 3 = \tfrac{5}{2} \times 3$. Now operate as in the case when the multiplier is a fraction. The multiplier is $\tfrac{5}{2}$. Then $\tfrac{5}{2}$ means that something is divided into two equal parts and then five of these equal parts are taken. Apply this concept to 2 and 3. If 3 is divided into two equal parts, the size of each part is $1\tfrac{1}{2}$. Take five of these equal parts. Thus:
$$5 \times 1\tfrac{1}{2} = 1\tfrac{1}{2} + 1\tfrac{1}{2} + 1\tfrac{1}{2} + 1\tfrac{1}{2} + 1\tfrac{1}{2} = 7\tfrac{1}{2}$$
The commutative law can be applied too. Thus:
$$2\tfrac{1}{2} \times 3 = 3 \times 2\tfrac{1}{2} = 2\tfrac{1}{2} + 2\tfrac{1}{2} + 2\tfrac{1}{2} = 7\tfrac{1}{2}$$
This, however, is not a basic explanation; it may be used as a check for the correct answer or to increase the pupils' understanding of the result.

MIXED NUMBERS TIMES MIXED NUMBERS

There are relatively few times when one will have to multiply a mixed number times a mixed number in daily life. This being so, careful attention should be given to the size of the mixed numbers and the kinds of word problems required for pupils' work. For example, one might have a situation in which a person needed $3\tfrac{1}{2}$ lengths of material (building material or picture framing), each length being $2\tfrac{1}{2}$. Let us consider rationalizing this example: $3\tfrac{1}{2} \times 2\tfrac{1}{2}$ (feet). Using the distributive law,
$$3\tfrac{1}{2} \times 2\tfrac{1}{2} = (3 + \tfrac{1}{2}) \times 2\tfrac{1}{2} = (3 \times 2\tfrac{1}{2}) + (\tfrac{1}{2} \times 2\tfrac{1}{2})$$

The $3 \times 2\frac{1}{2}$ is the case of an integer times a mixed number, and $\frac{1}{2} \times 2\frac{1}{2}$ is the case of a fraction times a mixed number. The answer is the sum of these two parts.

Now:
$$3 \times 2\frac{1}{2} = 2\frac{1}{2} + 2\frac{1}{2} + 2\frac{1}{2} = 7\frac{1}{2}$$

and:
$$\frac{1}{2} \times 2\frac{1}{2} = \frac{1}{2} \times \frac{5}{2} = \frac{5}{4} \text{ or } 1\frac{1}{4}$$

so:
$$3 \times 2\frac{1}{2} = 7\frac{1}{2} + 1\frac{1}{4} = 8\frac{3}{4} \text{ (feet)}$$

Another explanation is to change both mixed numbers to improper fractions. Thus:

$$3\frac{1}{2} \times 2\frac{1}{2} = \frac{7}{2} \times \frac{5}{2} = \frac{35}{4} = 8\frac{3}{4}$$

This leads to the final consolidation of the six cases into one case: fraction $\times$ fraction. This can be shown as:

$$6 \times \tfrac{1}{2} = \tfrac{6}{1} \times \tfrac{1}{2} = \tfrac{6}{2} = 3$$
$$\tfrac{1}{3} \times 6 = \tfrac{1}{3} \times \tfrac{6}{1} = \tfrac{6}{3} = 2$$
$$\tfrac{1}{4} \times \tfrac{3}{4} = \tfrac{3}{16}$$
$$2 \times 2\tfrac{1}{2} = \tfrac{2}{1} \times \tfrac{5}{2} = \tfrac{10}{2} = 5$$
$$2\tfrac{1}{2} \times 4 = \tfrac{5}{2} \times \tfrac{4}{1} = \tfrac{20}{2} = 10$$
$$2\tfrac{1}{2} \times 1\tfrac{1}{2} = \tfrac{5}{2} \times \tfrac{3}{2} = \tfrac{15}{4} = 3\tfrac{3}{4}$$

At this juncture we can establish a rule for the case of fraction $\times$ fraction:

$$\frac{\text{numerator} \times \text{numerator}}{\text{denominator} \times \text{denominator}}$$

All cases of multiplication involving fractions can be reduced to this one easy rule.

The authors recommend that each of the six basic types of multiplication of rational numbers presented in this section be taught so that children thoroughly understand the processes. In so doing children should be taught to use a variety of approaches and eventually to discover the one easy rule stated in the last paragraph.

One aspect of the multiplication of rational numbers which has been poorly taught by some teachers is "cancellation." Long, difficult examples have been used and children have been encouraged to complete work which was not meaningful to them.

In this example:

$$\frac{3}{4} \times \frac{6}{9} = \frac{\overset{1}{\cancel{3}}}{\underset{2}{\cancel{4}}} \times \frac{\overset{\overset{1}{\cancel{3}}}{\cancel{6}}}{\underset{\underset{1}{\cancel{3}}}{\cancel{9}}} = \frac{1 \times 1}{2 \times 1} = \frac{1}{2}$$

Children must be directed to discover that the bar (—) in each fraction can be extended thus,

$$\frac{3}{4} \times \frac{6}{9} = \frac{3 \times 6}{4 \times 9}.$$

Then they must recall (work with equivalent fractions) that the value of a fraction is unchanged when both numerator and denominator are divided by the same number. Using $\dfrac{3 \times \square}{\square \times 9}$, one can rename the fraction as $\frac{1}{3}$ (each term $\div$ 3). Then $\dfrac{\square \times 6}{4 \times \square}$ can be renamed $\frac{3}{2}$ (each term $\div$ 2). Then

$$\frac{1 \times \overset{1}{\cancel{3}}}{2 \times \underset{1}{\cancel{3}}} \text{ (each term } \div \text{ 3)} = \frac{1 \times 1}{2 \times 1} = \frac{1}{2}$$

Fractions can be renamed (reduced) before the multiplication operation proceeds. This simplifies the operation.

8.9 Division of Rational Numbers

Several basic concepts involved in the division process with whole numbers may be used as a model for presenting and understanding division of rational numbers. The measurement and partition concepts are particularly applicable to division of rational numbers. Inverse processes, used to rationalize the division algorithm, likewise apply to division of rational numbers. These include repeated subtractions as another way of taking apart and division as the inverse of multiplication. Each of these concepts will be discussed in connection with the six cases of division of rational numbers which follow:

1. Integer divided by a fraction
2. Fraction divided by an integer
3. Fraction divided by a fraction
4. Integer divided by a mixed number
5. Mixed number divided by an integer
6. Mixed number divided by a mixed number

Each of these cases will now be discussed as ordered.

INTEGER DIVIDED BY A FRACTION

The language of measurement will be used to introduce the division of an integer by a fraction. Let us first consider a social situation requiring this type of operation. For example:

Lynn wishes to share an apple pie with her five friends so that each will have one-sixth of the pie. How many sixths will there be in the one pie?

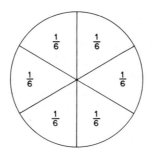

Using a diagram of a cir-
cle and the language of
measurement, we can an-
swer the question.

There are six one-
sixth pieces in the
pie.

The story problem and diagram of a circle will help children understand why the quotient of $1 \div \frac{1}{6}$ is 6, a number much larger than the dividend. Then with the use of fraction kits, pupils will discover the meaning of six equal parts or six congruent regions.

This particular case can be extended by using a common denominator approach to the division of fractional numbers. The number sentence would be $1 \div \frac{1}{6} = \frac{6}{6} \div \frac{1}{6}$. The standard expression for division could also be used:

$$\frac{6}{\frac{1}{6}\overline{)\frac{6}{6}}}$$
$$\frac{6}{6}$$

FRACTION DIVIDED BY AN INTEGER

Consider the example $\frac{1}{2} \div 4$. The divisor is 4, which is an integer. In this case the language of partition is used, while the language of measurement cannot be used. Thus, $\frac{1}{2} \div 4$ means: $\frac{1}{2}$ is divided into four equal parts; what is the size of each of the equal parts? This can be illustrated as shown.

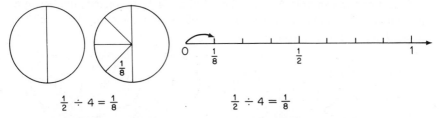

$$\frac{1}{2} \div 4 = \frac{1}{8} \qquad\qquad \frac{1}{2} \div 4 = \frac{1}{8}$$

The language of cutting pies is helpful here. That is, I have $\frac{1}{2}$ pie and wish to give each of four people an equal part; what part of a pie does each person get? In other words, $\frac{1}{2}$ of a pie is to be divided into four equal parts; what is the size of each of the equal parts? The answer is $\frac{1}{8}$. That is, each of the four persons will receive $\frac{1}{8}$ of a pie, and this will use the entire half of a pie.

Observe that the language of measurement cannot be used here. Thus, $\frac{1}{2} \div 4$ cannot be interpreted as: how many fours are there in $\frac{1}{2}$? There are not any fours in $\frac{1}{2}$.

FRACTION DIVIDED BY A FRACTION

Division of a fraction by a fraction will be a difficult learning experience for children unless the subject is carefully introduced. Situations in which this case of division usually occur involve measurement. For example, I have one-half of a pie and wish to give one-eighth of the pie to each person; how many individuals can I serve? Using a picture of one-half pie,

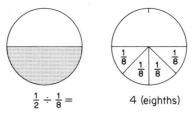

$$\frac{1}{2} \div \frac{1}{8} = \qquad 4 \text{ (eighths)}$$

we can divide the one-half into eighths as shown. There are four one-eighths in the one-half pie.

Using a ruler or a number line, we can show the division as illustrated here.

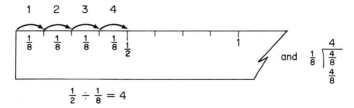

$$\frac{1}{2} \div \frac{1}{8} = 4$$

INTEGER DIVIDED BY A MIXED NUMBER

Consider the example $6 \div 1\frac{1}{2}$. The divisor is $1\frac{1}{2}$, a mixed number. The measurement concept of division should be used: How many $1\frac{1}{2}$'s are there in 6? The work is illustrated here.

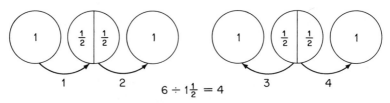

$$6 \div 1\frac{1}{2} = 4$$

The division can also be shown using a ruler.

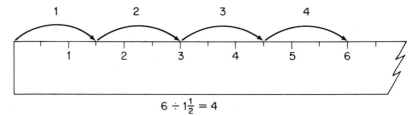

$$6 \div 1\frac{1}{2} = 4$$

By actual count there are four $1\frac{1}{2}$'s in 6. The language of partition cannot be used.

An alternative explanation is to change $1\frac{1}{2}$ to an improper fraction, $\frac{3}{2}$, and ask: How many $\frac{3}{2}$'s are there in 6?

MIXED NUMBER DIVIDED BY AN INTEGER

Consider the example $4\frac{1}{2} \div 2$. The divisor is 2, which is an integer. Either the language of partition or the language of measurement can be used. Using the language of partition: $4\frac{1}{2}$ is divided into two equal parts; what is the size of each of the equal parts? This can be illustrated as shown.

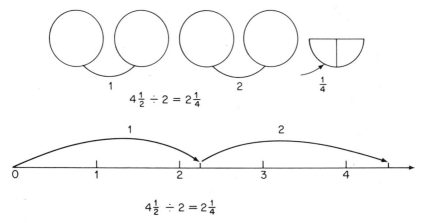

$$4\frac{1}{2} \div 2 = 2\frac{1}{4}$$

$$4\frac{1}{2} \div 2 = 2\frac{1}{4}$$

An alternative method is to change $4\frac{1}{2}$ to an improper fraction. Then: $4\frac{1}{2} \div 2 = \frac{9}{2} \div 2$. Divide $\frac{9}{2}$ into 2 equal parts; what is the size of each part?

MIXED NUMBER DIVIDED BY A MIXED NUMBER

Consider the example $4\frac{1}{2} \div 2\frac{1}{4}$. The divisor is $2\frac{1}{4}$, which is a mixed number. Using the language of measurement, how many times is $2\frac{1}{4}$ contained in $4\frac{1}{2}$?

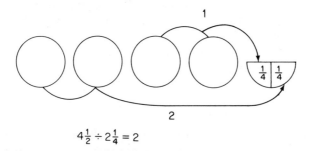

$$4\frac{1}{2} \div 2\frac{1}{4} = 2$$

An alternative method is to change $2\frac{1}{4}$ to an improper fraction. Then: $4\frac{1}{2} \div 2\frac{1}{4} = 4\frac{1}{2} \div \frac{9}{4}$. How many times is $\frac{9}{4}$ contained in $4\frac{1}{2}$?

All six cases can be consolidated to fit the case:

$$\text{fraction} \div \text{fraction.}$$

$$6 \div \tfrac{1}{2} = \tfrac{6}{1} \div \tfrac{1}{2}, \qquad\qquad 6 \div 1\tfrac{1}{2} = \tfrac{6}{1} \div \tfrac{3}{2}$$
$$\tfrac{1}{2} \div 4 = \tfrac{1}{2} \div \tfrac{4}{1}, \qquad\qquad 4\tfrac{1}{2} \div 2 = \tfrac{9}{2} \div \tfrac{2}{1}$$
$$\tfrac{1}{2} \div \tfrac{1}{8} = \tfrac{1}{2} \div \tfrac{1}{8}, \qquad\qquad 4\tfrac{1}{2} \div 2\tfrac{1}{4} = \tfrac{9}{2} \div \tfrac{9}{4}$$

After these conversions have been made, the rule can be given: invert the divisor and multiply. Thus:

$$6 \div \tfrac{1}{2} = \tfrac{6}{1} \div \tfrac{1}{2} = \tfrac{6}{1} \times \tfrac{2}{1} = \tfrac{12}{1} = 12$$
$$\tfrac{1}{2} \div 4 = \tfrac{1}{2} \div \tfrac{4}{1} = \tfrac{1}{2} \times \tfrac{1}{4} = \tfrac{1}{8}$$
$$\tfrac{1}{2} \div \tfrac{1}{8} = \tfrac{1}{2} \times \tfrac{8}{1} = \tfrac{8}{2} = 4$$
$$6 \div 1\tfrac{1}{2} = \tfrac{6}{1} \div \tfrac{3}{2} = \tfrac{6}{1} \times \tfrac{2}{3} = \tfrac{12}{3} = 4$$
$$4\tfrac{1}{2} \div 2 = \tfrac{9}{2} \div \tfrac{2}{1} = \tfrac{9}{2} \times \tfrac{1}{2} = \tfrac{9}{4} = 2\tfrac{1}{4}$$
$$4\tfrac{1}{2} \div 2\tfrac{1}{4} = \tfrac{9}{2} \div \tfrac{9}{4} = \tfrac{9}{2} \times \tfrac{4}{9} = \tfrac{36}{18} = 2$$

The operation of division has been defined to be the inverse of the operation of multiplication.

To give meaning to this rule, consider the following argument: the example $3 \div \tfrac{1}{5}$ means: how many times is $\tfrac{1}{5}$ contained in 3? This can be illustrated as shown.

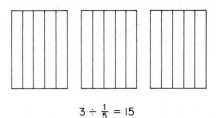

$$3 \div \tfrac{1}{5} = 15$$

Each unit contains 5 fifths, so 3 units contain 3×5 fifths $= 15$ fifths. So:

$$3 \div \tfrac{1}{5} = 3 \times \tfrac{5}{1} = \tfrac{3}{1} \times \tfrac{5}{1} = 15$$

Now consider $3 \div \tfrac{2}{5}$. The divisor is $\tfrac{2}{5}$, which is twice as large as $\tfrac{1}{5}$, so 2 will be contained in 3 only $\tfrac{1}{2}$ as many times as $\tfrac{1}{5}$ is contained in 3. Thus:

$$3 \div \tfrac{2}{5} = \tfrac{3}{1} \times \tfrac{5}{2} = \tfrac{15}{2} = 7\tfrac{1}{2}$$

To find how many times $\tfrac{1}{5}$ is contained in 3, simply multiply 3×5 or $3 \times \tfrac{5}{1}$. To find how many times $\tfrac{2}{5}$ is contained in 3, simply multiply 3×5 and then divide by 2, or:

$$3 \times \tfrac{5}{2} = \tfrac{15}{2} = 7\tfrac{1}{2}$$

This idea can be extended:

$$3 \div \tfrac{3}{5} = 3 \times \tfrac{5}{3} = \tfrac{15}{3} = 5$$

and so on. When teaching by this rule, one should stress the importance of inverting the *divisor*.

Some of the examples in division can be explained in other ways. Thus, $3 \div \tfrac{1}{2}$ can be explained by successive subtraction: how many times can $\tfrac{1}{2}$ be subtracted from 3, successively? In this case: $3 - \tfrac{1}{2} = 2\tfrac{1}{2} - \tfrac{1}{2} = 2$, and so on. By actual count $\tfrac{1}{2}$ can be subtracted 6 times from 3, successively, so

$3 \div \frac{1}{2} = 6$. Not all examples can be explained in this way. For instance, $\frac{7}{2} \div \frac{2}{6}$ could not be explained as successive subtraction.

Also, to explain the rule "invert the divisor and multiply" we can appeal to algebra:

$$a \div \frac{b}{c} = \frac{a}{\dfrac{b}{c}} = \frac{a \times \dfrac{c}{b}}{\dfrac{b}{c} \times \dfrac{c}{b}} = \frac{a \times \dfrac{c}{b}}{1} = a \times \frac{c}{b}$$

Substituting numbers:

$$6 \div 1\tfrac{1}{2} = \frac{6}{\frac{3}{2}} = \frac{6 \times \frac{2}{3}}{\frac{3}{2} \times \frac{2}{3}} = 6 \times \tfrac{2}{3} = 4$$

8.10   Problems Involving Fractions

Many problems in measurement involve fractions.

Example 1. What is the total of $\frac{1}{2}$ gallon and $\frac{1}{4}$ gallon?

Solution.

$$\tfrac{1}{2} \text{ gal.} + \tfrac{1}{4} \text{ gal.} = \tfrac{2}{4} \text{ gal.} + \tfrac{1}{4} \text{ gal.} = \tfrac{3}{4} \text{ gal.}$$

Example 2. Find the perimeter of a rectangle that is $6\frac{3}{4}$ inches long and $2\frac{1}{2}$ inches wide.

Solution.

$$6\tfrac{3}{4} + 2\tfrac{1}{2} + 6\tfrac{3}{4} + 2\tfrac{1}{2} = 6\tfrac{3}{4} + 2\tfrac{2}{4} + 6\tfrac{3}{4} + 2\tfrac{2}{4} = 16\tfrac{10}{4} = 18\tfrac{2}{4} =$$
$$18\tfrac{1}{2} \text{ perimeter in inches}$$

Alternate solution.

$$6\tfrac{3}{4} \text{ in.} + 2\tfrac{1}{2} \text{ in.} = 6\tfrac{3}{4} \text{ in.} + 2\tfrac{2}{4} \text{ in.} = 8\tfrac{5}{4} \text{ in.} = 9\tfrac{1}{4} \text{ in.}$$

$$2 \times 9\tfrac{1}{4} \text{ in.} = \frac{\overset{1}{\cancel{2}}}{1} \times \frac{37}{\underset{2}{\cancel{4}}} = \frac{37}{2} \text{ in.} = 18\tfrac{1}{2} \text{ in.}$$

Alternate solution.

$$P = 2L + 2W$$
$$= 2(6\tfrac{3}{4}) + 2(2\tfrac{1}{2})$$
$$= 2(\tfrac{27}{4}) + 2(\tfrac{5}{2})$$
$$= \tfrac{27}{2} + 5$$
$$= 13\tfrac{1}{2} + 5$$
$$= 18\tfrac{1}{2} \text{ perimeter in inches}$$

Many of these applications involve direct use of the four fundamental processes of addition, subtraction, multiplication, and division.

Three types of problems involving fractions occur so often that they deserve special, organized consideration.

1. Finding a part of a number.
2. Finding what part one number is of another number.
3. Finding a number when a specified part of it is given.

These will be discussed in order.

1. Find $\frac{2}{3}$ of $12.

    Multiplication is indicated here.

$$\tfrac{2}{3} \times \$12 = \tfrac{2}{3} \times \frac{\$12}{1} = \$8$$

This is called finding a part of a number.

2. A baseball team played 150 games and won 100 of them. What part of its games did it win?

This is finding what part one number is of another number.

$$\tfrac{100}{150} = \tfrac{2}{3}$$

The team won $\frac{2}{3}$ of its games. To check this result, multiply $\frac{2}{3} \times 150$. The result is 100, so the answer is correct. Notice that the concept of a fraction as as indicated division and as a ratio is involved here.

3. A baseball team won $\frac{3}{4}$ of its games. If it won 60 games, how many games did it play?

This is finding a number when a specified part of it is given. In this example $\frac{3}{4}$ of the desired number is 60, and the question is: "What is the number?" There are two ways to solve this: We can reason as follows:

$$\tfrac{3}{4} \times ? = 60$$

Therefore, 60 is the product of two numbers, $\frac{3}{4}$ is one of the numbers, and it is desired to find the other number. Division is the inverse of multiplication, so:

$$60 \div \tfrac{3}{4} = \frac{\overset{20}{\cancel{60}}}{1} \times \frac{4}{\underset{1}{\cancel{3}}} = 80$$

The team played 80 games. To check this result,

$$\tfrac{3}{4} \times 80 = \frac{3}{\underset{1}{\cancel{4}}} \times \frac{\overset{20}{\cancel{80}}}{1} = 60$$

so the result is correct.

This method of solving this problem is similar to the algebraic method:

$$\tfrac{3}{4}x = 60$$

Divide both members of this equation by $\frac{3}{4}$:

$$\frac{\frac{3}{4}x}{\frac{3}{4}} = \frac{60}{\frac{3}{4}}$$

$$x = \frac{60}{\frac{3}{4}} = \frac{\overset{20}{\cancel{60}}}{1} \times \frac{4}{\underset{1}{\cancel{3}}} = 80$$

Another method of solving this problem is called the unit analysis method:

$\frac{3}{4}$ of the number $= 60$

$\frac{1}{4}$ of the number $= 60 \div 3 = 20$

$\frac{4}{4}$ of the number $= 20 \times 4 = 80$

In this method we proceed from $\frac{3}{4}$ of the number to $\frac{1}{4}$ of the number to $\frac{4}{4}$ of the number, and $\frac{4}{4}$ of the number is the number.

Both the division method and the unit analysis method are taught in elementary school.

Of these three types, the third type is hardest to teach. The same three types occur later in decimals, as shown in the following:

1. Find .3 of 50.
2. What decimal part of 100 is 25?
3. If .14 of a number is 200, what is the number?

The same three types occur still later in per cent:

1. Find 6% of $800.
2. 30 is what per cent of 120?
3. If 4% of a number is 20, what is the number?

These three types of problems occur so frequently that it is wise to stress them in connection with fractions, both for their own sake and because they arise again in connection with decimals and per cent.

8.11 Scale Drawings

A scale drawing furnishes opportunities for work with fractions. Children are asked to make a scale drawing of the basic floor plans of their homes. To do this they must measure the dimensions of the rooms, and then make a drawing to a predetermined scale.

House plans are often made to a scale of $\frac{1}{4}''$ = 1'. For drawings in elementary school a scale of $1'' = 12'$ is more appropriate. After measuring the rooms, the pupils must convert the measurements to the scale used in their drawings. This requires the liberal use of fractions. Sometimes the plan is drawn on graph paper of four squares to the inch. Then intermediate dimensions can be read from the graph paper.

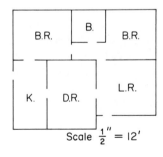

Scale drawings can be made for areas that have simple rectangular shapes, such as basketball courts, tennis courts, and football fields. A football field, for example, is 100 yards long and 145 feet wide. To a scale of $1'' = 40'$ how long and how wide should the scale drawing be?

8.12   Chapter Summary

An intuitive approach was used to introduce the teaching of fractions in the elementary school. Concrete objects, models, and pictures were suggested for building children's concepts of fractions and for performing basic operations with fractions.

The numbers shown by fractions are called *rational numbers*. They are abstract mathematical ideas like the counting numbers. Fractions are the numerals—the names for rational numbers.

The meaning of a fraction was extended to include ordering (points on a number line) and the order relation between pairs of its members ($\frac{1}{4} < \frac{2}{3}$). The common meanings of fractions (such as ordered pair, part of a unit, part of a set, a division, a ratio) were presented.

Congruent regions in a plane and the unit fraction concept were used to introduce addition and subtraction of rational numbers. The properties established for addition on whole numbers were applied to addition on rational numbers. Then subtraction was shown as the inverse of addition. An order for presenting the teaching of fractions to children was presented.

The system of whole numbers was also used as a model in discussing multiplication of rational numbers. Six basic types of cases were considered, and suggestions were given for helping children understand each case. Finally, after basic concepts were established and understood, the six cases were consolidated into one case: fraction $\times$ fraction.

Basic concepts involved in the division process with whole numbers were used as a model for presenting and understanding division of rational numbers. The measurement and partition concepts are particularly applicable to division of rational numbers. Inverse processes, used to rationalize the division algorithm, were applied to division of rational numbers. Six cases of division of rational numbers were presented, and methods for presenting each case to children were given. Then all six cases were consolidated to fit the case: fraction $\div$ fraction.

The chapter was concluded with a set of practical problems involving the use of fractions. Solutions and alternate solutions were given for each problem. Finally, fractions were applied to scale drawings.

QUESTIONS AND EXERCISES

1. Make a list of the five meanings of a fraction and show examples of each.
2. Read the following statements. Then make an example for each to show if the statement is true or false.
   (a) When the numerator of a fraction is not changed, multiplying the denominator by a number multiplies the fraction by that number.

(b) A number may be added to the numerator and denominator of a fraction without changing the value of the fraction.

(c) When several fractions have the same numerator, the fraction with the largest denominator is the largest.

(d) The numerator and denominator of a fraction may be divided by the same number without changing the value of the fraction.

(e) The same number may be subtracted from the numerator and denominator of a fraction without changing its value.

3. Illustrate with a line drawing, rectangle, or circle that:

(a) $\frac{4}{8} = \frac{1}{2}$ (b) $\frac{3}{4} = \frac{9}{12}$ (c) $\frac{1}{2} + \frac{1}{4} = \frac{3}{4}$ (d) $\frac{2}{3} = \frac{6}{9}$ (e) $\frac{2}{3} = \frac{12}{18}$

4. Agree or disagree with this statement: "All sums should be expressed in lowest terms" (addition of fractions). Use an example or story problem to prove your choice of answers.

5. Work these problems and identify the skills required for their computation.

(a)

$\frac{2}{5}$	$3\frac{1}{3}$	$2\frac{1}{2}$	$\frac{1}{3}$	$2\frac{2}{4}$	$3\frac{1}{2}$
$+\frac{2}{5}$	$+2\frac{1}{3}$	$+3\frac{1}{2}$	$+\frac{1}{6}$	$+2\frac{1}{2}$	$+4\frac{2}{3}$

(b)

$\frac{3}{5}$	$4\frac{1}{2}$	$3\frac{1}{4}$	$\frac{1}{2}$	$4\frac{1}{4}$	$3\frac{1}{2}$
$-\frac{2}{5}$	$-2\frac{1}{2}$	-1	$-\frac{1}{4}$	$-2\frac{7}{8}$	$-1\frac{2}{3}$

6. Use the product method to tell whether the fractions are equivalent. The first example is done.

(a) $\frac{4 \times 12}{6 \times 18}$ (b) $\frac{1}{2} \quad \frac{7}{14}$ (c) $\frac{3}{3} \quad \frac{6}{6}$ (d) $\frac{6}{9} \quad \frac{8}{12}$ (e) $\frac{12}{10} \quad \frac{6}{5}$ (f) $\frac{0}{4} \quad \frac{0}{1}$

7. Name the reciprocals of the following numbers:

(a) $\frac{5}{2}$ (b) $\frac{4}{5}$ (c) 3 (d) $\frac{3}{5}$ (e) 5 (f) $\frac{2}{3}$

8. Use a rectangle or circle drawing to show solutions for the examples.

(a) $2 \times \frac{3}{4}$ (b) $\frac{1}{2} \times \frac{1}{4}$ (c) $\frac{2}{3} \times 9$ (d) $\frac{1}{2} \times 1\frac{1}{2}$

9. Work the examples. Then list the skills and concepts pupils should learn in order to understand the solutions.

(a) $3 \times \frac{1}{8}$ (b) $\frac{1}{4} \times 2$ (c) $1\frac{1}{2} \times \frac{3}{4}$ (d) $4 \times \frac{3}{4}$ (e) $\frac{1}{2} \times \frac{1}{3}$

10. A man put 1 gallon of antifreeze into the radiator of his car and 3 gallons of water. What part of the mixture is water? What part is antifreeze?

11. There are six types of examples involved in multiplication of fractions. Identify each type and make an illustration for each.

12. How would you show the relationship between common fractions and decimals?

13. Use a flannel board to show the solution of these problems without inversion.

(a) $\frac{6}{8} \div 2$ (b) $\frac{3}{6} \div 3$ (c) $\frac{1}{2} \div \frac{1}{8}$ (d) $2 \div \frac{1}{4}$

14. Write these examples in equation form.

(a) 3 is what part of 4?

(b) 1 is what part of 3?

(c) What part of $\frac{3}{4}$ is $\frac{1}{4}$?

(d) What part of a foot is 3 inches?

15. Find the number when:

(a) $\frac{1}{2}$ of the number is 16.

(b) $\frac{3}{4}$ of the number is 8.

(c) $\frac{1}{8}$ of the number is 4.

(d) $\frac{1}{3}$ of the number is 12.

16. The library was open for three hours each day. If each person was on duty for $\frac{1}{2}$ hour, how many people would be needed each day?

17. The girls in Miss Jones' room had a long piece of material $\frac{2}{3}$ of a yard wide, from which they wanted to make sashes $\frac{1}{6}$ of a yard wide. How many sashes could they make?

18. Mother found she could make $2\frac{1}{2}$ recipes of candy from $\frac{3}{4}$ pound of butter. How much butter did each recipe use?

19. The teacher has 6 science books. Each child will read half of a book. How many children will it take to read all six books?

20. Use line drawings to show the solutions to these examples:

(a) $1 \div \frac{1}{6}$ (b) $2\frac{1}{2} \div \frac{3}{4}$ (c) $2 \div \frac{1}{8}$ (d) $\frac{2}{3} \div \frac{1}{6}$

SELECTED REFERENCES

Capps, Lelon R., "Division of Fractions," *The Arithmetic Teacher*, IX (January, 1962), 10–16.

Crumley, Richard D., "Teaching Rate and Ratio in the Middle Grades," *School Science and Mathematics*, LX (January, 1960), 143–50.

Heddens, James W., and Michael Hynes, "Division of Fractional Numbers," *The Arithmetic Teacher*, XVI (February, 1969), 99–103.

Gunderson, Ethel, and Agnes Gunderson, "Fraction Concepts Held by Young Children," *The Arithmetic Teacher*, IV (October, 1957), 168–73.

Johnson, John T., "Decimal versus Common Fractions," *The Arithmetic Teacher*, III (November, 1956), 201–3.

Mueller, Francis J., "On the Fraction as a Numeral," *The Arithmetic Teacher*, VIII (May, 1961), 234–38.

Riess, Anita P., "New Approach to the Teaching of Fractions in the Intermediate Grades," *School Science and Mathematics*, LXIV (February, 1964), 111–19.

Stephens, Lois, and Wilbur H. Dutton, "Retention of the Skill of Division of Fractions," *The Arithmetic Teacher*, VII (January, 1960), 28–31.

Trimble, H. C., "Fractions Are Ratios Too," *The Elementary School Journal*, XLIX (January, 1949), 285–90.

Vance, Irvin E., "A Natural Way to Teach Division of Rational Numbers," *The Arithmetic Teacher*, XVI (February, 1969) 91–93.

Van Engen, Henry, "Rate Pairs, Fractions, and Rational Numbers," *The Arithmetic Teacher*, VII (December, 1960), 389–99.

9

Rational Numbers
Expressed as Decimals

9.1 Meaning of Decimals

Rational numbers may be expressed as fractions or as decimals. The numerals $\frac{1}{2}$ and 0.5 are different ways to express the same rational number. You may have been taught to say "common fraction" for $\frac{1}{2}$ and "decimal fraction" for 0.5. The decimal notation is simply a useful notation for fractions whose denominators are powers of ten. Thus:

$$\frac{3}{10} = .3 \qquad \frac{3}{100} = .03 \qquad \frac{3}{1000} = .003$$

The decimal notation is a logical extension of the concept of place value developed with whole numbers for our base ten numeration system. Study the chart at the top of p. 196 which shows place values for whole numbers and decimals.

Note the double line in the chart. This shows the *decimal point* separating the places whose value is ones or greater (left of the point) from those whose value is tenths or smaller (right of the point). In France, Germany, Italy, and the Scandinavian countries a comma is used in decimal fractions instead of the point, as in 5,20 in place of 5.20. In England the point is placed midway between the top and bottom of the number, as in 25·25.

Algebraic exponent notation for decimals and whole numbers has been shown on the top line of the chart. Either $(\frac{1}{10})^1$, $(\frac{1}{10})^2$, or 10^{-1}, 10^{-2} may be used to show the decimal values.

Pupils should be taught the meaning of a decimal fraction by using several

10^5	10^4	10^3	10^2	10^1	10^0	$(\frac{1}{10})^1$	$(\frac{1}{10})^2$	$(\frac{1}{10})^3$	$(\frac{1}{10})^4$	$(\frac{1}{10})^5$
100,000	10,000	1000	100	10	1	$\frac{1}{10}$	$\frac{1}{100}$	$\frac{1}{1000}$	$\frac{1}{10,000}$	$\frac{1}{100,000}$
Hundred–thousands	Ten–thousands	Thousands	Hundreds	Tens	Ones	Tenths	Hundredths	Thousandths	Ten–thousandths	Hundred–thousandths
100,000	10,000	1000	100	10	1	0.1	0.01	0.001	0.0001	0.00001

teaching aids, each extending their depth of understanding. Three aids are suggested: (1) a ruler marked off in tenths, (2) line drawings, and (3) a place-value chart. Each of these will be discussed briefly.

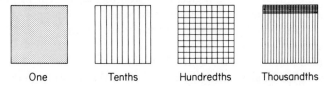

The ruler shows each inch marked off into ten tenths. This work can be related to the type of number line shown here.

By using the ruler, children should discover that while tenths would be convenient and accurate for some measurement, hundredths or thousandths would be required for scientific measurement. This exploration could lead to the discussion of measuring instruments (discussed in Chapter 6) used to measure thousands or ten-thousandths.

Line drawings or charts should be used to show rectangular regions marked off into tenths, hundredths, and thousandths.

One   Tenths   Hundredths   Thousandths

Pupils can dicover that *one whole rectangular region* can be lined to show tenths, hundredths, and thousandths. Each fractional part can be identified as $\frac{1}{10}$ or .1, $\frac{1}{100}$ or .01, and $\frac{1}{1000}$ or .001. Zeros are used as place holders, similar to work with whole numbers. Place values can be shown with the use of a place-value chart.

The chart shows three slips of paper in the hundredths column and two bundles of ten slips each in the tenths column. Ten hundredths = one tenth, so the tenths column shows two bundles of ten slips each, representing 2

ONES	TENTHS	HUNDREDTHS
	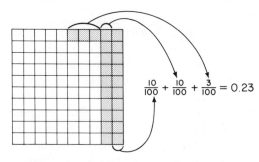	
		= 0.23

tenths or 20 hundredths. Using the line drawing to show the same amount, one would have a representation as illustrated here.

$$\frac{10}{100} + \frac{10}{100} + \frac{3}{100} = 0.23$$

Children should identify some of the decimal fractions used in daily living: odometer in an automobile, weather reports (rainfall in inches), averages for baseball or basketball teams, interest rates, United States money, diameter of wire, thickness of metals, and many uses in scientific measurement. Gradually, they should develop an appreciation of the usefulness and the accuracy which decimal fractions provide.

The basic idea of decimal notation was formulated about the year 1600. Credit for this discovery is usually divided between Simon Stevin of Belgium and John Napier of Scotland.

9.2 Reading and Writing Decimal Fractions

Beginning work in reading and writing decimal fractions should be based upon some model which relates decimals to whole numbers, fractions, and our place-value system. For example, 2.5 may be recorded as illustrated here.

SEE	THINK	WRITE	SAY
1 1 0·5 ⊘⊘▽ ½	2 ones and 5 tenths	2.5	two and five tenths

In this situation, we should encourage pupils to make a connection with whole numbers and fractional parts of a whole number. Then the thought process, the abstract form, and correct vocabulary are stressed.

Gradually we extend the pupils' understanding of place value to the right of the one's place. Each time a digit is moved one place to the right of the decimal point, the value of the digit is divided by 10. Thus .5 to .05 ($\frac{5}{10} \div 10$ = $\frac{5}{10} \times \frac{1}{10} = \frac{5}{100}$), and .05 to .005 ($\frac{5}{100} \div 10 = \frac{5}{100} \times \frac{1}{10} = \frac{5}{1000}$).

.5	or	$\frac{5}{10}$
.05	or	$\frac{5}{100}$
.005	or	$\frac{5}{1000}$
.0005	or	$\frac{5}{10000}$

Beginning with .5, each succeeding decimal fraction named is 10 times smaller than the preceding fraction.

To read a number such as .0250, start with the decimal point and move to the right in order to identify the place values and size of the fraction. Thus, the denominator is ten-thousands $\overline{10,000}$ and the numerator is (read as a whole number) $\underline{250}$. The decimal fraction is read two hundred fifty ten-thousandths $\frac{250}{10,000}$. This procedure is especially helpful in reading a decimal fraction such as .200. By saying tenths, hundredths, thousandths, one arrives at the name thousandths. The number is read two hundred thousandths ($\frac{200}{1000}$). Some pupils may try to read the decimal as two tenths, using an equivalent form. Decimal fractions are read as they are written unless an equivalent form is called for or a rounding off procedure established. How would you read the number 4.0025? Start with 4 *and* (the "and" is reserved for the decimal point).

Tenths	Hundredths	Thousandths	Ten-thousandths
0	2	5	0

Differences exist between the decimals .25 and .250. While .25 is equivalent to .250, there are situations where .250 ≠ .25. If a measurement is given as .25 inch, this may mean that the measurement is correct to the nearest hundredth of an inch. If .250 inch were used, the measurement may mean correct to the nearest thousandth of an inch. Then .250 is a more precise measurement than .25.

A complex decimal is a combination of a decimal and a common fraction, such as .04$\frac{1}{2}$, which is read four and one-half hundredths. Note that the $\frac{1}{2}$ in this example means half of a hundredth. Since the $\frac{1}{2}$ follows the 4 it might be erroneously construed to be in the thousandths place. Actually, it is supposed to be in the hundredths place, but that place is already occupied by the 4, so the $\frac{1}{2}$ must be written as shown.

A mixed decimal is a combination of an integer and a decimal fraction, such as 4.25. Using expanded notation, $4.25 = 4 + \frac{2}{10} + \frac{5}{100} = 4 + \frac{20}{100} + \frac{5}{100} = 4\frac{25}{100}$. Read 4.25 as "four *point* two five" or "four *and* twenty-five hundredths."

9.3 Addition of Decimals

Addition of decimal fractions follows the procedures used in adding fractions and whole numbers. The properties established for fractions in the last chapter hold for addition with decimals.
Thus:

$$.5 + .4 = .4 + .5 \qquad \text{Commutative property}$$
$$(.6 + .3) + .2 = (.2 + .3) + .6 \qquad \text{Associative property}$$
$$.7 + 0 = 0 + .7 = .7 \qquad \text{Identity element}$$

As in the work with fractions, begin the addition algorithm by adding decimals with the same denominator. Thus:

In fractions we add $\frac{1}{2}$

$$\frac{\frac{1}{2}}{\frac{2}{2} = 1}$$

In decimals we add   .5

$$\frac{.5}{1.0}$$

Then, $.5 + .7 = 1.2$ or $\begin{array}{r} .5 \\ .7 \\ \hline 1.2 \end{array}$, relating to fractions $\frac{5}{10} + \frac{7}{10} = \frac{12}{10} = 1\frac{2}{10}$ when needed. Extending the process to include mixed decimals, we have examples such as these:

	1	1
1.2	1.5	10.2
+ 1.3	4.6	15.4
2.5	6.1	6.5
		32.1

The steps are essentially the same as those used in addition of fractions. The child must think $\frac{2}{10} + \frac{3}{10} = \frac{5}{10}$, $\frac{5}{10} + \frac{6}{10} = \frac{11}{10}$, and $\frac{2}{10} + \frac{4}{10} + \frac{5}{10} = \frac{11}{10}$, carrying a whole number in each of the last two examples.

Extending the work to include hundredths and thousandths should not be difficult if presented first with like denominators and then with unlike denominators. Add examples like these,

	1	1	1
.21	.25	1.25	4.26
.32	.50	4.55	6.32
.33	.35	3.15	7.54
.86	1.10	8.95	18.12

	1	11	1
Then: .114	.322	.415	1.14
.211	.136	.382	3.62
.123	.414	.645	3.15
.448	.872	1.442	7.91

$$
\begin{array}{cc}
1 & 1\,1 \\
1.46 & 6.16 \\
4.31 & 4.14 \\
\underline{4.72} & \underline{5.93} \\
10.49 & 16.23
\end{array}
$$

Finally combine unlike denominators or decimals expressed in different units, such as: .5 + .25 + .425. Pupils must understand place values to the right of the decimal point and must be able to recognize .5 as $\frac{5}{10}$, .25 as $\frac{25}{100}$, and .425 as $\frac{425}{1000}$. With these prerequisite understandings they can recognize the necessity for establishing a common denominator.

$$
\begin{array}{ccc}
\frac{5}{10} & \frac{500}{1000} & .500 \\[4pt]
\frac{25}{100} & \frac{250}{1000} \quad \text{then} & .250 \\[4pt]
\frac{425}{1000} & \frac{425}{1000} & .425 \\[4pt]
& \frac{1175}{1000} = 1\frac{175}{1000} & 1.175
\end{array}
$$

Later, with maturity and experience, the pupils can use a short cut:

$$
\begin{array}{r}
.5 \\
.25 \\
\underline{.425} \\
1.175
\end{array}
$$

They are able to align the decimal fractions in proper place values without writing in the zeros. Teaching children to "keep the decimal points in a straight line," while helpful, is not a meaningful way to present decimals expressed in different units.

In business operations and in measurement procedures, we do not usually add decimals with different units. Workers are told to use hundredths, thousandths, or other specific units. This type of work requires accuracy expressed as specific units obtained by writing decimals consistently as hundredths or thousandths and rounding off to meet the required accuracy. However, standardized tests, arithmetic textbooks, and examinations used for a variety of civil services include working with decimal fractions expressed in different units. Teachers, therefore, must provide meaningful practice for this aspect of decimal fractions.

9.4 Subtraction of Decimals

Subtraction, an inverse process, would be presented along with the addition algorithm. When pupils add decimals with the same denominator (.5 + .4 = .9), they should then be able to subtract .5 − .4 = .1 or

$$
\begin{array}{r}
.5 \\
-\,.4 \\
\hline
.1
\end{array}
$$

traction process is then extended to include hundredths, thousandths, and ten-thousandths without regrouping:

$$
\begin{array}{r}
.45 \\
-\,.15 \\
\hline
.30
\end{array}
\qquad
\begin{array}{r}
.625 \\
-\,.414 \\
\hline
.211
\end{array}
\qquad
\begin{array}{r}
.4132 \\
-\,.2121 \\
\hline
.2011
\end{array}
$$

Regrouping in subtraction of decimals is practically the same as the process used with whole numbers except that place values are different (parts of a whole expressed in tenths, hundredths, and so forth). With the use of a place-value chart or a hundredths board, pupils should demonstrate their understanding of regrouping, first in the tenths place and then in the hundredths and thousandths places. For example, $.40 - .15 = .25$ is illustrated here.

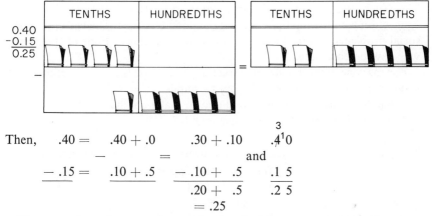

Then,

$$
\begin{array}{l}
.40 = \quad .40 + .0 \qquad .30 + .10 \qquad .\overset{3}{4}{}^{1}0 \\
\quad - \qquad\qquad\qquad = \qquad\qquad \text{and} \\
-\,.15 = \quad .10 + .5 \quad -\,.10 + .5 \qquad .1\ 5 \\
\hline
\qquad\qquad\qquad\qquad\quad .20 + .5 \qquad .2\ 5 \\
\qquad\qquad\qquad\qquad = .25
\end{array}
$$

The extension of regrouping to the hundredths or ten-thousandths place would follow the same general model shown above. For example:

$$
\begin{array}{l}
.426 \qquad .400 + .20 + .6 \qquad .300 + .120 + .6 \\
\quad = \quad - \qquad\qquad\qquad = \quad - \\
.234 \qquad .200 + .30 + .4 \qquad .200 + .30 \ + .4 \\
\hline
.192 \qquad\qquad\qquad\qquad\quad .100 + .90 \ + .2 = .192
\end{array}
$$

Relating new work with decimals to known work with fractions may help some pupils understand the new step quickly. Thus:

$$
\begin{array}{l}
\tfrac{6}{10} \qquad\qquad .6 \qquad\qquad 4\tfrac{2}{4} \qquad\qquad 4.50 \quad (\tfrac{2}{4} = .50) \\
\ - \qquad \text{so} \qquad\quad \text{or} \qquad\qquad \text{so} \\
\tfrac{3}{10} \qquad\qquad -.3 \qquad\quad -2\tfrac{1}{4} \qquad\quad -2.25 \quad (\tfrac{1}{4} = .25) \\
\hline
\tfrac{3}{10} \qquad\qquad .3 \qquad\qquad 2\tfrac{1}{4} \qquad\qquad 2.25
\end{array}
$$

Then regrouping with a whole number, the work might include:

$$
\begin{array}{l}
\qquad\qquad 2\tfrac{5}{4} \qquad\qquad\qquad 2 \\
3\tfrac{1}{4} = \quad \cancel{3}\tfrac{1}{4} \quad \text{so} \quad 3.25 = \cancel{3}.{}^{1}25 \\
-1\tfrac{2}{4} \quad -1\tfrac{2}{4} \qquad\quad -1.50 \qquad 1.50 \\
\hline
\qquad\qquad 1\tfrac{3}{4} \qquad\qquad\qquad\quad 1.75
\end{array}
$$

9.5   Multiplication of Decimals

Instruction pertaining to multiplication of decimals should begin with the identification of the main cases involving the use of decimals. These are:

1. Integer × decimal fraction
2. Decimal fraction × integer
3. Decimal fraction × decimal fraction
4. Integer × mixed decimal
5. Mixed decimal × integer
6. Mixed decimal × mixed decimal

Then each case can be studied in relation to skills and concepts learned in connection with the multiplication of common fractions. The use of practical social problems to introduce each case is recommended. Four of these cases will now be considered.

For case one, integer × decimal fraction, we can use the concept of measurement to make the work meaningful to pupils.

If one-half yard of ribbon is required to make one headband, how much ribbon would be needed for four headbands?

$$4 \times \tfrac{1}{2} \text{ or } 4 \times .5 = 2.0 \text{ (yards of ribbon)}$$

Then with the approach used in multiplication of fractions we can think:

What is 4 × 5 apples?
What is 4 × 5 tenths?
What is $4 \times \tfrac{5}{10}$?
What is 4 × .5?

Repeated additions could also be used, thus:

$$\tfrac{1}{2} \text{ yd.} + \tfrac{1}{2} \text{ yd.} + \tfrac{1}{2} \text{ yd.} + \tfrac{1}{2} \text{ yd.} = 2 \text{ yds.}$$
and $.5 + .5 + .5 + .5 = 2.0$ (yds.)

The second case, decimal fraction × integer, should be introduced by reviewing the same procedures used to teach common fractions. For example $\tfrac{1}{2} \times 6$ is interpreted as:

First divide the 6 into two sets.   Then take one of the sets.

The product is three. $\dfrac{1}{\underset{1}{\cancel{2}}} \times \overset{3}{\cancel{6}} \times \dfrac{1 \times 3}{1} = 3$

To continue: $\dfrac{\overset{1}{\cancel{5}}}{\underset{\underset{1}{\cancel{2}}}{\cancel{10}}} \times \overset{3}{\cancel{6}} = \dfrac{1 \times 3}{1} = 3$

$.5 \times 6 = 3.0$

Placing the decimal point in the correct place in the product must be established in a meaningful way. Children can discover that:

$$2 \times .3 \quad = .6$$
$$.2 \times .3 \quad = \tfrac{2}{10} \times \tfrac{3}{10} = \tfrac{6}{100} = .06$$
$$.2 \times .03 \quad = \tfrac{2}{10} \times \tfrac{3}{100} = \tfrac{6}{1000} = .006$$
$$.02 \times .03 = \tfrac{2}{100} \times \tfrac{3}{100} = \tfrac{6}{10000} = .0006$$

Thus:

Units $\times$ tenths = tenths = .6
Tenths $\times$ tenths = hundredths = .06
Tenths $\times$ hundredths = thousandths = .006
Hundredths $\times$ hundredths = ten-thousandths = .0006

At this juncture, or perhaps after the other two cases are developed, children should be able to discover a rule to assist them in placing the decimal point in the product.

There are as many places of decimals in the product as in the sum of the number of places of decimals in the two factors (multiplier and multiplicand).

Thus in the example:

$$
\begin{array}{r}
1.5 \\
\times\ 3.2 \\
\hline
3\,0 \\
4\,5 \\
\hline
4.8\,0
\end{array}
$$

There is one place in each factor, so $1 + 1 = 2$. Count two places in the product and place the decimal point 4.80. Discuss starting from the right and counting to the left in placing the decimal point. All six cases can be brought under this one rule.

The third case, decimal fraction $\times$ decimal fraction is difficult to introduce to pupils. However, using a word problem involving some practical aspect of measurement will prove helpful.

Suppose we have one-fourth cup of sugar needed for a bread recipe and we wish to make only one-half of the recipe. How much sugar would be needed?

$$\tfrac{1}{2} \text{ of } \tfrac{1}{4} \quad \text{or } \tfrac{1}{2} \times \tfrac{1}{4} = \tfrac{1}{8} \text{ (cup)}$$

Then:

$$\frac{5}{10} \times \frac{25}{100} = \frac{\overset{1}{\cancel{50}}}{\underset{4}{\cancel{100}}} \times \frac{\overset{1}{\cancel{25}}}{\underset{2}{\cancel{100}}} = \frac{1 \times 1}{4 \times 2} = \frac{1}{8}$$

Finally, for the case of mixed decimal $\times$ mixed decimal, we will encounter difficulty writing a word problem to cover the case. Perhaps we would need six and one-half lengths of cloth, each length being one and one-half yards long. How much material would we need?

$$6\tfrac{1}{2} \times 1\tfrac{1}{2} = 6.5 \times 1.5 = 9.75 \text{ (yds.)}$$

Consider rationalizing the last example using the distributive principle of multiplication.

Thus: $(6.5) \times (1.5) = (6 + .5)(1 + .5)$
$= (6 \times 1) + (6 \times .5) + (.5 \times 1) + (.5 \times .5)$
$= 6 + 3.0 + .5 + .25$
$= 9.75$

9.6 Division of Decimals

Division with decimals may be meaningfully presented by comparing the work to that presented with common fractions. As in common fractions, there are six cases.

1. Integer ÷ decimal fraction
2. Decimal fraction ÷ integer
3. Decimal fraction ÷ decimal fraction
4. Integer ÷ mixed number
5. Mixed number ÷ an integer
6. Mixed number ÷ mixed number

$$
\begin{array}{r}
1.0 \\
- .2 \\
\hline
.8 \\
- .2 \\
\hline
.6 \\
- .2 \\
\hline
.4 \\
- .2 \\
\hline
.2 \\
- .2 \\
\hline
0
\end{array}
$$

Consider the example, 1 divided by .2. Using the language of measurement: how many times is .2 contained in 1? Using subtraction we see that .2 can be subtracted from 1 a total of 5 times. There are five .2 contained in one.

For the case decimal fraction divided by decimal fraction (.8 ÷ .2), a number line may be used to illustrate the process.

$$
.2\overline{)\,.8} \atop \begin{array}{r} 4 \\ \underline{8} \\ 0 \end{array}
$$

From the drawing, pupils discover that $.8 \div .2 = 4$. This example has been explained by using the language of measurement.

Consider now the case of a decimal fraction divided by an integer: $0.6 \div 2$. The language of partition will be used. Divide .6 into 2 equal parts. What is the size of each of the equal parts?

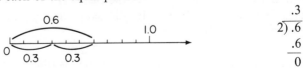

$$
2\overline{)\,.6} \atop \begin{array}{r} .3 \\ \underline{.6} \\ 0 \end{array}
$$

Each part will be 0.3.

Continuing the work on this example by relating to multiplication, we find that:

$$.6 \div 2 = \frac{6}{10} \div \frac{2}{1} = \frac{6}{10} \times \frac{\overset{3}{\cancel{1}}}{\underset{1}{\cancel{2}}} = \frac{3}{10} \text{ or } .3$$

Another explanation which should contribute to pupils' understanding of division of a decimal fraction by an integer involves the use of United States money. If an individual has $40.80 and wishes to divide it equally among eight persons, how much will each receive? The thought process is that of partition.

$$\begin{array}{r} 5.10 \\ 8\overline{)\$40.80} \\ 40 \\ \hline 8 \\ 8 \\ \hline 0 \\ 0 \\ \hline \end{array}$$

Division of a decimal fraction by a decimal fraction requires further discussion. Consider: $.4\overline{)8.4}$ or $\frac{8.4}{.4}$. A fundamental principle of fractions is that the numerator and denominator of a fraction can be multiplied by the same number without changing the value of the fraction. So we choose to make the divisor an integer. To do this, .4 must be multiplied by 10; then $10 \times .4 = 4.0 = 4$. If the divisor is multiplied by 10, then the dividend must be multiplied by 10: $8.4 \times 10 = 84$.

Combining both steps we get:

$$\frac{8.4}{.4} = \frac{8.4 \times 10}{.4 \times 10} = \frac{840}{4.0} = \frac{84}{4}$$

Then using the standard algorithm:

$$\begin{array}{r} 21 \\ 4\overline{)84} \\ 8 \\ \hline 4 \\ 4 \\ \hline 0 \end{array}$$

The same result can be obtained by using the rule:

Move the decimal point in the divisor to the right to make the divisor an integer. Move the decimal point in the dividend the same number of places to the right. Then proceed with the division.

This rule provides for multiplying both divisor and dividend by the same *power of ten*. Since a division example can be expressed in fraction form, this is equivalent to multiplying numerator and denominator by the same number. This procedure does not change the value of the fraction.

The moving of the decimal point can be shown in various ways, and then the example can be rewritten:

$$.4\overline{)8.4} \longrightarrow 4\overline{)84} \quad \text{and} \quad .4\overline{)8.4}, \quad 4\overline{)84}$$

Other examples are: $.37\overline{)42.6} \longrightarrow 37\overline{)4260}$ and $.023\overline{)0.0625} \longrightarrow 23\overline{)62.5}$ Note that in one example $(.37\overline{)42.6}\,)$ the divisor and dividend were multiplied by 100. In the other example $(.023\overline{)0.625}\,)$ divisor and dividend were multiplied by 1,000.

The same examples can be written as:

$$\frac{42.6}{.37} = \frac{42.6 \times 100}{.37 \times 100} = \frac{4260}{37} = 37\overline{)4260}$$

and

$$\frac{.0625}{.023} = \frac{.0625 \times 1000}{.023 \times 1000} = \frac{62.5}{23} = 23\overline{)62.5}$$

Dividing an integer by a mixed number occurs in measurement problems. For example:

An individual has 6′ of rope, and desires to cut the rope into 1.5′ pieces. How many pieces of rope can be secured?

$6' \div 1.5' = 1.5\overline{)6.0}.$ The quotient is 4. There are 4 one and one-half foot pieces of rope in the six-foot piece. Using common fractions the example may be written $6 \div 1\frac{5}{10}$.

Then, $6 \div 1\frac{5}{10} = 6 \div \frac{15}{10} = \overset{2}{\cancel{6}} \times \frac{10}{\underset{5}{\cancel{15}}} = \frac{20}{5} = 4.$

Working with the fifth case, mixed number divided by an integer, a social problem can be used to help pupils rationalize the process. Suppose we have $20.80 and we wish to divide the money equally among four individuals. How much money will each person get?

$$\$20.80 \div 4 = 4\overline{)\$20.80}$$

$$\begin{array}{r} \$5.20 \\ 4\overline{)\$20.80} \\ \underline{20} \\ 8 \\ \underline{8} \\ 0 \\ \underline{0} \end{array}$$

Note that the decimal point does not have to be changed in the dividend and is placed in the hundredths position in the quotient.

The sixth case, mixed number divided by a mixed number, is difficult to rationalize. Consider the situation where an individual has $40.80 and wishes give each person $5.10. How many individuals will receive this amount? Dividing, we see that eight will each receive $5.10. Again we can write the example as common fraction, $40\frac{80}{100} \div 5\frac{10}{100}$.

$$\begin{array}{r} 8 \\ 5.10\overline{)\$40.80} \\ \underline{40.80} \end{array}$$

Then, $40\frac{80}{100} \div 5\frac{10}{100} = \frac{4080}{100} \div \frac{510}{100} = \frac{\overset{1}{\cancel{4080}}}{\cancel{100}} \times \frac{\overset{1}{\cancel{100}}}{\cancel{510}} = \frac{408}{51} = 8$

Sometimes a quotient is desired to a predetermined precision. Consider the example:

Find the quotient $\frac{32.65}{1.2}$ to the nearest hundredth:

$$32.65 \div 1.2 = 1.2\overline{)32.6\,50}$$

$$
\begin{array}{r}
2\,7.20 \\
\hline
24 \\
\hline
86 \\
84 \\
\hline
25 \\
24 \\
\hline
10 \\
\end{array}
$$

Since the remainder is 10, more than half of the divisor of 12, the quotient is expressed to the nearest hundredth as 27.21.

9.7 Changing Decimals to Fractions and Changing Fractions to Decimals

Two kinds of reduction are taught in connection with decimal fractions:
1. Changing a decimal fraction to an equivalent common fraction.
2. Changing a common fraction to an equivalent decimal fraction.

DECIMAL FRACTIONS TO COMMON FRACTIONS

Example 1. Change .25 to a common fraction in lowest terms.
Solution. $.25 = \frac{25}{100} = \frac{5}{20} = \frac{1}{4}$

Example 2. Change .375 to a common fraction in lowest terms.
Solution. $.375 = \frac{375}{1000} = \frac{75}{200} = \frac{15}{40} = \frac{3}{8}$

Example 3. Change .0625 to a common fraction in lowest terms.

Solution. $.0625 = \frac{625}{10000} = \frac{125}{2000} = \frac{25}{400} = \frac{5}{80} = \frac{1}{16}$

In the above examples, each decimal fraction was changed to a common fraction with a denominator that was a power of ten. Then the principle, divide both numerator and denominator by the same number, was applied.

Example 4. Change $.06\frac{1}{4}$ to a common fraction in lowest terms.
First solution. $.06\frac{1}{4} = .0625 = \frac{625}{1000} = \frac{1}{16}$

Second solution. $.06\frac{1}{4} = \frac{6\frac{1}{4}}{100} = \frac{6\frac{1}{4} \times 4}{100 \times 4} = \frac{25}{100} = \frac{1}{16}$

Both numerator and denominator are multiplied by 4, in order to make the numerator an integer. Then the reduction is completed.

COMMON FRACTIONS TO DECIMAL FRACTIONS

To change a common fraction to a decimal fraction, divide the numerator by the denominator. This illustrates the meaning of a common fraction as an indicated division.

Example 1. Change $\frac{1}{4}$ to a decimal fraction.

Solution. $\frac{1}{4} = .25$

$$\begin{array}{r} .25 \\ 4\overline{)1.00} \\ \underline{8} \\ 20 \\ \underline{20} \\ 0 \end{array}$$

Example 2. Change $\frac{3}{16}$ to a decimal fraction.

Solution.

$$\begin{array}{r} .1875 \\ 16\overline{)3.0000} \\ \underline{1\ 6} \\ 1\ 40 \\ \underline{1\ 28} \\ 120 \\ \underline{112} \\ 80 \\ \underline{80} \\ 0 \end{array}$$

Example 3. Change $\frac{1}{7}$ to a decimal fraction.

Solution.

$$\begin{array}{r} .142857 \\ 7\overline{)1.000000} \\ \underline{7} \\ 30 \\ \underline{28} \\ 20 \\ \underline{14} \\ 60 \\ \underline{56} \\ 40 \\ \underline{35} \\ 50 \\ \underline{49} \\ 1 \end{array}$$

In this example, the quotient repeats:

$$\tfrac{1}{7} = .142857142857142857\ldots$$

When a common fraction is expressed in decimal form, one of two things happens: it either terminates or it repeats. Thus, $\frac{3}{8} = 0.375$; in this case it terminates. Or: $\frac{1}{3} = 0.333\ldots$ and $\frac{1}{7} = 0.142857\ldots$. In these cases they repeat. The fraction $\frac{1}{3}$ can be written:

$$.3\tfrac{1}{3}, \quad .33\tfrac{1}{3}, \quad .333\tfrac{1}{3}, \quad .3333\tfrac{1}{3}$$

or:

$$.3\ldots, \quad .33\ldots, \quad .333\ldots$$

where the dots indicate repetition of the preceding digits. Also, $\frac{1}{7}$ can be written: $.142857\tfrac{1}{7}$ or $.142857\ldots$.

An interesting project for pupils studying decimals is the following. Change fractions of the form $\frac{1}{n}$, where n is a prime number, to decimal form. (Note: a prime number is a number greater than 1 that is divisible by itself and 1, and by no other number.)

Thus:

$$\frac{1}{7} = .142857\ldots$$
$$\frac{1}{17} = .0588235294117647\ldots$$

Here $\frac{1}{7}$ repeats after 6 places, and $\frac{1}{17}$ repeats after 16 places. One might conclude that $\frac{1}{n}$ repeats after $n - 1$ places, where n is a prime number. However:

$$\frac{1}{13} = .076923\ldots$$

which repeats after 6 places, so it is not true that $\frac{1}{n}$ repeats after $n - 1$ places. Consider $\frac{1}{13}$. Here $n - 1 = 12$, and $\frac{1}{13}$ repeats after 6 places, and 6 is a factor of 12.

It can be shown that $\frac{1}{n}$ repeats after $n - 1$ places, or after a factor of $n - 1$ places, where n is a prime number.

It is interesting, then, to change:

$$\tfrac{1}{2}, \ \tfrac{1}{5}, \ \tfrac{1}{7}, \ \tfrac{1}{9}, \ \tfrac{1}{11}, \ \tfrac{1}{13}, \ \tfrac{1}{17}, \ \tfrac{1}{19}, \ \tfrac{1}{23}, \cdots$$

to decimal form and test this theorem. Exercises such as this encourage the pupil to look for patterns, which is an activity that is both desirable and valuable.

9.8 Scientific Notation

In algebra the exponent notation affords a brief method of writing certain products. Thus:

$$10^2 = 10 \times 10 = 100$$
$$10^3 = 10 \times 10 \times 10 = 1000$$

This notation can be extended:

$$10^1 = 10 \qquad\qquad 10^6 = 1,000,000$$
$$10^2 = 100 \qquad\qquad\qquad \cdot$$
$$10^3 = 1,000 \qquad\qquad\qquad \cdot$$
$$10^4 = 10,000 \qquad\qquad\qquad \cdot$$
$$10^5 = 100,000 \qquad\quad 10^{10} = 10,000,000,000$$

and so on. Notice the pattern. We see that 10^2 is equal to 1 followed by 2 zeros, 10^3 is 1 followed by 3 zeros, 10^4 is 1 followed by 4 zeros, and so on.

Thus, 10^{23} is 1 followed by 23 zeros. This notation is useful in writing certain kinds of large numbers in abbreviated form. Thus:

$$93,000,000 = 93 \times 1,000,000 = 93 \times 10^6$$
$$5,000,000,000 = 5 \times 1,000,000,000 = 5 \times 10^9$$

It is customary to express the integral part of such an expression as a units digit. Thus, 93,000,000 can be written 93×10^6, but a preferable form is 9.3×10^7. This amounts to dividing 93 by 10 and multiplying 10^6 by 10. Some examples are:

$$112,000,000 = 1.12 \times 10^8$$
$$231,400,000 = 2.314 \times 10^8$$

Notice the pattern. A rule can be formulated as follows:

If an arrow is placed where we wish the decimal point to be, we can count all digits to the right of this position to determine the exponent of 10.

For example:

$$8,120,000,000,000 = 8,120,000,000,000$$
$$= 8.12 \times 10^{12}$$

This is called scientific notation. Notice particularly that 5,000,000 can be written in this way, 5×10^6, but 5,000,001 cannot be written in this way. The single digit 1 at the end of 5,000,001 precludes the use of this notation; the number must terminate in a zero.

Junior high students find the slide rule both a useful tool and a means of enlarging their mathematical understandings. San Carlos school district, California; Project PLAN classrooms, Brittan Acres.

This notation can be extended from large numbers to small numbers. Observe the following pattern:

$$10^4 = 10,000$$
$$10^3 = 1000$$
$$10^2 = 100$$
$$10^1 = 10$$
$$10^0 = 1$$
$$10^{-1} = \tfrac{1}{10} = .1$$
$$10^{-2} = \tfrac{1}{10^2} = \tfrac{1}{100} = .01$$
$$10^{-3} = \tfrac{1}{10^3} = \tfrac{1}{1000} = .001$$
$$10^{-4} = \tfrac{1}{10^4} = \tfrac{1}{10,000} = .0001$$

To express a small number in the scientific notation, place an arrow where it is desired that the decimal point shall be, and count all digits to the left up to the decimal point to find the negative exponent that is to be used for 10. Some examples will illustrate the idea:

$$.0023 = .0023 = 2.3 \times 10^{-3}$$

$$.00023 = .00023 = 2.3 \times 10^{-4}$$

$$.000023 = .000023 = 2.3 \times 10^{-5}$$

$$.00000000235 = .00000000235 = 2.35 \times 10^{-9}$$

Very large numbers and very small numbers occur quite often in science. The number of molecules in one liter of any gas at certain standard conditions of temperature and pressure is 6.04×10^{23}, which in the ordinary notation would be written:

$$604,000,000,000,000,000,000,000$$

Also, two spherical particles, each 1 gram, with centers 1 centimeter apart, attract each other with a force of 6.66×10^{-8} dyne, which in the ordinary notation would be written .0000000666. Observe that the discussion of the scientific notation is related to the ideas of base 10 and place value.

One of the authors asked a graduate student, who is working toward his Ph.D. in Electrical Engineering, to describe the vacuum system he uses for work with thin-plate coating for transistors. Using one "torr" of pressure = 1 mm of mercury (Hg), his vacuum system will pump to a pressure of 10^{-9} torr = .000000001 mm Hg!

In scientific work it is customary to place a zero to the left of the decimal point in a number such as 0.06. This number is ordinarily written .06 in elementary school arithmetic.

9.9 Problems Involving Decimals

As in the case of common fractions three types of problems involving decimal fractions occur frequently. They are:

1. Finding a decimal part of a number.
2. Finding what decimal part one number is of another number.
3. Finding a number when a specified decimal part of it is given.

Example 1. Find .3 of 240.
Solution.

$$.3 \times 240 = 72.0 = 72$$

Example 2. What decimal part of 240 is 72?
Solution.

$$\frac{72}{240} = .3$$

Example 3. If .3 of a number is 72, what is the number?
First solution.

$$.3 \times ? = 72$$
$$\frac{72}{.3} = 240$$

Second solution.

$$.3 \text{ of the number} = 72$$
$$.1 \text{ of the number} = \frac{72}{3} = 24$$
$$1.0 \text{ of the number} = 10 \times 24 = 240$$

These same three types will occur again, in connection with per cent.
Decimal fractions may occur in finding averages.

Example 4. Find the average, correct to the nearest tenth:

$$36.2, \ 14.8, \ 27.9, \ 33.5, \ 29.2, \ 31.6$$

Solution.

$$\frac{36.2 + 14.8 + 27.9 + 33.5 + 29.2 + 31.6}{6} = \frac{173.3}{6}$$
$$= 28.87$$
$$= 28.9 \text{ correct to the nearest tenth.}$$

Decimal fractions may occur in the measurements of areas of rectangles and volumes of boxes.

Example 5. Find the area of a rectangular metal plate that is 8.62 inches long and 2.03 inches wide, correct to the nearest hundredth of a square inch.
Solution. $A = lw$

$$
\begin{array}{r}
8.62 \\
\times\ 2.03 \\
\hline
2586 \\
1724 \\
\hline
17.4986
\end{array}
$$

The area, correct to the nearest hundredth of a square inch, is 17.50 square inches.

Example 6. Find the volume of a box that is 21.3 inches long, 17.8 inches wide, and 6.9 inches deep, correct to the nearest tenth of a cubic inch.

Solution.

$$V = lwh$$
$$V = 21.3 \times 17.8 \times 6.9 = 2616.066$$

The volume, correct to the nearest tenth of a cubic inch, is 2616.1 cubic inches.

Decimal fractions occur, of course, in problems involving money.

Example 7. An electronics assembler earns $2.78 per hour. How much will he earn in a 40-hour week?

Solution.

$$40 \times \$2.78 = \$111.20, \text{ his earnings in a 40-hour week.}$$

9.10   Chapter Summary

Rational numbers may be expressed as fractions or as decimal fractions—fractions whose denominators are powers of ten.

Since decimal notation is a logical extension of the concept of place value developed with whole numbers for our base ten numeration system, basic principles and postulates developed with whole numbers have been applied to decimals. Place-value charts, number lines, and line drawings have been used to show how basic concepts may be taught with understanding.

The four fundamental operations used with decimals have been related to the same operations used with common fractions. By so doing, we relate the new work to familiar work with fractions and provide numerous opportunities to discover relationships and to enlarge concepts.

Emphasis was placed upon meaningful placement of the decimal point in addition and subtraction of decimals. This involved working with decimals having the same denominators and specifying the intended size of denominators.

In multiplication of decimals, stress was placed upon rationalizing the placement of the decimal in the product, rather than routine counting of decimal places in both factors.

A variety of examples involving the division of decimals was presented. The movement of the decimal point in numerator and denominator was compared to similar work involved with common fractions (multiplying numerator and denominator by the same number).

Numerous practical applications of work with decimals and word problems were used throughout the chapter to show the importance of motivating pupils' work and to encourage pupil discovery of meaningful uses for decimals.

QUESTIONS AND EXERCISES

1. Write each example as a decimal fraction.
   (a) One hundred three and forty-six hundredths.
   (b) Two hundred four ten-thousandths.
   (c) Thirty-three thousandths.
2. What is the perimeter of a rectangle with $L = 2.5''$ and $W = 1.75''$?
3. Write examples of two complex decimals.
4. Mark the statements T (true) or F (false) and justify your answer for each.
   (T) (F) In 550.15, the 5 on the far left is located in a place that has a place value 1000 times that of the 5 on the right.
   (T) (F) One hundred and twenty-two thousandths and one hundred twenty-two thousandths are expressions of the same number.
   (T) (F) The numeral .825 is often written as 0.825 in technical work.
   (T) (F) The decimal fraction 0.125 may be interpreted as 125 compared to 1000.
5. Explain placing the decimal point in the product for each example:

   (a) $\begin{array}{r} .15 \\ \times\ .5 \\ \hline .075 \end{array}$ (b) $\begin{array}{r} .15 \\ \times\ .25 \\ \hline 75 \\ 30 \\ \hline .0375 \end{array}$ (c) $\begin{array}{r} .125 \\ \times\ .12 \\ \hline 250 \\ 125 \\ \hline .01500 \end{array}$

6. Write two examples showing how the language of partition and the language of measurement may be used in division with decimals.
7. Rationalize moving the decimal point in this example: $.4\overline{)8.4}$
8. Work the following examples and identify the type or case:
   (a) Find .3 of 24.
   (b) What decimal part of 250 is 50?
   (c) If .3 of a number is 27, what is the number?
   (d) What is the average of these numbers to the nearest hundredth? 30.15, 42.61, 12.10, 14.35.
9. Round off to the nearest thousandth:
   (a) .7146   (b) 2.9996   (c) .0084   (d) 6.0047
10. Arrange the numbers in order of size, largest first: 2.15, 2.35, 2.36, 2.03, 2.348, 2.02.
11. State the fractions as decimals and the decimals as fractions.
    (a) $\frac{1}{2}$ (b) $\frac{1}{5}$ (c) $\frac{1}{8}$ (d) $\frac{3}{4}$ (e) $\frac{2}{3}$
    (f) $.33\frac{1}{3}$ (g) .40   (h) .25   (i) .55   (j) $.66\frac{2}{3}$
12. In the number 50.25, the 5 left of the decimal point is how many times the 5 to the right of the decimal point.
13. Place the decimal in the quotient without working the examples.
    (a) $.2\overline{)6.2}$ (b) $.6\overline{)5.48}$ (c) $.16\overline{).814}$ (d) $2.6\overline{)12.9}$
    (e) $.50\overline{)100.2}$ (f) $3.4\overline{).2140}$ (g) $1.6\overline{)64.}$ (h) $2.5\overline{)5}$

14. Arrange the following decimal fractions from smallest to largest: 4.4, 4.12, 4.49, 4.62, 4.78.

SELECTED REFERENCES

American Petroleum Institute, *Mathematics in the Petroleum Industry*. New York: The Institute, 1965, pp. 1–23.

Eicholz, Robert E., *et al.*, *School Mathematics I*. Reading, Mass.: Addison-Wesley Publishing Company, 1967, pp. 193–260.

Grossnickle, Foster E., *et al.*, *Discovering Meanings in Elementary School Mathematics*. San Francisco: Holt, Rinehart and Winston, Inc., 1968, pp. 270–90.

Holmes, Emma E., *Mathematics Instruction for Children*. Belmont, Calif.: Wadsworth Publishing Company, 1968, pp. 302–36.

Johnson, John T., "Decimal versus Common Fractions," *The Arithmetic Teacher*, III (November, 1956), 201–3.

Jones, Emily, "Historical Conflict—Decimal versus Vulgar Fractions," *The Arithmetic Teacher*, VIII (April, 1960), 184–88.

Marks, John L., *Teaching Elementary School Mathematics for Understanding*. New York: McGraw-Hill Book Company, 1965, Chap. X.

National Council of Teachers of Mathematics, *Topics in Mathematics*, *Twenty-ninth Yearbook*. Washington, D. C.: The Council, 1964, pp. 287–332.

Sauble, Irene, "Teaching Fractions, Decimals, and Per Cent: Practical Applications," *Arithmetic*, *1947*, Supplementary Education Monographs, No. 63. Chicago: University of Chicago Press, 1947, pp. 33–48.

Spitzer, Herbert F., *Teaching Elementary School Mathematics*. Boston: Houghton Mifflin Company, 1964, Chap. xvii.

Trueblood, Cecil R., "Promoting Problem-Solving Skills through Nonverbal Problems," *The Arithmetic Teacher*, XVI (January, 1969), 7ff.

Wilson, Patricia, *et al.*, "A Different Look at Decimal Fractions," *The Arithmetic Teacher*, XVI (February, 1969), 95–98.

10

Per Cent and Making Relative Comparisons

In the last chapter we stated that rational numbers may be expressed as fractions or as decimals. This chapter will present per cent (a subset of decimals or "decimal fractions") and the uses of per cent in making relative comparisons in business transactions and in selected areas of daily living.

10.1 Meaning of Per Cent

Per cent is derived from the Latin word *per centum*, which means "by the hundred." The term per cent means hundredths. The symbol % is derived from 0/0 which is a rearrangement of 100. Thus, 6% means 6 hundredths. The term is always used in connection with something, such as 6% of $2000, 6% of the population of a city, 6% of 324, or 6% of 400 square feet.

A per cent is a fraction whose denominator is 100:

$$6\% = \tfrac{6}{100}$$

Since $\tfrac{6}{100} = .06$, it follows that:

$$6\% = \tfrac{6}{100} = .06$$

so there are three ways of expressing six per cent.

The term 6% should not be taught as a new kind of number, since it is nothing more or less than $\tfrac{6}{100}$ or .06. However, it should be taught as a convenient and useful terminology. To say that an investment earns 6%

per year is a convenient and useful way of saying that each $100 will earn $6 in one year.

An important concept to teach is that 100% of any number equals the number. For example, 100% of 30 is 30, and 100% of 250 is 250. The per cents that cause the most difficulty in teaching are the small per cents, such as $\frac{1}{2}$% and $\frac{1}{4}$%, and the large per cents, such as 200% and 300%. The symbol $\frac{1}{2}$% means $\frac{1}{2}$ of 1%. The symbol 200% means 2 times 100%.

A good visual aid to use in introducing the concept of per cent is a hundredths board. This is a square divided into ten rows of ten squares each. The small squares can be turned over, their backs being of a different color from their fronts. The diagram illustrates 6%, or six hundredths.

6 % of 100

10.2 Ratio and Per Cent

In the chapter on rational numbers we showed that a fraction such as $\frac{1}{4}$ could be thought of as an ordered pair of numbers. Since per cent is a subset of rational numbers, per cent is also an ordered pair of numbers. So 5% is read 5 per cent and means 5 to 100. The ordered pair (5, 100) is interpreted as a ratio or relative comparison. Rate pair is another name for each ordered pair of a proportional relation.[1]

The language of ratio is useful in talking and thinking about rational numbers, including per cent. For example we can compare two sets by thinking of the ratio of the sets: 3 boys compared to 5 girls = 3 to 5 or 3: 5. Another example might be a baseball player's ratio of number of hits to times at bat: 3 to 4 = 3: 4.

Ratios can be compared in other ways. We can compare two basketball teams thus:

	Won	*Played*	*Ratio*
Team A	10	15	10: 15
Team B	12	16	12: 16

We can think (using familiar work with rational numbers) that team A won $\frac{10}{15}$ or $\frac{2}{3}$ of their games. Team B won $\frac{12}{16}$ or $\frac{3}{4}$ of their games. Then comparing the two teams, we say Team B has a better record than Team A because $\frac{3}{4} > \frac{2}{3}$. The ratio of 12 to 16 is greater than the ratio of 10 to 15. As we shall see later, these ratios can be expressed in per cents.

When two ratios are equal, such as 2: 4 = 1: 2, this is called a *proportion*.

[1] Rate pairs are ordered pairs used to solve rate and comparison problems. A name of a rate pair is a ratio. See *Seeing Through Mathematics, Book 1* (Chicago: Scott, Foresman & Company, 1962) p. 173.

A proportion has two middle numbers (means) and two end numbers (extremes).

$$2 : 4 = 1 : 2$$

means (inner), extremes (outer)

To check on their equality, the product of the means should be equal to the product of the extremes. Thus, $2 \cdot 2 = 4 \cdot 1$. Computing with ratio, then, may help pupils visualize sets and suggest alternative ways of reasoning. For example: The ratio of field goals scored in a basketball game to field goals attempted was $3 : 5$. There were 60 field goals attempted. How many field goals were scored?

If there are n shots, the ration of scored to attempted is $n : 60$, and using means $\times$ extremes, $n : 60 = 3 : 5$

$$5n = 3 \times 60$$
$$5n = 180$$
$$n = 36$$

Fractional notation may be used thus:

$n : 60 = 3 : 5$

$$\frac{n}{60} = \frac{3}{5}$$ Using cross-products rule

$$5n = 180$$
$$n = 36$$

To find per cent of the basket shooting, change $3 : 5$ to $\frac{3}{5}$ or 60%. The team made 60 per cent of their shots.

The solutions of per cent problems can be obtained by applying the proportion models just described. Before applying these models, however, we should present ways to use proportion in scale drawings and measurement.

10.3 Using Ratio and Proportion in Scale Drawing and Measurement

In order to make a line drawing or picture for a very large or a very small object, we use a scale. Study these examples:

1 : 100

1. A football field has been drawn so that $1'' = 100$ yds. What are the dimensions of the field?

2. The African Veldt (wart-hog) is drawn so that $1'' = 4'$. About how tall is the wild hog at the shoulders?

In order to find an answer for the questions given in each example an individual would have to estimate or use a ruler marked off into inches.

The language of ratio is also used to compare different units of measure, such as:

$$1 \text{ ft.} = 12 \text{ in.} \qquad 12:1$$
$$1 \text{ yd.} = 3 \text{ ft.} \qquad 3:1$$
$$1 \text{ hr.} = 60 \text{ min.} \qquad 60:1$$
$$1 \text{ day} = 24 \text{ hrs.} \qquad 24:1$$

In working examples such as these, one may wish to think in terms of ratio ideas or per cent. Returning to the drawing of the football field, we could ask question such as these:

1. What is the ratio of width to length?
2. How many lines (each 10 yds. apart) will be needed to mark off the playing area?
3. What per cent of the field has been lined?

Reductions, changing from per cent to decimal fractions or from decimal fractions to common fractions, must be taught so that pupils can use the kind of notation appropriate for their thought processes and for the problem being studied. We now turn to this aspect.

10.4 Reduction

Since 6%, $\frac{6}{100}$, and .06 are merely three ways of writing the same number, we need to teach how to:

1. Change a per cent to a decimal fraction.
2. Change a decimal fraction to a per cent.
3. Change a per cent to a common fraction.
4. Change a common fraction to a per cent.

These reductions will be discussed in this order.

1. To change a per cent to a decimal fraction, remove the per cent sign and move the decimal point two places to the left.

Some examples are:

$$8\% = .08$$
$$35\% = .35$$
$$100\% = 1.00$$
$$150\% = 1.50$$
$$1000\% = 10.00$$
$$\tfrac{1}{2}\% = .00\tfrac{1}{2} = .005$$
$$\tfrac{1}{4}\% = .00\tfrac{1}{4} = .0025$$
$$4\tfrac{1}{2}\% = .04\tfrac{1}{2} = .045$$

2. To change a decimal fraction to a per cent, move the decimal point two places to the right and annex a per cent sign.

Some examples are:

$$.07 = 7\%$$
$$.65 = 65\%$$
$$1.00 = 100\%$$
$$1.25 = 125\%$$
$$6.50 = 650\%$$
$$.005 = .5\% = \tfrac{1}{2}\%$$
$$.0075 = .75\% = \tfrac{3}{4}\%$$
$$.0475 = 4.75\% = 4\tfrac{3}{4}\%$$

This rule is the inverse of the previous rule.

3. To change a per cent to a common fraction, first change the per cent to a common fraction with a denominator of 100, and then reduce this common fraction if possible.

Some examples are:

$$8\% = \tfrac{8}{100} = \tfrac{2}{25}$$
$$50\% = \tfrac{50}{100} = \tfrac{1}{2}$$
$$62.5\% = \tfrac{62.5}{100} = \tfrac{625}{1000} = \tfrac{5}{8}$$
$$100\% = \tfrac{100}{100} = 1$$
$$200\% = \tfrac{200}{100} = 2$$
$$\tfrac{1}{2}\% = \frac{\tfrac{1}{2}}{100} = \frac{\tfrac{1}{2} \times 2}{100 \times 2} = \tfrac{1}{200}$$
$$\tfrac{1}{4}\% = \frac{\tfrac{1}{4}}{100} = \frac{\tfrac{1}{4} \times 4}{100 \times 4} = \tfrac{1}{400}$$

4. To change a common fraction to a per cent, first change the common fraction to a decimal fraction, and then change the decimal fraction to a per cent by rule 1 above.

Some examples are:

$$\tfrac{1}{2} = .5 \quad = 50\%$$
$$\tfrac{1}{3} = .33\tfrac{1}{3} \quad = 33\tfrac{1}{3}\%$$
$$\tfrac{3}{4} = .75 \quad = 75\%$$
$$\tfrac{1}{8} = .125 \quad = 12.5\% = 12\tfrac{1}{2}\%$$
$$\tfrac{5}{16} = .3125 = 31.25\%$$
$$1 = 1.00 \quad = 100\%$$
$$2 = 2.00 \quad = 200\%$$
$$1.5 = 1.50 = 150\%$$
$$\tfrac{1}{500} = .002 \quad = .2\% = \tfrac{1}{5}\%$$

10.5   Three Common Types of Problems

As in the case of common fractions and decimal fractions, the three commonly occurring types of problems in per cent are:

1. Finding a per cent of a number (Case 1).
2. Finding what per cent one number is of another (Case 2).
3. Finding a number when a specified part of it is given (Case 3).

Pupils should have ample background experiences, obtained while working similar problems with common fractions and with decimal fractions, to understand the three cases of per cent just enumerated. We will use the proportion models and a standard model to present examples and solutions for each case.

Example 1. Interest on a savings acount is 5% annually. What is the interest on $300?

Solution. (Find 5% of $300.)

by proportion: $5: 100 = n: \$300$
$$100n = 5 \times \$300$$
$$100n = \$1500$$
$$n = \$15$$

by fraction notation: $5: 100 = n: \$300$
$$\frac{5}{100} = \frac{n}{\$300}$$
$$100n = \$1500$$
$$n = \$15$$

by standard practice: The product of two numbers, .05 and $300, is desired.

$$5\% \times \$300 = .05 \times \$300 = \$15.00 = \$15$$

Example 2. If A earns $15 on an investment of $300, what is the per cent earned?

Solution. (What per cent of $300 is $15?)

by proportion: $n: 100 = \$15: \$300$
$$\$300n = \$15 \times 100$$
$$\$300n = \$1500$$
$$n = 5 = 5\%$$

by fraction notation: $\dfrac{n}{100} = \dfrac{\$15}{\$300}$
$$\$300n = \$1500$$
$$n = 5 = 5\%$$

by standard practice: This means what part of $300 is $15? Division is indicated:

$$\frac{\$15}{\$100} = \frac{5}{100} = 0.5 = 5\%$$

Example 3. If A receives $200 for selling a car, and $200 was 5% of the sale, what was the price of the car?

Solution. (Finding a number when a specified per cent is given.)

by proportion: $5: 100 = \$200: n$

$$5n = 100 \times \$200$$
$$5n = \$20,000$$
$$n = \$4,000$$

by fraction notation: $\dfrac{5}{100} = \dfrac{\$200}{n}$

$$5n = \$20,000$$
$$n = \$4,000$$

by standard practice: The product of two numbers is $200, and 5% is one of the numbers. What is the other number? Division is the inverse of multiplication.

$.05 \times$ a number $= \$200$

$$\text{the number} = \frac{\$200}{.05} = \frac{40\ 00}{.05)\overline{\$200.00}} = \$4,000$$

Alternate solution.

$$5\% \text{ of the number} = \$200$$
$$1\% \text{ of the number} = \$40$$
$$100\% \text{ of the number} = \$4000$$

(This is called the unit analysis method.)

Many kinds of problems involving the use of per cent do not come under the three types (cases) just presented. However, these three types occur so frequently in daily business practice that they deserve special study.

10.6   Commission

A salesman may sell merchandise on a commission basis. The commission is expressed as rate. For example, a salesman receives 5% of the retail price of all that he sells. If he sells $2,000 worth of merchandise he receives:

$$5\% \text{ of } \$2,000 = .05 \times \$2,000 = \$100$$

as his commission. The commission rate in this case is 5%. Using the language of per cent, 5% is the rate, $2,000 is the base, and $100 is the percentage. Then,

$$\text{rate} \times \text{base} = \text{percentage}$$

Using the proportion model:

$$5: 100 = n: \$2,000$$
$$100n = \$10,000$$
$$n = \$100$$

Three situations arise in selling on commission:

1. The commission is known, the value of goods sold is known, and the salesman's commission is required.
2. The value of goods sold is known, the salesman's commission in dollars is known, and his commission rate in per cent is required.
3. The salesman's commission rate is known, his commission in dollars is known, and the value of goods sold is required.

Observe that these three situations classify into Case 1, Case 2, and Case 3. The proportion, fraction, or standard models may be used to find solutions for each example. We will use only the standard methods to find solutions for the next four examples.

Example 1. A salesman's commission rate is 15%. He sells $20,000 worth of merchandise. How much does he receive?

Solution. $15\% \times \$20,000 = .15 \times \$20,000 = \$3,000$

Example 2. A salesman sells $30,000 worth of merchandise. He receives $3,000. What is his commission rate?

Solution. $\dfrac{3000}{30,000} = \dfrac{1}{10} = .1 = .10 = 10\%$

Example 3. A salesman's commission rate is 20%. He received $500 in the month of January. How much merchandise did he sell in January?

Solution. $20\% \times$ dollar value of goods sold $= \$500$

$$\frac{\$500}{.20} = \$2,500 \text{ of goods sold}$$

This solution uses the division method.

Alternate solution.

20% of the value of the goods sold $= \$500$
1% of the value of the goods sold $= \$25$
100% of the value of the goods sold $= \$2,500$

This is the unit analysis method.

Consider the following situation:

Example 4. An automobile salesman receives a 10% commission and a flat salary of $200 per month. How many automobiles must he sell per year, at $3,000 each, to make an average monthly salary of $900 per month?

Solution. He earns: $10\% \times \$3,000 = \$300$ per automobile. His flat salary is $200 per month, and he wishes to earn $900 per month, so he must earn:

$$\$900 - \$200 = \$700 \text{ per month on sales.}$$

He must sell:

$$\frac{700}{300} = 2\tfrac{1}{3} \text{ automobiles per month,}$$

or,

$$12 \times 2\tfrac{1}{3} = 28 \text{ automobiles per year.}$$

This problem can be solved in any one of several slightly different ways.

The solution given is typical. There are two reasons for considering problems such as this. One reason is that it is important for its own sake, but another reason is that it illustrates the fact that not all problems involving commission can be classified as simple one-step instances of Case 1, Case 2, or Case 3.

The following sections will illustrate many applications of per cent in financial transactions.

10.7 Discounts

A common application of per cent is found in situations involving discounts.

Example 1. A stero high-fidelity set sells for $800. A discount of 12% is allowed for cash. Find the cash price.

Solution. The discount is:
$$12\% \times \$800 = .12 \times \$800 = \$96.00$$
The case price is:
$$\$800 - \$96 = \$704$$

Alternate solution. Let 100% represent the usual retail price. The discount is 12%, so the cash price is:
$$100\% - 12\% = 88\% \text{ of the retail price.}$$
$$88\% \times \$800 = \$704$$

Example 2. A stereo high-fidelity set sells for $1,000. A cash discount of $150 is allowed. What is the per cent discount rate?

Solution. Per cent discount rate $= \dfrac{150}{1000} = \dfrac{15}{100} = 15\%$

Example 3. A stereo high-fidelity set sells for a cash discount rate of 10%. If the cash discount in dollars is $90, what is the usual retail selling price?

Solution. Selling price $= \dfrac{\$90}{.10} = \$900$

Alternate solution.
$$10\% \text{ of the selling price} = \$90$$
$$1\% \text{ of the selling price} = \$9$$
$$100\% \text{ of the selling price} = \$900$$

Notice that these three examples can be classified as Case 1, Case 2, and Case 3. Sometimes two (or more) successive discounts are allowed. The first discount may be one offered to all good customers, and the second discount may be for cash. For instance, a radio may retail for $50, and a discount of 5% may be allowed to motel chains that buy 100 or more of the radios. A further discount of 2% may be given for paying within 10 days. In this case, $5\% \times \$50 = \$2.50$. Then:
$$\$50 - \$2.50 = \$47.50$$
Finally:
$$2\% \times \$47.50 = \$.95$$
so:
$$\$47.50 - \$.95 = \$46.55, \text{ final cost of one radio.}$$

Notice that these discounts are taken successively. The first discount of 5%
is subtracted from the retail price before the second discount is taken.

Is it better for the purchaser to receive successive discounts of 5% and
2%, or a single discount of 5% + 2% = 7%? To answer this question,
consider the radio of the previous paragraph. Here:

$$7\% \times \$50 = \$3.50 \text{ and } \$50 - \$3.50 = \$46.50$$

which is less than $46.55, the price after two successive discounts. A little
thought will reveal why this is true. In the case of the single discount of 7%,
the entire discount is computed on the first price, $50, while in the case of the
two successive discounts the 5% discount is computed on this price, but
the second discount, 2%, is computed on a smaller value, so the total discount
is less.

Several kinds of problems arise in connection with successive discounts.
These will be illustrated by examples.

Example 1. A TV set sells for $500, less 10% for cash. Find the cash price.
  Solution. 10% × $500 = .10 × $500 = $50 discount
$$\$500 - \$50 = \$450 \text{ cash price}$$
  Alternate solution. 100% − 10% = 90%
$$90\% \times \$500 = .90 \times \$500 = \$450 \text{ cash price}$$

Example 2. A TV set sells for $400, less successive discounts of 10% fol-
lowed by 5%. Find the discount price.
  First solution.
$$10\% \times \$400 = .10 \times \$400 = \$40$$
$$\$400 - \$40 = \$360$$
$$5\% \times \$360 = .05 \times \$360 = \$18.00$$
$$\$360 - \$18 = \$342 \text{ discount price}$$
  Second solution.
$$100\% - 10\% = 90\%$$
$$90\% \times \$400 = .90 \times \$400 = \$360$$
$$100\% - 5\% = 95$$
$$95\% \times \$360 = .95 \times \$360 = \$342 \text{ discount price}$$
  Third solution.
$$100\% - 10\% = 90\%$$
$$100\% - 5\% = 95\%$$
$$90\% \times 95\% = .90 \times .95 = .8550 = 85.5\%$$
$$85.5\% \times \$400 = .855 \times \$400 = \$342 \text{ discount price}$$
The explanation here is that:
$$(\$400 \times .90) \times .95 = \$400 \times (.90 \times .95)$$
by the associative law for multiplication.

Example 3. Find the single discount equivalent to two successive discounts of 10% followed by 5%.

Solution. See the third solution of Example 2, above.

$100\% - 10\% = 90\%$

$100\% - 5\% = 95\%$

$90\% \times 95\% = .90 \times .95 = .855 = 85.5\%$

$100\% - 85.5\% = 14.5\%$ single discount equivalent to two successive discounts of 10% and 5%.

To verify this result:

$$14.5\% \times \$400 = .145 \times \$400 = \$58.00$$

$$\$400 - \$58 = \$342 \text{ discount price}$$

10.8 Taxes

A city or state sales tax is often stated as a per cent. The amount of the sales tax on small amounts of money is often printed on a card, for the convenience of sales persons in retail stores. On larger amounts of money the computation of sales tax requires the use of per cent by the sales persons.

Example 1. Compute the sales tax on an automobile that has a retail price of $2,865.95, if the sales rate is 4%.

Solution.

$4\% \times \$2,865.95 = .04 \times \$2,865.95 = \$114.64$ rounded off to nearest cent

Example 2. If the sales tax on a couch is $16, and if the retail price is $400 before adding the sales tax, find the sales tax rate.

Solution. $\dfrac{16}{400} = \dfrac{4}{100} = 4\%$

Example 3. If the sales tax on a refrigerator is $11.96, and if the sales tax rate is 4%, find the retail price of the refrigerator, before adding the sales tax.

Solution.

$$\frac{\$11.96}{.04} = \$299 \text{ retail price before tax}$$

Income taxes are based on per cent. A partial income tax table for a married taxpayer is shown.

MARRIED TAXPAYERS FILING JOINT RETURNS (1968)

Income over—	but not over—	Tax	of excess over—
$ 1,000	$ 2,000	$ 140, plus 15%	$ 1,000
2,000	3,000	290, plus 16%	2,000
3,000	4,000	450, plus 17%	3,000
4,000	8,000	620, plus 19%	4,000
8,000	12,000	1,380, plus 22%	8,000
12,000	16,000	2,260, plus 25%	12,000
16,000	20,000	3,260, plus 28%	16,000
20,000	24,000	4,380, plus 32%	20,000
(Not over $1,000 . . . 14%)			

10.9   Interest

Interest is a charge for the use of money. If a person borrows $1,000 for 1 year at 6%, the interest is $60. In a situation such as this there is a borrower and a lender. The borrower pays $60 for the loan of the money. The basic arithmetic problem involved here is the computation of the interest charge for a given amount of money for a given length of time at a given interest rate. When an interest rate of 6% is quoted in a situation such as this, the rate is on an annual basis; thus, 6% means 6% per year. In this illustration $1,000 is the principal, 1 year is the time, 6% is the rate, and $60 is the interest.

Interest = principal × rate × time (in years)

Algebraically, this is written:

$$i = prt$$

Example 1.   Find the interest on $2,000 for 3 years at 7%.

Solution. $i = prt$

$i = \$2,000 \times 7\% \times 3$

$i = \$20,000 \times .07 \times 3$

$i = \$420$

Example 2.   Find the interest on $2,000 for 9 months at 7%.

Solution. $i = prt$

$i = \$2,000 \times .07 \times \dfrac{9}{12}$

$i = \$105$

Example 3.   Find the interest on $2,000 for 45 days at 7%.

Solution. $i = prt$

$i = \$2,000 \times .07 \times \dfrac{45}{360}$

In most business transactions, when the time is given in days a 360-day year is used.

$$i = \$17.50$$

Example 4.   Find the interest on $2,000 at 7%, from March 8 to July 2.

Solution. One must count the days. This can be done with a calendar or a specially prepared table of days listing the number of days in each month.

March	23 days (31 − 8)
April	30 days
May	31 days
June	30 days
July	2 days
	116 days

$i = prt$

$= \$2,000 \times .07 \times \dfrac{116}{360}$

$= \$45.11$

Certain short cuts can be developed for special uses in computing interest.

Consider the problem of finding the interest on any amount of money for 60 days at 6%:

$$i = prt$$
$$= p \times .06 \times \frac{60}{360}$$
$$= p \times \frac{6}{100} \times \frac{60}{360}$$
$$= p \times \frac{1}{100}$$
$$= .01p$$

This yields the rule:

To find the interest on any given amount of money for 60 days at 6%, move the principal two places to the left.

    Example 5. Find the interest on $3,148.96 for 60 days at 6%.
    Solution. $i = .01p$
             $i = \$31.4896 = \$31.49$ to the nearest cent

10.10   Compound Interest

Consider the situation in which a person deposits $1,000 in a building and loan association, or other investment, that pays 4 per cent compounded annually, for a period of three years. The depositor is the lender, and the association is the borrower.

    Draw a line diagram:

$1,000	.	.	.
0	1 year	2 years	3 years

4% compounded annually

The zero on the diagram indicates today, or the day on which the deposit is made. At the end of one year the $1,000 has earned $4\% \times \$1,000 = \$40$ interest. If this interest is not withdrawn, but is left on deposit, we say that the investment begins to earn compound interest, or interest on interest.

$1,000	$1,040	.	.
0	1	2	3

4% compounded annually

The line diagram now shows $1,040 on deposit. The interest on $1,040 for 1 year at 4% is $4\% \times \$1,040 = \$41.60$. Leave this interest on deposit. Continuing this procedure for three years, the line diagram becomes:

$1,000	$1,040	$1,081.60	$1,124.86
0	1	2	3

4% compounded annually

If the interest is left on deposit, the amount on deposit accumulates more and more rapidly as time goes on. In 18 years the original deposit of $1,000 will become $2,025.82, or more than double the original amount. At 6%, money will double in less than twelve years, in this manner.

Next, consider the situation when the interest is compounded semi-annually. If $1,000 is deposited, then at the end of six months the interest for six months is:

$$\$1,000 \times .04 \times \tfrac{1}{2} = \$20$$

If this interest is left to accumulate, the line diagram looks like this:

$1,000 $1,020   .   .   .

0   1   2   3
4% compounded semi-annually

Each six months to compute the interest the amount on deposit is multiplied by $4\% \times \tfrac{1}{2} = 2\%$. This is described as 4% compounded semi-annually. At the end of three years the line diagram is:

$1,000 $1,040.40 $1,082.43 $1,112.16
       $1,020 $1,061.21 $1,104.08

0   1   2   3
4% compounded semi-annually

Observe that the amount on deposit accumulates more rapidly at 4% compounded semi-annually than it does at 4% compounded annually. The more frequently the interest is compounded the faster the amount on deposit accumulates. At 4% compounded quarterly, the interest is computed four times per year, or every three months. At this rate $1,000 would amount to $1,126.83 at the end of three years. Savings accounts in banks operate on the general principle of the preceding example.

Compound interest is involved in purchasing a home by monthly payments. Suppose, for example, that a home costs $35,000—and a $10,000 down payment is made. The balance due is $35,000 − $10,000 = $25,000. Suppose that the monthly payment is $150 and the interest rate is 6%. Part of this payment is used to retire the principal, and the rest of the payment is used for interest. At the end of the first month, $25,000 has been used by the buyer for one month.

$$i = prt$$
$$= \$25,000 \times 6\% \times \tfrac{1}{12}$$
$$= \$125$$

Of the first payment, then, $125 is for interest and the remainder, $150 − $125 = $25, is used to retire the principal. The outstanding debt is:

$$\$25,000 - \$25 = \$24,975$$

When the second monthly payment is made, the buyer has had the use of $24,975 for one month, so the interest is:

$$i = \$24,975 \times 6\% \times \tfrac{1}{12}$$
$$= \$124.88$$

Notice that his interest is a little less than the interest for the first month. Of the $150 payment $124.38 is for interest, so the remainder,

$$\$150 - \$124.88 = \$25.12$$

is used to retire the principal. Notice that his amount is a little more than in the case of the first payment. The outstanding principal after the second payment is:

$$\$24,875 - \$25.12 = \$24,849.88$$

This process is repeated until the home is paid for in full.

Observe that in the early months of the contract most of the monthly payment is for interest, and a relatively small amount is used to retire the principal. Near the end of the contract, the reverse is true: most of the payment is used to retire the principal, and a relatively small amount is for interest. Near the middle of the time, about half of the payment is for interest and about half for principal.

10.11 Bank Discount

Sometimes a person borrows money from a bank, or other lending agency, and the bank discounts a rate signed by the borrower. A person may go to a bank and say, "I should like to borrow $1,000." The bank requires that he sign a note that reads, "In one year I promise to pay $1,000," or words to that effect. Let us assume that the bank's discount rate is 7%. The bank computes $7\% \times \$1,000 = \$70$, and subtracts $70 from $1,000. The remainder is $930. The borrower receives $930 cash, and pays back $1,000 at the end of one year. This is a commonly used method of leading money, being used most generally for relatively small amounts of money for relatively short periods of time. If the time is two years, the computation is:

$$\$1,000 \times .07 \times 2 = \$140, \text{ and } \$1,000 - \$140 = \$860$$

In this case the borrower would receive $860 cash, and he would pay back $1,000 at the end of two years.

A little reflection shows that this method would result in ridiculous results for long periods of time. Thus, for 20 years:

$$\$1,000 \times .07 \times 20 = \$1,400$$

and

$$\$1,000 - \$1,400 = -\$400$$

The rate 7% in this transaction should be called a discount rate. It is not an interest rate. As a matter of fact, a 7% discount rate is equivalent to an interest rate of slightly more than 7%. In the first example considered in this section, $930 cash was received by the borrower. Now:

$$7\% \times \$930 = \$65.10 \text{ and } \$930 + \$65.10 = \$995.10$$

so at a 7% interest rate the borrower would pay back only $995.10, instead of $1,000. Therefore, a 7% discount rate is slightly more than a 7% interest rate.

An interesting problem arises in connection with discounting a note. It will be illustrated by an example.

Example. A person wishes to receive $1,000 cash, at a bank that discounts rates at 7%. If the term is one year, for how much should the note be made?

Solution. A line diagram is:

$$\frac{\$1,000 \qquad\qquad\qquad\qquad ?}{0 \qquad\qquad\qquad\qquad\qquad 1 \text{ year}}$$
$$7\% \text{ discount rate}$$

Let 100% represent the amount of the note. Then $100\% - 7\% = 93\%$, and this represents the amount of cash received. The situation is this: 93% of a number is $1,000; find the number.

$$\frac{\$1000}{.93} = \$1,075.27$$

This result can be proved, as follows:

$$7\% \times \$1,075.27 = \$75.27. \quad \$1,075.27 - \$75.27 = \$1,000.$$

This example can be solved algebraically:

$$X - .07X = \$75.27$$
$$.93X = \$1,000$$
$$X = \frac{\$1,000}{.93} \; \$1,075.27$$

Notice that 100% is used in per cent in arithmetic somewhat like X is used in algebra.

10.12 Installment Buying

If an automobile is purchased by making monthly payments, per cent is involved. The procedure will be illustrated by examples.

Example 1. The cash price of an automobile is $2,000. A trade-in is valued at $800. If the carrying charge rate is 6%, find the monthly payment for a 12-month contract.

Solution.

$$\$2,000 - \$800 = \$1,200 \text{ cash balance owed}$$
$$6\% \times \$1,200 = \$72 \text{ carrying charge}$$
$$\frac{\$1,200 \times \$72}{12} = \frac{\$1,272}{12} = \$106 \text{ monthly payment}$$

Example 2. Find the monthly payment on the automobile in Example 1 for an 18-month contract.

Solution.

$$18 \text{ months} = 1\tfrac{1}{2} \text{ years}$$
$$\$1,200 \times 6\% \times 1\tfrac{1}{2} = \$108 \text{ carrying charge}$$
$$\frac{\$1,200 + \$108}{18} = \frac{\$1,308}{18} = \$72.67 \text{ monthly payment}$$

Example 3. Find the monthly payment on the automobile in Example 1 for a 24-month contract.

Solution. 24 months = 2 years

$$\$1,200 \times 6\% \times 2 = \$144 \text{ carrying charge}$$
$$\frac{\$1,200 + \$144}{24} = \frac{\$1,344}{24} = \$56 \text{ monthly payment}$$

Radios, television sets, refrigerators, stoves, and many other items of merchandise are commonly sold on installment contracts that are entirely analogous to the example of the automobile. The guiding factor in such transactions is the carrying charge rate. The carrying charge rate is not an interest rate. The equivalent interest rate in the example of the automobile is much greater than 6%. This fact should cause no undue alarm. Items such as these are sold in this way. An alternative is to pay cash.

Buying a home, discounting a note, and purchasing an automobile illustrate three commonly used ways of paying a loan. There are others, but these three are quite typical.

10.13   Chapter Summary

In this chapter per cent has been presented as a subset of decimal fractions. The language of ratio and proportion was introduced to provide alternative ways of reasoning and to relate work with per cent with principles used in work with common fractions.

Many practical uses of per cent were presented and the three common types (cases) of problems were identified. The elementary school teacher should use many visual aids and manipulative materials to add understanding to arithmetic. Actual business forms should be used to make the applications of per cent interesting and meaningful. We recommend the use of automobile contracts, a building and loan association deposit book, a savings account deposit book, an income tax form, a sales tax chart used in variety stores, and an application for a loan at a bank or at a credit union. Secure copies of a newspaper from a local publisher and help children discover the many uses made of per cent in each major section of the newspaper.

QUESTIONS AND EXERCISES

1. Write these decimal fractions as per cent.

   (a) .08   (b) .35   (c) 1.50   (d) $\dfrac{1}{.002}$ (e) $\dfrac{1}{.004}$

2. Change the per cent to a common fraction.
   (a) 8% (b) 62.5% (c) 100% (d) $\frac{1}{2}\%$ (e) $\frac{1}{4}\%$
3. Change the common fractions to per cent.
   (a) $\frac{1}{2}$ (b) $\frac{1}{3}$ (c) $\frac{1}{4}$ (d) $\frac{1}{8}$ (e) $\frac{3}{4}$
4. Use the hundreds board shown in this chapter to make an explanation of these examples:
   (a) $\frac{1}{10}$ of 100   (b) $\frac{1}{100}$ of 100   (c) $.8\%$ of 100
   (d) 20% of 100   (e) 50% of 100   (f) 5% of 100
5. Find a per cent of a number for these examples:
   (a) 5% of 200   (b) 3% of 60   (c) $1\frac{1}{2}\%$ of 40
   (d) 6% of 250   (e) $4\frac{1}{2}\%$ of 300   (f) 25% of 415
6. What per cent of 200 is 20? Of 150 is 75? Of 60 is 20? Of 400 is 100?
7. If 5% of a number is 25, what is the number?
8. What is the difference between per cent and percentage?
9. Use the proportion model to secure answers for each case shown in the examples on commission in section 10.6.
10. Identify three situations in which a commission is used and computed in business transactions.
11. Would you rather buy a car receiving discounts of 5% and 2% or a single discount of 7%?
12. Find the single discount equivalent to two successive discounts of 10% followed by 5%.
13. If city sales taxes are computed at the rate of 5% per dollar, what happens in stores where small purchases necessitate the buyer paying tax on fractional parts of a dollar, that is, one cent on $15\cancel{c}$?
14. Find the interest on:
    (a) \$2,000 for 30 days at 8%.
    (b) \$1,000 at 7% from May 8 to July 8.
    (c) \$2,000 for 6 months at 6%.
15. Study a local newspaper to discover common interest rates—for the borrower and for the investor.
16. How much interest would \$10,000 earn if left at 4% for ten years compounded annually?
17. What is meant by a discount rate of 7%?
18. Suppose you purchase a car and borrow money from a credit union at the rate of 1% per month on the unpaid balance. What is the annual interest rate? What is the "truth in lending" law?
19. Write each example as a proportion.
    (a) 4 is 25% of 16.   (b) 5% of 40 is 2.
    (c) 250% of 50 is 125.   (d) 100 is 10% of 1000.
20. Solve for n.
    (a) $\dfrac{1}{5} = \dfrac{n}{100}$ (b) $\dfrac{1}{2} = \dfrac{n}{100}$ (c) $\dfrac{3}{5} = \dfrac{n}{100}$ (d) $\dfrac{2}{1} = \dfrac{n}{100}$

SELECTED REFERENCES

Crumley, R. D., "Teaching Rate and Ratio in the Middle Grades," *School Science and Mathematics*, LX (February, 1960), 143–50.

Grossnickle, Foster E., *et al.*, *Discovering Meanings in Elementary School Mathematics*. San Francisco: Holt, Rinehart & Winston, Inc., 1968, Chap. xvi.

Hauck, E., "Concrete Materials for Teaching Percentage," *The Arithmetic Teacher*, I (December, 1954), 9–12.

Holmes, Emma E., *Mathematics Instruction for Children*. Belmont, Calif.: Wadsworth Publishing Company, 1968, Chap. xi.

Howard, C. F., and E. Dumas, *Teaching Contemporary Mathematics in the Elementary School*. New York: Harper & Row, Publishers, 1968, Chap. xvi.

Kessler, Rolla V., "The Equation Method of Teaching Percentage," *The Arithmetic Teacher*, VII (February, 1960), 90–92.

Marks, J. L., *et al.*, *Teaching Elementary School Mathematics for Understanding*. New York: McGraw-Hill Book Company, 1965, pp. 328–50.

Nelson, Jeanne, "Per Cent: A Rational Number or a Ratio?" *The Arithmetic Teacher*, XVI (February, 1969), 105–9.

Riedesel, C. Alan, *Guiding Discovery in Elementary School Mathematics*. New York: Appleton-Century-Crofts, 1967, Chap. x.

Sanders, Walter J., "The Use of Models in Mathematics Instruction," *The Arithmetic Teacher*, XI (March, 1964), 157–65.

Spencer, Peter L., and Marguerite Brydegaard, *Buiding Mathematical Competence in the Elementary School*. San Francisco: Holt, Rinehart & Winston, Inc., 1966, pp. 214–54.

Swenson, Esther J., *Teaching Arithmetic to Children*. New York: The Macmillan Company, 1964, Chap. xvii.

Van Engen, Henry, "Rate Pairs, Fractions and Rational Numbers," *The Arithmetic Teacher*, VIII (December, 1960), 389–99.

11

An Introduction to Algebra

No sharp or definitive boundary line exists between arithmetic and algebra. Arithmetic is initially concerned with measuring and dealing with concrete elements, but inevitably this leads to making generalizations and becoming abstract regarding such elements.

11.1 Number Sentences

Our introduction to an algebraic concept is the study of number sentences.

You are familiar with sentences in English. They are arrangements of words that express a complete thought. This is also true in mathematics.

Examples.

1. California is a state of the United States.
2. The prime factors of 12 are 4 and 3.
3. $4 + 8 = 12$

The first and third sentences are true, and the second is false, but all of the sentences are called "statements" because they are definitely true or false. Now consider the following examples:

1. He is older than Jane.
2. $\Box + 5 = 14$

3. _____is the capital of California.

Since we cannot determine whether these sentences are true or false, they are called "open sentences." An open sentence expresses a condition that, when satisfied, produces a true statement. An open sentence contains one or more variables. In the first example, "he" is the variable. When we establish the identity of "he," we will be able to tell whether the sentence is true or false. The second sentence is either true or false, depending upon what we replace the $\square$ with. In mathematics, the symbol $\square$ stands for a definite yet unspecified number. The symbol $\square$ is called a variable. In the primary grades teachers often use "frames" such as $\square$, $\triangle$, $\bigcirc$, or $\Diamond$ to represent variables. In the upper grades, letters such as X, N, Y are used more often than frames to denote variables. Whether you use a frame, a letter, or a blank is unimportant so long as it is understood that "the symbol used represents an unspecified number." The third sentence in our list of examples is likewise true or false, depending upon what we replace the _____ with.
Consider the examples:

1. $6 > 2$
2. $5 > 6$
3. $\square < 6$

The first and second sentences are additional examples of "statements" because they are definitely true or false. The first sentence is true, the second sentence is false. However, the third sentence is an open sentence, involving the variable $\square$. It could be converted into a true statement by many replacements for the variable.

A number sentence which contains the symbol "$=$" is called an equation, and a number sentence which contains the symbols "$<$" or "$>$" is called an inequality.

A set of numbers, the members of which are the permissible replacements of the variable in an open number sentence, is called the replacement set or "domain" of the variable. From the replacement set, the subset of numbers that makes the sentence true is selected. This subset is called the "solution set" for the sentence, and each number in this set is said to be a solution of the open sentence.

Consider the sentence, $\square + 5 > 17$ where the domain of the variable is given by the set, $A = \{11, 12, 13, 14, 15\}$. Try 11: $11 + 5 > 17$ or $16 > 17$. Since this sentence is false, 11 is not a solution. Try 12: $12 + 5 > 17$ or $17 > 17$. Since this sentence is false, 12 is not a solution. Try 13: $13 + 5 > 17$ or $18 > 17$. Since this sentence is true, 13 is a solution. By continuing this process, it can be shown that 14 and 15 are also solutions; thus the solution set is $\{13, 14, 15\}$.

Consider the sentence $\square - 3 < 6$, if the domain of the variable is given by the set, $B = \{0, 1, 2, 3, \ldots\}$. B is an infinite set. Further, let us assume we shall accept only those solutions which are such that $\square - 3$ is a whole number. Following the same replacement procedure employed in the previous example, the solution set is $\{8, 7, 6, 5, 4, 3\}$. Had the example just illustrated been $\square - 3 > 6$ with the same set, B, as a domain and the condition that $\square - 3$ be a whole number, the solution set would have been $\{10, 11, 12, 13. \ldots\}$. This set is infinite.

Sometimes the solution set is the empty set, that is, no replacement from the domain will yield a true sentence. Consider $\square + 5 = 4$, in which the domain is the set of whole numbers. Since there is no whole number which when added to 5 will yield 4, there is no replacement for $\square$. The solution set is thus the empty set, or $\{\ \}$, or $\varnothing$.

Since a statement is a sentence that is either true or false (but not both), a false statement can be made true by adding or removing a corresponding negative word or phrase such as "not." It is also possible to change a true statement to a false statement by supplying a negative word. This same technique can be used in number sentences by the "slant bar," $/$, when superimposed on a symbol translates the original symbol as "not." The following examples show how the slant bar is used:

1. $7 \neq 5 + 1$
2. $9 \not< 7$
3. $7 \not> 9$

The first example says seven is not equal to five plus one, the second example says nine is not less than seven, and the third says seven is not greater than nine.

Consider now the sentences, "John is a good basketball player *and* John is a good student." When two simple sentences are joined by the connective "and," the compound sentence thus formed is defined to be true if, and only if, *both* parts are true.

A compound sentence could have been formed which reads: "John is a good basketball player *or* John is a good student." When two simple sentences are joined by the connective "or," the sentence is considered true if, and only if, at least *one* part is true.

Similarly in mathematics we use compound number sentences. For example:

1. $3 < 5$ *and* $9 = 5 + 4$. Since both parts are true sentences, the compound sentence "$3 < 5$ *and* $9 = 5 + 4$" is true.
2. $4 < 5$ *or* $9 = 5 \times 2$. Since $4 < 5$ is a true sentence, the compound number sentence "$4 < 5$ *or* $9 = 5 \times 2$" is true since one of its parts is true.
3. $4 > 5$ *or* $10 = 3 \times 3$. Since neither sentence is true, the compound sentence "$4 > 5$ *or* $10 = 3 \times 3$" is false.

Consider the example $\square < 4$ or $\square = 4$, where the domain of the variable is the set of whole numbers.

$\quad\quad\quad \square < 4$ is true if $\square$ is a member of the set $\{0, 1, 2, 3\}$.

$\quad\quad\quad \square = 4$ is true if $\square$ is a member of the set $\{4\}$.

The union of the two sets, $\{0, 1, 2, 3\}$ and $\{4\}$, namely, $\{0, 1, 2, 3, 4\}$, is the solution set for the "or" compound sentence. A short, concise, mathematical way of writing $\square < 4$ or $\square = 4$ is $\square \leq 4$ which is read, "$\square$ is less than 4 *or* $\square$ is equal to 4". The symbol $\leq$ is regarded as a combination of the symbols "$<$" and "$=$."

Another example of a compound open sentence is: $\square > 4$ or $\square = 4$ where the domain of the variable is the set of whole numbers. $\square > 4$ is true if $\square$ is a member of the set $\{5, 6, 7, \ldots\}$. $\square = 4$ is true if $\square$ is a member of the set $\{4\}$.

The union of the two sets, $\{5, 6, 7, \ldots\}$ and $\{4\}$, namely, $\{4, 5, 6, 7, \ldots\}$, is the solution set for the "or" compound sentence.

A short way of writing $\square > 4$ or $\square = 4$ is $\square \geq 4$, which would be read, "$\square$ is greater than 4 *or* $\square$ is equal to 4."

Find the solution set of the open sentence: $5 + \square \leq 9$, if the domain of $\square$ is $\{2, 3, 4, 5\}$.

If $\square$ is replaced by 2, the sentence becomes $5 + 2 \leq 9$, which is true because $5 + 2$ is less than 9.

If $\square$ is replaced by 3, the sentence becomes $5 + 3 \leq 9$, which is true because $5 + 3$ is less than 9.

If $\square$ is replaced by 4, the sentence becomes $5 + 4 \leq 9$, which is true because $5 + 4 = 9$.

If $\square$ is replaced by 5, the sentence becomes $5 + 5 \leq 9$, which is not true because $5 + 5$ is neither less than 9 nor equal to 9.

Thus the solution set $= \{2, 3, 4\}$.

11.2 Ordered Pairs

When objects are paired, the order in which they are paired may or may not be important. For example, the order in which one adds sugar and cream to a cup of coffee may not be important, but the order in which one puts on his underwear and outer garments is important. When the order *is* important, we use the symbol (a, b) to indicate that a is paired with b, and to note that a is considered first. The symbol (a, b) is read, "the ordered pair a, b." The letters a and b used in (a, b) are called the first and second components, respectively, of the ordered pair.

To illustrate the relationship between two ordered pairs, we define two ordered pairs to be equal if, and only if, they have identical first components and identical second components: $(a, b) = (c, d)$ if, and only if, $a = c$ and $b = d$.

Thus, $(a, b) = (a, b)$ but $(a, b) \neq (b, a)$ unless $a = b$. This leads us to a discussion of open sentences with more than one variable.

Consider the solution of the open sentence:

$$\triangle + \square = 6$$

Because there are two variables, each solution to this problem will be an ordered pair of numbers yielding a true sentence when the components of the ordered pair are used as replacements for the appropriate variables. The solution set for the above open sentence is the set of all ordered pairs the sum of whose components is six. The solution set would be $\{(0, 6), (1, 5), (2, 4)$ $(3, 3), (4, 2), (5, 1), (6, 0)\}$ or the members of the solution set may be listed in a table as indicated.

$\triangle$	$\square$
0	6
1	5
2	4
3	3
4	2
5	1
6	0

Consider the set of whole numbers as the replacement set for each of the variables in the sentence:

$$\square + \triangle + \diamondsuit = 8$$

Since there are three variables in this number sentence, each solution contains three numbers, and can be regarded as an ordered triple the sum of whose components is eight.

Following the analogy of listing the ordered pairs comprising a solution set, an incomplete solution set for the above open sentence is indicated:

$$\{(0, 0, 8), (0, 1, 7), (0, 2, 6), (0, 3, 5)\}$$

There are many more ordered triples, the sum of whose components is eight.

Consider the inequality, $\square + \triangle > 5$. Here again, if the replacement set is the set of whole numbers, our solution set can be seen to be an infinite set illustrated as follows:

$$\{(0, 6), (1, 5), (2, 7), (7, 2), \ldots\}.$$

11.3   Open Sentence Solving

One method of finding solutions for some open sentences with one variable is to use trial and error. For example, consider

$$(\square + 5) - 2 = 5$$

where the replacement set for ☐ is the set of whole numbers. The expression (☐ + 5) shows that the sum of (☐ + 5) is to be determined first then 2 is to be subtracted.

For what whole number (if any) is the sentence true? Let us try 9 as a possibility. When ☐ is replaced by 9, the resulting sentence is $(9 + 5) - 2 = 5$ or $12 = 5$, which is false. The number 9 for ☐ gives a solution which is too large for a solution. Try 6 for ☐. When ☐ is replaced by 6 the resulting sentence is $(6 + 5) - 2 = 5$ or $9 = 5$, which is false.

Trying a smaller value of ☐, namely 2, we get $(2 + 5) - 2 = 5$ or $5 = 5$, thus the solution set is {2}.

11.4   Problem Solving

Number sentences are useful in finding solutions of verbal problems. To write number sentences for problems, one must be able to translate verbal sentences into mathematical language.

Some typical verbal phrases and their mathematical translations follow.

The sum of a number and 5	☐ + 5
A number decreased by 5	☐ − 5
The product of 3 and a number	3 × ☐
A number divided by 3	$\frac{☐}{3}$
A number 10 is the sum of a number and 5.	$10 = ☐ + 5$

Now consider the situation:

I have ☐ books, and you have 10 more books than I. Together we have 20 books. How many books do I have?

Solution. Let us list our facts:

Number of books I have	☐
Number of books you have	☐ + 10
Number of books we have	☐ + (☐ + 10)
Number of books we have	20

Sentence: $☐ + (☐ + 10) = 20$
The replacement set is {0, 1, 2, 3, 4, . . .}.
If ☐ is replaced by 5, the sentence is true, and false when replaced by any other number. I thus have 5 books.

Not all verbal problems can be solved by sentences involving equations, but a great majority of them can.

11.5   Set of Integers

Up to now we have had little trouble solving number sentences.

Consider the number sentence $6 + ☐ = 4$. What is ☐ to be? We must now make a further demand and thus justify our extension of the set of whole numbers.

Let us rename 6 as $4 + 2$; then we have the above number sentence becoming $(4 + 2) + \square = 4$, and then using the associative property for addition, we have

$$4 + (2 + \square) = 4.$$

This sentence would be true if $2 + \square = 0$. To meet this need, the number $^-2$ is invented to have the property $2 + {}^-2 = 0$. We further assume that this new number has the same properties for addition and multiplication that the whole numbers have. The number $^-2$ is called the opposite of 2 or the additive inverse of 2. Also 2 is the opposite, or additive inverse, of $^-2$. So we write $^-(^-2) = 2$.

The number sentence that provoked this invention is thus:

$$4 + (2 + {}^-2) = 4$$
$$(4 + 2) + {}^-2 = 4$$
$$6 + {}^-2 = 4$$

Using the idea of subtraction developed in Chapter 3, we conclude $4 - 6 = {}^-2$. However, in order to make subtraction always possible, we need an additive inverse for each whole number. We invent the following, $^-6$ will be the additive inverse of the whole number 6, and $^-10$ will be the additive inverse of the whole number 10. The additive inverse of 0 is $^-0$ so that $0 + {}^-0 = 0$, yet from our experience with whole numbers, we have $0 + 0 = 0$; thus we conclude 0 is its own additive inverse. We have a set of new numbers, $A = \{{}^-1, {}^-2, {}^-3, {}^-4, \ldots\}$, and when this set is joined with the set of whole numbers, we have

$$I = \{\ldots {}^-4, {}^-3, {}^-2, {}^-1, 0, 1, 2, 3, \ldots\}$$

and this set is called the set of "integers." It is customary to refer to the set $A = \{{}^-1, {}^-2, {}^-3, {}^-4, \ldots\}$ as the set of negative integers. It is also customary to refer to the set $\{1, 2, 3, \ldots\}$ as the set of positive integers.

Consider the number sentence:

$$({}^-5 + {}^-9) + (5 + 9) = \square$$

$$({}^-5 + {}^-9) + (5 + 9) = ({}^-5 + {}^-9) + (9 + 5) \quad \text{commutative property for addition}$$

$$= {}^-5 + [{}^-9 + (9 + 5)] \quad \text{associative property for addition}$$

$$= {}^-5 + [({}^-9 + 9) + 5] \quad \text{associative property for addition}$$

$$= {}^-5 + [0 + 5] \quad \text{additive inverse}$$

$$= {}^-5 + 5 \quad \text{additive identity}$$

$$= 0 \quad \text{additive inverse}$$

We thus have, $({}^-5 + {}^-9) + (5 + 9) = 0$, and thus

$${}^-5 + {}^-9 = {}^-(5 + 9) = {}^-14.$$

For the above example and examples similar to it, we conclude with the definition:

If a and b are positive integers, then $^-a + {}^-b = {}^-(a + b)$.

Consider the number sentence $5 + {}^-9 = \square$

$\quad\quad 5 + ({}^-5 + {}^-4) = \square$ from the above definition

$\quad\quad (5 + {}^-5) + {}^-4 = \square$ associative property for addition

$\quad\quad\quad\quad\quad 0 + {}^-4 = \square$ additive inverse

$\quad\quad\quad\quad\quad\quad\quad {}^-4 = \square$ additive identity

Thus: $5 + {}^-9 = {}^-4$.

Working many examples similar to this example leads to the definition:

If a and b are nonnegative integers with $b > a$, then $a + {}^-b = {}^-c$, where c is a positive integer and $a + c = b$.

11.6 Order of Integers and the Number Line

Since order has been established for the whole numbers (now called the nonnegative integers), the necessity to fit the negative integers into an order scheme exists.

The set $I = \{\ldots {}^-5, {}^-4, {}^-3, {}^-2, {}^-1, 0, 1, 2, 3, \ldots\}$ is represented on the number line and its extension with "equally spaced" points on the number line as shown here.

The number of intervals from the point A to the point B is the "distance" from A to B. The distance is a number. This distance is always represented as a nonnegative integer. The distance from A to C is 3; this is the same as the coordinate of point C. The distance from A to B is 3; yet the coordinate of point B is $^-3$. We designate this distance to point B in terms of its coordinate by writing $|{}^-3|$ to mean 3. The expression $|{}^-3| = 3$ is read, "the absolute value of $^-3$ is 3." Also, $|3|$ is 3. Likewise, $|{}^-6| = 6$ and $|4| = 4$.

11.7 Subtraction of Integers

For each a, b, c in the set of integers, if $b + c = a$, then $a - b = c$.

With addition already defined for the set of integers, subtraction is accomplished as illustrated in the following examples.

Example 1. Solve $4 - {}^-2 = \square$.

$\quad\quad 4 - {}^-2 = \square$ if ${}^-2 + \square = 4$ and since

$\quad\quad {}^-2 + 6 = 4$, then $4 - {}^-2 = 6$

Thus, the solution set is $\{6\}$.

Example 2. Solve $^-9 - {}^-6 = \square$.
$^-9 - {}^-6 = \square$ if $^-6 + \square = {}^-9$ and since
$^-6 + {}^-3 = {}^-9$, then $^-9 - {}^-6 = {}^-3$
Thus, the solution set is $\{^-3\}$.

Example 3. Solve $4 - 6 = \square$.
$4 - 6 = \square$ if $6 + \square = 4$ and since
$6 + {}^-2 = 4$, then $4 - 6 = {}^-2$.
Thus, the solution set is $\{^-2\}$.

11.8   Multiplication of Integers

We assume, first, that the negative integers follow the same properties for multiplication as did the whole numbers. Consider the example: $6 \times (5 + {}^-5)$

$$6 \times (5 + {}^-5) = (6 \times 5) + (6 \times {}^-5) \quad \text{distributive rule}$$
$$6 \times 0 = (6 \times 5) + (6 \times {}^-5) \quad \text{additive inverse}$$
$$0 = (6 \times 5) + (6 \times {}^-5) \quad \text{renaming}$$
$$0 = 30 \qquad + (6 \times {}^-5) \quad \text{renaming}$$

Since $30 + (6 \times {}^-5) = 0$, then $(6 \times {}^-5)$ is the additive inverse of 30. The additive inverse of 30 is $^-30$, thus

$$(6 \times {}^-5) = {}^-30$$

We conclude: If a, b, and c are nonnegative integers, then $a \times {}^-b = {}^-c$ where $a \times b = c$.

Consider the example: $(5 + {}^-5) \times {}^-6$

$$(5 + {}^-5) \times {}^-6 = (5 \times {}^-6) + ({}^-5 \times {}^-6) \quad \text{distributive rule}$$
$$0 \times {}^-6 = (5 \times {}^-6) + ({}^-5 \times {}^-6) \quad \text{additive inverse}$$
$$0 = {}^-30 \qquad + ({}^-5 \times {}^-6) \quad \text{renaming}$$

Since $^-30 + ({}^-5 \times {}^-6) = 0$, then $({}^-5 \times {}^-6)$ is the additive inverse of 30. The additive inverse of $^-30$ is 30, thus

$$({}^-5 \times {}^-6) = 30$$

We conclude: If a, b, and c are nonnegative integers, then $^-a \times {}^-b = c$, where $a \times b = c$.

11.9   Division of Integers

Division is defined in terms of multiplication. That is, for all a, b, c, in the set of integers, $b \neq 0$

$a \div b = c$ if and only if $c \times b = a$.

Illustrate:

$$({}^+10) \div ({}^+2) = \square; \text{ if } \square \times ({}^+2) = {}^+10, \text{ thus } \square = 5$$
$$({}^+10) \div ({}^-2) = \square; \text{ if } \square \times ({}^-2) = {}^+10, \text{ thus } \square = {}^-5$$

$(^-10) \div (^+2) = \square$; if $\square \times (^-2) = {}^-10$, thus $\square = {}^-5$
$(^-10) \div (^-2) = \square$; if $\square \times (^-2) = {}^-10$, thus $\square = {}^+5$

11.10 Functions

Many elementary school teachers play a game referred to as "what's my rule?" to illustrate the concept of a function. The game could be illustrated as follows. If the tickets to a basketball game cost $1 per person, how much will tickets cost for two persons? For three persons? For four persons? And so on. We could arrange the information in a table as follows:

Number of Persons to Basketball Game	Total Cost of Tickets
1	$1.00
2	2.00
3	3.00
4	4.00
5	5.00
6	6.00
7	7.00
8	8.00

The rule, multiply the number of people attending the basketball game by $1 to find the total cost of any number of tickets, is soon discovered.

If we let the letter Y represent the cost in dollars of any number of tickets, and the letter X represent any number of persons attending the basketball game, we could then represent the relationship between the number of persons and the cost of tickets by the mathematical sentence $Y = X$.

In this sentence, X could be replaced with the set of values: $\{1, 2, 3, 4, \ldots 8\}$. This set of values is called the "replacement set" for X. Any symbol such as X that holds a place for a number from a certain set, as we used the symbol $\square$, in number sentences, is called a variable.

We can properly say that Y is a function of X, because any value of Y we might be interested in determining depends on the value of X taken from the replacement set. The set of ordered pairs of numbers resulting from assigning values to X is a set of mathematical "relations."

In the example under discussion, Y is a function of X because the number of tickets bought (X) determines the cost (Y). The resulting ordered pairs of numbers, or relations, are called the solution set. The solution set for this example is $\{(1, 1), (2, 2), (3, 3), (4, 4), (5, 5), (6, 6), (7, 7), (8, 8)\}$.

Shown in tabular form, it would appear:

X	Y
1	1
2	2
3	3
4	4
5	5
6	6
7	7
8	8

In the solution set, we do not have any negative values, because we have neither a negative number of people nor a negative number of dollars.

Let us look at a similar example with tickets costing $1.50 per ticket. Suppose Y again represents the cost of tickets and X represents the number of people buying tickets. Thus the new mathematical sentence would be $Y = 1.50X$. We can then determine that the solution set would be $\{(1, 1.50), (2, 3), (3, 4.50), \ldots\}$. Another way of writing the function determined by $Y = 1.50X$ is to write it: $\{(X, Y) \mid Y = 1.50X\}$. It is read: "The set of ordered pairs X and Y is such that Y is equal to 1.50 times X."

If we know in a given situation that Y is a function of X, we commonly use the notation $Y = f(X)$ which is read "Y equals f of X." This is an abbreviation for saying "Y is a function of X." For example, in considering the first function described with the tickets to the basketball game we can write $Y = f(X)$. The "domain" of the function is defined to be the set of number replacements for X, and the "range" of the functions is defined to be the unique set of numbers comprising the values of Y resulting from the replacements for X.

A formal definition of a function would be a set of ordered pairs of real numbers with no two of the pairs having the same first component.

As a further example, if the sentence were $y = x^2$, we might write it: $\{(x, y) \mid y = x^2\}$. If we selected $\{1, 2, 3, 4\}$ as our domain, then the set $\{1, 4, 9, 16\}$ would constitute the range. The function would then be the set $\{(1, 1), (2, 4), (3, 9), (4, 16)\}$.

Finally, in our discussion of a sentence similar to $y = x^2$ we might shorten our discussion to a statement "find $f(2)$." We find $f(2)$ by substituting 2 for x in the sentence. Thus, $f(2) = 2^2 = 4$. We say, for the function f, as defined by the equation $y = x^2$, with domain equal to the set $\{1, 2, 3, 4\}$ we can write:

$$f(1) = 1^2 = 1$$
$$f(2) = 2^2 = 4$$
$$f(3) = 3^2 = 9$$
$$f(4) = 4^2 = 16$$

We have found the corresponding values of y constituting the range.

11.11   Rectangular Coordinate System

We have seen the number line as a useful device for understanding and developing our concept of number relations.

We will now develop a system for locating our ordered pairs used in the discussion of the function concept.

We draw a number line in any direction.

			B	A
-2	$^-1$	0	1	2

On the number line above, we can name the point B as 1. How would we then name the point designated A?

We draw another number line perpendicular to the number line already drawn through the point labeled 0, using the same unit length.

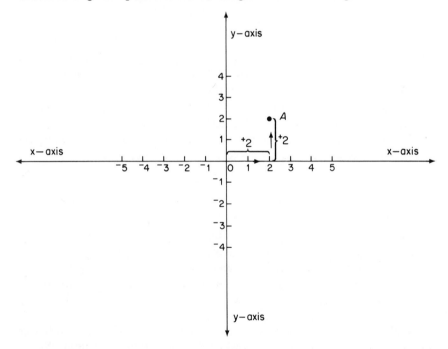

On this new vertical line we define "up" as a positive direction, and "down" as the negative direction, from the point at 0 as a starting point. The point A is located by moving two units to the right and then two units vertically.

To standardize the method of naming points such as A, mathematicians have named the horizontal number line the x-axis and the vertical number line the y-axis. The two numbers needed to locate a point such as the point A is also called an ordered pair. The first number named in the ordered pair indicates the number of units to the right or left of the y-axis, and the second number named in the ordered pair indicates the number of units up or down from the *x*-axis. The point at 0 where the two axes cross or intersect is called the "origin." The ordered pair naming the point *A* is written (2, 2). The understood signs of the numbers constituting the number pair are positive if not indicated. This system of locating or naming points is called a "rectangular coordinate system."

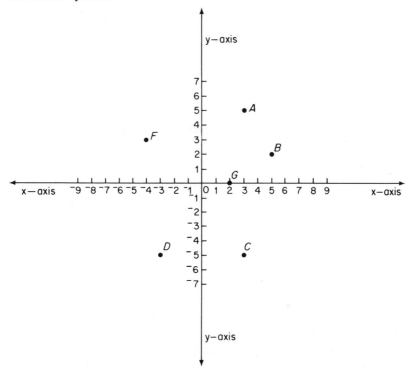

Other points located by their positions in relation to an *x*-axis and a *y*-axis are illustrated here. The point *A* has "coordinates" (3, 5), *B* (5, 2), *C* (3, ⁻5), *D* (⁻3, ⁻5), *F* (⁻4, 3), and *G* (2, 0).

We can also use the rectangular coordinate system to "graph" a function. An example would be our graph of the function $\{(x, y) \mid y = x\}$. We record once again in tabular form our ordered pairs.

x	*y*
1	1
2	2
3	3
4	4
5	5
6	6
7	7
8	8

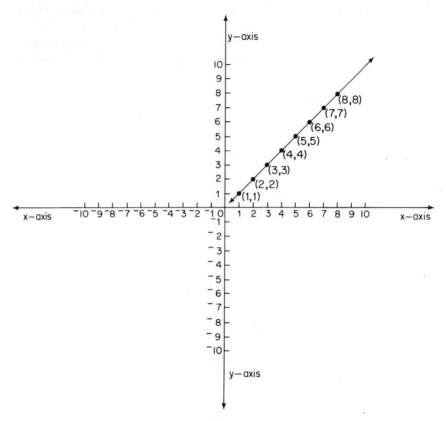

The points located on our "number plane" as indicated in the illustration represent the plotting of our solution set, or function. By connecting the points as indicated, we now have represented what is called the graph of the function $y = x$.

This system is also called the Cartesian coordinate system in honor of its developer, the seventeenth-century mathematician, Rene Descartes.

11.12   Chapter Summary

Number sentences such as $6 + 1 = 8$ and $15 > 12$ are called statements. A statement must be either true or false. The first statement $6 + 1 = 8$ is a false statement, while $15 > 12$ is a true statement.

A number sentence such as $\square + 3 = 7$ with a domain equal to $\{0, 1, 2, 3, \ldots\}$ is called an open number sentence. The symbol $\square$ is called a variable, and it represents a definite but unspecified number from the set $\{0, 1, 2, \ldots\}$. The set designated is called the domain of the variable $\square$. When the symbol

☐ is replaced by a numeral for a number from the domain, the resulting sentence is either true or false.

A number from the domain of the variable occurring in an open sentence is called a solution of the open sentence provided a true statement results when the variable is replaced by a numeral for that number. The set of all such solutions of an open sentence is called a solution set.

A solution of an open sentence in two variables consists of an ordered pair of numbers from a specified set of ordered pairs of numbers. A solution set again contains the set of all solutions of an open sentence.

A number sentence expressing an equality of two numbers is called an equation, whereas a number sentence expressing an inequality of two numbers is called in inequality.

The set of elements $\{\ldots, ^-3, ^-2, ^-1, 0, 1, 2, \ldots\}$ describes the system of integers. We assume the new numbers have the same properties for addition and multiplication that the whole numbers have. The set of integers has an additive inverse for each element. It solves the problem, $2 + \square = 0$. The additive inverse of 2 is $^-2$ and solves the problem.

This chapter also describes and defines the operations involving addition, subtraction, multiplication, and division as they apply to the set of integers. In addition, if a and b are nonnegative integers with $b > a$, then $a + {^-b} = {^-c}$, where c is a positive integer and $a + c = b$. For subtraction, for each a, b, and c in the set of integers, if $b + c = a$, then $a - b = c$. For multiplication if a, b, and c are nonnegative integers, then $a \times {^-b} = {^-c}$ where $a \times b = c$, and $^-a \times {^-b} = c$, where $a \times b = c$. Finally, division was defined in terms of multiplication.

The concept of function, its meaning, related vocabulary, and some of its relationships within the structure of mathematics were presented. We saw that the graph of a function of x has exactly one value of y for any value of x and can be plotted or graphed on a rectangular coordinate system.

Just as many problems involving fractions are impossible to a fourth grader but are easily solved by an eighth grader who has studied rational numbers, so as a result of this chapter you may now be able to see many problems that can be easily solved although they formerly appeared improbable if not impossible. As should now be clear, algebra is a generalization of arithmetic.

QUESTIONS AND EXERCISES

1. Write as simple an expression as you can for each of the following:
   Example: $[5 + (4 - 2)] + 6 = [5 + 2] + 6 = 7 + 6 = 13$
   (a) $9 + (5 - 4) + 3$
   (b) $5 + [3 + (4 - 1)] - 4$

    (c) $[5 + (2 + 3)] + [2 \times (2 + 4)]$

    (d) $\dfrac{5 + 3}{2} + \left[3 + \dfrac{4 + 1}{2}\right]$

2. Translate the following sentences into number sentences.
   (a) If ten is subtracted from fourteen, the result is four.
   (b) Seventeen is larger than twelve.
   (c) Eight is less than sixteen.
   (d) Ten is the product of five and two.
   (e) Seventeen is not equal to the sum of five and four.
   (f) The sum of six and seven is less than the product of six and seven.

3. Translate the following number sentences into word sentences.
   (a) $15 + 3 = 16 + 2$ **(b)** $5 \times 2 > 3$
   (c) $18 < 7 + 2$ **(d)** $14 \neq 8 + 2$
   (e) $17 \not< 12$ **(f)** $(5 + 2) > (3 + 1)$

4. Label each of the following either true or false.
   (a) ">" is read "is greater than."
   (b) "=" says, the "same as."
   (c) "<" is read "is greater than."

5. Translate the following sentences into number sentences using a frame ($\square$) for the variable.
   (a) Seven plus this number is equal to sixteen.
   (b) The sum of two and this number is greater than ten.
   (c) Fifteen is less than this number minus five.

6. Translate the following into verbal sentences.
   (a) $8 + \square = 15$ **(b)** $14 < \square - 3$
   (c) $\square + 8 > 15$

7. For each of the following open sentences, find the solution set. The domain of the variable is the set of whole numbers, $W = \{0, 1, 2, 3, \ldots\}$.
   (a) $\square - 5 = 22$ **(b)** $\square + 5 > 12$ **(c)** $8 < \square - 2$
   (d) $5 \times \square > 20$ **(e)** $\square + 3 = 3$

8. Find the solution set for each of the following number sentences. The domain of the variable is the set of whole numbers $\{0, 1, 2, 3, \ldots\}$.
   (a) $5 + \square \geq 9$ **(b)** $\square + 2 \leq 7$
   (c) $3 \times \square \leq 12$ **(d)** $12 + \square \leq 13$

9. Using the following set as the replacement set of each variable, list the solution sets of each of the following number sentences as ordered pairs. $A = \{3, 4, 5, 6, 7\}$
   (a) $\square + \triangle = 10$ **(b)** $\square - \triangle = 2$ **(c)** $\square + \triangle \leq 2$

10. By guessing, and recording your guesses, find the solutions. Use the domain of your guesses as the set of whole numbers.
    (a) $(5 + \square) - 3 = 20$ **(b)** $(\square - 5) + 6 = 21$
    (c) $[2 \times (\square + 4)] - 9 = 30$

11. Solve the following problems. For each problem, list the numbers involved and write the number sentence, and then the solution set.
    (a) John had $5.00 in the bank, and then he earned $3.00 mowing the lawn. How much money does he still need to buy a sweater that costs $11.50?
    (b) George had $20.50 saved. He spent $5.00 for a shirt, and $3.25 for a baseball bat. How much does he still have to spend?
    (c) A family has three weeks' vacation. It will take them 2 days to reach their camp site and 2 days to return home. How many days can they spend at the camp site?
12. For each of the following number sentences, make up a verbal problem. A solution set is unnecessary.
    (a) $\square + 5 = 30$ (b) $5 \times \square = 25$
    (c) $(2 \times m) + 5 < 26$
13. What is the additive inverse of:
    (a) 7   (b) $^-(^-5)$ (c) $^-10$ (d) $^-(6 + 3)$
14. What integer will make these sentences true?
    (a) $^-5 + \square = 0$ (b) $\square + (4 + 3) = 0$
    (c) $^-\square + (2 + 6) = 0$ (d) $7 + {^-(6 + 1)} = \square$
15. Find the sum of each of the following by using the definition which applies and any properties necessary.
    (a) $9 + {^-2}$ (b) $^-12 + {^-27}$ (c) $(23 + 13) + {^-13}$
    (d) $38 + ({^-14} + {^-5})$ (e) $^-8 + ({^-3} + {^-7})$
16. With a number line, use one of the symbols $(<, =, >)$ in the frame to make each of the following sentences true.
    (a) $18 \square 25$ (b) $^-18 \square 25$
    (c) $(32 + {^-12}) \square {^-92}$ (d) $^-(6 + 7) \square ({^-11} + {^-2})$
    (e) $^-({^-9} + {^-6}) \square 25$ (f) $({^-2} + {^-6}) \square {^-(10 + {^-2})}$
17. Give the value of each of the following.
    (a) $|{^-12}|$ (b) $|4 + 6|$ (c) $^-|{^-8} + {^-5}|$
    (d) $|25 + {^-10}|$ (e) $^-|16 + {^-16}|$
18. Give a simpler name for each of the following.
    (a) $^-6 \times {^-3}$ (b) $^-5 \times (4 - 8)$
    (c) $^-2 \times ({^-3} - {^-7})$
19. Draw a set of rectangular coordinates and locate all of the following points:
    (a) $A(3, 5)$ (b) $B({^-4}, 6)$ (c) $C(5, 0)$
    (d) $D(0, 5)$ (e) $E({^-5}, 0)$ (f) $F(0, {^-4})$
    (g) $G({^-4}, {^-3})$ (h) $H(5, {^-3})$
20. If the domain of a function $f(x)$ is $\{0, 1, 2, 3, 4\}$ and the rule defining the function is $y = 2x + 3$, find the set, F, comprising the range of the function.
21. In example 20, above, consider the function written in the form of a set

builder $\{(x, y) \mid y = 2x + 3\}$. Taking the same domain given in example 20, construct a table of values, showing the domain and range and then graph the function using rectangular coordinates.

22. Consider the function described by

$$f(x) = \frac{5}{3 - x}$$

What value of x in the domain would be inadmissable? Give a reason for your answer.

23. Tickets for a football game are $5 per ticket. If x represents the number of fans attending the game and y the total cost of tickets sold for the game:

   (a) write a mathematical sentence showing this relation,

   (b) put (a) in the form of a set builder, and

   (c) construct a table of values.

24. There are three more girls than boys in each classroom in a particular school. If x represents the number of boys in any classroom, and y the number of girls in any classroom:

   (a) write a mathematical sentence showing this relation,

   (b) put (a) in the form of a set builder,

   (c) construct a table of values, and

   (d) graph the function.

SELECTED REFERENCES

Haag, Vincent H., *Structure of Algebra*. Reading, Mass.: Addison-Wesley Publishing Company, 1964.

Hosford, Philip L., *Algebra for Elementary Teachers*. New York: Harcourt, Brace & World, Inc., 1968.

Jones, Burton W., *Elementary Concepts of Mathematics*, 2nd ed. New York: The Macmillan Company, 1963.

Keedy, Mervin L., Richard E. Jameson, and Patricia L. Johnson, *Exploring Modern Mathematics*, Book 1. New York: Holt, Rinehart & Winston, Inc., 1963.

McFadden, Myra, J. W. Moore, and W. J. Smith, *Sets, Relations, and Functions*. New York: McGraw-Hill Book Company, 1963.

McFarland, Dora, and Eunice M. Lewis, *Introduction to Modern Mathematics for Elementary Teachers*. Boston: D. C. Heath and Company, 1966.

Spitzer, Herbert F., *Teaching Elementary School Mathematics*. Boston: Houghton Mifflin Company, 1964.

12

An Introduction to Plane Geometry

Modern programs in mathematics are introducing geometric concepts in the elementary grades that in traditional programs were usually reserved until secondary school. The approach used in the elementary grades is intuitive; that is, children discover geometry in the development of their own observations about shapes and figures in their physical world.

In a modern approach, geometry is defined as the study of space and locations in space. Vocabulary is introduced only when necessary to help express ideas. The building blocks to build on are geometric concepts such as the point, space, curve, line, line segment, ray, and angle. These concepts are fundamental to a study of geometry and must be understood before children can express geometric ideas. Some concepts are undefined terms; we can attach meaning to them only by assuming particular properties about them. Other concepts are assumed to be true and are called axioms or postulates.

12.1 Introduction

The Babylonian and Egyptian civilizations are credited with the first uses of geometry. The Egyptians, faced with many problems in such areas as surveying and navigation, recorded some of their observations in these areas. Later, the Greeks tried to organize and relate the isolated facts that the Egyptians had recorded in the process of "earth (geos) measure (metron)." As a result of the Greeks' efforts there evolved a mathematical system that is now called *Euclidean geometry* or *plane geometry*. Because of this influence, geometry developed as the first mathematical system to embody the *deductive reasoning* process, a process that lies at the foundation of present-day "pure mathematics." Plane geometry, the mathematical model of our *real* world, as man perceives it in its "flatness," is an excellent prototype of an abstract mathematical system.

12.2 Elements of Plane Geometry

The basic *undefined elements* of geometry are *points, lines,* and *planes.* No attempt is made to define the *elements.* Instead, we accept these elements as representing concepts with which we are familiar. We say a point has position only; a line has length only; and a plane a flat surface. In the real world, we make a "point" on a piece of paper with a sharp pencil; the edge of a book is a "line"; and the top of a table is a "plane."

In our modern concept of geometry, we think of a line as a *set of points*; a plane is the *universal set* of all points under discussion, that is, the plane is the surface upon which we develop the results of geometry; and *geometric figures* are subsets of the plane. In order to discuss and represent points, lines, and geometric figures, we shall adopt the notation of using capital letters to

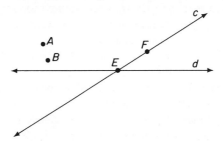

identify points and lower case letters to identify lines. *A, B, E,* and *F* are points on the plane; $F \in c$; $c \cap d = E$.

12.3 Axioms

Relations exist between points and lines that are generally accepted but are not proven. These assumptions or *axioms* are necessary for the further development of our mathematical system. The axioms establish the building blocks for the logical development of geometry.

Axiom 1: Two distinct points determine a unique line.

Axiom 2: Two distinct lines have at most one point in common.

We shall illustrate the first two axioms.

The line *a* goes through two points *C* and *D*. In set notation, $C \in a, D \in a$. If another line *b* were drawn through the same two points *C* and *D*, we would find that a and *b* would coincide; that is, $a = b$. Illustrating axiom 1, the points *C* and *D* determine one, and only one, line.

Using set notation, *C* and *D* are points, *a* and *b* are lines, and *P* is a place such that $\{C, D\} \subset P$, $a \subset P$, and $b \subset P$. Then if $C \neq D$, $C \in a \cap b$, and $D \in a \cap b$, then $a = b$.

In illustrating axiom 2, we consider two cases:

Case 1: Two distinct lines that have exactly one point in common.

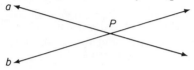

The lines *a* and *b* *intersect* at point *P*. In set notation, $a \cap b = \{P\}$.

Case 2: Two distinct lines that do not have any points in common.

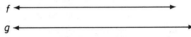

We say the lines *f* and *g* are "parallel," and use the notation, $f \parallel g$. In set notation, $f \cap g = \varnothing$. One might argue that *f* and *g* will intersect if extended far enough.

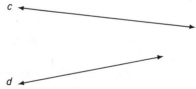

Although *c* and *d* do not intersect as illustrated, it is apparent they would intersect if extended far enough. To avoid any concern over the matter of extension, we have axiom 3:

Axiom 3: A line extends indefinitely.

On the basis of this axiom, if *c* and *d* did intersect after extension, then *c* and *d* would not be parallel. In conclusion, then, given any two lines, they either coincide, are parallel, or intersect at exactly one point.

SUBSETS OF A LINE

A line is a set of points which are determined by two distinct points and which extend indefinitely in either direction. We illustrate the indefinite extension by placing arrowheads on the ends.

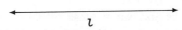

l

A point on a line separates the line into two parts called *rays*. A *ray* is a subset of a line having one endpoint.

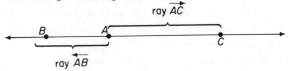

A *line segment* is a subset of a line consisting of two points called the *endpoints* of the segment together with all points between the endpoints.

The segment with endpoints A and B is denoted by $\overline{AB}$ or $\overline{BA}$ whereas line l can be denoted AB or BA (without the bars). Note that $\overline{AB} \subset l$ and that $\overline{AB} \cap \overrightarrow{BC} = \varnothing$.

A set of points is collinear if, and only if, there is a line containing all the points of the set.

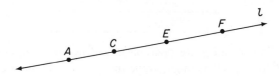

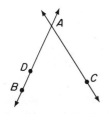

$A, C, E,$ and F are collinear since $A \in l, C \in l, E \in l,$ and $F \in l$.

A further example would be the following illustration:

Assume $\{A, B, C\}$ is a set of *noncollinear* points. Find (a) $AB \cap AC$, (b) $\overline{AB} \cap \overline{DA}$.
$AB \cap AC = \{A\}, \overline{AB} \cap \overline{DA} = \overline{DA}$

12.4 Angles

Consider the set of noncollinear points $\{A, B, F\}$ and the union of the two rays $\overrightarrow{AB}$ and $\overrightarrow{AF}$ having a common endpoint A. This set forms an *angle*. The rays $\overrightarrow{AB}$ and $\overrightarrow{AF}$ are called sides and the common endpoint A is called the vertex.

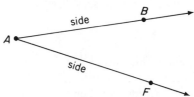

In general, an *angle* is a point set formed by the union of two rays. If the union of the two sides of the angle is a line, the angle is called a straight angle.

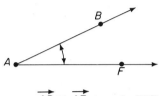

We should note that the two segments $\overline{AF}$ and $\overline{AB}$ with a common endpoint A determine an angle with vertex A. The sides of the angle are the rays obtained by extending $\overline{AB}$ and $\overline{AF}$ in the directions from A to B and A to F.

The angle indicated is denoted by the symbol $\angle BAF$ or $\angle FAB$ or simply $\angle A$.

$$\overrightarrow{AB} \cup \overrightarrow{AF} = \text{angle } BAF$$

Note that the point which is the vertex occupies the central position in the name of the angle.

12.5 Congruence

The concept of congruence is an undefined concept in the same manner that point and line are undefined. Intuitively, we say that two geometric objects are *congruent* if they have the same size and shape.

If two lines intersect, they form four angles with a common vertex, as shown in the first diagram below. $\angle FOC$, $\angle COG$, $\angle AOG$, $\angle FOA$ are the names of the four angles formed.

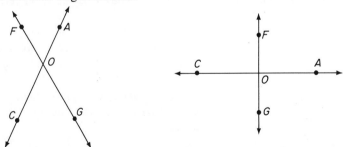

If all four angles are congruent, we say that the lines are *perpendicular*, as shown in the diagram, above, of the perpendicular lines FG and CA. If the line CA is perpendicular to FG, we write $CA \perp FG$, and any of the four congruent angles is called a *right angle*.

12.6 Angle Measurement

The "measure" of an angle is determined by the "amount of turning" between the rays that form the angle. Angles can vary in size.

In order to measure, or relate angles by sizes, we introduce a basic *unit* of angular measurement as an angle of one degree, written 1°, according to the following definition.

Definition: An angle of 1° is an angle with an opening which is $\frac{1}{180}$ of a straight angle.

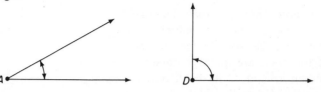

$\angle A$ is an angle of approximately 30° ($\frac{1}{6}$ of 180°) and $\angle D$ appears to be 90° ($\frac{1}{2}$ of 180°).

Using degree measure, we can define the following types of angles.

Definitions:

1. A *right angle* is a 90° angle.
2. An *acute angle* is an angle that is less than 90°.
3. An *obtuse angle* is an angle that is greater than 90° and less than 180°.
4. A *straight angle* is an angle that is equal to 180°.
5. An angle that is *bisected* is an angle that is divided into two equal angles.
6. *Perpendicular* lines are lines that meet at right angles.

12.7 Angle Pairs

Two angles are said to be *adjacent* if the angles have the same vertex and a common side between them.

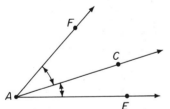

$\angle CAE$ and $\angle FAC$ are adjacent.

If, for example, $\angle FAE = 60°$ and $\angle CAE = 20°$ then $\angle FAC = \angle FAE - \angle CAE = 60° - 20° = 40°$.

Vertical angles or *opposite angles* are angles formed by two intersecting lines and are not adjacent.

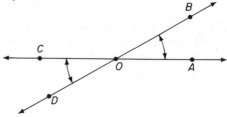

$\angle BOA$ and $\angle COD$ are vertical or opposite angles, as well as $\angle BOC$ and $\angle DOA$. In a high school geometry class it is not difficult to show that $\angle BOA$ and $\angle COD$ would always be equal.

Complementary angles are two angles whose degree measurement have a sum of 90°. For example, if $\angle A = 35°$ and $\angle B = 55°$, then $\angle A$ and $\angle B$ would be called complementary angles.

Suppose $\angle B$ and $\angle F$ are each complements of a third angle $\angle C$, then by definition, $\angle B + \angle C = 90°$, and $\angle F + \angle C = 90°$ so that $\angle B = \angle F$, hence, we say, *two angles which are complements of the same angle are equal.*

Supplementary angles are two angles whose degree sum is 180°. Thus is an $\angle A = 150°$ and $\angle B = 30°$, then $\angle A$ and $\angle B$ are called supplementary. It can also be shown that *two angles which are supplements of the same angle are equal.*

Also easily shown is that *if equal supplementary angles are adjacent, they would determine right angles.*

12.8 Closed Plane Figures: Polygons and Circles

In this section we will form *geometric figures* by forming *set unions* of line segments.

A figure formed by taking the set union of line segments which are connected by the intersection or overlapping of end points is called a polygon path.

Note the following illustrations:

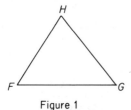

Figure 1

Polygon path $FGH = $
$\overline{FG} \cup \overline{GH} \cup \overline{FH}$

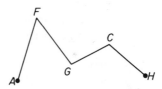

Figure 2

Polygon path $AFGCH = $
$\overline{AF} \cup \overline{FG} \cup \overline{GC} \cup \overline{CH}$

Note that in Figures 1 and 2 any two line segments of the path are either disjoint or have common endpoints. Also, in Figure 1 each segment endpoint or *vertex of the polygon path* is shared by two segments, whereas in Figure 2 the path has two unattached endpoints at A and H. Polygon paths that resemble Figure 1 which have no unattached endpoints are called *closed polygons* or more simply *polygons.*

In general, a *closed geometric figure* is a figure which separates the plane into disjoint subsets or regions.

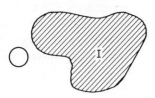
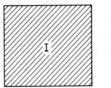

Many figures similar to the figures illustrated here could be cited to separate the plane into *interior* and *exterior* regions. In the figures illustrated I is the interior (inside) and 0 the exterior (outside). Thus, if C is a closed figure, then it follows in each case illustrated that $O \cup C \cup I =$ plane, and if $I \cap C = \varnothing$, $I \cap O = \varnothing$, and $C \cap O = \varnothing$, then the closed path is not a part of either interior or exterior.

12.9   Polygon Classification

Polygons are classified according to the number of *sides* or *line segments* which form the polygon.

Since the least number of line segments necessary to form a polygon is three, we begin our classification with three-sided polygons, called *triangles*.

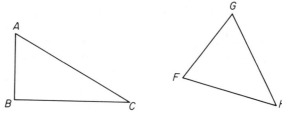

Our classification list includes the polygons most commonly used in our discussion of plane geometry.

NUMBER OF SIDES	NAME	NUMBER OF SIDES	NAME
3	Triangle	8	Octagon
4	Quadrilateral	9	Nonagon
5	Pentagon	10	Decagon
6	Hexagon	15	Pentadecagon
7	Heptagon		

If the sides are equal, and the angles have the same measure in a given polygon, the polygon is called a *regular polygon*. We illustrate the triangle (Figure 1) and the quadrilateral (Figure 2).

Figure 1 represents the regular triangle, more commonly called an *equilateral triangle*; and Figure 2 represents the regular quadrilateral, more commonly called the *square*.

In Figure 2, a line segment such as $\overline{AB}$ or $\overline{CF}$ is called a *diagonal*. It is determined by drawing a line segment between two nonadjacent vertices.

Most of the properties of polygons with more than three sides can be deduced from the properties of triangles, so our primary concern will be with triangles.

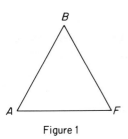

Figure 1

$$\overline{AB} = \overline{BF} = \overline{AF}$$
$$\angle A = \angle B = \angle F$$

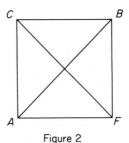

Figure 2

$$\overline{AF} = \overline{FB} = \overline{BC} = \overline{AC}$$
$$\angle A = \angle F = \angle B = \angle C$$

12.10 Triangles

A triangle is determined by any three *noncollinear* points such as A, B, and F. $\overline{AB} \cup \overline{BF} \cup \overline{AF}$ determine a triangle with vertices A, B, and F, and sides $\overline{AB}$, $\overline{BF}$, and $\overline{AF}$. The triangle is named $\triangle ABF$.

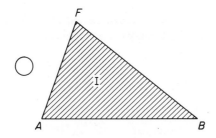

The interior, I, of $\triangle ABC$ is the result of (interior of $\angle A$) $\cap$ (interior of $\angle B$) $\cap$ (interior of $\angle C$).

12.11 Theorems

Much of the discussion in a geometry text concerns itself with the investigation of geometric relationships. It will be proposed that *if* certain conditions are true, *then* certain other conditions will also be true. These proposals are called *theorems* and are in the form of implications, that is, $p \rightarrow q$ (p implies q). In each theorem, if p is true, it will be our goal to prove that q is true, which will establish the validity of $p \rightarrow q$. Further, it will be necessary to make use of an important property of the implication relation, that of transitivity. Symbolically, if p, q, and r are statements, $p \rightarrow q$ is true and $q \rightarrow r$ is true, then the implication $p \rightarrow r$ is also true.

12.12   Congruent Triangles

Two triangles, $\triangle ABC$ and $\triangle FGH$, are said to be congruent ($\cong$) if all of their parts can be made to coincide, that is to say, congruent triangles have the same size and same shape.

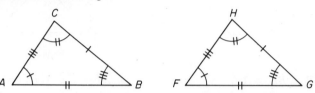

If $\triangle ABC \cong \triangle FGH$, it could mean that the following conditions are true, namely, $\angle A = \angle F$, $\angle B = \angle G$, $\angle C = \angle H$, $\overline{AB} = \overline{FG}$, $\overline{BC} = \overline{GH}$, $\overline{AC} = \overline{FH}$. Note the symbols on the sides and angles of the respective triangles to denote what pairs of angles and sides are equal.

An important axiom that applies to triangle congruency is the axiom that "a geometric figure can be moved without changing its size or shape." If the validity of this axiom is accepted, then it can be shown that to prove two triangles congruent one of the following theorems can suffice.

Theorem 1. If three sides of one triangle are equal, respectively, to three sides of another triangle, then the triangles are congruent.

If $\overline{FG} = \overline{AB}$, $\overline{GH} = \overline{BC}$, and $\overline{FH} = \overline{AC}$, $\triangle FGH \cong \triangle ABC$. This is called the side, side, side theorem, or abbreviated, *s.s.s.*

Because of the uniqueness of the congruency of triangles, it is implied that $\angle F = \angle A$, $\angle G = \angle B$, $\angle H = \angle C$. We say that the angles named represent *corresponding parts* and would be equal by the nature of the congruency. Note that the equal angles are opposite the sides that are equal.

Theorem 2. If two sides and the angle included between them of one triangle are equal, respectively, to two sides and the angle included between them of another triangle, then the triangles are congruent.

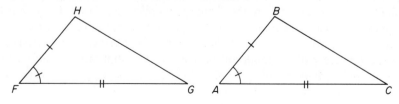

If $\overline{FG} = \overline{AC}$, $\overline{FH} = \overline{AB}$, and $\angle F = \angle A$, $\triangle FGH \cong \triangle ABC$. This theorem is commonly named the *s.a.s.* theorem. In the two triangles the corresponding parts would be: $\overline{GH} = \overline{BC}$, $\angle H = \angle B$, $\angle G = \angle C$.

Theorem 3. If two angles and the side included between them of one triangle equal, respectively, two angles and the side included between them of another triangle, then the triangles are congruent.

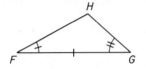 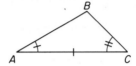

If $\angle F = \angle A$, $\overline{FG} = \overline{AC}$, $\angle G = \angle C$, $\triangle FGH \cong \triangle ABC$. This theorem is commonly named the *a.s.a.* theorem. In the two triangles the corresponding parts would be: $\overline{FH} = \overline{AB}$, $\angle H = \angle B$, and $\overline{HG} = \overline{BC}$.

An application of the use of theorems in proving original problems dealing with congruency of triangles would be illustrated by the figure shown here. In the figure, assume $\overline{AG} = \overline{AF}$ and $\angle FAB = \angle GAB$. Show that $\triangle ABF \cong \triangle ABG$.

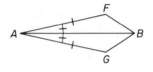

Proof: 1. $\overline{AG} = \overline{AF}$ and $\angle FAB = \angle GAB$ 1. Assumed
      2. $\overline{AB} = \overline{AB}$ 2. Identical side
      3. $\triangle AFB \cong \triangle ABG$ 3. *s.a.s.*

12.13 Parallel Lines

Recall in Section 12.3 above that two distinct lines that do not have any points in common are said to be parallel ($\parallel$).

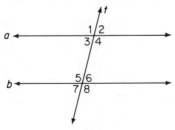

Assume that the lines a and b are parallel. The third line t, that intersects both of these lines, is called a *transversal*.

Lines a and b need not be parallel in order for t to be called a transversal, because, by definition, if any two lines on a plane are intersected by a third line, the third line is a transversal.

In the figure, $\angle 2$ and $\angle 6$, $\angle 4$ and $\angle 8$, $\angle 1$ and $\angle 5$, $\angle 3$ and $\angle 7$, by pairs, are named *corresponding angles*. Also, $\angle 3$, $\angle 4$, $\angle 5$, and $\angle 6$ are all referred to as *interior angles*, while the pairs, $\angle 3$ and $\angle 6$, and $\angle 4$ and $\angle 5$, are called *alternate interior angles*.

If we assume at this point that when lines a and b are drawn parallel to each other that $\angle 3 = \angle 6$ and $\angle 4 = \angle 5$, that is, the pairs of *alternate interior angles* are equal, we can prove a most important theorem in plane geometry, namely, the theorem which we will discuss next, theorem 4.

Theorem 4. The sum of the angles of a triangle is 180°.

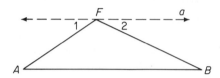

Proof: A line, labeled a, is drawn parallel to AB.

 1. $\angle 1 = \angle A$, $\angle B = \angle 2$. This is because of the equality of pairs of alternate interior angles.
 2. $\angle 1 + \angle AFB + \angle 2 = 180°$. They form a straight angle through point F.
 3. $\angle A + \angle AFB + \angle B = 180°$. This results from substituting for $\angle 1$, $\angle A$ and for $\angle 2$, $\angle B$.

Many other theorems of this type can be proven by a similar method.

One of the most important theorems of plane geometry is known as the *Pythagorean theorem*, which will be illustrated here without proof.

Pythagorean theorem. The square of the hypotenuse (side opposite the right angle in a right triangle) is equal to the sum of the squares of the other two sides.

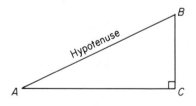

The theorem states, $\overline{AB}^2 = \overline{BC}^2 + \overline{AC}^2$

Suppose $\overline{BC} = 3$ inches, $\overline{AC} = 4$ inches; find $\overline{AB}$.

$$\overline{AB}^2 = \overline{BC}^2 + \overline{AC}^2$$
$$\overline{AB}^2 = 3^2 + 4^2$$
$$\overline{AB}^2 = 9 + 16$$

$$\overline{AB}^2 = 25$$
$$\overline{AB} = \sqrt{25} = 5 \text{ inches}$$

Suppose $\overline{AB} = 13$ inches, $\overline{BC} = 5$ inches; find $\overline{AC}$.

$$\overline{BC}^2 + \overline{AC}^2 = \overline{AB}^2$$
$$5^2 + \overline{AC}^2 = 13^2$$
$$25 + \overline{AC}^2 = 169$$
$$\overline{AC}^2 = 144$$
$$\overline{AC} = \sqrt{144} = 12 \text{ inches}$$

12.14   Similar Triangles

In contrast to congruent triangles, two triangles are *similar* if they have the same shape. *Two triangles are similar if they have equal angles and if their corresponding sides are proportional.* We illustrate this definition by an example.

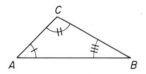 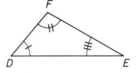

If $\angle A = \angle D$, $\angle B = \angle E$, $\angle C = \angle F$ and if the ratios, $\dfrac{\overline{AB}}{\overline{DE}} = \dfrac{\overline{BC}}{\overline{EF}} = \dfrac{\overline{AC}}{\overline{DF}}$, then the triangles are said to be similar, which is written $\triangle ABC \sim \triangle DEF$. An example illustrating an application of this definition would be to find the lengths of $\overline{DF}$, and $\overline{FE}$, knowing that $\overline{AB} = 10$ inches, $\overline{BC} = 8$ inches, $\overline{AC} = 4$ inches, and $\overline{DE} = 5$ inches.

Solution: $\quad \dfrac{\overline{AB}}{\overline{DE}} = \dfrac{\overline{BC}}{\overline{FE}}$

$$\frac{10}{5} = \frac{8}{\overline{FE}} \qquad \overline{FE} = 4 \text{ inches}$$

also $\qquad \dfrac{\overline{AB}}{\overline{DE}} = \dfrac{\overline{AC}}{\overline{DF}} \qquad \overline{DF} = 2 \text{ inches}$

It can also be shown that two triangles will be similar if only the angles of the two triangles are equal by pairs.

12.15   Circles

If we take a fixed point in a plane and find the set of points equally distant from the fixed point, we get a closed curve called a *circle*. The fixed point is called the *center* and the fixed distance the *radius*.

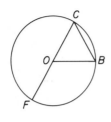

In the first example of a circle shown here 0 is the center of the circle and $\overline{OB}$ is a radius, and $\overline{OC}$ is a radius. A *chord*, represented by $\overline{CB}$, is a segment connecting any two points on the circle. The portion of the circle between *B* and *C* is called an *arc* and is designated $\overset{\frown}{BC}$. The chord $\overline{COF}$ drawn through the center is called a *diameter*. The arc of the circle formed by the diameter is called a *semicircle*.

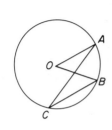

In the second circle, if 0 is the center of the circle and $\overline{OA}$ and $\overline{OB}$ are radii, then the angle at the *center* of the circle, namely $\angle AOB$, is called a *central angle*, and the angle formed at *C* by the chords $\overline{AC}$ and $\overline{CB}$ is called an *inscribed angle*. The size of a central angle has the same angle measure as it arc. In this figure if $\overset{\frown}{AB}$ = 60° ($\frac{1}{6}$ of the circle), then $\angle AOB$ is 60°. In like manner, the inscribed angle at *C* has the same measure as one-half of the $\overset{\frown}{AB}$. Thus if $\overset{\frown}{AB}$ = 60°, then $\angle BCA$ = 30°.

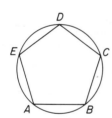
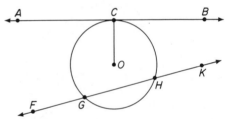

In the third figure the polygon is said to be inscribed in the circle, or the circle is said to be circumscribed about the polygon. If the polygon were *regular*, this would result in $\overset{\frown}{AB} = \overset{\frown}{BC} = \overset{\frown}{CD} = \overset{\frown}{DE} = \overset{\frown}{AE}$.

In the fourth figure the line *AB* is a *tangent* line to the circle at *C*. A *tangent* line to a circle has at least two important properties: One, it does not intersect the circle regardless of how far it is extended, only touching it at one point; and second, it is perpendicular to the radius drawn to the point of tangency (*C*).

The line *FK* intersecting the circle in two points regardless of how far extended is called a *secant*.

12.16   Areas of Closed Figures

We have already discussed the idea of congruency. Two congruent polygons are said to be equal in area, but two polygons equal in area are not necessarily congruent.

To find a way to measure what we call area, we must have a *basic unit of measure*. Many choices are available but we use as the basic unit of measurement of area, *the square*. *The number of squares that is contained in the polygon represents the area of a polygon*. The size of the polygon being measured, that is, a field, a floor, a sheet of paper the shape of a rectangle, will determine the size of square to be used. The square may be a square with a side of one inch, known as a square inch, it may be a square with a side of one foot, known as a square foot, or even a square with a side of one mile, known as a square mile.

12.17 Area of a Rectangle

To find the area of a rectangle is to find the number of squares of some basic size it contains.

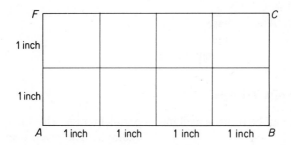

In the rectangle *ABCF* which is four inches long and two inches wide, if the length is divided into four equal parts and the width divided into two equal parts, the rectangle will be divided into 8 squares of an inch on a side. If this process were repeated with a great number of rectangles, the conclusion could be reached that the area of a rectangle can be found by finding the product of the length (or base) and the width (height) if both of these measures are in the same unit; that is, both in inches, feet, or whatever unit.

Example. Find the area of a rectangle whose length is 3 feet and width is 2 feet.

Solution. Area = length × width
= 3 feet × 2 feet
= 6 square feet

12.18 Area of a Parallelogram

The figure *ABCF* at the top of p. 268 is a parallelogram.

If we extend *AB* and construct *CY* to the extension at *Y* to form a rectangle *KYCF*, it can be determined that △*BYC* ≅ △*AKF* in order to see

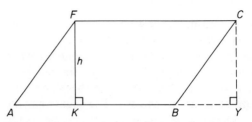

that the area of the figure $\triangle AKF + \square KBCF \cong \triangle BYC + \square KBCF$. The area given by $\triangle AKF + \square KBCF$ is the parallelogram and the area given by $\triangle BYC + \square KBCF$ is the area of the rectangle. We conclude, to find the area of the parallelogram is to find the area of the rectangle. The area of the rectangle is the base $KY \times$ height CY, but since we can substitute AB, the base of the parallelogram, for its equal KY and for CY its equal h, the area of the parallelogram is the product $AB \times h$.

Example. Find the area of a parallelogram whose base is 4 feet and whose height is 3 feet.

Solution. Area = base × height
= 4 feet × 3 feet
= 12 square feet

12.19   Area of a Triangle

Any triangle can be transformed into a parallelogram. This figure is a typical example. The given triangle is ABF.

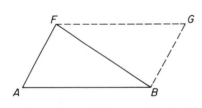

If lines are drawn through F parallel to AB and through B parallel to AF intersecting at G, a parallelogram is formed. $\triangle ABF \cong \triangle BFG$. Since $\triangle ABF \cong \triangle BFG$, the $\triangle ABF$ has one-half the area of parallelogram $ABGF$. The area of the parallelogram is the product of the base and its height. The area of the triangle ABF is, therefore, one-half of the product of the base and its height.

Example. What would be the area of a triangle whose base is 4 inches and whose height (altitude) is 2 inches?

Solution. Area = $(\frac{1}{2})$ base × height
= $(\frac{1}{2})$ 4 inches × 2 inches
= 4 square inches

12.20   Area of a Trapezoid

The figure $ABCF$ shown at the top of p. 269 is called a trapezoid. It is different from a parallelogram in that it has two parallel sides AB and

CF which are called bases. Its height is a line drawn from *F* perpendicular to *AB*. By drawing diagonal *BF*, two triangles are created. By finding the areas of these two triangles and finding the sum we shall have found the area of the trapezoid. The area will turn out to be one half the height multiplied by the sum of the bases. Written as a formula it will be:

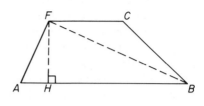

$$\tfrac{1}{2}(FH)(AB + CF).$$

Example. Find the area of a trapezoid whose bases are 10 inches and 6 inches and whose height is 4 inches.

Solution. Area = $\tfrac{1}{2}\,h$(base + base)
$$= \tfrac{1}{2} \times 4 \times (10 + 6)$$
$$= 2 \times (10 + 6)$$
$$= 8 \text{ square inches}$$

12.21   Area of a Circle

The distance around a circle is called the circumference and in all cases the length of the circumference divided by the diameter gives the approximate value 3.14159 to five decimal places. The value 3.1416 is always referred to as π. By employing a regular polygon the area of a circle can be determined to be the product of π and the square of the radius.

Example. Find the area of a circle whose radius is 5 inches:

Solution. Area = $\pi \times$ radius²
$$= 3.1416 \times 5^2$$
$$= 3.1416 \times 25$$
$$= 78.54 \text{ square inches}$$

Other closed plane figures have areas that can be determined by employing triangles and other plane figures whose areas are easily determined.

12.22   Chapter Summary

Modern programs in mathematics are introducing geometric concepts in the elementary grades. The approach used in these programs is intuitive.

In these modern programs, geometry is defined as the study of space and locations in space. The building blocks are the geometric concepts such as the point, space, curve, line, line segment, ray, and angle.

The basic undefined elements of geometry are points, lines, and planes. No attempt is made to define the elements, but only to accept these elements as representing concepts with which the pupils are familiar.

We consider a line as a set of points, a plane, the universal set of points under discussion, and geometric figures as subsets of the plane.

Certain relations between points and lines are generally accepted but are not proven. The assumptions or axioms are necessary for the development of the mathematical system.

A line is defined as a set of points which are determined by two distinct points and which extend indefinitely in both directions. A ray is a subset of a line having one endpoint and a line segment is a subset of a line with two endpoints.

The union of two rays forms an angle. The rays are called sides, and the common endpoint is called the vertex.

The concept of congruence is a undefined concept, but, intuitively, we say that two geometric objects are congruent if they have the same size and shape.

If two lines intersect and form four congruent angles, the lines are said to be perpendicular and the angles right angles.

The measure of an angle is determined by the amount of turning between the rays that form the angle. The basic unit of angular measurement is the degree (°).

A right angle has a measure of 90°, an acute angle less than 90°, an obtuse angle greater than 90° and less than 180°, and the straight angle 180°. Complementary angles are a pair of angles whose combined measure is 90°, and supplementary angles are a pair of angles whose combined measure is 180°.

Two angles are said to be adjacent if the angles have the same vertex and a common side between them. Two angles are said to be vertical angles or opposite angles if they are formed by two intersecting lines and are not adjacent.

A figure formed by taking the set union of line segments which are connected by the intersection or overlapping of endpoints is called a polygon path. If the figure has no unattached endpoints it is called a closed polygon or simply a polygon.

Polygons are classified by the number of sides. The triangle with three sides, the quadrilateral with four sides, and the pentagon with five sides are among the most commonly employed polygons. If the sides are equal, and the angles have the same measure, the polygon is called a regular polygon.

Much of the discussion in geometry concerns itself with the investigation of geometric relationships. It is proposed that if certain conditions are true, then certain other conditions will be true. These proposals are called theorems.

Many theorems could be considered for discussion. Among them are the theorems concerning the congruency of triangles, namely, two triangles are congruent if the three sides of one triangle are equal, respectively, to three sides of another triangle (*s.s.s.*). Two triangles are congruent if two sides and the angle included between them of one triangle are equal, respectively, to two sides and the angle included between them of another triangle (*s.a.s.*). Finally, two triangles are congruent if two angles and the side included between them of one triangle equal, respectively, two angles and the side included between them of another triangle (*a.s.a.*).

Because of the uniqueness of the congruency of triangles it is implied that the corresponding parts of the figures would be equal by the nature of the congruency.

Two distinct lines that do not have any points in common are said to be parallel.

One of the important theorems in plane geometry depending upon parallel lines is the theorem that the sum of the angles of a triangle is 180°.

Another important theorem is the Pythagorean theorem which states that the square of the hypotenuse (side opposite the right angle in a right triangle) is equal to the sum of the squares of the other two sides.

In contrast to congruent triangles, two triangles are similar if they have equal angles and if their corresponding sides are proportional.

If we take a fixed point in a plane and find the set of points equally distant from the fixed point, we get a closed curve called a circle. The fixed point is called the center and the fixed distance the radius.

A segment joining any two points on the circle is a chord, and the part of the circle between the two points is called an arc. A diameter is a chord drawn through the center and the arc of the diameter is a semicircle.

An angle of a circle formed at the center by two radii is called a central angle, and an angle formed by two chords emanating from the same point is called an inscribed angle.

A polygon is said to be inscribed in a circle if it lies within the circle and its vertices are on the circle.

A line that touches a circle in one point regardless of its length is a tangent line. A secant is a line that represents a chord extended in either or both directions.

The basic unit used to measure the amount of space occupied by a polygon is the square. Depending upon the extent of the space to be measured, the square employed in measuring the space might be a square foot, a square inch, or even a square yard.

The amount of space or area of a rectangle can be found by finding the product of the length and width, both expressed in the same linear unit.

The area of a parallelogram is found by finding the product of its base and height, both expressed in the same linear unit.

The area of any triangle is found by finding the product of its base and height, both expressed in the same linear unit divided by two.

The area of a trapezoid is found by finding the product of the sum of the bases and height, all expressed in the same linear unit divided by two.

The distance around a circle is called the circumference and is found in all cases to be the product of the diameter and π, which always has the fixed approximate value of 3.1416.

Finally, the area of any circle is found to be the product of π and the square of the radius.

QUESTIONS AND EXERCISES

1. Complete each of the following statements:
   (a) The elements of a line are _____ .
   (b) If l is a line and P is an element of l, then $P \in$ _____ .
   (c) The line represented in the diagram is a _____ .

   $$\bullet \quad \bullet \longrightarrow$$
   $$C \quad\quad D$$

   (d) Suppose that A and B are two points and l is a line such that $A \in l$, and $B \in l$. Then $\{A, B\} \subset$ _____ .
2. Answer true or false. Write the correct statement in case of a false answer.
   (a) A line CD is a point set.
   (b) Let $\{C, D, F, G\}$ be contained in l, then there exists a line m distinct from a line l that contains $\{F, G\}$.
   (c) A line CD is determined by a point C.
3. Complete each of the following statements:
   (a) If $\{C, D, E\}$ is a set of collinear points, then there is a line l such that _____ $\subset m$.
   (b) Consider a point C on a line l. How many rays does l contain that have C as endpoints.
   (c) Let C, F, G be collinear, and assume that C is not between F and G. Are $\overrightarrow{CA}$ and $\overrightarrow{CB}$ the same ray?
4. Assume l and q are lines such that $l \cap q \neq \varnothing$. Is $l \| q$? Explain.
5. Assume that the set $\{A, C, B, F\}$ is a set of collinear points.

   $$\longleftarrow \bullet \quad\quad \bullet \quad\quad \bullet \quad\quad \bullet \longrightarrow$$
   $$\quad C \quad\quad A \quad\quad F \quad\quad B$$

   Find:
   (a) $\overline{AB} \cup \overline{CA} =$ _____
   (b) $\overrightarrow{CA} \cap \overleftrightarrow{AC} =$ _____
   (c) $\overline{CA} \cap \overline{FB} =$ _____
6. Find the degree measures of each of the following:
   (a) $\frac{3}{5}$ of a right angle.
   (b) $\frac{1}{3}$ of a straight angle.
   (c) Two adjacent angles together are $96°$; one of them is $24°$. Find the other.
   (d) Two angles are complementary; one is twice the other. Find each angle.

7. Find each of the following angles in the figure if $\overline{AB} \perp \overline{AC}$.

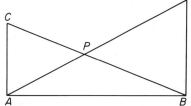

(a) $\angle ABF$ if $\angle ABC = 35°$, and $\angle FBC = 50°$.
(b) $\angle FAC$ if $\angle BAF$ is $45°$.
(c) $\angle APC$ if $\angle FPB$ is $40°$.
(d) $\angle APC$ if $\angle APB$ is $120°$.

8. In each of the examples illustrated indicate:
(a) Whether the figure is closed.
(b) Whether the figure is a polygon path.
(c) Whether the figure is a polygon.
(d) The interior and exterior (if they exist).
(e) The name of the polygon if it is a familiar type.

(a)   (b)   (c)

(d)   (e)

9. Given: $\overline{AB} = \overline{CF}$ and $\angle 2 = \angle 1$
Prove: $\triangle ABC \cong \triangle ACF$

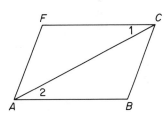

10. $\triangle ABC$ is similar to $\triangle FGH$. If $\angle A = 50°$, $\angle B = 30°$, and $\angle E = 100°$. Find the measures of all of the other angles.

11. Referring to the figure here, identify each of the following:

(a) diameter
(b) radius
(c) central angle
(d) inscribed angle
(e) arc
(f) Using the central $\angle COF = 40°$, find the measure of $\angle 1$, $\angle 2$, $\angle 3$.

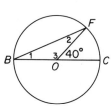

12. Show that a triangle whose sides have the following lengths are right triangles.
    (a) 3, 4, 5   **(b)** 9, 12, 15   **(c)** 5, 12, 13
13. Find the measure of the supplement and the complement of each of the following angles.
    (a) $\angle F = 70°$ **(b)** $\angle G = 40°$ **(c)** $\angle C = 10°$
14. If two lines, a and b, are drawn such that $a \cap b \neq \varnothing$ and $a \neq b$, what can be said about the intersection of a and b?
15. In $\triangle ABC$, $\angle B = 90°$, $\overline{AB} = 3$ inches, and $\overline{AC} = 5$ inches. Find $\overline{BC}$.
16. Given the figure shown here with BH drawn parallel to FC:
    If $\angle BAC = 110°$ and $\angle HAF = 130°$ find:
    (a) $\angle CAF$
    (b) $\angle C$

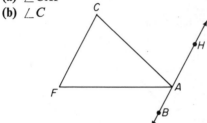

17. Suppose in a rectangle $FGHW$, $\overline{FG} = 5$ inches and $\overline{GH} = 6$ inches. Find:
    (a) the area of rectangle $FGHW$ **(b)** the area of triangle FGH
18. Find the area of the figure illustrated here.

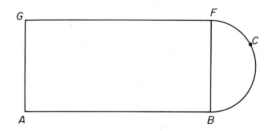

ABFG is a rectangle and BCF is a semicircle with BF a diameter. $\overline{AB} = 20$ inches, $\overline{BF} = 10$ inches. Use $\pi = 3.142$.

19. In the figure, $\overline{AB} \parallel \overline{FG}$ and $\angle A = \angle G = 90°$.
    If $\overline{AB} = 10$ inches, $\overline{FG} = 4$ inches, $\overline{BC} = 14$ inches, find $\overline{FC}$.

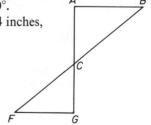

20. Find the area of a rectangle with a diagonal of 13 inches if the base is equal to 12 inches.

21. Find the area of a trapezoid if the lower base is 14 inches, the upper base is 10 inches, and the altitude is 6 inches.

22. Find the area of a circle with diameter 10 inches if $\pi = 3.14$.

SELECTED REFERENCES

Banks, J. Houston, *Elements of Mathematics*. Boston: Allyn and Bacon, 1965.

Brumfiel, Charles F., Robert E. Eicholz, and Merrill E. Shanks, *Fundamental Concepts of Elementary Mathematics*. Reading, Mass.: Addison-Wesley Publishing Company, 1962.

Hacker, Sidney G., Wilfred E. Barnes, and Calvin L. Long, *Fundamental Concepts of Arithmetic*. Englewood Cliffs, N.J.: Prentice-Hall, Inc., 1963.

National Council of Teachers of Mathematics, *Insights into Modern Mathematics*. Washington, D. C.: The Council, 1964.

Peterson, John A., and Joseph Hashisaki, *Theory of Arithmetic*. New York: John Wiley & Sons, Inc., 1963.

School Mathematics Study Group, "Concepts of Informal Geometry," in *Studies in Mathematics*, Vol. V. New Haven: Yale University Press, 1960.

School Mathematics Study Group, "Intuitive Geometry," in *Studies in Mathematics*, Vol. VII. New Haven: Yale University Press, 1961.

Wheeler, Rurie E., *Modern Mathematics: An Elementary Approach*. Belmont, Calif.: Wadsworth Publishing Company, 1966.

13

Logic, Probability, Odds, and Permutations

13.1 Mathematical Logic

Most mathematical educators agree that the topic of logic should be introduced and explored in the elementary grades. However, this important aspect of mathematics is ignored in most textbooks and developed haphazardly in others. We will explore the ramifications of mathematical logic as they may be implemented in the grades.[1]

Logic, as generally interpreted, refers to the ability to think correctly. In mathematics, we are concerned with the ability to formulate and deduce correct proofs from given numerical or symbolic statements. Drawn to its furthest extension, logic entails the formulation of proofs for mathematical formulas and theorems. In the elementary school, we should be more concerned with the presentation of the mechanics of logic and the provisions for the acquisition of a few rules that will allow pupils to formulate simple proofs.

Pupils should first be exposed to the concept that all mathematical sentences or expressions are one of two kinds—atomic or molecular. An atomic

---

[1] This topic has been prepared with the assistance of James Bowen. For detailed coverage on teaching logic in elementary schools see: James Bowen, *Use of An Educational Game in Teaching Abstract Thinking in Mathematical Logic* (unpublished doctoral dissertation, University of California, Los Angeles, 1969).

statement contains one thought or expression. An example would be $5 - 3 = 2$. A molecular statement contains more than one thought or expression. An example is $8 + 3 = 11$ and $5 + 6 = 11$. The word "and" is called a connective and joins the two atomic parts of the molecular expression. A distinction is made between atomic and molecular statements in logic because the students must learn to manipulate expressions to arrive at proofs. This is done through knowledge of the basic connective words with which the common rules of logic are associated. The pupils should become familiar with five basic connectives and their corresponding symbols. They are: not ($\neg$); both ... and ($\wedge$); either ... or ($\vee$); if ... then ($\rightarrow$); and only if ... then ($\leftrightarrow$). Symbols for connectives may vary from author to author; the above, however, are common in usage and acceptable. For logical purposes then, all mathematical expressions are reduced to atomic or molecular statements joined together by connectives. Most connectives found in print (but, however, so, and the others) can easily be translated to mean one of the five standard logic connectives.

The individual parts of a molecular expression are known as its variables. In presenting logic to elementary pupils, the teacher must make the pupils aware that they are usually dealing with relevant or related variables. That is, the mathematical expressions, or one of their components, are related to each other so that they interact with one another and call for a conclusion. Logic is deductive reasoning, and one idea flows from another. Given the statements: (1) $A \rightarrow B$, and (2) A, it is apparent that statement 2 is related to 1 (it has the same symbol A). Letters of the alphabet are efficient symbols for statements. Statement 1 reads "if A then B" and statement 2 reads "A." A conclusion is called for because of the words *if* and *then*. The conclusion naturally is B since statement 2 indicates A is true. Had the second statement read "not A" ($\neg A$), there would have been no conclusion. There is no rule in logic that states that when the first part of an "if ... then" statement is false that the conclusion is false. We must only conclude what the rules of logic allow us to conclude. Had the second statement read C, there would be no conclusion because it is in no way related to either atomic part of statement 1.

Mathematical sentences for the above example would be:

1. $3 + 3 = 6 \longrightarrow 6 - 3 = 3$
2. $3 + 3 = 6$

The conclusion drawn is $6 - 3 = 3$. It is more efficient when working with youngsters to have them develop the skill of translating mathematical expressions (even in story form) into symbolic form. The manipulations become much easier for the students. They can then concentrate on a few symbols and their logical implications. Young children, especially, find it difficult to comprehend that we are not necessarily proving the "truthfulness" of statements in logic. Rather, we are interested in their form, transition, and usage. It is entirely possible to arrive at an untruth in logic. Consider the statements:

1. If you have 5¢ and I have 5¢ then we have 20¢ together.
2. I have 5¢ and you have 5¢.

The conclusion drawn is that together we have 20¢. The statements are not altered by logic. We are really stating that the "process" of thinking used was correct. Advanced logic allows children to indicate truthfulness of whole expressions, but we are never guaranteed that we have truth. We must be content with proving the validity of the statements. Indicating whether a proof is possible from a given set of statements is what logic promises to do. The teacher should always ask the conclusion that can be drawn from the variables. There are only two situations in logic when "truth" can be assessed. The first is when a negation is used in a statement (not, no, can't, ≠, |<) and thus makes the expression false. The second is when two variables conflict with one another. Obviously, one of the statements must be false.

Children must receive sufficient practice in symbolizing mathematical statements before they are ready to handle the formal rules of logic. This can be done by exercises in recognizing complete thoughts. A thought becomes an atomic expression, which can be symbolized by any letter of the alphabet. It also becomes a variable that the student can manipulate.

After the children have been presented the concepts of variables, connectives, symbolization, relevancy, truthfulness, and conclusions, they should be ready to proceed to simple one-step proofs. Some authors of textbooks on logic introduce the rules of inference one at a time. Then by a process of combining one rule with the next, the children gain proficiency in manipulating more complex statements. This process, however, is lengthy and worthwhile only if a rigorous attempt is going to be made by the teacher to spend a great deal of time with logic. The method suggested here is that all the rules of logic are presented in one-step fashion. Many of the rules are intuitive in nature, and elementary children should not have a great deal of difficulty in their comprehension. After all the rules are presented and careful explanation follows them, combinations of rules might be attempted and the difficulty graduated according to the abilities of the children. Formal rules of logic may be found in textbooks treating logic. In many cases the sophistication of the language will have to be reduced to the pupils' level.

Ideally, logic should be part of each year's mathematical experience for the youngsters. At the fifth grade level, children should be involved in using the rules of inference to conclude rather complex proofs.

The following example is offered as evidence that computational skills alone as offered in the elementary school will not allow children to arrive at correct conclusions. However, with limited training in the elements involved in logic and a repertoire of a few rules of inference, the children can handle the problem effectively.

Example. If Bob is 16, then Carl is not 17. Carl is 17 and Helen is not 15. Either Helen is 15 or Bob is 16. Therefore, Carl is not 17.

Correctly symbolized, the problem becomes:

∴ ¬C

1. B → ¬C   C = Carl is 17
2. C ∧ ¬D   B = Bob is 16
3. D ∨ B   D = Helen is 15

Solution.

4. ¬D   A rule of logic states that in a both . . . and statement, both atomic sentences are true and may be used separately. Consequently we simplify the D from line 3.

5. B   A rule of logic states that in an either . . . or statement, if one atomic sentence is proven to be false, the other atomic sentence is true. Consequently, ¬D from line 4 proves B to be true.

6. ¬C   A rule of logic states that in an if . . . then statement, when the first atomic sentence is found to be true, the second atomic sentence is true. Consequently, B from line 5 proves ¬C from line 1.

Our conclusion is that Carl is not 17. The problem is logically valid. In referring to truth in the rules, we are not concerned with the "inherent truth" of the statement. Rather, we are concerned with its truthfulness of form (the manner in which it interacts with the connectives). Children, as well as teachers, often fail to see the distinction.

The extensions of logic in the classroom are innumerable, even though most have not been attempted. Aside from working with numerals and mathematical expressions and equations, other experiences can be provided for the children. Any use of logic will result in actual use of mathematics or a better understanding of it. The teacher may provide the children with opportunities to translate English sentences into logical symbols and concluding proofs (as shown in the example). Many uses of logic can be derived from the news media. Cartoons, articles, commercials, and so forth can often be translated in symbolic form and conclusions inferred from the information included or excluded. Pupils may use the information excluded from certain commercials to infer that the conclusions drawn from the information included are invalid. Teachers have sometimes used the pupils' knowledge of logic to solve disputes on the playground. Rules of games are often scrutinized as to their logical construction. Care must be taken in using these suggestions, however, because our everyday language does not include frequent usage of the exact connectives that we use in logic. A rule of thumb when looking for materials to use in the classroom is to observe the source and find out if a conclusion is being asked for. Some sources are clearly not deductive in nature and as such, are outside the realm of logical manipulations.

Once children acquire a background in logic, they can advance in depth and sophistication. Truth tables may be introduced, procedures for indirect proofs and conditional proofs may be explored, and methods of discovering inconsistencies may be utilized. The degree of complexity advances into the proving of complex theroms. However, it would be an atypical group of elementary children who would arrive at this level of mastery.

A game sold commercially adds additional appeal to the area of logic. The WFF'N PROOF game begins at a very elementary level of logical interpretation and increases in complexity as it introduces advanced games for knowledgeable players. The rules of inference are introduced through this game approach, and the children move at their own rate of speed.

Through a combined effort on the part of elementary teachers, children who have a continuing exposure to logic will be better prepared to handle advanced mathematics.

13.2   A Look at Probability

The word probability is used extensively in everyday conversation. We talk of the chance that U.C.L.A. will win a basketball game or that it might rain tonight. We are interested in a future event, of which the outcome is uncertain and about which we want to make a kind of prediction.

All mathematical probabilities are measured on a scale from 0 to 1. The value 0 is assigned to any event that certainly will not occur; that is, the probability is 0 that the Earth and Sun will collide tonight. The value 1 is assigned to events that are certain to occur; that is, the probability is 1 that the sun will rise in the east. Events that may occur or may not occur are assigned fractional probabilities between 0 and 1.

To appreciate the meaning of probability from a basic point of view, consider one of the simplest phenomena of chance, the toss of a coin. There are two possible outcomes, a head or a tail. It is certain that a head or a tail will occur on any one toss of the coin. If we assume we have an "honest" coin, that is, one that is not specially weighted or that does not have two heads, we can say that the outcome of having a heads or a tails turn up is equally likely. Thus we assign $\frac{1}{2}$ to each as its probability.

Another example of probability use would be in the rolling of a die. A die is a perfect cube with six faces having one to six dots. If we roll it once, the set of possible outcomes is the set $\{1, 2, 3, 4, 5, 6\}$. If we assume the equal likelihood of any number of dots turning up, we say that the probability is $\frac{1}{6}$ of any number turning up on the roll of a die. The denominator, 6, in the fraction always represents the total number of possibilities, and the 1 represents the number of ways the possibility can occur.

In discussing probability we use the word *event* to refer to the possible outcomes of a happening. Thus, we should say that the total number of possible events in the case of the die is 6.

We have the following definition, then, to agree with our intuitive notion of chance in the simplest situation.

Definition.

$$\text{Probability of event occurring} = \frac{\text{Number of ways event can occur}}{\text{Total number of possible events}}$$

The definition is based on a large number of trials of any event occurring. In the illustration of tossing the coin we might find that out of five tosses heads could turn up four times. However, if we were to toss a coin 1,000 times, we would come closer to 500 heads or 500 tails, that is, the probability of one out of two.

Consider the example of the tossing of two coins:

Toss	First Coin	Second Coin
First	Heads	Tails
Second	Tails	Heads
Third	Heads	Heads
Fourth	Tails	Tails

We see that two coins can come down in four possible ways. Thus, the probability of having a pair of heads, for example, is $\frac{1}{4}$.

Consider the example of tossing three coins:

Toss	First Coin	Second Coin	Third Coin
First	Heads	Heads	Heads
Second	Heads	Heads	Tails
Third	Heads	Tails	Heads
Fourth	Heads	Tails	Tails
Fifth	Tails	Heads	Heads
Sixth	Tails	Heads	Tails
Seventh	Tails	Tails	Heads
Eighth	Tails	Tails	Tails

The total number of possible "events" is eight. What are the number of ways that all coins are heads? One out of eight possible, or $\frac{1}{8}$. What are the chances that two coins will be heads and one tails? Three, or $\frac{3}{8}$. What are the chances that two coins will be tails and one heads? Three, or $\frac{3}{8}$. Finally, there is one chance of having all coins turn up tails, or $\frac{1}{8}$. The sum of the probabilities, namely, $\frac{1}{8} + \frac{3}{8} + \frac{3}{8} + \frac{1}{8} = 1$.

To check experimentally how well these probabilities work, a pupil might take a coin and make a record of the results of tossing the coin at least one hundred times.

Toss	Heads	Tails
First		
Second		
Third		
Hundredth		

You may conclude after this experiment that the chances of getting a head or a tail is $\frac{1}{2}$ or "one chance out of two."

Another example of probability would be to ask what is the probability that a letter of the alphabet picked at random (by pure chance) will be a vowel.

Solution: Since there are five vowels in the alphabet, and twenty-six letters in the alphabet, you may agree the solution of the problem is five chances out of twenty-six or $\frac{5}{26}$.

13.3 Odds

If from a bag containing 3 white balls and 2 green balls, a ball is drawn at random (by pure chance), a white ball can be drawn in 3 ways and fail to be drawn in 2 ways. We say that the odds in favor of drawing a white ball are 3 to 2. This statement is the same as saying that the probability of drawing a white ball is $\frac{3}{5}$. In general, the odds that an event will occur is the ratio of the probability that the event will occur to the probability that it will not occur.

Consider the example of the roll of a die. What are the odds that a 6 will turn up on the first roll? The probability that a 6 will turn up on the first roll is 1 out of 6, and the probability is 5 out of 6 that a 6 will not turn up. The odds, therefore, are $\dfrac{\frac{1}{6}}{\frac{5}{6}}$ that a 6 will turn up. $\frac{1}{6} \div \frac{5}{6} = \frac{1}{5}$. The odds are 1 to 5 that a 6 will turn up and 4 to 5 that a 6 will not turn up.

13.4 Permutations

In order to understand *permutations* we need to state a principle often times referred to as the principle of *choices*. The principle stated is that if a certain operation can be performed in m ways and if, after this operation has been performed, a second operation can be performed in n ways, then the total number of ways in which the two operations can be performed in the order named is $m \times n$.

To illustrate the principle, imagine having 6 baseball pitchers and 3 catchers. How many different batteries can be formed?

Solution: The pitcher can be selected in 6 ways and the catcher in 3 ways. Thus the battery can be selected in $6 \times 3 = 18$ different ways.

Another example would be the girl who has 5 sweaters, 3 blouses, and 4 skirts. How many different ensembles, each consisting of sweaters, blouses, and skirts, could she select?

Solution: The sweater can be selected in 5 ways, the blouses in 3 ways and the skirts in 4 ways; thus the ensembles can be selected in $5 \times 3 \times 4 = 60$ different ways.

Let us consider a set of three marbles of different colors and designate these marbles by the letters a, b, and c, respectively.

Let us now list the different arrangements of the three marbles in a row which can be formed from the three marbles. They are:

$$
\begin{array}{ccc}
a\ \ b\ \ c & b\ \ a\ \ c & c\ \ a\ \ b \\
a\ \ c\ \ b & b\ \ c\ \ a & c\ \ b\ \ a
\end{array}
$$

Each of these arrangements is called a *permutation*.

The number of different arrangements or permutations could have been found in the marble problem without listing the permutations as follows. In forming any permutation the marble for the first position can be chosen in 3 ways, then the marble for the second position can be chosen in 2 ways, and then the marble for the third position can be chosen in 1 way. Following the principle of choices we can conclude that $3 \times 2 \times 1 = 6$ will give us the number of different permutations possible.

Finally, a pupil has an arithmetic book, an English book, a geography book, and a history book. In how many ways can he arrange these books in a row on his desk.

Solution: Following the principle of choices we conclude that $4 \times 3 \times 2 \times 1 = 24$ represents the number of arrangements or permutations of the four books that can be made.

13.5   Chapter Summary

Suggestions have been made for introducing and exploring the topic of logic in the elementary grades. Ideally, simple logic should be part of each year's mathematical experience for children. By the fifth grade level, pupils should be involved in using the rules of inferences to conclude proofs. The extensions of logic in the classroom are innumerable, and several practical suggestions were made. Pupils who have had a continuing exposure to logic should be better prepared to handle advanced mathematics.

Some practical applications of probability were presented. All mathematical probabilities are measured on a scale from 0 to 1. The value 0 is assigned to any event that will not occur; the value 1 is assigned to any event that is certain to occur. By definition, the probability of a particular event occurring is the ratio of the number of ways the event can occur to the total number of possible events.

We say that the odds are in favor of an event occurring or the odds are against an event occurring. By definition, the odds that an event will occur is the ratio of the probability that the event will occur to the probability that the event will not occur.

The number of different arrangements of the elements of a set is the same as the number of permutations of the elements of the set.

QUESTIONS AND EXERCISES

1. A basketball coach has nine first-string players, all of whom can play any of the five positions on the team. How many different teams can he form?

2. How many different two-digit numbers can be formed using the digits 3, 6, 7, 8, 9?

3. A baseball manager has 4 pitchers and 2 players for each of the other 8 positions. How many different teams could he put on the field?

4. A high school boy has 5 pairs of slacks, 3 sport coats, and 4 sweaters. How many different ensembles, each consisting of slacks, sport coat, and sweater, could he select?

5. A card is drawn at random from a full pack of 52 cards. What is the probability that it is a club?

6. If two pennies are tossed simultaneously, what is the probability that they will both fall heads up?

7. In a roll of one die, what is the probability that the number of dots obtained will not exceed four?

8. Construct a table showing all the possible results when four coins are tossed. What is the probability of at least two heads? Of at least two tails?

9. How many three-letter "words" can be formed from our alphabet if none is to contain any single letter more than once?

10. In a raffle of an automobile a man holds 7 chances out of a total of 3,000. What are the odds against his winning the automobile?

11. The probability of an event happening is $\frac{5}{8}$. What are the odds in favor of it?

12. May is older than Bob and Carl is not older than Bob. If Carl is not older than Bob, then Bob is 13. If Mary is older than Bob, then she is not 12?

    What may be concluded from the above statements?

    Answer: Nothing—invalid.

13. Ken can run the mile in 6.4 minutes and cannot seem to achieve well in the high jump. If Ken goes out for the track team, he'll have to do well on the high jump. If he can run the mile under 7 minutes, he can make the baseball team.

    What may be concluded from the above statements?

    Answer: Ken can make the baseball team, but not the track team.

14. If John works with Pete and Helen works with Margaret, the script will be finished by Friday. John will either work with Dave or he will work alone. Helen will either finish painting or she will work with Margaret. John has decided not to work alone and Helen can't paint because the brushes weren't cleaned. Margaret and John are cousins.

    What may be concluded from the above statements?

    Answer: The script will be finished by Friday.

15. Given the statement A B (either A or B) and the possibility that A is either true or false and B is either true or false, under what conditions may the whole statement (A B) be true?

    Answer: When A is true and B is true.

    When A is true and B is false.

    When A is false and B is true.

16. "If you use Clean-o toothpaste," says the television commercial, "you'll never have cavities. If you don't have cavities, people will like you. If people like you, you'll always have friends." Cathy used Clean-o toothpaste for six months, but didn't gain any friends.

    How do you evaluate the above situation?

    Answer: It's logical, but false: otherwise Cathy would have gained some friends.

SELECTED REFERENCES

Brumfiel, Charles, Robert Eicholz, Merrill Shanks, and P. G. O'Daffer, *Principles of Arithmetic.* Reading, Mass.: Addison-Wesley Publishing Co., 1963.

Cameron, Edward, and Edward T. Browne, *College Algebra.* New York: Holt, Rinehart & Winston, 1956.

Copi, Irving M., *Introduction to Logic*. New York: The Macmillan Company, 1954.

Chase, Stuart, *Guides to Straight Thinking*. New York: Harper & Row, Publishers, 1956

Johnson, Donovan A., and William H. Glenn, *The World of Statistics*. St. Louis: Webster, 1961.

Reese, Paul K., and Fred W. Sparks, *Algebra and Trigonometry*. New York: McGraw-Hill Book Company, 1962.

Schaaf, William A., *Basic Concepts of Elementary Mathematics*. New York: John Wiley & Sons, Inc., 1960.

Suppes, Patrick, and Shirley Hill, *First Course in Mathematical Logic*. New York: Blaisdell Publishing Company (Ginn and Co.), 1964.

14

Evaluation in Elementary School Mathematics

During the past decade a major thrust has been made to improve the mathematics curriculum in elementary and secondary schools. Few professional educators or mathematicians would deny that progress has been made or that the curriculum reform movement will continue during the next decade. A remarkable aspect of this development has been the continuing progress despite the inertia of some schools to accept change and the alarming inadequacy of evaluation procedures to determine the success of new programs.

Neither the schools nor the mathematical profession should allow these conditions to continue. At least five major aspects of evaluation need to be injected into mathematics education:

1. Redefining the role of evaluation
2. Inserting appropriate evaluation procedures into curriculum development
3. Building evaluation procedures into instructional practices
4. Involving pupils in evaluation
5. Using empirical methods to test principles used in curriculum work in mathematics

Each of these aspects will be discussed.

14.1   New Roles for Evaluation

Three major factors are responsible for the need to redefine the role of evaluation in mathematics education: (1) the accelerating development of assessment and evaluation instruments in an unorganized way by semiprofessional and professional groups; (2) the current emphasis upon innovation at all levels of education and the need for evaluation expertise; and (3) the beginning of a technology for evaluation of educational programs by the American Educational Research Association[1] and the Research and Development Center.[2]

NEW EVALUATION INSTRUMENTS

The development of new evaluation instruments for use in mathematics education has been a sporadic enterprise. Several examples will be given to show the validity of this statement.

1. The meaningful approach to teaching arithmetic received its original impetus from psychologists who proved the advantages of learning with understanding instead of learning by isolated drill. While this approach to teaching has been widely accepted by psychologists and the teaching profession, comparatively few standardized achievement tests or even teacher-made classroom tests contain adequate provision for measuring pupil understanding of basic mathematical concepts.[3]

2. Governmental and private corporations have initiated vast new production lines for new curricula in mathematics and instructional materials. With few exceptions provision for evaluation has either been lacking or inadequate.

3. New textbooks prepared for elementary school children are beginning to incorporate procedures for helping pupils and teachers appraise understanding of basic mathematical concepts. The establishment of adequate objectives for directing the teaching-learning process involved, however, has been only partially achieved.

4. The National Assessment Program, directed by the Committee on Assessing the Progress of Education (CAPE), has initiated the development of sophisticated polling techniques to show the national educational strengths and weaknesses. The mathematical "exercises" (not tests) may not reflect much of the current emphasis upon "new mathematics" or upon "discovery techniques" stressed in these programs.

---

[1] See *American Educational Research Association Monograph Series on Curriculum Evaluation* (Washington D. C.: The Association, 1967), pp. 4–10.
[2] Research and Development Center, University of California, Los Angeles.
[3] Wilbur H. Dutton, *Evaluating Pupils' Understanding of Arithmetic* (Englewood Cliffs, N. J.: Prentice-Hall, Inc., 1964), pp. 109–13.

The dangers as well as the accomplishments are becoming apparent as the program begins. The results will be publicized for broad categories, such as the ability of nine-year-old children to tell time (for upper-income families of the rural Southwest). As this provocative enterprise gets underway, individual states are doing assessments of their own and are publicizing results of pupils' achievement by districts and by schools. In most instances these tests have been inadequately prepared and are not valid measures of pupil achievement or of teaching efficiency. Individual states have not followed procedures developed for the national model. The collecting of data and releasing of information pertaining to findings has, in some cases, been motivated more by political objectives than by the need for objective curriculum improvement.

5. The international study of achievement in mathematics has been undertaken by UNESCO with twelve major nations participating. The project has been exploratory in nature and has striven to develop procedures for making large studies of this type. The need for educational studies to establish procedures of research and quantitative assessment is quite apparent. The project has pointed out the role of education in promoting or hindering social and economic development in any country. A definite attempt is being made to provide for an exchange of information on different patterns of educational organization, curricula, and teaching methods.

While other examples of the sporadic development and use of evaluation instruments could be given, the writers of this textbook contend that there is little quality control of mathematical materials being produced at the present time. Assessment programs at state, national, and international levels are exploratory in nature. These programs are detrimental to curriculum improvement work when they emphasize the retention of traditional content and antiquated instructional practices. These educational activities are initiating drastic changes in the role of evaluation in curriculum improvement work in mathematics.

EDUCATIONAL INNOVATION

Educational innovation has created the need for new concepts of evaluation. Concepts, procedures, and instruments used in the past must be reexamined. Are these concepts or procedures appropriate for the current demands for innovation in education at all learning levels? Some of the important aspects of educational innovation will be examined and implications for evaluation given.

1. A major responsibility of the elementary school has been to "educate" all of America's children. The fact that between 20 and 30 per cent have been labeled slow learners or retarded learners is receiving considerable attention. Each individual needs to succeed in the mastery of mathematical skills and concepts appropriate for his maturity level and ability.

2. Many elementary schools have become program-centered, losing track of their primary purpose of meeting the needs of children. We should no longer use evaluation instruments which perpetuate the belief that elementary schools are satisfactorily carrying out mathematics programs appropriate for all children. Such factors as individualized learning, readiness for learning, sequencing instruction, and retention of mathematical concepts must be realistically used and carefully evaluated with new procedures.

3. The time-worn concepts of intelligence testing and ability groupings are being challenged. Language ability, environmental factors, self image, and attitude have much to do with a child's performance on an intelligence test or performance in school. In place of these older concepts of intelligence we need new concepts of readiness for mathematics, language development, and a genuine concern for identifying each child's potential. Acceptance of these new concepts of intelligence and the influences of environment necessitates new techniques of evaluation.

4. Too much emphasis has been placed upon mastery of subject matter, use of computational skills, and ranking of students in terms of knowledge and ability. Very little attention has been given to individual diagnosis, recording, and prescription of new learning based upon these data. Many new diagnostic techniques are needed which can be used by teachers in self-contained classrooms, in connection with team teaching, and in mathematics laboratories where high-speed computers and electronic data processing machines are available. Much more emphasis must be placed upon appropriate evaluation instruments which can be used to direct individualization of instruction.

5. A major thrust of the new mathematics for elementary school children is the emphasis placed upon "discovery." This concept of meaningful pupil participation in discovering the structure of our number system or in discovering how mathematicians solve problems or develop new mathematical systems cannot be evaluated with antiquated achievement tests. While new techniques for appraising pupil progress in meaningful discovery work are being developed, there must also be considerable clarification of the concept of discovery in order that appropriate evaluation work can be accomplished.

While educational innovation continues and pressures are placed upon elementary schools to change their programs, new concepts are continually being formed as to the role of the school, the flexibility of the curriculum, the meaning of intelligence, the appropriate ways to learn, and the structure of knowledge. As these new concepts develop, new methods of evaluation are devised, often without careful study of the changes they make in the relevance and logic of traditional structures. Continued emphasis, therefore, must be placed upon clarifying and strengthening the basic concepts which should permeate instructional programs in elementary school mathematics; only then can a meaningful approach to evaluation be achieved.

A NEW TECHNOLOGY FOR EVALUATION

In a recently published monograph on evaluation, Ralph Tyler, Robert Gagne, and Michael Scriven identify the need for professional tools and tactics in evaluation work.[4] They believe that more attention must be given to diagnostic testing, to task analysis, and to evaluation of goals. Bringing these processes together, according to these leaders, would constitute the beginnings of a technology of evaluation. This technology would draw from instructional technology, psychometric-testing technology, social-survey technology, communication technology, and others. The contributions of evaluation technology could be used in areas other than education.

Many professional organizations have recognized the need for developing an evaluation technology. The American Educational Research Association (AERA), however, has the broad research purview and measurement skill needed for this important task. They are committing their organization to this work, and a Committee on Curriculum Evaluation is actively working on the project. Hopefully, the National Council of Teachers of Mathematics will join other professional organizations in supporting this timely project. Assistance should also be secured from consulting agencies such as: the American Institute for Research; the Center for Instructional Research and Curriculum Evaluation, University of Illinois; the Educational Testing Service; the Institute for Administrative Research, Teachers' College, Columbia University; and the Research and Development Center, University of California, Los Angeles.

AERA has sorted out many important concepts needed as "building stones" in the development of program evaluation. Thus, the beginning of a technology for evaluation is well underway. Major aspects of curriculum evaluation in elementary school mathematics will now be discussed.

14.2 Curriculum Evaluation

The term *curriculum* has several meanings, depending upon the degree of specificity desired. A broad definition of curriculum which has been used since the 1940's is: "all experiences provided for children under the direction of the school." Recently a curriculum has been defined as an educational program. A curriculum may be a lesson or a curricular program for an

---

[4]Ralph Tyler, *et al. Perspectives of Curriculum Evaluation* (Chicago: Rand McNally and Co., 1967), p. 4.

elementary school. The curriculum can be specified in terms of what the teacher will do, in terms of what the pupil will do, or in terms of student achievement.

Stake, in the AERA monograph on evaluation 1967,[5] has characterized educational programs by their purposes, their content, their environments, their methods, and the changes they bring about. While rather complex, each characteristic can be identified, specified, and evaluated.

Curriculum evaluation in mathematics requires collecting, processing, and interpreting data pertaining to the educational program being considered. Two kinds of data are needed: (1) objective data on goals, environments, personnel, methods, content, and outcomes; and (2) personal judgments pertaining to the quality and appropriateness of the goals and other factors covered in (1). Evaluation, when carefully done, leads to the improvement of all aspects of curriculum work.

Since elementary school teachers should be actively involved in curriculum improvement work in mathematics, several indispensable aspects of curriculum evaluation will be presented. Teachers are the first to be drafted for putting new curriculum changes into practice. Unfortunately, they are seldom asked to participate in the formulating of objectives and in the evaluating of results based upon these objectives. While much of the basic curriculum work can and should be done by professional staff members, teachers need to know how to influence desirable curriculum improvement practices.

The contributions of the current curriculum reform movement in mathematics are easy to identify: (1) updating of content; (2) introducing of new content; (3) emphasis on inquiry in teaching and learning; and (4) stimulation of personnel to work on mathematics projects.

The weaknesses of the new programs are, likewise, easy to state: (1) inadequate statements of course or program objectives; (2) no built-in plan for evaluation; (3) little attention given to sequencing of instructional materials; and (4) only minor provision for children who have learning difficulties and who constitute about one-third of the total elementary school population. We must be alert to recognize that these weaknesses are tied in with the unanswered question of what elementary education is supposed to do in the new context of this century. This question can only be answered by cooperative efforts of subject-matter specialists, professional curriculum workers, and the general public which supports education.

Turning our attention again to the contributions of the reform movement in mathematics, we must make use of the new mathematical content; we st experiment with the inquiry methods of learning; and we must en- e subject-matter specialists to continue their efforts to improve their

ational Research Association Monograph Series on Curriculum Evaluation
C.: The Association, 1967), pp. 4–5.

disciplines. In addition to these efforts, we must initiate new curriculum improvements procedures which will provide for self-renewal. This would involve the testing of new instructional programs as well as new theories of curriculum. In order to accomplish these important tasks, professional educators, subject-matter specialists, and curriculum experts will have to work together as a team. Curriculum improvement would be carried on as a continuous program. To insure this continuity as well as continuous improvement, two important aspects of evaluation must be provided for: (1) "formative evaluation," which takes place at an intermediate stage of curriculum development and permits important changes to be made in curriculum work; and (2) "summative evaluation," which provides for terminal evaluation so that general conclusions or findings can be reported and used—in practice as well as in further program development.

The weaknesses of the new mathematical programs will now be discussed. In this section only the topics of course objectives and evaluation will be considered. The sequencing of instructional materials and provision for individual differences in learning will be covered in the next section on instructional practices (14.3).

Ideally, we should have a national group of leading citizens and educators who would give continued attention to the formulation of educational objectives.[6] The fact that there are no clear statements of aims for elementary education or for elementary mathematics education has meant that *there is no external criterion against which to determine the effectiveness of new mathematical programs*. Teachers become enmeshed in this controversy over objectives because they are expected to use new instructional materials and to produce "good" results even though the producers (curriculum investigators) and the consumers (parents and children) have no clearly defined objectives and have not reached agreement upon many aspects of mathematics education.

How can the problem of ends, means, and evaluation be resolved? Several practical suggestions are offered:

1. Curriculum investigators working on mathematics curricula should be required to submit statements of objectives as well as plans for evaluating their attainment.

2. The National Council of Teachers of Mathematics should take a leadership role in formulating educational objectives for elementary school mathematics along with the cooperation of one or two leading professional groups such as ASCD (Association of Supervision and Curriculum Development) and National Elementary School Principals.

3. The *Instructional Objectives Exchange* located in the Center for School Evaluation, University of California, Los Angeles, should be used. This

---

[6]See John I. Goodlad, *School Curriculum Reform in the United States* (New York: The Fund for the Advancement of Education, 1964), pp. 80–82.

exchange is designed so that curriculum workers may send in statements of objectives for appraisal or may withdraw statements of behavioral objectives for use in curriculum development work.

4. Having secured or developed behavioral objectives for some aspect of mathematics education (a grade level or a division such as primary-age children), a variety of experimental programs need to be planned to find "ways" to achieve these objectives.

The four suggestions just presented lay the ground work for curriculum development and instruction being "wed" so that ends, means, and evaluation are integral parts of educational improvement.

14.3   Evaluating Instructional Practices

RATIONALE FOR EVALUATION OF TEACHING

The discussion which follows in this section is based upon a rationale which includes the establishment of new criteria for determining success in teaching, the consideration of flexibility in teaching methods, and the importance of self-evaluation in teaching.

Teacher-preparation institutions, particularly U.C.L.A., are searching for new criteria for determining teacher effectiveness. In brief, emphasis is shifting from what the teacher does to what the pupil does. Instead of judging a teacher's competence by the procedures followed in the classroom, we try to determine the results he produces in pupils.

The good teacher is one who guides learning experiences so that desirable changes take place in the learner. Each teaching situation should be considered an experiment in which certain procedures are followed and certain outcomes are predicted. Successes and failures are studied in terms of the objectives established for the instruction. Methods of instruction are regarded as a *means* which must be tested to see if established objectives produce the effects desired. The method must be appraised in terms of pupil progress. Failure to achieve the desired effect might indicate something inadequate in the method or that the new learning was not appropriate for the children.

INSTRUCTIONAL PARADIGM FOR MATHEMATICS LESSON

The successful teacher is one who: (1) can attain results appropriate for the pupil; (2) can make a task analysis; (3) can select appropriate objectives; (4) can use appropriate teaching procedures; and (5) can measure (evaluate) his own success.

Appropriate Learnings.   Deciding upon appropriate learnings for children is dependent upon the teacher's understanding of each child and his mathematical needs. The teacher may use the child's cumulative record to obtain general information about his achievement in mathematics. Probably the best procedure is to use informal preassessment techniques. Before presenting regrouping in subtraction to nine-year-old children, the teacher would have to obtain information about the child's understanding of place value, renaming numbers, and basic subtraction facts. These informal procedures could be used:

1. Ask a child to show with counters several ways to rename 14; that is, $10 + 4$, $4 + 10$, $7 + 7$, $8 + 6$, $6 + 8$.
2. Have the child use a place-value holder to identify the values of 45 (four tens and five ones) or 132 (one hundred, three tens, two ones).
3. Write a few subtraction facts on the chalkboard and ask the child to give the answers orally ($12 - 6$, $24 - 3$, $14 - 7$, $21 - 10$).
4. Then present the new step (regrouping) $34 - 5$. This would give some indication about the child's recognition of the new learning required. Some children might know the new step or would be able to find a correct response by renaming 34 as $20 + 14$ and taking away 5 to secure $20 + 9$ or 29 or

$$
\begin{array}{r}
\overset{\overset{\displaystyle 1}{\displaystyle 2}}{\cancel{3}}\,4 \\
-\ 5 \\
\hline
29
\end{array}
$$

Task Analysis.   The task analysis in this learning situation involved knowing the entrance skills needed by the child before presenting the new step—regrouping 34 so that 5 could be subtracted.

Formulating Objectives.   Selecting or formulating appropriate objectives for each learning experience should involve several important considerations:

1. We cannot teach skills or understandings unless they are specified. We need to know what the pupil will do in order to learn. Stating the objective in terms of expected behavior of the pupils is called a "behavioral statement" or "behavioral objective." The teacher states the behavior expected (minimal standards of performance) and the conditions under which the behavior will take place. For example:

Given a subtraction example such as $25 - 6$, the child will be able to give a correct response and show his understanding by demonstrating the work with a place-value chart.

Using a clock, the child will be able to demonstrate (by turning the clock hands) telling time to the hour; that is, one o'clock, seven o'clock, or any hour requested.

2. The teacher should be able to distinguish between immediate and long-term objectives. This involves thinking about the overall learning as

well as the generalization aspects. In the first objective dealing with subtraction the child should be able to work several examples similar to $25 - 6$, should be able to make and work examples of his own, and should be able to retain these new learnings for use in work with three-place numerals in the minuend and two-place numerals in the subtrahend.

Selecting Learning Experiences. When objectives for a lesson have been stated "behaviorally," the kinds of learning activities are usually indicated. In the two objectives shown in the section on formulating objectives, the lesson on subtraction would involve work with concrete objects and a place-value chart. Telling time (to the hour) would necessitate using aids such as a Judy Clock and an actual alarm clock.

The learning principles used to direct the teaching-learning experiences would vary according to the teacher's particular "teaching style." Recommendations on desirable learning principles have been given in Chapter 1. These should be reviewed at this time.

Evaluating Results. A successful teacher uses theory and principles to direct his teaching practices. He also tests his practice and his theory by evaluating his work to see if teaching objectives have been achieved and his work has been effective.

Evaluation is a continuous process that takes place before the lesson starts, as the lesson advances, and after the lesson closes. The desirable mathematics teacher studies the results of the previous lesson before beginning the new lesson. He may decide, during the lesson, that his objective is too difficult for the child or group. The lesson would then be changed at that point (possibly more work on renaming numbers such as 15 as $10 + 5$ for understanding regrouping). Finally, at the close of the lesson the teacher should be able to identify strengths and weaknesses of the procedures used. He should be able to record the steps to take in teaching the next lesson.

This completes the discussion of the main components of an instructional paradigm for teaching. The importance of evaluation to each aspect of the paradigm has been stressed.

14.4 Pupil Involvement in Evaluation

A number of factors are important when discussing the involvement of pupils in evaluating their own work in mathematics. These factors include the philosophy of the teacher, the type of mathematics curriculum being used, and the kind of instructional program being used.

If the teacher believes in pupil-teacher planning, individualizing of instruction, and a discovery approach to learning, there will be numerous opportunities for pupils to become involved in evaluating their work in mathematics. A teacher who believes that the class should be taught as one group

The key to profitable individualized instruction is periodic meetings between teacher and student. Here evaluation of prior work is made as well as planning for next steps. San Carlos school district, California; Project PLAN classrooms, Brittan Acres.

and who uses the textbook as the main source of content for the course will not provide many opportunities for pupil self-evaluation.

When the mathematics curriculum is organized around the needs and interests of pupils as well as the important concepts identified by subject-matter specialists, there probably will be carefully planned procedures for directing pupils' use of self-evaluation throughout most learning experiences.

Likewise, when the instructional program is designed to carry out a curriculum organized around pupil needs and interests, evaluation procedures will be woven into the pupils' daily work in mathematics. In team teaching children should have many opportunities to work with the teacher in diagnosing difficulties, planning corrective work, checking papers and recording achievement, and becoming involved in discovering new mathematical relationships and concepts. Classrooms using individualized programs (some with computers to assist in storage and retrieval of achievement data) will probably have many ways for pupils to evaluate their own work for most learning units. In individualized mathematical programs, pupils usually have some pattern to follow which includes "check points" or "test points" where they must work with the teacher or take a test before advancing to the next unit of work.

The advantages of pupil self-evaluation are: motivation of work, building skills and attitudes to help the learner become increasingly independent in his work, improving the pupil's ability to locate and remove deficiencies based upon understanding, and efficiency in teaching and learning because pupils will be able to evaluate their work and do much of the record keeping.

14.5   Standardized Tests and Teacher-made Tests

Two main types of tests are used to collect data about pupil achievement in mathematics: standardized tests (formal tests), and teacher-prepared tests (usually informal). The characteristics of these two types are given in the table.

TWO MAJOR TYPES OF TESTS: BASIC APPLICATIONS OF EACH

Formal Tests	*Teacher-prepared Tests*
Content covers topics widely taught in nation. Test prepared by experts to cover a sample of skills and abilities.	Paper and pencil tests or application tests to test local curriculum or teacher objective.
Standardized procedures for administering.	Not standardized but may be standardized for a specific school system.
Accurate interpretation.	Interpretations made in terms of individuals or groups.
Retesting with alternate from.	Retesting when necessary, usually no alternate forms.
Careful recording of results—norms and grade expectancies.	Data recorded largely for teacher use.
Application made to daily program and larger goals of the school.	Application made to specific work with individuals and groups—may apply to overall program.
Valid for survey purposes and may not cover teacher's specific goals or local school curriculum.	Valid coverage of teacher's specific goals or the school curriculum.

STANDARDIZED TESTS

Standardized tests have an important place in the evaluation of a school's mathematics program or a pupil's achievement of specific learning levels. Since the tests have been standardized with average pupils and norms established on the performance of this average population of children, they should be used primarily for survey purposes. Only when a careful study is made of test items to discover their validity for specific age groups and instructional practices, can the results be used in a diagnostic way. Thus there will be many test items which are not appropriate for any particular group, class, or school.

Some of the widely used standardized tests include:

1. California Arithmetic Test, California Test Bureau.
2. Contemporary Mathematics Test, California Test Bureau.
3. Functional Evaluation of Mathematics, American Guidance Service.
4. Iowa Tests of Educational Development, Science Research Associates.
5. Metropolitan Achievement Tests, Harcourt, Brace, & World, Inc.
6. Sequential Tests of Educational Progress, Educational Testing Service.
7. SRA Achievement Series, Science Research Associates.
8. Stanford Achievement Tests, Harcourt, Brace, & World, Inc.

SEMI-STANDARDIZED TESTS

The publishers of leading mathematics textbooks have prepared tests which parallel their textbooks. These tests contain items which measure pupil achievement, skills, and understanding. They are especially helpful to teachers in that the test items may be used as models for informal tests used in connection with each learning unit. Some of these tests may be used as diagnostic instruments if the teacher selects and uses items appropriate for his pupils and the work being studied.

TEACHER-PREPARED TESTS

Teachers should be encouraged to use appropriate evaluation techniques for each stage of the sequential development of mathematical concepts. The teacher must evaluate the specific outcomes of his teaching. Some pupils will be at the mastery level in a process such as division of a whole number by a fraction, while other pupils will just be starting work on multiplication of fractions. The teacher must tailor the evaluation work to fit the children in his class.

One might ask, what type of test item should be used? The answer is not one type, but many. Use the type of test item which is easiest to administer, to score, and to interpret. The following criteria should be helpful in the preparation of test items or informal tests to use as part of the instructional paradigm discussed in an earlier section:

1. Construct the test or test item around specific objectives.
2. The behavior tested should be measurable. Can the teacher tell the difference between a child who demonstrates the behavior and a child who does not?

3. Use a variety of techniques to secure valid data for cognitive, psycho-motor, and affective domains.

4. The teacher should be concerned with determining pupil readiness, diagnosing learning deficiencies, removing deficiencies, and directing sequential learning.

5. Emphasis should be placed upon pupil understanding, concept development, and discovery learning.

Each chapter in this book has included suggestions for helping children understand new skills and concepts in mathematics as they are encountered in the teaching-learning process. The examples which follow are for the purpose of helping the teacher use a variety of procedures in evaluating pupils' mathematical learning.

Checklists. List the types of behavior to stress or appraise. The teacher then observes individual pupils to determine strengths and weaknesses. The statements below are some of the behaviors related to multiplication.

———1. Hesitates when multiplying with 7, 8, or 9.

———2. Counts on fingers or with a pencil while working with difficult facts.

———3. Uses a zero to show place values for writing numbers in partial product.

———4. Repeats part of multiplication table to find correct fact.

———5. Avoids higher-decade addition, in adding partial products, by adding easy facts and then counting.

Rating Scales. Instead of a check placed before the behavior observed, the rating scale provides for an appraisal of the behavior by using a rating: $N = $ never, $L - $ little, $F = $ frequently.

———1. Shows ability to work independently.

———2. Asks for help from neighbors.

———3. Shows persistence in working on difficult problems.

In addition to samples of observation techniques, a few sample test items useful in teacher-made tests include the following:

Short Answer. If the short hand of a clock is between seven and eight, and the long hand is on six, what time is it?

Multiple Choice. Seven million, eight hundred four thousand forty-five is written:

(a) 7,840,450   (b) 7,804,045   (c) 7,840,045   (d) 7,800,045

Matching.

1. partial product	———(a)	465
2. multiplier	———(b)	$\times$ 82
3. multiplicand	———(c)	930
4. product	———(d)	3720
5. place values	———(e)	38130

True-false.
1. Both numerator and denominator of a fraction may be multiplied by the same number without changing the value of the fraction.
2. If the numerator of a fraction is unchanged, dividing the denominator by a number divides the fraction by that number.

Application. Place the answers to the problems below on the appropriate spot on the ruler. Use the marks shown after each item.
(a) At 2.5 in. put an *X*.
(b) At 1.75 in. put an *O*.
(c) At .75 in. plus .50 in. put a *Y*.

EVALUATING ATTITUDES TOWARD ARITHMETIC

Attitudes can be stated behaviorally and measured. For example: given the choice (during free time) between going to a reading center or going to the mathematics center to work, a child will choose to go to the mathematics center three out of four times.

Since attitudes are so important to individual success in mathematics, a section on evaluating pupils' attitudes has been included as part of the teacher's informal testing work.

Attitudes are indicators of favorable or unfavorable feelings one has toward some object, subject, person, or idea. Both children and adults have definite feelings toward arithmetic and mathematics. In general, individuals are ambivalent about these subjects, liking some aspects and disliking other aspects.

Factors which cause pupils to like mathematics have been identified as success in the subject, good teachers, the challenge it presents, enjoyment in working on interesting problems, and recognizing the practical values of the subject.

Dislike for mathematics seems to be caused by boring drill, difficult "story" or "word" problems, failures in a variety of classroom situations, and lack of understanding of certain aspects of the work.

Attitudes toward mathematics are acquired as children progress through the elementary school program. While each learning level seems to influence children's feelings toward mathematics, the crucial stages seem to be those which cause children unusual stress or strain. The transition from primary-level work to longer assignments or difficult regrouping in subtraction found in middle grades represents one crucial stage. Unfavorable attitudes are likewise developed when children encounter multiplication or division of fractions. Junior high school years are difficult for some children because of the changes from self-contained classrooms to departmentalized teaching, because of the difficulties encountered in advanced work, or because of the teachers.

Because attitudes are so important in influencing children's work in mathematics, considerable attention should be given to collecting data about children's attitudes so that teachers can provide for the development of positive feelings toward each aspect of mathematics. The scale which follows should be a useful tool to help teachers discover pupil attitudes toward arithmetic. The scale may also be used to help the teacher assess his own feelings toward this subject.

A Study of Attitude Toward Arithmetic

Check (X) *only the statements which express your feeling toward arithmetic*

———— 1. I feel arithmetic is an important part of the school curriculum.

———— 2. Arithmetic is something you have to do even though it is not enjoyable.

———— 3. Working with numbers is fun.

———— 4. I have never liked arithmetic.

———— 5. Arithmetic thrills me and I like it better than any other subject.

———— 6. I get no satisfaction from studying arithmetic.

———— 7. I like arithmetic because the procedures are logical.

———— 8. I am afraid of doing word problems.

———— 9. I like working all types of arithmetic problems.

————10. I detest arithmetic and avoid using it at all times.

————11. I have a growing appreciation of arithmetic through understanding its values, applications, and processes.

————12. I am completely indifferent to arithmetic.

————13. I have always liked arithmetic because it has presented me with a challenge.

———— 14. I like arithmetic but I like other subjects just as well.

————15. The completion and proof of accuracy in arithmetic gave me satisfaction and feelings of accomplishment.

Before scoring your attitude scale, place an (*X*) on the line below to indicate where you think your general feeling toward arithmetic might be:

11	10	9	8	7	6	5	4	3	2	1

Strongly favor   *Neutral*   *Strongly against*

Use the spaces below to write *two things you like most* about arithmetic or mathematics and two things you like least about these same subjects.

Like most

1. _____

_____

2. _____

_____

Like least

1. _____

   _____

2. _____

   _____

Method of Scoring Arithmetic Attitude Test

Place the scale value for the items you checked on the test in the left margin of the page. Total all items checked and divide by the total number of items you checked. This will give you an average score on the test. Compare this average with the estimated placement shown on the line indicating your general feeling toward arithmetic. Individual items will reveal highly favorable or unfavorable attitudes.

Scale Value	Test Item
7.2	1
3.3	2
8.7	3
1.5	4
10.5	5
2.6	6
7.9	7
2.0	8
9.6	9
1.0	10
8.2	11
5.2	12
9.5	13
5.6	14
9.0	15

14.6   Research in Mathematics Curriculum Work

The main focus for change in mathematics educational practice has been upon the curriculum. This emphasis no doubt will continue for at least another decade. Hopefully, much more attention will be given to clarification of aims, preparation of instructional materials, teacher preparation, and appropriate evaluation procedures. But most important of all, there must be a plan developed which will coordinate all of the factors just mentioned. When this is accomplished, curriculum improvement work will be systematized so that continuous evaluation will be accomplished and adjustments made in appropriate segments regularly. Until this advanced stage of curriculum work is reached, we will have to accept the dangers of hit-or-miss tactics, considerable mediocre development work, and acceptance of programs that are not effective or desirable.

Some educational leaders, Sizer,[7] Gagne,[8] and Cronbach,[9] believe that a major shortcoming of current curriculum development work is the absence of systematic investigations of the effects of introduction of new curricula and courses of study. Gagne asks questions which emphasize the concern of these educators: "How can one test the principles used in curriculum design by empirical methods? What kinds of evidence can be sought to determine the extent to which a curriculum promotes the learning expected of it?"

The work of Gagne cannot be discussed at length in this chapter. The reader is urged to explore the work cited in the last footnote.

Gagne defined three important terms (content, curriculum, and curricular units) in specific ways. Content is defined as *descriptions of the expected capabilities of students in specified domains of human activity*. A unit of content is defined as *a capability to be acquired under a single set of learning conditions*, among these conditions being certain specified prerequisite capabilities. Finally, *a curriculum is a sequence of content units arranged in such a way that the learning of each unit may be accomplished as a single act*, provided the capabilities described by specified prior units (in the sequence) have already been mastered by the learner.[10]

Thus Gagne defines the curriculum so that it may be of any length, depending on the number of units. The curriculum is specified when: (1) the terminal objectives are stated; (2) the sequence of prerequisite capabilities is described; and (3) the initial capabilities assumed to be possessed by the student are identified.

An example of the method of specifying a curriculum derived from a hierarchy of capabilities, beginning with educational objectives that describe human performance, has been given for the "addition of integers" by Gagne. The work of the American Association for the Advancement of Science, *A Process Approach*, is also available. This curriculum[11] contains exercises on observation, classification, measurement, quantification, prediction, and inference. Each of these exercises is designed to build upon the others as a good curriculum should.

Several important implications of the specified curriculum for research in mathematics curriculum improvement work are:

[7]T. R. Sizer, "Classroom Revolution: Reform Movement or Panacea?" *Saturday Review*, XLVIII (June 19, 1965), 52f.

[8]Robert M. Gagne, "Curriculum Research and the Promotion of Learning," in *Perspectives of Curriculum Evaluation* (Skokie, Ill.: Rand McNally, 1967), pp. 19–38.

[9]L. J. Cronbach, "The Logic of Experiments in Discovery," in *Learning by Discovery* (Skokie, Ill.: Rand McNally, 1966), pp. 65–78.

[10]Robert M. Gagne, *op. cit.*, p. 23.

[11]American Association for the Advancement of Science, *An Evaluation Model and Its Application* (Washington D. C.: The Association, 1965).

1. The design of a curriculum can be based upon empirical data. The correctness of a sequence of content units can be tested by repeated trials of what students can achieve. These data can then be used in rearranging the sequence of instruction.
2. Successive tryouts and systematic testing are possible, thus making curriculum development a continuous process.
3. The plan provides for a methodology of content control which makes possible extended studies of learning.
4. The method of curriculum development described provides new opportunities for studies designed to relate individual differences to learning variables.

14.7 Chapter Summary

Five major aspects of evaluation should be injected into mathematics education: (1) redefining the role of evaluation; (2) inserting appropriate evaluation procedures into curriculum development; (3) building evaluation procedures into instructional practices; (4) involving pupils in evaluation; and (5) using empirical methods to test principles used in curriculum work in mathematics. Practical suggestions were given for teachers conducting informal evaluation and for discovering data about pupil attitudes toward mathematics.

QUESTIONS AND EXERCISES

1. Write several exercises for some aspect of fractions (adding or multiplying). Then ask a pupil to recite orally "how he thinks" or works the examples. Record the pupil's reasoning and thought processes for use in planning lessons for him.
2. Take the attitude test included in this chapter. Find out the results by scoring the test with the scale provided.
3. Locate a course of study for some large school system or state. Study the provisions made for evaluation of the total program or for any one instructional process.
4. Visit an elementary school in your area. Observe pupils as they work independently after an arithmetic lesson. Note work habits such as counting on fingers or marking on the page to obtain partial answers. Then try to prepare a check-list of work habits for one age level.
5. As a teacher or prospective teacher, complete the following tasks.
   (a) Given an instructional material (textbook or course of study), formulate a behavioral objective for a lesson.
   (b) Devise a test with items that represent the population of items inferred by the objective stated above.

(c) Teach a lesson, then formulate new objectives based on pupil deficiencies revealed in the lesson.

(d) Given an objective, propose in writing three ways for achieving the objective (selecting learning opportunities that differ in prerequisite skills or appeal to pupil interests).

SELECTED REFERENCES

Abramson, D. A., "Curriculum Research and Evaluation," *Review of Educational Research*, XXXVI (1966), 388–95.

American Association for the Advancement of Science, Commission on Science Education, *An Evaluation Model and Its Application*. Washington, D. C.: The Association, 1965.

Bloom, B. S., *et al.*, *A Taxonomy of Educational Objectives: Handbook I, The Cognitive Domain*. New York: Longmans, Green, 1956.

Brownell, W. A., *The Evaluation of Learning under Dissimilar Systems of Instruction*, Award Paper. Chicago: American Psychological Association, 1965.

Cox, R. C., "Item Selection Techniques and Evaluation of Instructional Objectives," *Journal of Educational Mesaurement*, II (1965), 181–86.

Cronbach, L. J., "Course Improvement through Evaluation," *Teacher's College Record*, LXIV (1963), 672–83.

Dutton, Wilbur H., *Evaluating Pupils' Understanding of Arithmetic*. Englewood Cliffs, N. J.: Prentice-Hall, Inc., 1964.

———, and Reginald Hammond, "Two In-Service Mathematics Programs for Elementary School Teachers," *California Journal of Educational Research*, XVII, No. 2 (March, 1966), 63–67.

Gagne, R. M., and Staff, University of Maryland Mathematics Project, "Some Factors in Learning Non-metric Geometry," *Monographs of the Society for Research in Child Development*, XXX (1965), 42–49.

Husen, Torsten, *International Study of Achievement in Mathematics*. New York: John Wiley Sons, Inc., 1967.

Madden, Richard, "New Directions in the Measurement of Mathematical Ability," *The Arithmetic Teacher*, XIII (May, 1966), 375–79.

National Society for the Study of Education, *Measurement and Understanding*, *Forty-fifth Yearbook, Part I*. Chicago: University of Chicago Press, 1946, XLV, pp. 7–43.

———, *The Teaching of Arithmetic*, *Fiftieth Yearbook, Part II*, "Testing Instruments and Practices in Relation to Present Concepts of Teaching Arithmetic." Chicago: University of Chicago Press, 1951, L, pp. 186–200.

Payette, R. F., *Report of the School Mathematics Study Group Curriculum Evaluation*. Princeton. N. J.: Educational Testing Service, 1961.

Popham, W. James, *Objectives and Instruction*. Paper presented at the annual meeting of the American Educational Research Association, Los Angeles, California, February 5–8, 1969, pp. 1–5.

———, *Probing the Validity of Arguments against Behavorial Goals.* Paper presented at the annual meeting of American Educational Research Association, Chicago, February 7–10, 1968, pp. 1–7.

———, *Selecting Appropriate Educational Objectives* (film). Los Angeles: Vimcet Associates, 1967.

Tyler, Ralph W., "The Objectives and Plans for a National Assessment of Educational Progress," *Journal of Educational Measurement,* III (1966), 1–4.

———, *Some Persistent Questions on the Defining of Objectives.* Pittsburgh: University of Pittsburgh Press, 1964, pp. 77–83.

Wrightstone, J. W., *et al.,* *Evaluation in Modern Education.* New York: American Book Company, 1956.

Index